Real Estate Investing For Dummies®

by Eric Tyson and Robert Griswold

Eric and Robert's Principles for Success

- **Real estate is a proven wealth-building vehicle.** Investing in rental properties can generate current income and significant tax benefits as well as build equity from appreciation over the years.
- **Although many people can succeed at investing in real estate, rental property investing isn't for everyone.** Take account of your investment preferences and personal temperament before buying property. Do you have the time to devote to real estate investing? Are you comfortable troubleshooting problems or hiring a property manager?
- **Make sure you're financially fit before investing in rental properties.** Pay particular attention to your monthly budget and make sure that you have adequate insurance coverage. Most successful real estate investors build their real estate investment portfolio through saving money and then gradually buying properties over the years.
- **Don't underestimate the importance of establishing good credit.** The best returns on real estate rely upon the use of credit to obtain the leverage of using OPM (other people's money).
- **Your first (and often one of the best) real estate investment is buying a home to live in.** Real estate is the only investment that we know of that you can live in or rent to produce income. You can also derive large tax-free profits when you sell your principal residence at a higher price than you paid for it.
- **Among residential property options, our top recommendations are small apartment buildings and single-family homes.** Residential property is an attractive investment and is easier to understand, purchase, and manage than most other types of property. Attached housing makes more sense for investors who don't want to deal with building maintenance and security issues.
- **Have your real estate team in place before you begin your serious property searching.** Line up a real estate agent, loan officer, tax advisor, lawyer, and so on early because the real estate investor with the best resources can identify the properties to ignore and those worthy of careful consideration. Move quickly — the speed at which you can close a transaction is an advantage in any type of market.
- **Look for properties in the path of progress.** Areas where new development or redevelopment is heading are where to be. The best real estate investment properties are ones that are well located and physically sound but cosmetically challenged and poorly managed.
- **You won't get rich trying to find no-money-down real estate investment deals.** Don't believe infomercial hucksters. Don't expect to buy top-notch rental properties that way.
- **Making at least a 20 to 25 percent down payment provides access to the best financing terms.** You can make smaller down payments — even as low as 10 percent or less — but you'll often pay a much higher interest rate, loan fees, and private mortgage insurance. Leverage, or the use of the lenders' money to cover the majority of your acquisition costs, can boost your rates of return. But too much leverage can be dangerous if the rental market turns and your debt expenses are high.

(continued)

Real Estate Investing For Dummies®

by Eric Tyson and Robert Griswold

(continued)

- **For low entry costs, consider real estate investment trusts (REITs) and lease options.** You can buy these exchange-traded securities (which can also be bought through REIT focused mutual funds) for a thousand dollars or less. With lease options, you begin by renting a property you may be interested in purchasing later, and a portion of your monthly rent goes towards the future purchase. If you can find a seller willing to provide financing, you can keep your down payment to a minimum.
- **We prefer the adage of "Location, location, value."** It clearly emphasizes location but also the importance of finding good value for your investment dollar. Owning real estate in up and coming areas with new development or renovated properties enhances finding and keeping good tenants and leads to greater returns. Another great opportunity are properties in great locations but with extensive deferred maintenance, especially aesthetic issues that can be inexpensively addressed.
- **Make real estate investments close by.** Buy property within two hours away by your favorite mode of transportation. Venture further only when you really know another real estate market and regularly find yourself there for other reasons or you've found an excellent property manager.
- **Any decision about where to invest starts with an evaluation of the overall region's economic trends.** If the area isn't economically sound, then the likelihood for successful real estate investments are diminished.
- **You're purchasing a future income stream or cash flow when you buy an investment property.** What you pay for a property and the cash flow it generates makes a significant difference in the success of your investment. The key is identifying which properties sellers have under-priced.
- **Don't rely on the seller's numbers when evaluating a property's potential.** Speak directly with the seller to determine the history of the property and their motivation for selling. But, don't rely on historic operating results offered by the seller or broker. Develop your own numbers through evaluating the property with a team of qualified professionals who are specialists in the physical and fiscal management of real estate.
- **The buy-and-flip real estate investment strategy can work, but it also has a downside.** Buying and flipping can be a way to make quick money in real estate if you time your investments correctly in a rapidly rising real estate market. However, flipping can cause your profits to be taxed as ordinary income and you could lose during a market downturn.
- ***Bottom line:* Real estate professionals, and you, should value a property based on the projected net operating income (NOI).** Project the NOI preferably for the next few years. Projecting the NOI is time consuming and requires a lot of experience, especially if you plan property changes to increase income and/or reduce expenses.

Praise for Eric Tyson's Real Estate and Investing Titles

"You won't find a better how-to-sell-your-home book than this one. The authors have included practical knowledge you won't find anywhere else. . . . On my scale of one to 10, it rates a solid 10."

— Bob Bruss, Tribune Media Services, on *Home Buying For Dummies*

" . . . takes you step by step through the process . . . humorous insights that keep the pages turning. This is a reference you'll turn to time after time."

— *St. Petersburg Times,* on *Home Buying For Dummies*

". . . *Home Buying For Dummies* . . . takes a holistic approach to home buying."

— *San Jose Mercury News*

". . . *Home Buying For Dummies* provides a much-needed emotional stabilizer."

— Knight-Ridder News Service

"The humorous *Home Buying For Dummies* by Ray Brown and Eric Tyson is a favorite . . . because the editorial is so good. They check their facts very well. They set out to make you understand this subject and make it fun reading and informative."

— *Minneapolis Star Tribune*

"Eric Tyson . . . seems the perfect writer for a *For Dummies* book. He doesn't tell you what to do or consider doing without explaining the why's and how's — and the booby traps to avoid — in plain English."

— *Chicago Tribune*

"*House Selling For Dummies* by Eric Tyson and Ray Brown is fun . . . and also filled with practical advice."

— *Charlotte Observer*

"*Home Buying For Dummies* and *House Selling For Dummies* . . . go into surprising depth on their topics without straying from their mission of explaining the processes simply."

— *Washington Post*

"In *Investing For Dummies,* Tyson handily dispatches both the basics . . . and the more complicated."

— *The Capital-Journal*

Praise for Robert Griswold's Property Management For Dummies

"Robert Griswold is the guru of smart property management. You won't find a better written, more practical book on the subject."

—Kenneth Harney, nationally-syndicated real est columnist, Washington Post Writers Group

"Anyone who is contemplating becoming a landlord — or for that matter anyone who already is — would do well to read Robert Griswold's book, *Property Management For Dummies*. . . . Mr. Griswold covers all the bases of property management. . . . Whether you have one rental or hundreds, this is a book to keep close by."

—Dave Liniger, Chairman of the Board, RE/MAX International, Inc.

"Robert Griswold is a national leader in the property management field. This is an outstanding reference guide authored by an experienced and outstanding property management professional."

—Dr. Rocky Tarantello, Tarantello and Associates, Newport Beach, CA

"If you're a first-time landlord, this is the only book you'll need. Robert Griswold is a real pro and simplifies every step of the process."

—Dick Barnes, Inman News Features

More Bestselling For Dummies Titles by Eric Tyson

Personal Finance For Dummies®

Discover the best ways to establish and achieve your financial goals, reduce your spending and taxes, and make wise personal finance decisions. *Wall Street Journal* bestseller with over 1 million copies sold in all editions and winner of the Benjamin Franklin best business book award.

Mutual Funds For Dummies®

This bestselling guide is now updated to include current fund and portfolio recommendations. Using the practical tips and techniques, you'll design a mutual fund investment plan suited to your income, lifestyle, and risk preferences.

Taxes For Dummies®

The complete, best-selling reference for completing your tax return and making tax-wise financial decisions year-round.

Home Buying For Dummies®

America's #1 real estate book includes coverage of online resources in addition to sound financial advice from Eric Tyson and frontline real estate insights from industry veteran Ray Brown. Also available from America's best-selling real estate team of Tyson and Brown — *House Selling for Dummies* and *Mortgages for Dummies*.

Small Business For Dummies®

Take control of your future and make the leap from employee to entrepreneur with this enterprising guide. From drafting a business plan to managing costs, you'll profit from expert advice and real-world examples that cover every aspect of building your own business.

Investing For Dummies®

Get back to basics with Eric Tyson's revised and updated bestselling guide to investing. You'll discover how to cut through the hype to find the real deals, how to calculate securities, how to flourish in any market, how new tax laws affect your investments, and much more.

Real Estate Investing
FOR
DUMMIES®

by Eric Tyson and Robert S. Griswold

Wiley Publishing, Inc.

Real Estate Investing For Dummies®
Published by
Wiley Publishing, Inc.
111 River St.
Hoboken, NJ 07030-5774
www.wiley.com

Published by Wiley Publishing, Inc., Indianapolis, Indiana

Published simultaneously in Canada

For general information on our other products and services, please contact our Customer Care Department within the U.S. at 800-762-2974, outside the U.S. at 317-572-3993, or fax 317-572-4002.

For technical support, please visit www.wiley.com/techsupport.

Wiley also publishes its books in a variety of electronic formats. Some content that appears in print may not be available in electronic books.

Library of Congress Control Number is available from the publisher.

ISBN: 0-7645-2565-4

Manufactured in the United States of America

10 9 8 7 6 5

1O/RV/RR/QU/IN

About the Authors

Eric Tyson, MBA, is a best-selling author and syndicated columnist. Through his counseling, writing, and teaching, he equips people to manage their personal finances better and successfully direct their investments. Eric is a former management consultant to Fortune 500 financial service firms and has successfully invested in real estate for more than two decades.

Eric earned his Bachelor's degree in economics at Yale and an MBA at the Stanford Graduate School of Business. Despite these handicaps to clear thinking, he had the good sense to start his own company, which took an innovative approach to teaching people of all economic means about investing and money.

An accomplished freelance personal finance writer, Eric is the author of the national bestsellers *Personal Finance For Dummies* and *Investing For Dummies,* co-author of *Home Buying For Dummies* and *Taxes For Dummies,* and was an award-winning columnist for the *San Francisco Examiner.* His work has been featured and quoted in dozens of national and local publications, including *Newsweek, The Wall Street Journal, Forbes, Kiplinger's Personal Finance Magazine,* the *Los Angeles Times,* and *Bottom Line/Personal;* and on NBC's *Today Show,* ABC, CNBC, PBS's *Nightly Business Report,* CNN, CBS national radio, Bloomberg Business Radio, and Business Radio Network. He's also been a featured speaker at a White House conference on retirement planning.

Despite his "wealth" of financial knowledge, Eric is one of the rest of us. He maintains a large inventory of bumblebee colored computer books on his desk for those frequent times when his computer makes the (decreasing amount of) hair on his head fall out.

Robert S. Griswold, MSBA, is a successful real estate investor and hands-on property manager with a large portfolio of residential and commercial rental properties who uses print and broadcast journalism to bring his many years of experience to his readers, listeners, and viewers.

He is the author of *Property Management For Dummies* and the host of a live weekly radio talk show, *Real Estate Today!,* now in its 14th year (`www.retodayradio.com`). Robert is also the real estate expert for NBC San Diego with a regular on-air live caller segment since 1995. He's also the lead columnist for the syndicated "Rental Roundtable" and "Rental Forum" columns published in dozens of major newspapers throughout the country and has been recognized twice as the #1 real estate broadcast journalist in the nation by the National Association of Real Estate Editors.

Robert's educational background includes having earned BS and two master's degrees in real estate, business economics, and finance from the University of Southern California. His real estate investing and managing professional designations include the CRE (counselor of real estate), the CPM (certified property manager), the CCIM (certified commercial investment member), and the GRI (graduate, Realtor Institute).

Mr. Griswold has been retained on hundreds of legal matters as an expert in the standard of care and custom and practice for all aspects of real estate ownership and management in both state and federal cases throughout the country. Robert is the president of Griswold Real Estate Management, managing residential, commercial, retail, and industrial properties throughout southern California and Nevada.

On a personal level, Robert enjoys travel (particularly cruises), sports, and family activities. He truly enjoys real estate and tries to keep life in perspective through humor!

Dedication

Eric: To my wife, Judy; my family — especially my parents, Charles and Paulina; my friends; and to my counseling clients and students of my courses for teaching me how to teach them about managing their finances.

Robert: I dedicate this book to my parents, Wes and Carol, for their unconditional love and infinite encouragement. I also couldn't have written this book without my best friend and wife, Carol, who has been there for me with her love, support, patience, and persistent attempts to bring the proper balance to my life. Finally, I want to praise and thank God for the wonderful gifts and incredible opportunities He has given me.

Authors' Acknowledgments

Writing a book from scratch is an enormous undertaking, and we couldn't have done it without some invaluable contributions from others. First and foremost we'd like to thank Mike Baker who worked his magic on each and every chapter, page, paragraph, and sentence. He is truly a gifted book editor. We also appreciate the efforts of Jennifer Bingham who did a masterful job as copy editor. And, Kathy Cox deserves special praise for believing in us and making this project happen.

We also would like to thank our technical reviewers Gene Trowbridge, CCIM, and Mark Keeney, plus CPA and real estate tax expert Vern Hoven, for their insightful review and comments. Additional thanks goes to Jim McKernney and Professional Publishing/TrueForms.com for supplying us with forms.

Robert is indebted to Anna Leitzke for her countless hours of assistance in background research. He is looking forward to sharing his real estate knowledge with his four great children — Sheri, Stephen, Kimberly, and Michael who make it all worthwhile.

Publisher's Acknowledgments

We're proud of this book; please send us your comments through our Dummies online registration form located at www.dummies.com/register/.

Some of the people who helped bring this book to market include the following:

Acquisitions, Editorial, and Media Development

Project Editor: Mike Baker

Acquisitions Editor: Kathy Cox

Copy Editor: Jennifer Bingham

Technical Reviewers: Mark Keeney, Gene Trowbridge

Editorial Manager: Jennifer Ehrlich

Editorial Assistants: Courtney Allen, Nadine Bell

Cover Photos: © Getty Images/Photodisc Green

Cartoons: Rich Tennant, www.the5thwave.com

Composition

Project Coordinator: Erin Smith

Layout and Graphics: Andrea Dahl, Joyce Haughey, Heather Ryan

Proofreaders: Dave Faust, TECHBOOKS Production Services

Indexer: TECHBOOKS Production Services

Publishing and Editorial for Consumer Dummies

Diane Graves Steele, Vice President and Publisher, Consumer Dummies

Joyce Pepple, Acquisitions Director, Consumer Dummies

Kristin A. Cocks, Product Development Director, Consumer Dummies

Michael Spring, Vice President and Publisher, Travel

Brice Gosnell, Associate Publisher, Travel

Kelly Regan, Editorial Director, Travel

Publishing for Technology Dummies

Andy Cummings, Vice President and Publisher, Dummies Technology/General User

Composition Services

Gerry Fahey, Vice President of Production Services

Debbie Stailey, Director of Composition Services

Contents at a Glance

Table of Contents

Part II: How to Get the Money: Raising Capital and Financing 79

Part III: Finding and Evaluating Properties 115

Introduction

Welcome to *Real Estate Investing For Dummies!* We're delighted to be your tour guides. Throughout this book, we emphasize three fundamental cornerstones, which we believe to be true:

- Real estate is one of the three time-tested ways for people of varied economic means to build wealth (the others are stocks and small business). Over the long-term, you should be able to make an annualized return of at least 8 to 10 percent per year investing in real estate.
- Investing in real estate isn't rocket science but does require doing your homework. If you're sloppy doing your legwork, you're more likely to end up with inferior properties or overpaying. Our book clearly explains how to buy the best properties at a fair (or even below-market value!) price. (Although we cover all types of properties, our book concentrates more on residential investment opportunities, which are more accessible and appropriate for nonexperts.)
- Although you should make money over the long-term investing in good real estate properties, you *can* lose money, especially in the short-term. Don't unrealistically expect real estate values to increase every year. When you invest in real estate for the long-term, which is what we advocate and practice ourselves, the occasional price declines should be merely bumps on an otherwise fruitful journey.

How This Book Is Different

If you expect us (in infomercial-like fashion) to tell you how to become an overnight multimillionaire, this is definitely not the book for you. And please allow us to save you money, disappointment, and heartache by telling you that such hucksters are only enriching themselves through their grossly overpriced tapes and seminars.

Real Estate Investing For Dummies covers tried and proven real estate investing strategies that real people, just like you, use to build wealth. Specifically, this books explains how to invest in single-family homes; detached and attached condominiums; small apartments including duplexes, triplexes, and multiple-family residential properties up to 20 to 30 units; commercial properties, including office, industrial, and retail; and raw (undeveloped) land. We also cover "indirect" real estate investments such as real estate investment trusts (REITs) that you can purchase through the major stock exchanges or a real estate mutual fund.

Unlike so many real estate book authors, we don't have an alternative agenda in writing this book. Many real estate investing books are nothing more than infomercials for high priced audiotapes or seminars the author is selling. The objective of our book is to give you the best crash course in real estate investing so that if you choose to make investments in income-producing properties, you may do so wisely and confidently.

Here are some good reasons why we — Eric Tyson and Robert Griswold — are a dynamic duo on your side:

Robert Griswold has extensive hands-on experience as a real estate investor who has worked with properties of all types and sizes. He is also the author of *Property Management For Dummies* (Wiley) and is the lead columnist for two popular syndicated real estate newspaper columns. He appears as the NBC-TV on-air real estate expert for southern California. And he is the host of the most popular and longest running (14 plus years) real estate radio show in the country — *Real Estate Today! with Robert Griswold* on Clear Channel Communications.

Mr. Griswold also holds Counselor of Real Estate (CRE), Certified Commercial Investment Member (CCIM), and Certified Property Manager (CPM) designations. Robert earned a bachelor's degree and two master's degrees in real estate and related fields from the University of Southern California's Marshall School of Business.

Eric Tyson is a financial counselor, lecturer, and co-author of the national bestseller, *Home Buying For Dummies* (Wiley), as well as the author of four other bestselling books in the *For Dummies* series: *Personal Finance, Investing, Mutual Funds,* and *Taxes* (co-author).

Eric has counseled thousands of clients on a variety of personal finance, investment, and real estate quandaries and questions. A former management consultant to Fortune 500 financial service firms, Eric is dedicated to teaching people to manage their personal finances better. Over the past two decades, he has successfully invested in real estate and securities, and started and managed several businesses. He earned an MBA at the Stanford Graduate School of Business and a bachelor's degree in economics at Yale.

Foolish Assumptions

Whenever an author sits down to write a book, he has a particular audience in mind. Because of this, he must make some assumptions about who his reader is and what that reader is looking for. Here are a few assumptions we've made about you:

- You're looking for a way to invest in real estate but don't know what types of properties and strategies are best.
- You're considering buying an investment property, be it a single-family home, a small apartment complex, or an office building, but your real estate experience is largely limited to renting an apartment or owning your own home.
- You may have a small amount of money already invested in real estate, but you're ready to go after bigger, better properties.
- You're looking for a way to diversify your investment portfolio.

If any of these descriptions hit home for you, you've come to the right place.

How This Book Is Organized

We've organized *Real Estate Investing For Dummies* into five parts. Here's what you'll find in each.

Part I: Understanding Real Estate as an Investment

In this part, we explain how real estate compares with other common investments, how to determine whether you've got what it takes to succeed as a real estate investor, how much money you'll need to invest in various types of real estate, and the tax advantages of real estate. We also cover how to fit real estate investments into your overall financial and personal plans. We discuss the range of real estate investments available to you — not only common ones such as single-family homes and small apartments — but also the more unusual such as foreclosures and tax sales. Finally, you'll want to work with the best professionals that you can, so we also detail how to interview and secure top agents, lawyers, and other real estate pros.

Part II: How to Get the Money: Raising Capital and Financing

You can't play if you can't pay. This part details how and where to come up with the dough you need to buy property. We also explain the common loans available through lenders and how you may be able to finance your real estate investment through the seller of the property. Finally, we share all of our favorite strategies for finding and negotiating the best deals when you need a mortgage.

Part III: Finding and Evaluating Properties

This section gets down to the brass tacks of helping you decide where and what to buy. We explain how to value and evaluate real estate investment properties: From choosing the best locations to projecting a property's cash flow, we have you covered. Finally, we hold your hand through the negotiation process, plus all of the ins and outs of purchase agreements, inspections, and closing on your purchase.

Part IV: Operating the Property

After you own a property, you have lots of opportunities to improve its value and manage it well. For starters, this important part covers how to be a landlording genius, find and keep the best tenants, and sign solid lease contracts. We also reveal many proven methods for boosting (legally, of course) a property's return and value. We won't let tax headaches get you down as we walk you through how to account for the annual cash flow on your property and how the tax advantages of depreciation allow you to legally pay lower taxes. Last but not least, we share strategies for deciding when and how to sell, including how to defer taxation on your sales' profits while expanding your real estate holdings if you so desire.

Part V: The Parts of Tens

This part contains other important chapters that didn't fit neatly into the rest of this book. Topics that we cover in this section include ten steps to a real estate fortune and ten ways to increase a property's return.

Appendix

This book is comprehensive, but it isn't a book of forms. The purchase and sale of real estate is complicated, and specific legal issues and practices vary throughout the country. We do include a purchase agreement to illustrate some of the key points. However, we recommend that you contact local real estate professionals for the forms that are specifically drafted for your area.

Icons Used in This Book

Throughout this book, you can find friendly and useful icons to enhance your reading pleasure and to note specific types of information. Here's what each icon means:

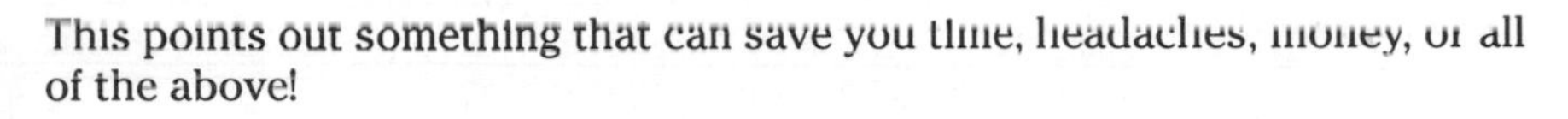
This points out something that can save you time, headaches, money, or all of the above!

Here we're trying to direct you away from blunders and boo-boos that others have made when investing in real estate.

This alerts you to hucksters, biased advice, and other things that could really cost you big bucks.

Potentially interesting but nonessential (skippable) stuff.

We use this icon to highlight when you should look into something on your own or with the assistance of a local professional.

This icon flags concepts and facts that we want to ensure you remember as you make your real estate investments.

Where to Go from Here

If you have the time and desire, we encourage you to read this book in its entirety. It provides you with a detailed picture of how to maximize your returns while minimizing your risks in the real estate market. But you may also choose to read selected portions. That's one of the great things (among many) about *For Dummies* books. You can readily pick and choose the information you read based on your individual needs.

Part I
Understanding Real Estate as an Investment

"I could rent you this one. It's got a pool in the backyard. Then I got a six bedroom with a fountain out front, but nothing right now with a moat."

In this part . . .

Real estate is just one of many available investment options, so in this part, we compare and contrast real estate investing with alternatives you may consider. We discuss the realities of investing in and managing rental properties (both the pros and the cons) and how to fit real estate into your overall personal financial plans. We also cover the gamut of real estate investments you have to choose from and how to begin to assemble a team of competent professionals to assist you with the process.

Chapter 1

Stacking Real Estate Up Against Other Investments

In This Chapter

- Getting started
- Contrasting real estate with other financial options
- Deciding whether real estate is really for you
- Arranging your overall investment and financial plans to include real estate

The vast array of choices available to Americans is both a privilege and a burden. Go to the grocery store in search of something as simple as bread and you'll know exactly what we mean. The same holds true in the investment field. You have tens of thousands of choices among mutual funds, stocks, bonds . . . the list is seemingly endless.

Allow us to help you through the cluttered investment world. In this book, we explain how, why, when, and where to invest successfully in real estate. And, even though we're advocates for investing in real estate, we also (in this chapter) take you through some issues to weigh if you're wondering whether you have what it takes to make money *and* be comfortable investing in real estate. We share our experience, insights, and thoughts on a long-term strategy for building wealth through real estate that virtually everyone can understand and actually achieve.

Let's Get Motivated!

It's never too early or too late to formulate your own plan into a comprehensive wealth-building strategy. For many, such a strategy can help with the challenges of funding future education for children and ensuring a comfortable retirement. The stock market and other diversified investments are essential to a proper asset allocation and diversification strategy, too.

The challenge involved with real estate is that it takes some real planning to get started. It sure is a lot easier to call your broker and purchase a few shares of your favorite stock than to purchase your first rental property. But buying property isn't that difficult. You just need a financial and real estate investment plan, a lot of patience, and the willingness to do some hard work, and you're on your way to building your own real estate empire!

The vast majority of people who don't make money in real estate make easily avoidable mistakes, which we will help you avoid.

In this chapter, we give you some information that can help you decide whether you have what it takes to make money and be comfortable with investing in real estate. We compare real estate investments to other investments you may be considering. We provide some questions you need to ask yourself before making any decisions. And finally, we offer guidance on how real estate investments can fit into your overall personal financial plans.

Robert's father retired a few years ago, after a successful career as a real estate attorney. Robert remembers the advice his father gave him nearly 25 years ago when Robert first entered the real estate field while attending college. He advised that Robert should plan to use his monthly income to primarily pay day-to-day living expenses and allocate money each month into long-term financial investments like real estate. This is solid advice that has served Robert well over the years.

Comparing Real Estate to Other Investments

You've surely considered or heard about many different investments over the years. To help you appreciate and understand the unique attributes of real estate, we compare and contrast real estate with other wealth building investments like stocks and small business.

Returns

Clearly, a major reason that many people invest in real estate is for the healthy total *returns* (which include ongoing profits and the appreciation of the property). Real estate generates robust long-term returns because, like stocks and small business, it's an ownership investment. By that, we mean that real estate is an asset that has the ability to produce income *and* profits.

Our research and experience suggest that total real estate investment returns are comparable to those from stocks (about 8 to 10 percent annually). Over the past 20 years, REIT stocks have appreciated an average annual return of

10.1 percent — not too shabby! (In Chapter 2, we discuss real estate investment trusts — REITs — which are publicly traded companies that invest in income-producing real estate such as apartment buildings, office complexes, shopping centers, and so on.)

And you can earn returns better than 10 percent per year if you select excellent properties in the best areas and manage them well. That said, investing in real estate is accompanied by:

- **Few home runs:** Your likely returns from real estate would not approach the "home runs" that the most accomplished entrepreneurs achieve in the business world.
- **Ups *and downs:*** You're not going to earn an 8 to 10 percent return every year. Although you have the potential for significant profits, owning real estate isn't like owning a printing press at the U.S. Treasury. Like stocks and other types of ownership investments, real estate goes through down as well as up periods. Most people who make money investing in real estate do so because they invest and hold property over many years.
- **Relatively high transaction costs:** If you buy a property and then want out a year or two later, you may find that even though it has appreciated in value, much (if not all) of your profit has been wiped away by the high transaction costs. Typically, the costs of buying and selling — which include real estate agent commissions, loan fees, title insurance, and other closing costs — amount to about 15 percent of the purchase price of a property. So, although you may be elated if your property appreciates 15 percent in value in short order, you may not be so thrilled to realize that if you sell the property, you may not have any greater return than if you had stashed your money in a lowly bank account.
- **Tax implications:** Last, but not least, when you make a profit on your real estate investment, the federal and state governments are waiting with open hands for their share. So, throughout this book we highlight ways to improve your after-tax returns. As we stress more than once, the profit you have left after Uncle Sam takes his bite (not your pretax income) is all that really matters.

Risk

Real estate doesn't always rise in value. That said, market values for real estate don't generally suffer from as much volatility as stock prices do. You may recall how the excitement surrounding the mushrooming of technology and Internet stock prices in the late 1990s turned into the dismay and agony of those same sectors' stock prices crashing in the early 2000s. Many stocks in this industry, including those of "leaders" in their niches, saw their stock prices plummet by 80 percent, 90 percent, or more. You don't see that kind of roller coaster experience with real estate market values.

Keep in mind though (especially if you tend to be concerned about shorter-term risks) that certain types of real estate in some areas can suffer from declines of 10 percent, 20 percent, or more. If you make a down payment of say, 20 percent, and want to sell your property after a 10 to 15 percent price decline, after you factor in transaction costs, you may find that all (as in 100 percent) of your invested dollars (down payment) are wiped out. So you can lose everything.

You can greatly reduce and minimize your risk investing in real estate through buying and holding property for many years (seven to ten or more).

Liquidity

Liquidity — the ease and cost with which you can sell and get your money out of an investment — is one of real estate's shortcomings. Real estate is relatively illiquid: You can't sell a piece of property with the same speed with which you whip out your ATM card and withdraw money from your bank account or sell a stock with a phone call or click of your computer's mouse.

We actually view this illiquidity as a strength, certainly compared with stocks that people often trade in and out of because doing so is so easy and seemingly cheap. As a result, many stock market investors tend to lose sight of the long-term and miss out on the bigger gains that accrue to patient buy-and-stick-with-it investors. Because you can't track the value of investment real estate daily on your computer, and because real estate takes considerable time, energy, and money to sell, you're far more likely to buy and hold onto your properties for the longer-term.

Although real estate investments are generally less liquid than stocks, they're generally more liquid than investments made in your own or someone else's small business. People need a place to live and businesses need a place to operate, so there's always demand for real estate (although the supply of such properties can greatly exceed the demand in some areas during certain time periods).

Income- and wealth-producing potential

Compared with most other investments, good real estate can excel at producing current income for property owners. So in addition to the longer-term appreciation potential, you can also earn income year in and year out. Real estate is a true growth *and* income investment.

The appreciation of your properties compounds tax-deferred during your years of ownership. You don't pay tax on this profit until you sell your property — and even then you can roll over your gain into another investment property and avoid paying taxes. (See the "Tax advantages" section later in this chapter.)

If you have property that you rent out, you have money coming in every month in the form of rents. Some properties, particularly larger multi-unit complexes, may have some additional sources, such as from coin operated washers and dryers. When you own investment real estate, you should also expect to incur expenses that include your mortgage payment, property taxes, insurance, and maintenance. It's the interaction of the revenues coming in and the expenses going out that will tell you whether you realize positive operating profit each month.

For income tax purposes, you also get to claim an expense that isn't really an out-of-pocket cost — depreciation. Depreciation enables you to reduce your current income tax bill and hence increase your cash flow from a property. (We explain this tax advantage and others later in the "Tax advantages" section.)

Unless you make a large down payment, your monthly operating profit may be small or nonexistent in the early years of rental property ownership. During soft periods in the local economy, rents may rise more slowly than your expenses (rents may even fall). That's why you must ensure that you can weather financially tough times. In the worst cases, we've seen rental property owners lose both their investment property and their homes. Please see the section "Fitting Real Estate into Your Financial Plans" later in this chapter.

How leverage affects your real estate returns

Real estate is different from most other investments in that you can borrow (finance) up to 70 to 90 percent or more of the value of the property. Thus, you can use your small down payment of 10 to 30 percent of the purchase price to buy, own, and control a much larger investment. So when your real estate increases in value (which is what you hope and expect), you make money on your investment as well as on the money that you borrowed. That's what is meant when it's said that the investment returns from real estate get magnified due to *leverage*.

Take a look at this simple example. Suppose that you purchase a property for $150,000 and make a $30,000 down payment. Over the next three years, imagine that the property appreciates 10 percent to $165,000. Thus, you have a profit (on paper) of $15,000 ($165,000 minus $150,000) on an investment of just $30,000. In other words, you've made a 50 percent return on your investment. (***Note:*** We ignore *cash flow* — whether your expenses from the property exceed the rental income that you collect or vice versa, and the tax benefits associated with rental real estate.)

Remember, leverage magnifies all of your returns and those returns aren't always positive! If your $150,000 property decreases in value to $135,000, even though it has only dropped 10 percent in value, you actually lose (on paper) 50 percent of your original $30,000 investment. (In case you care, and it's okay if you don't, some wonks apply the terms *positive leverage* and *negative leverage*.) Please see the "Income- and wealth-producing potential" section in this chapter for a more detailed example of investment property profit and return.

Over time, your operating profit, which is subject to ordinary income tax, should rise as you increase your rental prices faster than the rate of increase for your property's overall expenses. What follows is a simple example to show why even modest rental increases are magnified into larger operating profits and healthy returns on investment over time.

Suppose that you're in the market to purchase a single-family home that you want to rent out and that such properties are selling for about $200,000 in the area you've deemed to be a good investment. (***Important note:*** Housing prices vary widely across different areas but the following example should give you a relative sense of how a rental property's expenses and revenue change over time.) You expect to make a 20 percent down payment and take out a 30-year fixed rate mortgage at 6 percent for the remainder of the purchase price — $160,000. Here are the details:

Monthly mortgage payment	$960
Monthly property tax	$200
Other monthly expenses (maintenance, insurance)	$200
Monthly rent	$1,400

In Table 1-1, we show you what happens with your investment over time. We have assumed that your rent and expenses (except for your mortgage payment, which is fixed) increase 3 percent annually. We also assumed that your property appreciates a conservative 4 percent per year. (For simplification purposes, we have ignored depreciation in this example. If we had included the benefit of depreciation, it would further enhance the calculated returns.)

Table 1-1 How a Rental Property's Income and Wealth Build Over Time

Year	*Monthly Rent*	*Monthly Expenses*	*Property Value*	*Mortgage Balance*
0	$1,400	$1,360	$200,000	$160,000
5	$1,623	$1,424	$243,330	$148,960
10	$1,881	$1,498	$296,050	$133,920
20	$2,529	$1,682	$438,225	$86,400
30	$3,398	$1,931	$648,680	$0
31	$3,500	$1,000	$674,625	$0

Now, notice what happens over time. When you first bought the property, the monthly rent and the monthly expenses are about equal. By year five, the monthly income exceeds the expenses by about $200 per month. Consider why this happens — your largest monthly expense, the mortgage payment, doesn't increase. So, even though we have assumed that the rent increases just 3 percent per year, which is the same rate of increase assumed for your nonmortgage expenses, the compounding of rental inflation begins to produce larger and larger cash flow to you, the property owner. Cash flow of $200 per month may not sound like much, but consider that this $2,400 annual income is from an original $40,000 investment. Thus, by year five, your rental property is producing a 6 percent return on your down payment. (And remember, if you factor in the tax deduction for depreciation, your cash flow and return would be even higher.)

In addition to the monthly cash flow from the amount that the rent exceeds the property's expenses, also look at the last two columns in Table 1-1 to see what has happened by year five to your *equity* (the difference between market value and mortgage) in the property. With just a 4 percent annual increase in market value, your $40,000 in equity (the down payment) has more than doubled to $94,370 ($243,330 minus $148,960).

By years 10 and 20, you can see the further increases in your monthly cash flow and significant expansion in your property's equity. By year 30, the property is producing more than $1,400 per month cash flow and you're now the proud owner of a mortgage-free property worth more than triple what you paid for it!

After you get the mortgage paid off in year 30, take a look at what happens to your monthly expenses (big drop) and therefore your cash flow in year 31 and beyond (big increase).

Capital requirements

Although you can easily get started with traditional investments such as stocks and mutual funds with a few hundred or thousand dollars, the vast majority of quality real estate investments require far greater investments — usually on the order of tens of thousands of dollars. (We devote an entire part of this book — Part II, to be precise — to showing you how to raise capital and secure financing.)

If you're one of the many people who don't have that kind of money burning a hole in your pocket, don't despair. We present you with lower cost real estate investment options. Among the simplest low cost real estate investment options are real estate investment trusts (REITs). You can buy these as exchange traded stocks or you can invest in a portfolio of REITs through a REIT mutual fund (see Chapter 2).

Diversification value

An advantage of holding investment real estate is that its value doesn't necessarily move in tandem with other investments, such as stocks or small-business investments that you hold. You may recall, for example, the massive stock market decline in the early 2000s. In most communities around America, real estate values were either steady or actually rising during this horrendous period for stock prices.

However, real estate prices and stock prices, for example, *can* move down together in value. Sluggish business conditions and lower corporate profits can depress stock and real estate prices.

Ability to add value

Although you may not know much about investing in the stock market, you might have some good ideas about how to improve a property and make it more valuable. You can fix up a property or develop it further and raise the rental income accordingly. Perhaps through legwork, persistence, and good negotiating skills, you can purchase a property below its fair market value.

Relative to investing in the stock market, persistent and savvy real estate investors can more easily buy property in the private real estate market at below fair market value. You can do the same in the stock market, but the scores of professional, full-time money managers who analyze the public market for stocks make finding bargains more difficult. We help you identify properties that you can add value to in Part III.

Tax advantages

Real estate investment offers numerous tax advantages. In this section, we compare and contrast investment property tax issues with those of other investments.

Deductible expenses (including depreciation)

Owning a property has much in common with owning your own small business. Every year, you account for your income and expenses on a tax return. (We cover all the taxing points about investment properties in Chapter 16.) For now, we'd like to remind you to keep good records of your expenses in purchasing and operating rental real estate. (Check out Chapter 15 for more information on all things accounting.)

One expense that you get to deduct for rental real estate on your tax return — depreciation — doesn't actually involve spending or outlaying money. *Depreciation* is an allowable tax deduction for buildings, because structures wear out over time. Under current tax laws, residential real estate is depreciated over 27½ years (commercial buildings are depreciated now over 39 years).

Tax-free rollovers of rental property profits

When you sell a stock or mutual fund investment that you hold outside a retirement account, you must pay tax on your profits. By contrast, you can avoid paying tax on your profit when you sell a rental property if you roll over your gain into another like-kind investment real estate property.

The rules for properly making one of these 1031 exchanges are complex and usually involve third parties. We cover 1031 exchanges in Chapter 16. Make sure that you find an attorney and/or tax advisor who is an expert at these transactions to ensure that everything goes smoothly (and legally).

If you don't roll over your gain, you may owe significant taxes because of how the IRS defines your gain. For example, if you buy a property for $200,000 and sell it for $550,000, you not only owe tax on that difference, but you also owe tax on an additional amount, depending on the property's depreciation. The amount of depreciation that you deducted on your tax returns reduces the original $200,000 purchase price, making the taxable difference that much larger. For example, if you deducted $125,000 for depreciation over the years that you owned the property, you owe tax on the difference between the sale price of $550,000 and $75,000 ($200,000 purchase price minus $125,000 depreciation).

Installment sales

Installment sales are a complex method that can be used to defer your tax bill when you sell an investment property at a profit and you don't buy another rental property. With such a sale, you play the role of banker and provide financing to the buyer. In addition to collecting a competitive interest rate from the seller, you only have to pay capital gains tax as you receive proceeds over time from the sale. For details, please see Chapter 16.

Special tax credits for low-income housing and old buildings

If you invest in and upgrade low-income housing or certified historic buildings, you can gain special tax credits. The credits represent a direct reduction in your tax bill from expenditures to rehabilitate and improve such properties. These tax credits exist to encourage investors to invest in and fix up old or run-down buildings that likely would continue to deteriorate otherwise. The IRS has strict rules governing what types of properties qualify. See IRS Form 3468 to discover more about these credits.

Determining Whether You Should Invest in Real Estate

We believe that most people can succeed at investing in real estate if they're willing to do their homework, which includes selecting top real estate professionals. In the sections that follow, we ask several important questions to help you decide whether you have what it takes to succeed and be happy with real estate investments that involve managing property.

Do you have sufficient time?

Purchasing and owning investment real estate and being a landlord is time consuming. If you fail to do your homework before purchasing property, you can end up overpaying or buying real estate with a mess of problems. Finding competent and ethical real estate professionals takes time. (We guide you through the process in Chapter 4.) Investigating communities, neighborhoods, and zoning also soaks up plenty of hours (information on performing this research is located in Chapter 8), as does examining tenant issues with potential properties (see Chapter 9).

As for managing a property, you can hire a property manager to interview tenants and solve problems such as leaky faucets and broken appliances, but doing so costs money and still requires some of your time.

If you're stretched too thin due to work and family responsibilities, real estate investing may not be for you. You may wish to look into the less time-intensive real estate investments discussed in Chapters 2 and 3.

Can you deal with problems?

Challenges and problems inevitably occur when you try to buy a property. Purchase negotiations can be stressful and frustrating. You can also count on some problems coming up when you own and manage investment real estate. Most tenants won't care for a property the way property owners do.

If every little problem (especially those that you think may have been caused by your tenants) causes you distress, at a minimum, you should only own rental property with the assistance of a property manager. You should also question whether you're really going to be happy owning investment property. The financial rewards come well down the road, but you'll be living the day-to-day ownership headaches immediately.

Does real estate interest you?

In our experience, some of the best real estate investors have a curiosity and interest in real estate. If you don't already possess it, such an interest and curiosity *can* be cultivated — and this book may just do the trick.

On the other hand, some people simply aren't comfortable investing in rental property. For example, if you've had experience and success with stock market investing, you may be uncomfortable venturing into real estate investments. Some people we know are on a mission to start their own business and may prefer to channel the time and money into that outlet.

But even if you prefer other investments offering real growth potential, we hope you'll consider the diversification value that real estate offers. When the stock market tanked in the early 2000s, investors in real estate were grateful that their holdings were generally appreciating in value and offsetting their stock market losses.

Fitting Real Estate into Your Financial Plans

For most nonwealthy people, purchasing investment real estate has a major impact on their overall personal financial situation. So, before you go out to buy property, you should inventory your money life and be sure your fiscal house is in order. This section explains how you can do just that.

Ensure your best personal financial health

If you're trying to improve your physical fitness by exercising, you may find that eating lots of junk food and smoking are barriers to your goal. Likewise, investing in real estate or other growth investments such as stocks while you're carrying high-cost consumer debt (credit cards, auto loans, and so on) and spending more than you earn impedes your financial goals.

Before you set out to invest in real estate, pay off all your consumer debt. Not only will you be financially healthier for doing so, but you will also enhance your future mortgage applications.

Become your own landlord

Many real estate investors are actually involved in other activities as their primary source of income. Ironically, many of these business owners come to realize the benefits of real estate investing but miss the single greatest opportunity that is right before their eyes — the prospect of being their own landlord. Robert has advised many business owners that they should purchase the buildings occupied by their own businesses and essentially pay the rent to themselves. If you own a business that rents, do yourself a favor — become your own landlord!

Eliminate wasteful and unnecessary spending (analyze your monthly spending to identify target areas for reduction). This will enable you to save more and better afford making investments including real estate. Live below your means. As Charles Dickens said, "Annual income twenty pounds; annual expenditures nineteen pounds; result, happiness. Annual income twenty pounds; annual expenditure twenty pounds; result, misery."

Protect yourself with insurance

Regardless of your real estate investment desires and decisions, you absolutely must have comprehensive insurance for yourself and your major assets including:

- **Health insurance:** Major medical coverage protects you from financial ruin if you have a big accident or illness that requires significant hospital and other medical care.
- **Disability insurance:** For most working people, their biggest asset is their future income earning ability. Disability insurance replaces a portion of your employment earnings if you're unable to work for an extended period of time due to an incapacitating illness or injuries.
- **Life insurance:** If loved ones are financially dependent upon you, term life insurance, which provides a lump sum death benefit, can help to replace your employment earnings if you pass away.
- **Homeowners insurance:** Not only do you want homeowners insurance to protect you against the financial cost due to a fire or other home-damaging catastrophe, but such coverage also provides you with liability protection.
- **Auto insurance:** This coverage is similar to homeowners coverage in that it insures a valuable asset and also provides liability insurance should you be involved in an accident.

- **Excess liability (umbrella) insurance:** This relatively inexpensive coverage, available in million dollar increments, adds on to the modest liability protection offered on your home and autos, which is inadequate for more affluent people.

None of us enjoy spending our hard-earned money on insurance. However, having proper protection gives you peace of mind and financial security, so don't put off reviewing and securing needed policies. For assistance, see the latest edition of Eric's *Personal Finance For Dummies* (Wiley).

Consider retirement account funding

If you're not taking advantage of your retirement accounts such as 401(k)s, 403(b)s, SEP-IRAs, and Keoghs, you may be missing out on some terrific tax benefits. Funding retirement accounts gives you an immediate tax deduction when you contribute to them. And some employer accounts offer "free" matching money — but you've got to contribute to earn the matching money.

In comparison, you derive no tax benefits while you accumulate your down payment for an investment real estate purchase (or other investment such as for a small business). Furthermore, the operating profit or income from your real estate investment is subject to ordinary income taxes as you earn it. To be fair and balanced, we must mention here that investment real estate offers numerous tax benefits, which we detail in the "Tax advantages" section earlier in this chapter.

Think about asset allocation

With money that you invest for the longer-term, you should have an overall game plan in mind. Fancy-talking financial advisors like to use buzzwords such as *asset allocation.* This indicates what portion of your money you have invested in different types of investments, such as stocks and real estate for growth or lending vehicles such as bonds and CDs, which produce current income.

Here's a simple way to calculate asset allocation: Take your age and subtract it from 110. You get a number that you convert into a percentage. Invest that portion of your long-term money in ownership investments for appreciation. So, for example, a 40-year-old would take 110 minus 40 equals 70 percent in growth investments, such as stocks and real estate. If you wish to be more aggressive, you can take your age and subtract it from 120 so that a 40-year-old would have 80 percent in growth investments.

These are simply guidelines, not hard-and-fast rules or mandates. If you wish to be more aggressive and are comfortable taking on greater risk, you can invest higher portions in ownership investments.

When tallying your investments, determine and use your *equity* in your real estate holdings, which is the market value of property less outstanding mortgages. For example, suppose that prior to buying an investment property, your long-term investments consist of the following:

Stocks	$150,000
Bonds	$50,000
CDs	$50,000
Total	$250,000

So, you have 60 percent in ownership investments ($150,000) and 40 percent in lending investments ($50,000 + $50,000). Now, suppose you plan to purchase a $300,000 income property making a $75,000 down payment. Because you've decided to bump up your ownership investment portion to make your money grow more over the years, you plan to use your maturing CD balance and sell some of your bonds for the down payment. After your real estate purchase, here's how your investment portfolio looks:

Stocks	$150,000
Real estate	$75,000 ($300,000 property – $225,000 mortgage)
Bonds	$25,000
Total	$250,000

Thus, after the real estate purchase, you've got 90 percent in ownership investments ($150,000 + $75,000) and just 10 percent in lending investments ($25,000). Such a mix may be appropriate for someone under the age of 50 who desires an aggressive investment portfolio positioned for long-term growth potential.

Chapter 2

Covering the Landscape of Common Real Estate Investments

In This Chapter

- Keeping your investments close to home
- Looking at residential properties
- Getting to know commercial real estate
- Studying undeveloped land
- Comprehending real estate investment trusts (REITs)

If you lack substantial experience investing in real estate, you should avoid more esoteric and complicated properties and strategies. In this chapter, we discuss the more accessible and easy-to-master income-producing property options. In addition to discussing the pros and cons of each, we add insights as to which may be the most appropriate and profitable for you.

Investing Close to Home

The first (and one of best) real estate investments for many people is a home in which to live. In this section, we cover the investment possibilities inherent in buying a home for your own use, including potential profit to be had from converting your home to a rental, to fixing it up and selling it. We also give you some pointers on how to profit from owning your own vacation home.

Buying a place of your own

During your adult life, you're going to need a roof over your head for many decades. And real estate is the only investment that you can live in or rent to produce income. A stock, bond, or mutual fund doesn't work too well as a roof over your head!

Unless you expect to move within the next few years, buying a place probably makes good long-term financial sense. (Even if you need to relocate, you may decide to continue owning the property and use it as a rental property.) Owning usually costs less than renting over the long haul and allows you to build *equity* (the difference between market value and mortgage loans against the property) in an asset.

Under current tax law, you can also pocket substantial tax-free profits when you sell your home for more than you originally paid plus the money you sunk into improvements during your ownership. Specifically, single taxpayers can realize up to a $250,000 tax-free capital gain and married couples filing jointly, up to $500,000. In order to qualify for this *homeowners capital gains tax exemption,* you (or your spouse if you're married) must have owned the home and used it as your primary residence for a minimum of 24 months out of the past 60 months. The 24 months doesn't have to be contiguous. Additionally, the IRS now provides for pro-rata credit based on hardship or change of employment.

Some commentators have stated that your home isn't an investment, because you're not renting it out. We respectfully disagree: Consider the fact that many people move to a less costly home when they retire (because it's smaller and/or because it's in a lower cost area). Trading down to a lower priced property in retirement frees up equity that has built up over many years of homeownership. This money can be used to supplement your retirement income and for any other purpose your heart desires. Your home is an investment because it can appreciate in value over the years and you can use that money toward your financial or personal goals. *Home Buying For Dummies* (Wiley), which Eric co-wrote with residential real estate expert Ray Brown, can help you make terrific home buying decisions.

Converting your home to a rental

Turning your current home into a rental property when you move is a simple way to buy and own more properties. This approach is an option if you're already considering investing in real estate (either now or in the future), and you can afford to own two properties. Holding onto your current home when you're buying a new one is more advisable if you're moving within the same area, so that you're close by to manage the property. This approach presents a number of positives:

- You save the time and cost of finding a separate rental property, not to mention the associated transaction costs.
- You know the property and have probably taken good care of it and perhaps made some improvements.
- You know the target market because the house appealed to you.

Some people unfortunately make the mistake of holding onto their current home for the wrong reasons when they buy another. This situation often happens when homeowners must sell their homes in a depressed market. Nobody likes to lose money and sell their home for less than they paid for it. Thus, some owners hold onto their homes until prices recover. If you plan to move and want to keep your current home as a long-term investment property, you can. But turning your home into a *short-term* rental is usually a bad move because:

- You may not want the responsibilities of being a landlord, yet you force yourself into the landlord business when you convert your home into a rental.
- You owe tax on the sales' profit if your property is a rental when you sell it and don't buy another rental property. (You can purchase another rental property through a 1031 exchange to defer paying taxes on your profit. See the discussion in Chapter 16.)

If you've spent the last 24 months living in this home that you're converting to a rental property, you then have up to 36 months to dabble in the landlord biz and still preserve your ability to sell and take the $250,000 or $500,000 capital gains tax exclusion. If you find that being a landlord (either by self-managing or hiring a professional property manager) is a positive experience, you can keep the property as a rental long-term.

After you do sell, you can either take advantage of the lower long-term capital gains rates or you can do a 1031 deferred exchange. For tax purposes, you get to deduct depreciation and all of the write-offs during the ownership and you can shelter up to $25,000 in income from active sources as long as your adjusted gross income is $150,000 or less. Please see Chapter 16.

Serial home selling

Serial home selling is a variation on the tried-and-true real estate investment strategy of investing in well-located fixer-upper homes where you can invest your time, sweat equity, and materials to make improvements that add more value than they cost. The only catch is that you must actually move into the fixer-upper for at least 24 months to earn the full homeowners capital gains exemption of up to $250,000 for single taxpayers and $500,000 for married couples filing jointly (as we cover in the "Buying a place of your own" section earlier in this chapter).

Be sure to buy a home in need of that special TLC in a great neighborhood where you're willing to live for 24 months! But if you're a savvy investor, this is usually where you would've invested anyway.

Here's a simple example to illustrate the potentially significant benefits of this strategy. You purchase a fixer-upper for $275,000 that becomes your principal residence, and then over the next 24 months you invest $25,000 in improvements (paint, landscaping, appliances, decorator items, and so on) and you also invest the amount of sweat equity that suits your skills and wallet. You now have one of the nicer homes in the neighborhood and you can sell this home for a net price of $400,000 after your transaction costs. With your total investment of $300,000 ($275,000 plus $25,000), your efforts will have earned you a $100,000 profit completely tax-free. Thus, you've earned an average of $50,000 per year, which is not bad for a tax-exempt second income without strict office hours. Watch out Amway! (Note that many states also allow you to avoid state income taxes on the sale of your personal residence using many of the same requirements as the federal tax laws.)

Now, some cautions are in order here. This strategy is clearly not for everyone interested in making money from real estate investments. We recommend that you bypass this strategy if any of the following apply:

- You're unwilling or reluctant to live through redecorating, minor remodeling, or major construction.
- You dislike having to move every few years.
- You're not experienced or comfortable with identifying undervalued property and improving it.
- You don't have the budget to hire a professional contractor to do the work, and you don't have the free time or the home improvement skills needed to enhance the value of a home.

One final caution: Beware of transaction costs. The expenses involved with buying and selling property — such as real estate agent commissions, loan fees, title insurance, and so forth — can gobble up a large portion of your profits. With most properties, the long-term appreciation is what drives your returns. Consider keeping homes you buy and improve as long-term investment properties.

Vacation homes

A common way that people of means expand their real estate holdings beyond their primary home is to purchase a *vacation home* — a home in an area where they enjoy taking pleasure trips. For example, we know a family that lived in Pennsylvania and didn't particularly like the hot and humid summer weather. They enjoyed taking trips and staying in various spots in northern New England and eventually bought a small home in New Hampshire. Their situation highlights the pros and cons that many people face with vacation or second homes.

The obvious advantage this family enjoyed in having a vacation home is that they no longer had the hassle of securing accommodations when they wished to enjoy some downtime. Also, after they arrived at their home away from home, they were, well, home! Things were just as they expected — with no surprises, unless squirrels had taken up residence on their porch.

The downsides to vacation homes can be numerous, as our Pennsylvania friends found, including:

- **Expenses:** With a second home, you have the range of nearly all of the costs of a primary home — mortgage interest, property taxes, insurance, maintenance, utilities, and so on.
- **Property management:** When you're not at your vacation home, things can go wrong. A pipe can burst, for example, and it may be days or weeks until the mess is found. Unless the property is close to a kind person willing to keep an eye on it for you, you may incur the additional expense of paying a property manager to watch the property for you.
- **Lack of rental income:** Most people don't rent out their vacation homes, thus negating the investment property income stream that contributes to the returns real estate investors enjoy (see Chapter 1). If your second home is in a vacation area where you have access to plenty of short-term renters, you or your designated property manager could rent out the property. However, this entails all of the headaches and hassles of having many short-term renters. (But you do gain the tax advantages of depreciation and all expenses as with other rental properties.)
- **Obligation to use:** Some second homeowners we know complain about feeling forced to use their vacation homes. Oftentimes in marriages, one spouse likes the vacation home much more than the other spouse (or one spouse enjoys working on the second home rather than enjoying it).

Before we close out this section on vacation homes, there are a few tax tips we want to share with you, as found in the current tax code:

- If you retain your vacation home or secondary home as personal property, forgoing the large income streams and tax write-offs for depreciation and operating expenses associated with rental properties, you can still make a nice little chunk of tax-free cash on the side. The current tax code permits you to rent the property for up to 14 days a year — and that income is *tax-free!* You don't have to claim it. Yes, you read that right. And you can still deduct the costs of ownership, including mortgage interest and property taxes, as you do for all other personal properties.
- If you decide to maintain the property as a rental (you rent it out for more than 14 days a year), you, as the property owner, can still use the rental property as a vacation home for up to 14 days a year, or a maximum of

10 percent of the days gainfully rented, whichever is greater, and the property still qualifies as a rental. Also, all days spent "cleaning" or "repairing" the rental home don't count as personal use days — so that's why you paint for a couple hours every afternoon and spend the morning fishing!

Consult with your tax advisor for other tax-saving strategies for your second home or vacation home. And please see Chapter 16 for more tax related information on rental properties.

Before you buy a second home, objectively weigh all the pros and cons. If you have a spouse or partner with whom you're buying the property, have a candid discussion. For most people, buying a vacation home is more of a consumption decision than it is an investment decision. That's not to say that you can't make a profit from owning a second home. However, your total potential investment returns shouldn't be the main reason you buy a second home.

Investing in Residential Income Properties

Residential income property can be an attractive real estate investment for many people. Residential housing is easier to understand, purchase, and manage than most other types of property, such as office, industrial, and retail property. If you're a homeowner, you already have experience locating, purchasing, and maintaining residential property.

If you've been in the market yourself for a home, you know that in addition to single-family homes, you can choose from numerous types of attached or shared housing including apartment buildings, condominiums, townhomes, and cooperatives. In this section, we provide an overview of why some of these may make an attractive real estate investment for you.

Single-family homes

As an investment, single-family detached homes generally perform better in the long run than attached or shared housing. In a good real estate market, most housing appreciates, but single-family homes tend to outperform other housing types for the following reasons:

- Single-family homes tend to attract more potential buyers — most people, when they can afford it, prefer a detached or stand-alone home, especially for the increased privacy.
- Attached or shared housing is less expensive and easier to build *and to overbuild;* because of this surplus potential, such property tends to appreciate more moderately in price.

Because so many people prefer to live in detached, single-family homes, market prices for such dwellings can sometimes become inflated beyond what's justified by the rental income these homes can produce. To discover whether you're buying in such a market, compare the monthly cost (after tax) of owning a home to monthly rent for that same property. Focus on markets where the rent exceeds or comes close to equaling the cost of owning and shun areas where the ownership costs exceed rents.

Single-family homes that require just one tenant are simpler to deal with than a multi-unit apartment building that requires the management and maintenance of multiple renters and units. The downside, though, is that a vacancy means you have no income coming in. Look at the effect of 0 percent occupancy for a couple of months on your projected income and expense statement! By contrast, a vacancy in a four-unit apartment building (each with the same rents) means that you're still taking in 75 percent of the gross potential (maximum total) rent.

With a single-family home, you're responsible for all maintenance. You can hire someone to do the work, but you still have to find the contractors and coordinate and oversee the work. Also recognize that if you purchase a single-family home with many fine features and amenities, you may find it more stressful and difficult to have tenants living in your property who don't treat it with the same tender loving care that you might yourself.

The first rule of being a successful landlord is to let go of any emotional attachment to a home. But that sort of attachment on the tenant's part is favorable: The more they make your rental property their "home," the more likely they are to return it to you in good condition — except for the expected normal wear and tear of day-to-day living. (We discuss the proper screening and selection of tenants in Chapter 13.)

Attached housing

As the cost of land has skyrocketed in many areas, packing more housing units that are attached into a given plot of land keeps housing somewhat more affordable. In this section, we discuss the investment merits of condominiums, townhomes, and co-ops.

Condos

Condominiums are typically apartment-style units that are stacked on top of and/or side-by-side of one another, and that are sold to individual owners. When you purchase a condominium, you're actually purchasing the airspace and interior surfaces of a specific unit as well as a proportionate interest in the common areas — the pool, tennis courts, grounds, hallways, laundry room, and so on. Although you (and your tenants) will have full use and enjoyment of the common areas, remember that the homeowners association will actually own and maintain the common areas, as well as the building structures themselves, which typically include the foundation, roof, plumbing, electrical, and other building systems.

One advantage to a condo as an investment property is that of all the attached housing options, condos are generally the lowest-maintenance properties because most condominium associations deal with issues such as roofing, gardening, and so on for the entire building and receive the benefits of quantity purchasing. Note that you're still responsible for maintenance that is needed inside your unit, such as servicing appliances, interior painting, and so on.

Although condos may be somewhat easier to keep up, they tend to appreciate less than single-family homes or apartment buildings, unless the condo is located in a desirable urban area.

Condominium buildings may start out in life as condos or as apartment complexes that are then converted into condominiums.

Be wary of apartments that have been converted to condominiums. Although they're often the most affordable housing options in many areas of the country, and may also be blessed with an excellent urban location that can't easily be re-created, you get what you pay for in the long run. Our experience is that these converted apartments are typically older properties with a cosmetic makeover (new floors, new appliances, new landscaping, and a fresh coat of paint). However, be forewarned: The cosmetic makeover may look good at first glance, but the property probably still boasts 40-year-old plumbing and electrical systems, poor sound attenuation, and a host of economic and functional obsolescence.

Within a few years, most of the owner-occupants will have moved on to the traditional single-family home and will rent out their condos. You will then find the property is predominantly renter-occupied and has a volunteer Board of Directors that is unwilling to levee the monthly assessments necessary to properly maintain the aging structure. Within 10 to 15 years of the conversion, these properties may well be the worst in the neighborhood.

Townhomes

Townhomes are essentially attached or row homes — a hybrid between a typical "air space only" condominium and a single-family house. Like condominiums, townhomes are generally attached, typically sharing walls and a continuous roof. But townhomes are often two-story buildings that come with a small yard and offer more privacy than a condominium, because you don't have someone living on top of your unit.

As with condominiums, it's extremely important that you review the governing documents before you purchase the property to see exactly what you legally own. Generally, townhomes are organized as *planned unit developments* (PUDs) in which each owner has a *fee simple* ownership (no limitations as to transferability of ownership and the most complete ownership rights one can have) of their individual lot that encompasses their dwelling unit and often a small area of immediately adjacent land for a patio or balcony. The common areas are all part of a larger single lot, and each owner holds title to a proportionate share of the common area.

Co-ops

Cooperatives are a type of shared housing that has elements in common with apartments and condos. When you buy a cooperative, you own a stock certificate that represents your share of the entire building, including usage rights to a specific living space per a separate written occupancy agreement. Unlike a condo, you generally need to get approval from the cooperative association if you want to remodel or rent your unit to a tenant. In some co-ops, you must even gain approval from the association for the sale of your unit to a proposed buyer.

Turning a co-op into a rental unit is often severely restricted or even forbidden and, if allowed, is usually a major headache because you not only must keep your tenant satisfied but also the other owners in the building. Co-ops are also generally much harder to finance and a sale requires the approval of the typically finicky association board. Therefore, we highly recommend that you shun co-ops for investment purposes.

Apartments

Not only do apartment buildings generally enjoy healthy long-term appreciation potential, but they also often produce positive *cash flow* (rental income less expenses) in the early years of ownership. But as with a single-family home, the buck stops with you for maintenance of an apartment building. You may hire a property manager to assist you, but you'll still have oversight responsibilities (and additional expenses) in that event.

In the real-estate financing world, apartment buildings are divided into two groups, based on the number of units:

- **Four or fewer units:** You can obtain more favorable financing options and terms for apartment buildings that have four or fewer units, because they're treated as residential property.
- **Five or more units:** Complexes with five or more units are treated as commercial property and don't enjoy the extremely favorable loan terms of the one- to four-unit properties.

One way to add value, if zoning allows, is to convert an apartment building into condominiums. Keep in mind, however, that this metamorphosis requires significant research on the zoning front and with estimating remodeling and construction costs.

Deciding among the options

From an investment perspective, our top recommendations are apartment buildings and single-family homes. We generally don't recommend attached-housing units. If you can afford a smaller single-family home or apartment building instead of a shared-housing unit, buy the single-family home or apartments.

Shared housing makes more sense for investors who don't want to deal with building maintenance and security issues. Avoid shared housing units in suburban areas where the availability of undeveloped land makes building many more units possible. Attached housing prices tend to perform best in fully developed or built-out urban environments.

For higher returns, look for property where relatively simple cosmetic and other fixes may allow you to increase rents and, therefore, the market value of the property. Examples of such improvements may include but not be limited to:

- Adding fresh paint and flooring
- Improving the landscaping
- Upgrading the kitchen with new appliances and new cabinet/drawer hardware that can totally change the look
- Converting five-unit apartment buildings into four-unit buildings to qualify for more favorable mortgage terms (see the "Apartments" section, earlier in this chapter)

Look for property with a great location and good physical condition but with some minor deferred maintenance. Then you can develop the punch list of items with maximum results for minimum dollars — for example, a property with a large yard but dead grass, a two- or three-car garage but peeling paint or a broken garage door. You could also add a garage door opener to jazz up the property for minimum cost. You can also really add value to a property with a burnt-out, absentee, or totally disinterested owner who is tired of the property.

Unless you can afford a large down payment (25 percent or more), the early years of rental property ownership may financially challenge you:

- **Single-family home:** Making a profit in the early years from the monthly cash flow with a single-family home is generally the hardest stage. The reason: Such properties usually sell at a premium price relative to the rent that they can command (you pay extra for the land, which you can't rent). Also remember that with just one tenant, when you have a vacancy, you have no rental income.
- **Apartment buildings:** Apartment buildings, particularly those with more units, generally produce a small positive cash flow, even in the early years of rental ownership (unless you're in overpriced markets like California where it may take two to four years before you break even on a before-tax basis).

With all properties, as time goes on, generating a positive cash flow gets easier because your mortgage expense stays fixed while your rents increase faster than your expenses. Regardless of what you choose to buy, make sure that you run the numbers on your rental income and expenses (see Chapter 10) to see if you can afford the negative cash flow that often occurs in the early years of ownership.

Considering Commercial Real Estate

Commercial real estate is a generic term that includes properties used for office, retail, and industrial purposes. You can also include self-storage and hospitality (hotels and motels) properties in this category. If you're a knowledgeable real estate investor and you like a challenge, you need to know two good reasons to invest in commercial real estate:

- You can use some of the space if you own your own small business. Just as it's generally more cost-effective to own your home rather than rent over the years, so it is with commercial real estate if — and this is a big *if* — you buy at a reasonably good time and hold the property for many years.
- Your analysis of your local market suggests that it's a good time to buy. We discuss more on this point in a moment.

We'd like to be clear, though, that commercial real estate isn't our first recommendation, especially for inexperienced investors. Residential real estate is generally far easier to understand and also usually carries lower investment and tenant risks.

With commercial real estate, when tenants move out, new tenants nearly always require extensive and costly improvements to customize the space to meet their planned usage of the property. And you'll likely pay for the majority of the associated costs in order to compete with other building owners. Fortunes can quickly change — small companies can go under, get too big for a space, and so on. Change is the order of the day in the business world, and especially in the small business world.

So how do you evaluate the state of your local commercial real estate market? You must check out, over a number of years, the supply and demand statistics. How much total space (and new space) is available for rent, and how has that changed in recent years? What is the vacancy rate, and how has that changed over time? Also, examine the rental rates, usually quoted as a price per square foot. We help you cover this ground in Chapter 8.

One danger sign that purchasing a commercial property in an area is likely to produce disappointing investment returns is a market where the supply of available space has increased faster than demand, leading to higher vacancies and falling rental rates. (This is called *negative absorption,* and what you naturally want is a track record and projections showing *positive absorption* — when the supply of space isn't keeping up with the demand.) A slowing local economy and a higher unemployment rate also spell trouble for commercial real estate prices. Each market is different, so make sure that you check out the details of your area.

Uncovering Undeveloped Land

For prospective real estate investors who feel tenants and building maintenance are ongoing headaches, buying undeveloped land may appear attractive. If you buy land in an area that is expected to experience expanding demand in the years ahead, you should be able to make a tidy return on your investment. This is called *buying in the path of progress,* but of course the trick is to buy before it's obvious to all that new development is moving in your direction. (Check out Chapter 8 for a full discussion on the path of progress.)

You may even hit a home run if you can identify land that others don't currently see the future value in holding. However, identifying many years in advance which communities will experience rapid population and job growth isn't easy. Land prices in those areas that people believe will be the next hot spot already sell at a premium price. That's what happened in a matter of days when the San Diego Padres announced the location of their new baseball park downtown. The same story has been told in most major cities with new sports facilities (especially because these decisions often are disclosed well in advance of the municipality leadership vote or the ballot initiative). There's not much opportunity to get ahead of the curve — or if you guess wrong, you may own some costly land for a long time!

Investing in land certainly has other drawbacks and risks:

- **Care and feeding:** Land requires ongoing cash to pay the property taxes and liability insurance, and to keep the land clear and free of debris while it most likely produces little or no income. Although land doesn't require much upkeep compared with tenant-occupied property, it almost always does require financial feeding.
- **Opportunity costs:** Investing in land is a cash drain, and of course, it costs money to purchase land. If you buy the land with cash, you have the opportunity cost of tying up your valuable capital (which could be invested elsewhere), but most likely you will put down 30 to 40 percent in cash and finance the balance of the purchase price.
- **Costly mortgages:** Mortgage lenders require much higher down payments and charge higher loan fees and interest rates on loans to purchase land because they see it as a more speculative investment. Obtaining a loan for development of land is challenging and more expensive than obtaining a loan for a developed property.
- **Lack of depreciation:** You don't get depreciation tax write-offs because land isn't depreciable.

On the income side, some properties may be able to be used for parking, storage income, or maybe even growing Christmas trees in the northwest or grain in the Midwest! (After you make sure you've complied with local zoning restrictions and have the proper insurance in place.)

Although large-scale land investment isn't for the entry-level real estate investor, savvy real estate investors have made fortunes taking raw land and getting the proper entitlements and then selling (or better yet, subdividing and then selling) the parcels to developers of commercial and residential (primarily home builders) properties. If you decide to invest in land, be sure that you:

- **Do your homework.** Ideally, you want to buy land in an area that's attracting rapidly expanding companies and that has a shortage of housing and developable land. Take your time to really know the area. This isn't a situation in which you should take a hot tip from someone to invest in faraway property in another state. Nor should you buy raw land just because you heard that irresistible opening bid price advertised on the radio for the government excess land auction down at the convention center this Saturday.
- **Know all the costs.** Tally up your annual *carrying costs* (ongoing ownership expenses such as property taxes) so that you can see what your annual cash drain may be. What are the financial consequences of this cash outflow — for example, will you be able to fully fund your tax-advantaged retirement accounts? If you can't, count the lost tax benefits as another cost of owning land.

- **Determine what improvements the land may need.** Running utility, water, and sewer lines; building roads; landscaping; and so on all cost money. If you plan to develop and build on the land that you purchase, research these costs. Make sure that you don't make these estimates with your rose-tinted sunglasses on — improvements almost always cost more than you expect them to. (You need to check with the planning or building department for their list of requirements.)

  Also make sure that you have access to the land or ingress/egress. Some people foolishly invest in landlocked properties. When they discover the fact later, they think that they can easily get an easement. Wrong!

- **Understand the zoning and environmental issues.** The value of land is heavily dependent upon what you can develop on it. Never purchase land without thoroughly understanding its zoning status and what you can and can't build on it. This advice also applies to environmental limitations that may be in place or that could come into effect without any warning, diminishing the potential of your property (with no compensation).

  This potential for surprise is why you must research the disposition of the planning department and nearby communities. Attend the meetings of local planning groups, if any, because some areas that are antigrowth and antidevelopment are less likely to be good places for you to buy land, especially if you need permission to do the type of project that you have in mind. Through the empowerment of local residents who sit on community boards and can influence local government officials, zoning can suddenly change for the worse — sometimes you may find that your property has been *downzoned* — a zoning alteration that can significantly reduce what you can develop on a property and therefore the property's value. See "The dangers of downzoning" sidebar in this chapter for more details.

The dangers of downzoning

Robert owned raw land for many years in an area where a recent government action effectively downzoned his property from 4 acres to 2 acres. The multi-species conservation act designated huge swaths of undeveloped land as mitigation habitat for "endangered plant and animal species." This ordinance mandated that every parcel that wasn't already fully developed was subject to a development limitation of 2 acres. Luckily for Robert, he had subdivided the original 20 acres into 4 smaller parcels of 4 to 5 acres each or the entire 20 acres would've only been allowed usage of 2 acres. Still, Robert's 4- to 5-acre parcels are now limited to 2 acres of development unless Robert pays a "mitigation fee" which is currently over $20,000 per acre! This story illustrates the dangers of buying and owning vacant real estate in areas where conservation activists are prevalent.

Researching Real Estate Investment Trusts

Real estate investment trusts (*REITs*) are for-profit companies that own and generally operate different types of property, such as shopping centers, apartments, offices, warehouses, hotels, and other rental buildings (see Figure 2-1). These property-holding REITs are known as *equity REITs.* Some REITs, known as *mortgage REITs,* focus on the financing end of the business. Mortgage REITs lend to real estate property owners and operators or provide credit indirectly through buying loans (mortgage backed securities such as GNMAs).

Equity REIT managers typically identify and negotiate the purchase of properties that they believe are good investments and manage these properties directly or through an affiliated advisory and management company, including all tenant relations. Thus, REITs can be a good way to invest in real estate for people who don't want the hassles and headaches that come with directly owning and managing rental property.

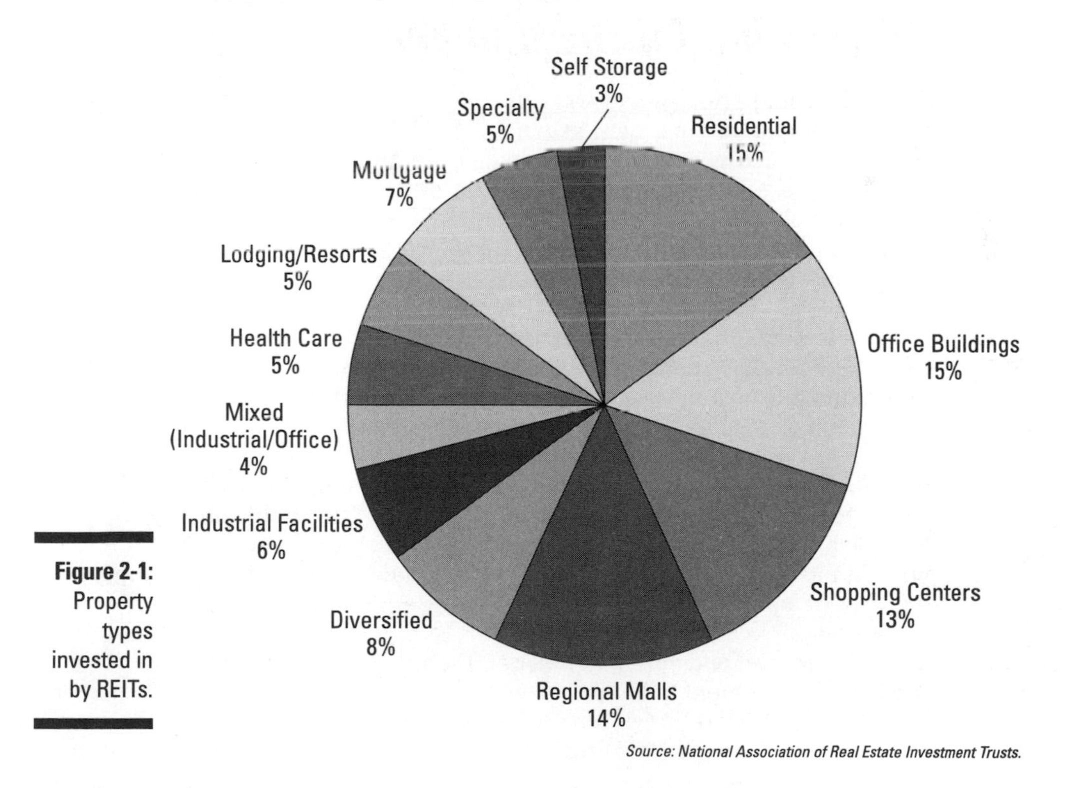

Figure 2-1: Property types invested in by REITs.

Distinguishing between public and private REITs

We recommend that investors not be shy about asking for full disclosure of the relationship between the REIT, its advisors, and the management companies because there are often conflicts of interest that aren't clearly disclosed or significant above-market fees paid that ultimately lower the cash flow and return on investment available for distribution.

Public REITs are traded on the major stock exchanges and thus must meet strict SEC reporting requirements. However, the latest trend towards private REITs raises some concerns. Because they're not publicly traded, they don't have the same disclosures as public REITs. This means an investor in a private REIT had better carefully scrutinize the prospectus and realize that the private REIT has the ability to make changes that may not be in the investor's best interests but that reward the private REIT sponsors or their affiliates.

Performing by the numbers

So what about performance? Over the long-term, REITs have produced total returns comparable to stocks in general. In fact, over the past 30 years, REIT returns have actually been slightly higher. Not only have REIT returns historically been as good or better than stock returns, but REITs have also generally been less volatile than stocks. In the context of an overall investment portfolio, REITs add diversification because their values don't always move in tandem with other investments.

For investments that move perfectly in lock step, their beta or correlation to the overall stock market is 1. For investments always moving in opposite directions, the correlation is 0. Over the long-term, the correlation between stocks and REITs has been about 0.6 (with foreign stocks, it's just 0.4).

One final attribute of REITs we'd like to highlight is the fairly substantial dividends that REITs generally pay. Because these dividends are generally fully taxable (and thus, not subject to the lower stock dividend tax rate), you should generally avoid holding REITs outside of retirement accounts if you're in a high tax bracket such as during your working years.

In case you care, and you may well not, the reason for the high dividends is the legal requirement in REIT charters that they have to distribute 95 percent of their income. In other words, REITs are only allowed to retain a maximum of 5 percent of their net income and everything else must be distributed to the shareholders.

Unlike direct real estate investments, investments in REITs are generally as easy to sell as are other securities such as stocks and bonds. Although this can be a benefit, it can also be tempting for trigger happy investors who are prone to making knee-jerk selling decisions as they try to time the market or become convinced that the latest talking head on the financial news channel thinks that you should sell today!

You can research and purchase shares in individual REITs, which trade as securities on the major stock exchanges. An even better approach is to buy a mutual fund that invests in a diversified mixture of REITs. Some of the best fund REITs charge one percent per year or less in management fees. Vanguard's REIT index fund charges just 0.24 percent per year in fees and has racked up annualized returns in excess of 13 percent since its inception in 1996.

In addition to providing you with a diversified, low-hassle real estate investment, REITs offer an additional advantage that traditional rental real estate doesn't. You can easily invest in REITs through a retirement account (for example, IRA or Keogh). As with traditional real estate investments, you can even buy REITs and mutual fund REITs with borrowed money (in nonretirement accounts). You can buy with 50 percent down, known as *buying on margin,* when you purchase such investments through a brokerage account.

Table 2-1 contains a short list of the best REIT mutual funds currently available.

Table 2-1 The Best REIT Mutual Funds

Fund	*Toll-Free Number*	*Web Site*
American Century Real Estate Investments	800-345-3533	www.americancentury.com
CGM Realty Fund	800-345-4048	www.cgmfunds.com
Cohen & Steers Realty Shares	800-437-9912	www.cohenandsteers.com
Fidelity Real Estate Investment	800-544-8888	www.fidelity.com
Frank Russell Real Estate Securities	800-787-7354	www.russell.com
Neuberger Berman Real Estate Fund	800-877-9700	www.nbfunds.com
SSGA Real Estate Equity Fund	800-647-7327	www.ssga.com

(continued)

Table 2-1 *(continued)*

Fund	*Toll-Free Number*	*Web Site*
Third Avenue Real Estate Fund	800-443-1021	`www.thirdavenuefunds.com`
T. Rowe Price Real Estate Fund	800-638-5660	`www.troweprice.com`
Undiscovered Managers Fund	888-242-3514	`www.undiscoveredmanagers.com`
Vanguard REIT Index Portfolio	800-662-7447	`www.vanguard.com`

If you really have your heart set on becoming the next Warren Buffett and you enjoy the challenge of selecting your own stocks, you can research and choose your own REITs to invest in. Both of the investment research publications, *Morningstar* and *Value Line,* which can be found at many local libraries, produce individual stock page summaries on various REITs. *Forbes* magazine also writes articles about the better REITs (visit their Web site at `www.forbes.com` for more information).

Remember, in regard to the mutual fund REITs listed in Table 2-1, that in addition to having a professional manager deciding what REITs to buy and when, you also enjoy a consolidated financial reporting. If you purchase individual REITs, you will have tax statements to deal with for each and every REIT you're invested in.

Chapter 3

Even More Real Estate Investments

In This Chapter

- Debunking no-money-down strategies
- Uncovering those buy-and-flip properties
- Mastering foreclosures and REOs
- Utilizing lease options
- Understanding probate and tax lien certificate sales and auctions
- Considering alternative real estate investments such as tenants in common and triple net

Although most real estate investors actually begin conventionally through buying a home for their own use and then purchasing a new home and renting out their first home, some folks have found that the best way to quickly become a real estate investor is to purchase income-producing properties in a more unconventional manner.

In this chapter, we take a brief look at some of the most common of these methods of acquiring real estate investment properties or participating in the real estate market, and we tell you what we think about whether you should pursue these options. We start off with a discussion on no-money-down deals and buying and flipping property. We then go over foreclosures, REOs, and lease options. We also cover some other, even more unusual ways to acquire real estate at below-market prices such as probate sales, tax lien sales, and even auctions. And besides REITs (discussed in Chapter 2), there are other avenues to passively invest in real estate, including triple net properties, notes and trust deeds, and limited partnerships, which we also discuss.

Purchasing with No Money Down

If you've ever had insomnia and turned on the television in the middle of the night, you've likely seen the late-night infomercial real estate gurus who claim to possess the true secrets of buying real estate significantly below market value — and they don't even use their own money! They tell viewers that anyone can buy real estate tomorrow using their no-money-down strategies. And it gets even better — they tell you that you can actually receive money from the seller to buy her property. Well, if it sounds too good to be true . . . it usually *is* too good to be true!

Although we do believe it's possible to find a buyer who is so motivated that she'll actually pay you to take a property off her hands, the reality is that the vast majority of such properties don't prove to be profitable for you in the long run. Ask yourself — why would anyone give away a property unless it had some really serious problems?

Reality or myth

The concept of buying real estate without using any of your own money is clearly dependent on finding an extremely motivated seller. And a certain number of motivated sellers exist in any market. A *motivated seller* is one who faces circumstances that don't allow him the flexibility to achieve full market value for his property.

The stock market is a relatively liquid market where buyers and sellers can enter or leave the market quickly with broad knowledge of current pricing. In contrast, real estate assets are *illiquid* — it can take a relatively long time to enter or leave the real estate market. Real estate is also unique: A share of your favorite stock always represents the same investment; not so with real estate. This creates the opportunity to profit from pricing inefficiencies between one property and another. Also, the ability to complete a real estate transaction quickly provides an additional factor that can affect the price.

The ethics of foreclosures

One of the most difficult moral dilemmas facing real estate investors is the ethics of negotiating with an owner facing a foreclosure. Are you helping her or are you a vulture seeking to profit upon the misfortune of another? You must walk a fine line in many of these situations.

Although there's some value to a distressed seller in a quick transaction that provides needed cash, pushing too hard for a bargain can be unethical. Robert uses the "pillow test" to guide his conscience: Can you fall asleep at night and not feel guilty about your moral and ethical conduct?

The following are examples of motivated sellers who may be willing to accept a no-money-down offer:

- **Relocating seller in a hurry:** An owner who's leaving the area may need to quickly sell his home so he can buy a replacement home in his new location. In order to complete the sale in a timely manner, he may be willing to lower the price to $10,000 below the *full market value* (the price he could have received if he were not in such a hurry).

  Finding a seller in a hurry is one of the most reliable ways to buy real estate with no money down.

- **Desperation and exasperation:** The owner of a property that has been vacant for an extended time period or that requires extensive renovation may be desperate to sell. The property may have a deadbeat tenant, or maybe it's vacant after being destroyed by the last tenant and the owner lacks the cash to make the significant investment in repairs. This type of seller may be willing to offer generous seller financing terms or even pay you to remove him from his liability.

But even when sellers find themselves in such positions, who will stamp "Desperate to Sell" on their forehead? Trying to determine a seller's motivation always takes work. Check out Chapter 11 for more on the subject.

Although, clearly, such real estate owners exist, they're not as common as some of the real estate investment gurus would have you believe. There are always anecdotal stories about an amazing success story, but there are many more untold stories of cocky novice real estate investors who found out the hard way that you get what you pay for.

Finding those unique properties

No-money-down sellers are in greater abundance in a weak real estate market (or *buyer's market*) because sellers have fewer options. The target market for no-money-down deals is a real estate market environment with highly motivated sellers facing dire consequences (including foreclosure, which we discuss later in this chapter) unless they dispose of their property.

Often your candidate for a no-money-down offer is a seller who has had some unfortunate circumstances such as an illness, a death in the family, a divorce, or a significant loss of income such that she can no longer afford to make the payments and handle the ongoing expenses of the property. Because of her compromised situation, such a property seller may not readily qualify for new or additional loans that would allow her to handle the cash flow dilemma she faces. Although home equity loans may be available in these circumstances, the owner may be so financially overwhelmed that she prefers to sell her property and downsize her financial obligations to a more manageable level.

Owners with significant equity (difference between the property's market value and outstanding loans) but limited options to tap that equity are good candidates for no-money-down transactions. Such an owner is likely to have cash flow problems, but the overall equity in the property can allow her to act as a lender to you (see Chapter 6).

The two most common *good candidates* (as opposed to the classic definition of folks who would be flexible out of desperation, as detailed above) for no-money-down scenarios are:

- Folks at or approaching retirement age who would prefer a steady income stream to a lump sum.
- Individuals who inherited the property and are looking for monthly income without the hassles of being a landlord.

Unfortunately, the infomercials and the real estate gurus have oversold the concept of no money down. Of course this is the best way to achieve incredible rates of return — earning a return without any investment! But the vast majority of properties that you can acquire with no money down are properties that you can't afford to own any more than the seller can.

Flipping Out over Buying and Flipping

In a solid real estate market, you often find properties appreciating at an annual rate of 3 to 5 percent — a solid and sustainable rate of appreciation that rewards investors with long-term investment horizons who take the buy-and-hold approach with their real estate assets. This buy-and-hold strategy works and should always be the foundation of your wealth building.

But in some areas, the demand for housing has been so great that the limited supply of new and existing properties available in the market is insufficient to meet the demand. It is in these markets of high demand and rapidly escalating prices that real estate speculators with a buy-and-flip strategy appear.

Flipping new and existing homes

A buy-and-flip strategy works with existing homes, but here's an example of how the *buy-and-flip* strategy works with new homes: Buyers know about the shortage of housing, and they look to make a quick profit by putting down a deposit on a new home that a builder hasn't even started. Basically, the buyers make a reservation on the property, betting that when the house is complete (or sooner), the market value will have risen to a point where they can make a quick profit by selling their stake before they close on the deal.

Investing in the first phase of a new residential home development is well-known for its potential to be quite profitable. Because each successive phase is traditionally priced at a higher level, the investor has built-in a return on his or her investment. Placing a deposit on a home to be built in the future is a variation on this strategy that often can result in a significantly higher return on investment because the holding deposit is often just 10 percent or less of the overall purchase price of the home.

For example, a home scheduled to be completed in six months that's selling for $350,000 might only require a holding deposit of $3,500. If the market value of that home increases by 10 percent to $385,000, the holder of the rights to purchase the home may be able to sell their position for up to the $35,000 in increased value for a phenomenal return on investment. Thus, in real estate markets where home values are rapidly increasing, merely controlling the real estate and then selling your position can be rewarding.

The buy-and-flip strategy can also work with existing homes that the investor can purchase from a motivated seller at a wholesale price that is below the market value. The investor may not even have to close escrow before finding a buyer willing to pay a retail price. There may be some minor cosmetic work or simple improvements needed before reselling, but typically, buy-and-flip investors really make their money when they buy at a discount and then locate a buyer at full market value. This is risky, but can also be rewarding.

Heeding the risks

There's nothing wrong with the buy-and-flip strategy, but we prefer the more conventional and lower-risk strategy of buy, fix, and flip. With the *buy, fix, and flip (or refinance) strategy,* you invest in properties where value can be added to the property through repairs, upgrades, and improvements that take a distressed property and turn it into a solid and well-maintained property.

We strongly prefer this method because it has proven throughout the years to be the lowest risk, highest probability way to make money in real estate. You can think of it as the tortoise in the old tortoise-and-the-hare story, where the hare is the fast money, high risk, high return strategy. The tortoise may be slow and steady, but he ends up winning in the long run. As an example, Robert is a conservative person by nature, yet he has acquired a significant real estate portfolio by simply purchasing well-located, but distressed properties and renovating, filling them up, and then refinancing. Please see Chapter 18 for more details on the buy, fix, and flip strategy.

You may be located in a market that has experienced rapid housing price increases, but be careful. If there is too much excess demand for new housing in the area, real estate speculators, not long-term investors or homeowners, can make up the majority of the purchasers. This can be dangerous when the majority of buyers in the market are looking for the quick profit rather than a long-term stable real estate investment. When enough of these speculators head for the exits and don't return, prices can quickly turn tail. The speculators are then forced to mitigate their losses by renting out their properties (sometimes for years) until the real estate market rebounds and they're able to sell the property to break even.

But we're pragmatists — we know that lightning may strike and you may run into a property that turns out to be a buy-and-flip candidate. So, we detail how to keep this possibility open when completing a purchase agreement in Chapter 11. And we also cover possible tax drawbacks in Chapter 16.

Finding Foreclosures and REOs

Would you rather buy real estate at retail or at wholesale? Obviously the answer is "wholesale!" Just like in the stock market, the concept of buy low, sell high also applies to real estate.

One of the best ways to maximize your chances of earning a good return on your investment is to buy a property at foreclosure or as an REO. Such investments will generally be a better value than a conventional purchase, but not without some increased risk! (And of course, other real estate investors are also scouring your local real estate market for great deals.)

Foreclosures are simply properties for which the owner has failed to meet his loan payment or other loan term obligations and the lender is forced to foreclose and *take title* (take over legal ownership and control of the property). Although more formal in a legal sense and more time consuming, a real estate foreclosure is similar to a lender repossessing the car from an owner who fails to make her monthly car payments.

After the lender completes the foreclosure process, the lender takes title, at which point it owns the property. The lender has to maintain and manage the property, so the property is turned over to the lender's in-house Real Estate Owned (REO) department with asset managers who inspect the property, repair any emergency items, and essentially operate the property until it can be sold — usually within a few months unless the borrower has redemption rights (see the "Redemption period" section later in the chapter). Some major lenders, like Bank of America, call the department holding their repossessed properties Owned Real Estate Operations (OREOs). No matter what the name, the savvy real estate investor willing to do the extensive due diligence to find the rare diamonds in the rough will be rewarded.

When considering foreclosures and REOs, be sure to perform the necessary research, including:

- Inspect the property and determine the physical condition and the cost of any needed work. Be careful to rule out environmental concerns.
- Review a preliminary title report to see whether there are any unpaid tax liens or encumbrances on the property.
- Appraise the property and establish your target price and a firm maximum bid so that the emotions of bidding don't lead you to overpay.

Foreclosures

The term *foreclosure* actually describes a process by which a lender takes title to a property on which a loan is in default. The two most common high-risk mistakes made by homeowners that lead to foreclosure are:

- **Failing to make the mortgage payments as required.** For example, some homeowners who overstretched and bought their homes using 100 percent financing (they made no down payment towards the home's purchase price) are living on the edge.
- **Borrowing too much when refinancing:** The record low interest rates combined with the tremendous increase in real estate values in most parts of the country in recent years has led many homeowners to refinance their properties. Although there's nothing wrong with refinancing, as long as you don't borrow too much, some lenders are promoting 110 to 120 percent loans that tempt homeowners to pull all of their equity — and more — out of their homes.

  The theory is that real estate values only increase, so you're simply tapping your future equity. However, one slight stumble with a loss of a job or a drop in income, a serious illness, death, or divorce can lead to a missed mortgage payment or two and ultimately, foreclosure.

But properties can also be subject to foreclosure for other reasons:

- **Owners fail to meet other loan requirements:** Examples include not maintaining proper insurance coverage or not keeping the property in good physical condition.
- **Absentee owners are unable to effectively manage the property:** Good property managers regularly visit and inspect their properties. This level of involvement isn't practical from a distance.

- **Owners walk away from serious problems:** Some properties fall into foreclosure because the property has serious and irreversible problems that are so bad that the current owner chooses to walk away rather than deal with them. Environmental hazards and serious physical problems where cost of repair can exceed the value of the property (such as cracked slabs), often top the list. (In Chapter 12, we cover research you can perform to help avoid these types of problems.)

Before you pursue foreclosure properties, determine the type of foreclosure process commonly used in your state. Check with your favorite lender, real estate agent, real estate attorney, or title company representative to find this information. Your state will fall under one of two categories:

- **Deed of trust state:** When a loan is placed in a deed of trust state, the property title is held in the name of a third party or trustee. If the loan payments aren't made as promised or the loan is in default for another reason, the trustee is empowered to foreclose or take back the property. No court action is necessary and thus a foreclosure in a deed of trust state can happen in 60 to 120 days. This process is referred to as nonjudicial foreclosure.
- **Mortgage state:** In these states, judicial foreclosure in a court of law is required for approval to foreclose. In a mortgage state, no trustee or third party is named. When a mortgage goes into default for nonpayment or other breach, the holder of the mortgage must go to court and seek legal remedies including judicial foreclosure. A judicial foreclosure can take much longer than a nonjudicial foreclosure.

Foreclosure properties aren't that hard to find. Whether you're in a deed of trust state or a mortgage state, the filing of a Notice of Default or a judicial foreclosure lawsuit are matters of public record. An additional public notice announcing a pending foreclosure sale must be published in a local legal newspaper. The timing of the publication prior to the sale varies by state. Many title companies and real estate firms track the Notices of Default and all the steps right through to the actual foreclosure. This information is public record and filed with the county recorder or equivalent, but subscribe to one of the local services offering this information via daily or weekly e-mails or faxes, because gathering this information on your own is time consuming.

Technically there are four steps, and thus four buying opportunities, for a property subject to the typical foreclosure process. Knowing these steps, which we outline in the following sections, and the techniques or negotiating points necessary at each step to motivate the owner or lender is essential to mastering one of the best strategies of buying real estate at below market or wholesale prices.

Preforeclosure

Every potential foreclosure begins when the owner misses a payment on her debt service or is notified in writing by the lender that a condition or term of her loan isn't being met. The *preforeclosure* stage is the period of time before the lender formally files the Notice of Default, which triggers the legal foreclosure process.

The period of time before the formal foreclosure begins is an important buying opportunity: You can get in ahead of your competitors to identify properties on which the owner is delinquent on mortgage payments or violating other conditions of her loan. The key is to track and locate these defaulting owners.

This is the time when you want to offer a solution to the owner that'll get him out of the property and preserve his credit status so he can purchase a home in the future. Also, every owner facing a mortgage delinquency needs some cash to pay for moving and relocation costs. Understanding the motivation of the owner and lender can allow you to formulate an investment strategy that meets everyone's needs and allows you to own a property before it becomes heavily exposed on the local multiple listing service!

Notice of Default

The first formal legal action in the foreclosure process is the filing of a Notice of Default (NOD). If the owner wasn't concerned when he first began missing loan payments, the filing of the Notice of Default should be a real wake-up call.

An owner who has received the Notice of Default is likely to be motivated to sell because she knows that the lender has begun the formal steps toward repossessing her property. But not all owners facing foreclosure are aware that the late charges, penalties, and hefty legal fees further erode their shaky financial position. They may not understand the logic that if they can't make their regular monthly payments, they're unlikely to catch up and pay all of the additional costs, which can literally double the delinquent amount.

The 60 to 90 days following the filing of the NOD is a great time to offer real solutions to an owner facing a foreclosure. Most owners truly believe that their financial problems are temporary, so make your offer sensitive to the fact that preserving the owner's credit record is a key consideration: If you can buy the property quickly at a discount and then cure the default or pay off the delinquent mortgage, the seller will only have the slow payments on his credit report rather than a foreclosure (or possibly a bankruptcy, which is often the only alternative for owners that are unwilling to voluntarily resolve their cash flow problems).

Determine the loan balance and the value of the property to ensure that the owner has equity. Generally, the more equity, the better, because this equity allows you to provide the owner with some quick cash so he can cover the costs of vacating the property and finding a new place to live. It is also this equity in the property that provides you with a profit potential after all of your costs of acquisition plus the required repairs and upgrades to maximize the resale value of the property.

Some real estate gurus recommend that you simply offer a nominal amount of cash to the owner facing a default and then begin making the payments on the existing loans or, in other words, purchase the property "subject to" the current loans. Be wary that the lender may not allow you to just step into the shoes of the original borrower and may still declare the loan to be in default. Have your legal advisor (see Chapter 4) look for an *assumption clause* in the loan documents that would allow you to properly assume the loan. Usually this requires a loan application and a fee. You may also want to watch out for a *due on sale clause* that accelerates the entire loan and makes it due immediately upon the transfer of the property to a new owner. Foreclosure transactions aren't risk free; your legal advisor can tell you the potential downside of your proposed transaction with a defaulting buyer.

Many of the problems that occur in buying foreclosures could've been avoided by structuring the purchase offer to require the owner to vacate the property immediately. It's very difficult for an owner to lose her home and it's often even more difficult for her to accept the fact that she's no longer the owner when she's still living in the property.

Foreclosure sale

Although the foreclosure process varies from state to state, the main difference is whether the loan is secured with a mortgage that requires a judicial foreclosure or by a deed of trust, in which case the nonjudicial process is used (for an introduction to these two types of states, see the "Foreclosures" section earlier in the chapter).

- **Judicial foreclosure:** In a judicial foreclosure, the lender files a lawsuit against the borrower to get the property. Like any other lawsuit, it begins with the serving of a summons and complaint upon the borrower along with any other parties with junior liens or encumbrances against the property. If the borrower responds, the court holds a hearing and rules that either the borrower has presented a legitimate issue (and alternate payment terms are arranged), or the lender is permitted to foreclose.

  The most common scenario is that the borrower doesn't respond and the lender receives a judgment by default and can proceed to have a referee appointed by the court. The lender then advertises the sale for 4 to 6 weeks and then, if full payment hasn't been made, a public sale is held, typically on the courthouse steps. The time frame for this entire judicial foreclosure process is usually between 4 and 6 months, although the process can take as little as 3 months to as long as 12 months.

- **Nonjudicial foreclosure:** In a nonjudicial foreclosure state, lenders are allowed to foreclose without a lawsuit, using the power of sale provisions of the deed of trust. The deed of trust actually has three parties to the original loan agreement — the borrower (grantor), the lender (beneficiary), and the trustee who actually holds title during the pendency of the loan. In the event the borrower defaults, the trustee files a Notice of Default and a Notice of Sale in a legal newspaper.

As with the judicial foreclose, if the loan in a nonjudicial foreclosure is not fully reinstated prior to the date and time of the trustee's sale, then the public auction or sheriff's sale occurs on the steps of a prominent public location in town such as a courthouse. If no one bids, the lender will bid the amount of their loan plus accrued penalties and fees and take title to the property. This is the most common scenario unless the property is desirable and has equity, in which case many interested bidders may compete in a free-for-all.

Bidding on and purchasing properties at the foreclosure sale can be exciting and even profitable if you do your homework and know everything about a property before you bid. But getting a little lazy or going with your gut feeling can lead to a disaster, and it often takes quite a few home runs to offset even one disaster. Something as simple as an unrecorded tax lien or latent physical problems like a cracked slab or expansive soil can turn your lemonade back into a lemon! Be sure to get a title report showing clear title and an owner's title insurance policy.

Redemption period

Some states allow the borrower the right to redeem her property after the sale during a *redemption period* in which she can pay the full amount owed, including the loan balance, late charges, legal fees incurred by the lender, and all of the costs of sale, and get title to the property back. The length of the redemption period varies from state to state. This is also an opportunity to reach an agreement with the borrower for her deed. If successful, the purchaser then essentially obtains the redemption rights of the borrower and has the right to redeem the property.

Even if you're the successful purchaser at the foreclosure sale, you still have to give the borrower the opportunity to redeem the property per the state-required redemption period. Don't make significant improvements only to have the borrower redeem the property — and thank you for renovating his distressed property from the worst on the block to the model home!

Because the majority of properties at a foreclosure sale end up with the lender (because most properties aren't desirable investment properties at this time due to foreclosure risks and limited due diligence, as we discuss in this section), there is a great opportunity to make a deal with the lender just after the foreclosure sale and before they've incurred the expense of hiring an agent to market and sell the property.

You may also be able to make a better deal if the property has significant deferred maintenance or code violations, because the local building inspector or code enforcement departments know when a deep-pocket lender has title to the property and they expect all citations for substandard conditions or code violations to be corrected immediately. You may be able to relieve the lender of this liability while allowing yourself to negotiate a favorable transaction.

Lender REO (Real Estate Owned)

Because titles to the majority of foreclosed properties end up with the lender, you may find that your next opportunity to purchase the property is from the lender's REO department that specializes in handling foreclosed properties. Some investors have found that this is one of the best times to buy a property because they're not dealing with an emotional or unreliable owner. Discovering the ins and outs of the lenders' policies and procedures of disposing of these foreclosed properties can be invaluable to your goal of buying real estate at below market prices.

The days of stealing prime REO properties from the Resolution Trust Corporation (RTC) are gone. The RTC was a quasi-federal government entity established by congress to dispose of the tremendous number of foreclosed assets of the major lenders during the real estate market downturn in the early '90s. Due to the numbers of properties and the relative inexperience and limited due diligence by the RTC in some areas of the country, a once-in-a-lifetime real estate investment opportunity did fall into the lap of savvy real estate investors who had large amounts of cash and could act quickly and then had the financial horsepower to ride out the market downturn.

Lender REOs remain one of the favorite strategies for the late-night infomercial gurus, but the reality is that the lenders are neither foolish nor benevolent. Although these nonperforming loans are a negative on their balance sheet, they're not going to sell a property below its market value just to "get it off their books."

The disposition specialists in the REO department are professionals who understand the real estate markets well and are usually wired into the best real estate brokers in the market. These real estate brokers are often compensated as a percentage of the sales price and thus also motivated to achieve the highest value as reasonably possible.

The only angle a real estate investor usually has with an REO is financing and the continued operating losses that often occur because the lender is merely holding the property and often isn't willing to take the time and make the investment necessary to enhance the property physically and reposition it to perform better in the market.

Sales are as-is, and lenders are often exempt from the standard disclosure rules.

When lenders have an excessive number of REOs, they become more flexible, but they're often limited by the Office of Thrift Supervision (OTS), a government agency that oversees many savings banks and savings and loan associations, and that routinely audits their loan portfolio and their REOs.

FHA/VA repos

Government agencies, such as the Federal Housing Administration (FHA) and the Department of Veterans Affairs (VA), guarantee loans made by lenders to qualified individuals. When these home buyers fail to make their payments, the lender goes through the foreclosure process and ultimately repossesses the house. The government pays the lender the guaranteed loan amount and then takes possession of the property.

These FHA and VA repos are then listed for sale through real estate agents approved by the Department of Housing and Urban Development (HUD). Typically, real estate investors don't find these properties as attractive as some other real estate investment opportunities, because they're usually offered at or just a shade under market prices. Qualified first-time home buyers should look for these FHA/VA repos, because they're often available with favorable financing, including low, or no, down payments.

Looking Into Lease Options

A *lease option* is an excellent way to control and eventually purchase a property without the significant cash investment in a down payment. A lease option, as you may imagine, is essentially two different types of contracts combined into a single agreement. You have a lease (rental agreement), which has all of the usual terms, but the tenant also has the unilateral right to buy the property under certain terms and conditions in the future.

A lease option obligates the owner to sell the property but doesn't obligate the tenant to buy. This is a unilateral contract until the tenant exercises the option and a bilateral contract is created. One of the key issues with lease options is the *option price* (purchase price) that the buyer must pay. This can be a fixed price based on current market value, but often, it's a future projected value based on anticipated appreciation with set time limits for exercising the option. For example, a home valued at $200,000 today may be offered as a lease option with an option price of $210,000 that can be exercised anytime in the next 12 months in a market where the seller expects appreciation of 5 percent per year. Of course, a savvy buyer doesn't exercise the option if the option price exceeds the market value of the property.

Lease options are much easier to find, and much more favorable deals can be made, when there are limited buyers, and sellers are anxious to sell. Lease options are most commonly used with single-family homes and condos, but the concept can be used with any type of property. Overall, in virtually all areas of the country, the demand for lease options is greater than the supply.

Remember that lease options aren't just a great way for real estate investors to buy property; they're also an opportunity for many first-time home buyers to ease into home owning. They're in high demand. So lease options are rarely advertised and you may even need to run your own ad seeking lease options. Another way to track down a possible lease option is to respond to ads with "house for rent." When you own a property that you want to use a lease option to sell, a small ad often brings a large response. Check out Chapter 16 for more information on using a lease option as an exit strategy.

One of the greatest advocates of the lease option is noted real estate columnist Bob Bruss, who has personally been using and writing about lease options for over 25 years. Bob has a monthly *Real Estate Newsletter* and a special report on using lease options to buy or sell your home or investment property. You can subscribe to his monthly newsletters or purchase his special reports online at www.bobbruss.com.

Probing Probate Sales and Auctions

A discussion of the more unusual real estate investments must include probate or sales of properties in estates. Also, auctions are becoming a more popular way to dispose of real estate, particularly because of the continued expansion of the Internet.

Probate sales

Even more reliable than taxes, death creates opportunities for the purchase of good real estate at attractive prices. Every day someone in your area dies and leaves behind real estate that his heirs may not have any desire to retain. These properties are sold in *probate sales* by executors of the estate with the assistance of probate attorneys (or by the public administrator if the owner dies without a trust or will).

Know the laws and rules regarding probate sales in your area, because waiting periods and even court confirmation may be required before the sale is finalized. Also, these sales are often subject to *overbids.* A potential buyer can use the overbid process to appeal directly to the court (before the court issues the order approving the probate sale) to outbid you and purchase the property for more than the current offer under consideration. Generally, the right to overbid requires an offer that exceeds the existing offer by at least 5 percent. Be aware that this possibility exists and be prepared to raise your bid. Just be careful not to get caught up in a bidding war and overpay for a property. Set a maximum price for yourself before you begin bidding.

Robert has a friend who bought a one-of-a-kind beachfront property in San Diego at significantly below market value from the estate of an elderly gentleman who died and left the property to his son. Apparently, the son had no interest in living near the ocean because of the noise and traffic that accompanies beachfront properties. So, the son contacted a real estate broker. He was anxious to sell the property, including the house and two rental units, for not much more than the value of the land alone. The real estate broker and Robert's friend were surfing buddies and because the broker owed Robert's friend a favor . . . the broker was glad to give him the first shot at this once-in-a-lifetime opportunity!

Real estate auctions

Real estate auctions, in which companies claim to be selling prime real estate at below-market prices, are a recent trend in some areas. Don't confuse these auctions with the foreclosure sales that are referred to as auctions in some regions. We're talking about public auctions where antiques or collectibles may also be sold on the same afternoon. Even new home builders have turned to private auctions to sell their new homes in areas where demand is high.

Private individuals, government entities, and lately, companies that specialize in auctions all use this method of selling real estate to the public. You can often find real estate auctioneers listed in your local yellow pages. Like any auction, the goal is to generate interest and competition among potential purchasers in order to drive up the sales price. Often a minimum or reserve price is set to protect the seller from giving the property away too cheaply.

These real estate auctions are promoted heavily in newspapers, on radio and television, and on the Internet with sample prices that sound enticing. They claim to have all types of properties and usually promote a few irresistible-sounding properties — like 10 acres of pristine land for only $5,000. Of course, who knows how far out into the boonies the property is located?

Our experience is that auctions are rarely great opportunities for investors, because too many people compete for the unusual, quality property. Plus, the reserve or minimum prices are set so close to the actual market value of the property that the buyer essentially pays retail under the illusion that she's buying at wholesale. But some good opportunities do arise now and then, so check out these auctions to see if you can find anything worth pursuing.

If you do find a property of interest in an auction, follow the same thorough due diligence process that applies to foreclosures and REOs (see "Finding Foreclosures and REOs" earlier in this chapter).

Unfortunately, proper due diligence isn't always possible due to the short time frame available before the sale or because the auctioneer doesn't provide enough information. For example, the best way to minimize the possibility that the property will contain some costly environmental hazards is to have a professional firm prepare a Phase I environmental report (see Chapter 12). But you're unlikely to be able to afford one for every property that interests you at an auction. This is just one example of the dangers in buying properties without a thorough and exhaustive due diligence investigation, so don't be rushed. Real estate is one investment that you can't easily get out of if you make a mistake. Remember — you don't want any surprises!

If you're the lucky buyer, you'll be required to immediately produce a certified funds check for at least 10 percent of the purchase price. Your final closing date will usually fall in the next 30 days.

The Internet is quickly becoming the preferred method of promoting real estate auctions. As with many Internet opportunities, great care should be taken to ensure that you're dealing with a reputable firm. *Never* even consider buying *any* real estate sight unseen no matter how good the deal seems!

Taking the Passive Approach

Many investors want the diversification and solid returns offered by real estate but aren't qualified for or interested in actively managing their real estate holdings. So these real estate investors often look for investment opportunities that require no management or even minimal interaction with a property manager. Besides REITs (discussed in Chapter 2), there are other avenues to passively invest in real estate, including tenants in common, triple net properties, notes and trust deeds, tax lien certificate sales, and limited partnerships. We discuss these options in this section.

Tenants in common

Recently, tenants in common real estate investments have been heavily promoted as the common man's opportunity to own a piece of institutional- grade, commonly known as *trophy,* properties that the average investor could never acquire on her own. Due to a March 2002 IRS real estate tax ruling, tenants in common (TIC) real estate ownership has been gaining momentum.

Tenants in common ownership is arranged by sponsors that form a TIC investment group for each property where the individual investor actually receives a title deed for an undivided fractional share in a large institutional-grade property. The TIC sponsors either already have purchased or at least control these properties. TIC sponsored properties available for investment include regional shopping malls or even class A high-rise office buildings in major metropolitan areas.

These TIC investments do have some limitations: For instance, there are often limits on the number of investors (married couples count as a single investor) and their financial strength; each investor is proportionately responsible for the debt on the property, if any; and each owner must actually hold a specific fractional deeded interest in the property. As an owner, all profits and losses must be shared and paid proportionately, and the TIC sponsor can't advance funds to cover any expenses. The IRS also requires each owner to have a vote equal to his percentage of ownership.

Don't feel too confident about your voting rights because you'll probably own a small percentage (sometimes as little as 1 or 2 percent of the total property), so you may find that the majority make decisions about management and leasing. Plus, the IRS requires unanimous approval of all co-owners to borrow against the property or sell — which may or may not coincide with your goals and needs.

Our advice is that although there are some advantages to TICs for real estate investors seeking passive tax-sheltered income, new real estate investors and those with modest assets who may need to liquidate or sell their interest should avoid them for now as the current TIC offerings are typically over-priced "retail" investments with extremely high sales commissions and costs. We believe that this relatively new product will evolve and, with more offerings from additional market players, the properties will become more competitively priced and the commissions and costs will fall significantly.

Paying for 1031 availability and "hassle free" management

These investment vehicles can be right for certain investors with significant net worth and no desire to directly own real estate — as long as they fully understand the benefits and drawbacks. The minimum investment for most TICs is measured in the hundreds of thousands of dollars, although some TIC sponsors are offering fractionalized ownership for as little as $50,000.

Traditionally, owners with significant equity either sell or exchange into a larger property or continue to hold and refinance the highly appreciated property to generate cash for additional real estate investments, which also offer additional tax benefits. But TIC candidates are usually real estate owners currently in or contemplating a 1031 tax-deferred exchange (see Chapter 16).

If you're considering a TIC as an alternative for your 1031 exchange, verify in advance with your tax advisor that your transaction will qualify. A 1031 tax-deferred exchange is limited to like-kind property with specific rules about how you hold title of both the relinquished and replacement properties. If the property being sold is directly owned, the transaction will most likely meet the requirements and not be taxable at the time of sale as long as the TIC property is a direct ownership of real estate and not a security. But many investors may find that the property they're selling is a partnership interest in real estate and won't qualify for the 1031 preferred tax treatment because the two investments aren't like-kind.

However, the TIC sponsors have targeted these owners of highly appreciated properties, who are considering a 1031 exchange, but are at a stage in their lives in which they're not interested in expanding their real estate empire. Or they may have used all of the tax benefits of depreciation (see Chapter 16) and really should sell their property and simply pay the capital gains.

A downside of these TIC investments is that they're often extremely expensive. Because the majority of the potential purchasers for these real estate investments are coming out of a tax deferred 1031 exchange, they're subject to tight time limits. The IRS requires 1031 exchanges to identify the replacement property within 45 days of the close of escrow of the property being sold. And the replacement property transaction must be completed within 180 days. Please see Chapter 16 for more details.

Thus, the syndicators of the tenants in common product are always standing by with a pending real estate acquisition for those buyers whose time limits are running short and who need to identify and close on a property within the time limits imposed by the IRS. TICs are only in such high demand now because the real estate market is in disequilibrium in many parts of the country with many more buyers than sellers, which makes it difficult to find new properties to purchase as required by the IRS to defer the reporting of capital gains through the 1031 exchange.

In exchange for this flexibility and readily available product, the syndicators have prepurchased these properties and roll them over to the tenants in common investors at a higher price. Further, the syndicators usually associate with financial advisors who receive hefty sales commissions of 5 to 7 percent and even as high as 10 percent of the investors' initial investment, plus a spread to the TIC sponsor to cover their internal marketing and administration costs. Then many TIC sponsors have separate "advisory firms" that are closely held by the principals of the sponsor and they commonly charge upfront, plus ongoing, consulting fees. Thus, the purchaser of a tenants in common real estate investment is paying top dollar for the property and is only receiving the benefit of about 90 percent of her gross investment because of commissions and fees paid upfront.

The TIC sales pitch also places a heavy emphasis on the desirability of eliminating the trials and tribulations often associated with an owner trying to manage his own property. TIC sponsored properties are professionally managed by the sponsor or a property manager of their choice.

Asking the right questions: Are TICs for you?

Be aware that TIC sponsors often provide attractive, teaser rates of return that are guaranteed only for the first couple of years. For example, a review of the private placement offering will indicate that investors will receive a 7 percent cash distribution per year for the first two years only. This is potentially an enticement for investors who have built up significant equity in their real estate holdings but haven't seen their cash flow increase as fast.

Also, like many other financial products, a lot of effort goes into the promotion and sales of TICs, often through "independent" investment advisors, which means there's a lot of overhead to cover. You'll typically get slick marketing materials and be referred to fancy Web sites or "free" seminars reminiscent of the late-night infomercial gurus. These promotional efforts are high on fluff and scarce on details.

You need to determine whether TICs are right for you by asking your investment advisor and the TIC sponsor for written answers to some basic questions before sending them your money:

- **Who's receiving commissions and how much?** The TIC sponsor receives a commission or spread right off the top, plus the investment advisors (broker) who refer their clients get a piece of the action too.
- **Was the offered property recently acquired and at what price?** Many TIC investors purchase the properties and then resell them within days or months at full retail or top of the market pricing, so it may be informative to know how much the TIC sponsor has made on the investment in addition to the commissions.
- **How much of my net investment is actually invested in the property?** At the end of the day, after everyone has been paid, how much of my investment actually is invested into the property?
- **What's the amount and timing of the cash distributions?** If based on a certain percentage rather than actual operating results, are the distributions guaranteed, and if so, for how long and by whom? Many TIC sponsors use an above-average cash distribution as a hook to entice new investors, but property performance may not generate enough cash to cover the distributions and investors may actually be required to cover operating losses. Where's that fact in the fancy brochure?

- **What are the charges for property and asset management?** Most TIC sponsors have affiliated property management firms that handle the day-to-day management — but at fees toward the high end of reasonable. Also, there may be another layer for an asset manager or advisory firm that supervises the property management company, and they're also often controlled or associated with the TIC sponsor.
- **How liquid is my investment, and does the sponsor offer a buyback or loan program?** Currently, there's no secondary market for TIC investments, so you're at the mercy of the TIC sponsor or possibly another investor who'd be willing to buy you out. Anyone buying a fractional ownership is going to expect and will receive a significant discount from the actual asset value. Have you ever tried to sell a timeshare interest at the price you paid originally from the developer?!

Of course, many investors are attracted to the fact that someone else (all TIC sponsors claim to be experts) is tracking down the properties and doing all of the due diligence, and there is definitely a price to be paid for these benefits. So follow the money and make sure you are comfortable with this investment, because it isn't easy to sell should your needs change.

Triple net properties

Triple net properties are another real estate option for investors looking to avoid the headaches of day-to-day management. For years, these properties have been the favorites of real estate investors who like the steady income stream and safety usually associated with bonds. These investments are sometimes referred to as *net leased* or *net net net properties.* Many investors are attracted to the minimal property management and maintenance requirements of triple net properties because the tenant is responsible for the majority of all operating costs and maintenance.

A triple net lease typically involves a fast-food franchise or restaurant chain or a local chain drugstore. The owner buys the building (usually from a developer who works exclusively with such companies), which is built precisely to the tenant's specifications, and the tenant then enters a long-term fixed-rent lease in which she pays for almost everything, including the property taxes, insurance, utilities, and most of the maintenance. The owner only retains responsibility for the building shell and often the major components like the roof, parking lot, and HVAC equipment. The owner should regularly inspect the property because she retains ultimate control — and thus the liability — if the tenant fails to properly maintain the building.

Lately, the returns available on these triple net properties have been low due to the perception that they're essentially a risk-free investment. However, should the tenant find that the location isn't profitable, you may find yourself owning a customized taco stand that requires a lot of modifications to be a viable location for another business.

Triple net real estate investments are suitable for some, but stay away from them unless you're really comfortable with the tenant and the location and are willing to accept relatively low rates of return. Also, look closely at the rent structure because most leases have many years of flat, fixed rental income with an occasional upward adjustment that's likely to be lower than the future market rent. Triple nets may make some sense if you can consistently earn a return that's higher than a comparable bond investment. But there's always risk with any single-tenant investment property, and fast-food and drugstore chains can (and do) go out of business. We advise investors interested in this type of investment to consider the diversification and lower risk associated with purchasing REITs (see Chapter 2) that hold triple net properties (among others) rather than a direct purchase of a triple net property.

Notes and trust deeds

Although the vast majority of real estate loans for purchasing or renovating properties come from conventional lenders, there are private sources of money that make loans backed by notes or trust deeds. Real estate investors have found that they can benefit from the strong demand for real estate in their area by acting as a lender. They purchase notes and trust deeds that are backed by pledged real estate. *Pledged real estate* is the collateral or security interest provided to the investors to protect them from nonpayment by giving them the ability to foreclose on the real estate. Besides the interest earned on the investment, the note or trust deed holder has the collateral of the underlying real property in the event of a default in the payment of the loan.

Real estate investors who buy and sell trust deeds are also often interested in making private *hard money loans* (loans on top of the first mortgage made by a traditional lender) to property owners or other real estate investors. These hard money loans are secured by the owner's equity in the property and offer potentially favorable returns for the lender willing to make loans to borrowers that often have poor credit. Although there's always increased risk when the borrower has credit issues, the terms can be quite attractive — typically above-market interest rates ranging from 10 to 15 percent, plus loan fees of 3 to 5 points (a point is 1 percent of the loan amount and is essentially prepaid interest), plus prepayment penalties that lock in the high interest rates or require a hefty payment for the privilege of refinancing.

Your loan is secured by a mortgage or Deed of Trust against the property, so it's extremely important to be conservative with the loan-to-value ratio or the amount of money you actually lend the borrower versus the fair market value of the property. At times, borrowers damage or neglect the property if they fall behind on the payments, so we advise real estate investors to limit their exposure to no more than 50 to 60 percent of the value of the property.

Although making and purchasing real estate notes and trust deeds can be a lucrative investment vehicle, acting as a real estate lender can be risky for the novice. Properties with latent problems or unrecorded tax liens are just some of the potential pitfalls. Should you decide that lending money on real estate offers you the high returns you're looking for without the headaches of ownership, proceed with caution. Also be sure that you have an experienced real estate advisor and/or your real estate attorney review the documents before making an agreement or advancing any funds (see Chapter 4).

The safest approach to making secured loans on property is to thoroughly evaluate the pledged collateral to protect your investment and determine the fair market value if you had to foreclose. Never make a loan on a property that you wouldn't be willing to own if that becomes your best way to protect your investment. Some lenders actually hope that the borrower does default so they can obtain the property for a fraction of its market value.

However, don't forget that in addition to the unpaid balance of your loan and accrued interest, there will be additional costs for legal fees and foreclosure costs in the event that the borrower defaults.

Tax lien certificate sales

Real estate owners who fail to pay their property taxes in a timely manner find that the local county will file a lien on their property. A *lien* is any legal claim or charge against real or personal property for the satisfaction of a debt or duty that includes the right to take the property if the obligation isn't discharged. The county will ultimately sell the property in a tax lien certificate sale auction to generate the funds necessary to satisfy the unpaid real estate property taxes, along with the accrued penalties and fees.

But local municipalities don't want to foreclose or wait for payment because they need the funds today to pay the costs of government, so they auction off these tax lien certificates to investors.

Tax lien certificates can be a good investment regardless of the economic cycle, because some property owners will always be unable to pay their property taxes. When you buy a real estate tax lien, you're simply providing the government entity with the funds for the delinquent taxes and buying the rights to collect those taxes from the property owner, plus penalties and a fixed rate of interest that can range from 12 to 24 percent per annum.

The property owner can't sell or pledge her real estate without paying the outstanding tax liens, so over 90 percent of the tax lien certificates are redeemed within 24 months (or the maximum allowable redemption period set by each state or county). Look for tax lien certificates in certain types of real estate, such as owner-occupied properties, because these tend to have nearly a 100 percent redemption rate. You may ultimately have to give the required legal notices and foreclose on the underlying real estate to achieve your return of capital and realize your return on investment, so always limit your purchase of tax lien certificates to properties that you're willing to own.

Tax lien certificates aren't available in every state, and you don't have any way to control the timing of the redemption. Savvy real estate investors that have done quite well with tax lien certificate sales generally buy multiple liens to spread out their anticipated payoffs. Also, they read the fine print of the government rules and regulations concerning these sales, because the rules vary greatly from state to state — and each county within a state may have different rules. Contact your county tax collector to see whether real estate tax lien certificates are a viable investment alternative in your area.

You have to devote the time necessary to really find out about the underlying properties even though finding information is difficult. The conventional sources of local real estate knowledge — brokers and agents — don't work in this market because it offers no opportunities for them to earn commissions.

Limiting the scope of limited partnerships

Limited partnerships have been available for many years. Prior to the extensive overhaul of the federal taxation of real estate investments in the 1980s, they were a common method of real estate investing. Up until that time, all losses from real estate were fully deductible and these loopholes created opportunities for aggressive tax management to avoid legal tax liabilities.

In 1986, Congress passed new tax regulations that eliminated the favorable tax treatment of most losses unless the real estate investor was an active participant. To qualify as an active participant, an individual must be involved in direct management decisions of the property, although the day-to-day rental activities of collecting rent, overseeing repairs, and paying bills can be delegated to a property manager.

Further, the federal tax code limited the deductibility of your passive losses against your earned income (salary, dividends, and interest) to a maximum of $25,000 as long as your adjusted gross income doesn't exceed $100,000. There is a phase out of the maximum $25,000 passive loss deduction at a ratio of $1 for every $2 in adjusted gross income between $100,000 and $150,000. For real estate owners with adjusted gross income exceeding $150,000, any passive losses are carried forward to future years or until the property is sold.

However, there is an extremely valuable exception for real estate investors that can meet the requirements to qualify as a real estate professional. We discuss this in Chapter 16.

Limited partnerships

Unlike a *general partnership,* in which every partner has full management authority and accountability, a real estate *limited partnership* is an investment program in which general partners manage property and accept unlimited liability, and the limited partners don't participate in management decisions and their liability for losses is limited to their investment. A limited partnership offers advantages to real estate investors who want to participate in the market while limiting their day-to-day involvement and liability.

The disadvantage of limited partnerships is that limited partners don't have any authority, so limited partnerships are passive investments. Current federal tax laws favor real estate investments in which the real estate investors qualify as active investors, and this book focuses on real estate investment strategies that qualify as active activities in order to garner the full tax benefits. If you're seeking a passive investment, please see the discussion of other real estate investments, especially REITs, in Chapter 2.

In a limited partnership, the general partner makes all the decisions of management and even decides when to sell the property. Upon disposition, many limited partnerships provide for the general partner to receive a portion of the appreciation (usually from 10 to 25 percent) right off the top — prior to distributions to the limited partners who get a share of the remaining realized appreciation based on their ownership percentage. This equity kicker for the general partner is typically in addition to brokerage fees upon acquisition and disposition, plus market rate or higher fees for property management and asset management.

Although some limited partnerships are formed by general partners who treat each partner as an equal, the majority are structured by general partners with the perspective of "Heads: I win! Tails: You lose!" Some limited partnerships are nothing more than a pure profit play for the general partner in which they get their money upfront — often while the limited partners are held captive and can only hope to see the return of their capital and some appreciation in the distant future.

Chapter 4

Building Your Team

In This Chapter

- Putting a team together first
- Hiring tax and financial advisors
- Seeking lending professionals
- Finding top real estate agents and brokers
- Adding appraisers and attorneys

There are some investments where you can simply turn your money over to professional money managers or financial advisors who then act on your behalf and make the day-to-day investment decisions, buying and selling investment assets within the portfolio. Mutual funds are an example of this type of passive investment. You send your money to your favorite mutual fund firm and periodically evaluate how your fund's managers are doing.

Passive investments in real estate aren't readily available (except for REITs, which we cover in Chapter 2, and TICs, which we discuss in Chapter 3). And for most real estate investors, real estate investing is hands on and complicated enough to require the services and knowledge of a team of professionals. Although you may be skilled in your chosen field, it's unlikely that you possess all of the varied and detailed skills and knowledge necessary to initiate and close a good real estate transaction.

Evaluate proposed real estate investments carefully and methodically before you make the ultimate purchase decision. The uniqueness of each potential real estate opportunity requires the investor to patiently critique the pending investment. You should understand the economic climate and potential for growth, the current physical condition of the property, the tenants, and the value of the property in the marketplace. Then you must ensure that the transfer of real estate is handled properly. This requires a team approach.

In this chapter, we discuss the different real estate professionals and service providers that you should consider teaming up with as you search for real estate investment opportunities and proceed with the purchase of property.

Establishing Your Team Early

Some real estate investors make the mistake of looking for a property to buy without spending enough time up front thinking about and identifying the pros whose help should be hired. But having your team in place before you begin your serious property searching is necessary for two reasons:

- **You can move quickly:** The speed at which you can close a transaction is an advantage in any type of market. In a buyer's market, some sellers are desperate for cash and need to close quickly. In a seller's market, sellers typically don't tolerate having their property tied up in a long escrow with a buyer who doesn't understand the current market conditions or how to properly evaluate the property. Sellers may be missing out on a better deal with a more qualified buyer.
- **You can effectively research the property before making an offer:** Prudent investors conduct research and gather information before they buy, so they know which property or properties are worthy of an offer. Typically, the real estate industry describes *due diligence* as the period of time after you place a property under contract (see Chapter 12). But you really need to perform due diligence even before making an offer. You don't want to waste time on a property that can't meet your goals.

  Some real estate investors like to make an offer and get a property under contract before they begin due diligence. We believe that this is a mistake and can lead to a reputation with sellers (and agents) that you're not a serious buyer (see the "Working with Real Estate Brokers and Agents" section later in the chapter). We recommend only making offers when you have done enough due diligence to feel comfortable that your further thorough review of the property interiors and books will probably not reveal any surprises that will lead to canceling the purchase.

  The most effective research is done with the assistance of real estate professionals to give you the advice and information you need to make an intelligent decision. This pre-offer period is critical and is the one real opportunity for a prospective buyer to investigate a property while retaining the ability to terminate the transaction without a significant monetary loss. You may invest time and several hundred to several thousand dollars to perform the necessary due diligence, but this is a small amount compared to the potential losses from the purchase of a bad property. (We cover this prepurchase research in Chapters 8 through 10.)

Adding a Tax Advisor

A tax advisor may not be the first person that you think to consult before making a real estate transaction. However, our experience is that a good tax advisor can provide terrific feedback on the potential benefits and pitfalls of different real estate investment strategies. Of course, make sure that your tax person has experience with real estate investing and understands your needs and specific goals in regard to your property investments. (We cover the ins and outs of real estate accounting and taxation in Chapters 15 and 16.)

TIP

Although you may pick up a lot of information about real estate and discover some of the advantages of property investing speaking with some tax people, don't rely on generic information ("Investing in real estate offers a terrific tax shelter," for example). You need specific feedback and ideas from a tax expert regarding your unique financial situation and which types of real estate investments will work best for you.

Based on your age, income, and other important factors, the benefits you seek from real estate may be entirely different from other investors. Many real estate investors are looking for immediate cash flow from their properties. But others have sufficient income currently from other sources and prefer to look at real estate as a wealth builder for their retirement years. And almost all real estate investors are looking for tax benefits.

The role of your accountant is to evaluate and recommend investments and tax strategies that will maximize your financial position. Remember the old adage that says, "It is not what you make that matters, but what you keep."

A good tax advisor with property investment experience can tell you whether your best real estate investment is the direct ownership of properties or perhaps owning triple net leased properties with lower returns but fewer management headaches. An accountant can inform his clients as to whether they can still meet the active participation required for certain tax benefits while hiring a property management company to handle the bulk of the day-to-day tenant/landlord issues.

You may also want to find out if you qualify for the added tax benefits that are available for some investors who qualify as real estate professionals. Achieving such qualification isn't easy, and the IRS may someday audit you. Meet with your tax advisor and get to know the benefits and pitfalls of your proposed real estate investments before you start making offers.

Finding a Financial Advisor

Over the years, Eric has written extensively about the financial planning profession and how individuals can best navigate important personal financial decisions with and without the help of such planners. In theory, all of us entering into major investments like real estate should seek holistic financial advice from a financial advisor who charges an hourly fee.

BEWARE

Steering you straight — to the poorhouse

Here are a couple of stories that highlight the conflicts of interest you may be subjected to when working with a "financial advisor."

While serving as an expert real estate witness, Robert had a case where a retired couple was given some self-serving advice by their financial planner. This couple owned their principal residence plus three other rental homes valued at $1 million. All of their real estate was owned free and clear and the rentals were in great condition with good long-term tenants. The properties provided a nice monthly income stream that was mostly tax-free due to their depreciation deduction (see Chapter 16). Although the real estate was clearly their largest asset, they also had nearly $500,000 in stocks, bonds, and IRAs and seemed to be fairly set. That was, until their new financial advisor told them that their retirement was at risk because they had too much invested in real estate. The planner's recommendation was to keep their own home as their real estate investment, but sell the three highly appreciated rental properties and invest the proceeds in mutual funds and other financial products from companies affiliated with the planner.

The planner failed to inform them of his relationship with the sponsors of the new investments and also failed to disclose the significant capital gains taxes that would be due upon sale. By the time they met with their accountant, it was too late — two of the three rental properties had been sold and over $200,000 in taxes was due. The accountant advised the couple to contact an attorney and file a lawsuit against the financial advisor. Although the couple prevailed, they recovered only a small portion of what they paid in taxes. Even worse — they lost the benefits of cash flow and appreciation on their real estate while now owning fully taxable investments.

In Eric's work as an hourly-based financial advisor, he often had clients come to him who were disappointed with the biased and confusing advice they got from various so-called financial planners. In one typical case, a widow had been told by an advisor to sell her two investment properties because he believed that the stock market would produce better returns. She set the wheels in motion to unload the properties but put the brakes on at the last minute after deciding she needed a second opinion. She met with Eric. The first thing that she noticed working with him is that he was far more thorough in examining her overall financial situation, including *all* of her investments, insurance, and resources for retirement. She also realized that she was happy with her real estate holdings and really didn't have any motivation to sell them. Furthermore, she found out from Eric that over the long-term, the returns from stocks and real estate were quite comparable. She thus decided to keep her life simple and stable and hold onto her nicely performing rental properties.

Don't get us wrong, selling real estate can make sense at times. However, you must ask a lot of questions and run any proposed investment strategies by a good tax advisor before you make the decision to liquidate your real estate and shift your investments to other opportunities.

In reality, many financial consultants sell investment and insurance products that provide them with commissions or manage money for an ongoing percentage in stocks, bonds, mutual funds, and the like. Such salespeople and money managers can't provide objective, holistic advice, especially on real estate transactions. When you buy property, it takes money away from these people to manage. Check out the "Steering you straight — to the poorhouse" sidebar in this chapter for more information on such conflicts of interest.

If you've worked with or can locate a financial advisor who sells her time and nothing else, just as a good tax advisor does, consider hiring her. A true financial advisor can help you understand how real estate investment property purchases fit with your overall financial situation and goals. (Please see Chapter 1 for details on this subject.)

Lining Up a Lender or Mortgage Broker

Before looking at specific real estate opportunities, you need a budget. And because your budget for real estate purchases is directly a function of how much you can borrow, you need to determine the limits on your borrowing power. If you can't afford a property, it doesn't matter what a great deal it is.

Reviewing roles

Postpone that appointment to look at investment properties until after you examine the loans available. You have two resources to consult:

- **Lender** is a generic term for any firm, public or private, that directly loan you the cash you need to purchase your property. This type of lender is often referred to as a *direct lender.* Most often, your list of possible lenders will include banks, credit unions, and private lenders (including property sellers). Lenders tend to specialize in certain types of loans. For instance, you don't go to a credit union that only offers car loans to finance a real estate investment property loan.
- A **mortgage broker** is a service provider that presents your request for a loan to a variety of different lenders in order to find the best financing for your particular needs. Just like real estate or insurance brokers, a good mortgage broker can be a real asset to your team (we cover mortgages in detail in Chapter 6, along with the advantages and disadvantages to working with mortgage brokers versus direct lenders in Chapter 7).

Lenders and mortgage brokers are in the business of making loans. That is how they make money. Their product is cash and they make money by renting it to people and businesses that pay them the money back plus *interest,* which is the cost of renting the money. Money is a commodity just like anything else and its availability and pricing are subject to an assortment of variables.

Lenders and mortgage brokers want to find you money for your next real estate purchase, but they're not objective advisors to provide counsel for how much you should borrow. They're trained to calculate the maximum that you *may borrow.* Don't confuse this figure with the amount that you *can truly afford* or that will fit best with your overall financial and personal situation.

So why is getting a loan so difficult at times? Because lenders want to make loans to those investors who are a good credit risk and who they think have a high probability of repaying the loan in full plus the interest. The lender has costs of doing business and needs to make a profit. Because the money they lend often belongs to their depositors, lenders need to be careful and selective about the loans they make. (See Chapter 7 for more information on the necessity of a good credit rating when investing in real estate.)

The lender requires collateral to protect them if the borrower doesn't make the debt service payments as required. *Collateral* is the real or personal property that is pledged to secure a loan or mortgage. If the debt isn't paid as agreed, the lender has the right to force the sale of the collateral to recover the outstanding principal and interest on the loan. Typically, the property being purchased is the pledged collateral for real estate loans or mortgages.

Building relationships

Relationships with lenders can take time to build, so begin looking for lenders that specialize in the types of properties within the geographic area that you have targeted. They can help you understand your financial qualifications or how much you will be able to borrow before you begin your search for an investment property. Get together with your lender or mortgage broker and provide them with your latest personal financial statement, which includes your income and expenses as well as your assets and liabilities and net worth.

Always be truthful with your lender. One way to sabotage a relationship with a lender is to exaggerate or stretch the truth about your current financial situation or about the potential for your proposed property acquisition. The lender will require supporting documents for your income and assets and will obtain a current credit report. The savings and loan abuses in the early 1990s have led to much tighter controls, so expect the lender to check and recheck every line item. When you don't oversell yourself or your proposed property, lenders are often more willing to work with you and even offer better terms.

Although lenders only make money by making loans and some lenders seem to be willing to lend money on any property at any price, the type of lender you should associate with is one who understands real estate cycles and your local real estate market.

We've found that lenders can also serve a valuable role by preventing you from making serious mistakes. Particularly in overheated seller's markets where prices are irrationally climbing with no fundamental economic support, your lender and the required appraisal can keep you from getting caught up in a buy-at-any-price frenzy. In these markets, lenders tend to be a little more conservative and will limit loan amounts and require larger down payments. These factors provide the lender with additional protection should market prices fall, but they're also a signal that the lender feels the loan exceeds the intrinsic value of the property that they'll be stuck with if you default. Smaller loan offers with higher down payments are a clue that you may be paying more than a property is worth or buying at the market's peak.

Working with Real Estate Brokers and Agents

Your investment team should include a sharp and energetic real estate broker or agent. All real estate brokers and agents are licensed by the state in which they perform their services. A real estate *broker* is the highest level of licensed real estate professional and a licensed real estate sales *agent* is qualified to handle real estate listings and transactions under the supervision of a broker. The vast majority of real estate licensees are sales agents.

A real estate agent must have his license placed under a supervising broker who's ultimately responsible for the actions of the sales agent. Real estate brokers often begin their careers as real estate agents, but it's possible to meet the more stringent qualifications and immediately qualify as a broker. Brokers and agents can perform the same functions; many real estate agents actually have more practical experience and hands-on market knowledge than the brokers they work for. Brokers that have many agents reporting to them often spend most of their time educating, supervising, and reviewing the transactions presented by their agents. So, if you have a problem with an agent, contact the broker — the buck stops with her!

Generally, you'll deal with real estate agents, but the added experience and dedication of a broker can be beneficial to you if you're involved in larger and/or more complicated transactions. Real estate agents are fine to handle the majority of real estate transactions, including the typical purchase or sale of an owner-occupied single-family home or condo. But whether you use a broker or an agent, make sure that this person has a solid track record with investment property transactions in your area. We refer to both real estate brokers and agents simply as agents throughout this chapter.

The implications of agency

When you deal with a real estate agent, you need to know who she represents. Real estate investors need to understand the concepts of dual agency and single agency and the implications of each:

- **Single agency:** This is when an agent only represents the buyer or the seller. The other party either represents herself or is represented by an agent who doesn't work for the same broker as the other agent. For example, a buyer's agent only has a fiduciary relationship with the buyer. The buyer's agent has a duty to promote the interests of the buyer and keep all information confidential unless legally required to disclose. The buyer's interest should be first and foremost, and no information is passed to the seller without your knowledge other than that information that directly affects your ability to perform on the contract as written.

  We strongly recommend that you work with an agent who operates as a single agency representative. A lot of money is involved in income property transactions, and you want to have someone looking out for your interests whether you're buying or selling an investment property.

- **Dual agency:** A situation in which the same individual agent represents both the seller and the buyer *or* when two different agents representing the seller and buyer are from the same firm (with the same broker). With any transaction, each agent involved owes a fiduciary duty of loyalty to each client he represents, but this is nearly impossible for one agent who is representing both the buyer and seller in the same transaction (and difficult as well if two agents work for the same broker).

  Avoid the inherent conflict of interest found with dual agency and establish a relationship with a single agency agent who represents only *your* interests. Dual agency makes it extremely challenging for one agent, or two agents working for the same broker, to be loyal to clients with opposing interests. For example, agents may hear confidential information from sellers about what their minimum acceptable price is, and the same agent or another agent from the same firm will hear from buyers that they're willing to pay more than what they first offered.

Agents, and especially their brokers, prefer dual agency — they generate more commissions by representing both sides of the transaction. That is why many agents will start out showing their clients only properties that are listed by their firms. However, this desire to capture a bigger share of the real estate commission has led to some serious conflicts of interest. Now most states either prohibit dual agency or at least require the agent to disclose the exact nature of the agency relationship prior to commencing the representation of a client by taking a listing, showing a property, or making an offer.

Compensation

Real estate agents are generally motivated to see the transaction go through because they're compensated when a sale is made. Compensation for agents is typically calculated as a percentage of the sales price paid for a property. So the agents actually have an interest in the property going for a higher price. Commissions vary based on the property and the size of the transaction:

- Individual residential properties, such as single-family homes and condos, have commissions of 5 to 6 percent of the sales price.
- Small multi-family and commercial properties are often in the 3 to 5 percent range.
- Larger investment properties have commissions of 1 to 3 percent.
- Raw land is usually at 10 percent, unless the acreage is large.

These commissions are typically split between the firm listing the property for sale and working with the seller and the agent representing the buyer. The actual proportion of the split varies, with the listing agent sometimes taking a smaller percentage than the buyer's agent if the commissions aren't evenly split. The commission actually is paid to the broker, and the agent receives his share based on his employment or commission agreement, which also often calls for the agent to cover some of his own expenses and overhead.

Real estate commissions can be a significant cost factor for real estate investors. Most listing agreements acknowledge that commissions aren't fixed by law and that they're always negotiable. Traditionally, the seller "pays" the commission to the real estate agents involved in the transaction, although because the buyer is the one paying for the property, we say that both the buyer and seller ultimately pay for the agent's commissions.

Real estate agents do add to the cost of purchasing property, but a good agent, like a good property manager, can justify the cost of her services by introducing you to properties that you would not otherwise have an opportunity to purchase. A good agent will earn her commissions.

Some real estate investors get a real estate license so that they can eliminate paying at least one-half of the real estate commission to agents. And there are times when you'll be able to use your sale's or broker's license to effectively reduce your transaction expenses and investment requirement by representing yourself in a transaction. This is particularly helpful when you're looking to sell a property in a strong seller's market.

How to find a good broker or agent

INVESTIGATE

The key to finding a good broker or agent to assist you in the purchase of investment real estate is to narrow the field down to those individuals who are the best. Look for folks with the following qualifications:

- **Full-time professional:** Because the commissions earned on the sale of a large income property can be so great, you will find that almost every broker or agent will claim that she can represent you. But you want to eliminate those brokers or agents who are greedy, incompetent, or simply mediocre. Although many part-time real estate professionals sell single-family homes and condos, you'll quickly find that the most qualified real estate investment property agents are full-time.
- **Expert in the geographic market and specific property type:** Find someone who knows your market and the specific property type you're seeking. This knowledge is especially important if you don't live nearby. Avoid brokers who aren't experts in your specific property type. For example, don't use a broker who specializes in single-family homes and condominiums unless that's your target market. Likewise, a commercial property broker is unlikely to have the best investment opportunities for your consideration with single-family investment property.

After narrowing down the candidates, many standard screening techniques can then be applied to pinpoint the top three that you should interview:

- **Verify the professional's license status:** Most states have an online broker and agent database, so this step is simple. Confirm that their real estate license is current with no citations or disciplinary action for past or pending violations. If you're using a real estate agent, check both the license status of the agent and her supervising broker. If state has disciplined the broker or agent, inquire further to understand the relevance to your transaction. A suspension or temporary revocation of a license is a serious issue — even if it was reinstated. The facts of the case may be material to your choice of a real estate professional.
- **Check references:** Get the names and numbers for three to five clients (in the geographical area where you're seeking property) that the broker or agent has worked with in the past year. Investment real estate transactions tend to be fewer than owner-occupied property transactions, so speaking with three to five clients from the last year maximizes your chances of speaking with clients other than the agent's all-time favorites.

  Don't just ask for the references; call them. And don't just ask generic questions about whether the client was happy with the broker or agent. Dig deeper — find an agent who you can work with on investments that are critical to your long-term wealth-building goals. Ask questions about the types of properties and the geographic locations involved. Ask questions like, "Did the broker or agent assertively represent you and take charge of the transaction or did you have to initiate conversations?"

Consider these traits when investigating potential brokers and agents as well:

- **Willingness to communicate with you:** The number one complaint about real estate professionals is that they don't keep their clients informed during transactions. You're looking for someone with experience who isn't necessarily the "top producer," because you want someone who can take the time to communicate regularly with you.
- **Interpersonal skills:** A broker or agent needs to get along with you and with a whole host of others involved in a typical real estate deal: other agents, property sellers, inspectors, lenders, and so on. An agent needs to know how to put your interests first without upsetting others.
- **Negotiation skills:** Putting a real estate deal together involves negotiation, so you want a broker or agent with negotiating skills and lots of experience in larger transactions. Is your agent going to exhaust all avenues to get you the best deal possible? Most people don't like the sometimes aggravating process of negotiation, so they hire someone else to do it for them. Be sure to ask the agent's former clients how the agent negotiated for them.
- **Reputation for honesty, integrity, and patience:** When it comes to the brokering of investment properties, the reputation of your representative can be critical. Brokers or agents with a track record of dealing fairly with their clients and their peers can greatly assist in gaining the cooperation of an adversarial seller. And gaining such cooperation is often needed to close a complicated transaction. Some strife is almost guaranteed when buying commercial investment real estate — there will be several opportunities where the transaction can unravel and only the trustworthiness, perseverance, and patience of the real estate professionals involved can keep the transaction on course.

Making the most of your agent

Some real estate investment books advise you to contact every broker or real estate agent who targets your preferred geographic area. Although casting a bigger net has some inherent attraction, our experience is that you should only work with one broker or agent at a time in a given market area.

Real estate agents can be a key source for new investment opportunities and general market information. This is where our advice in the previous section — find an experienced agent who specializes in the types of properties you're looking for and knows the local market — pays off. These agents know buyers and sellers and also possess contacts for other services and products that you'll need as your real estate investment portfolio expands.

Because agents only get paid for deals they close, they're not interested in investing time and energy with numerous potential buyers. They want serious buyers who will close the deal. A track record of not wasting the time of your professional team is your goal. Plus, if you garner a reputation of tying up properties and then renegotiating the deal or canceling the escrow, you'll find that your offers won't be accepted in the future. Sellers and their brokers don't want to waste time with phantom buyers.

You want to be the first one contacted about the best properties coming on the market, rather than one of many when everyone knows about the property from the Multiple Listing Service (MLS). The *MLS* is a service created and maintained by real estate professionals, which gathers all of the local property listings into a single place so that purchasers may review all available properties from one source. The MLS also deals with commission splitting and other relations between agents.

To get the best deals, timing is critical. You want your broker or agent to think of you first. If you're not interested in or not able to purchase a property at the time, explain your situation and thank them for thinking of you. A handwritten thank you note or simple gift also lets them know you appreciate their efforts — and keeps you at the top of their lists for the next opportunity.

In many metropolitan areas, looking at the properties on a Multiple Listing Service or in the newspaper isn't enough. The best deals are often the ones that don't make it into these sources. This is where the insider information from real estate sales agents can make you the bride and not the bridesmaid. (Of course, many brokers are themselves interested in investing in income producing properties, and they have the first chance at the best deals.)

Many owners of investment real estate don't want the disruption that can occur with openly listing the property. The management company and employees begin to worry about their jobs, and tenants become concerned that rents will be raised. These problems can be avoided by quietly talking to one or two top brokers in an area with the understanding that the potential transaction is to be kept confidential. This leads to some great opportunities for the top brokers and their clients.

And although having a real estate agent on your team is an excellent strategy that will give you a competitive edge, don't completely ignore the Multiple Listing Service or in-house listings of brokers. Such sources often include properties that other investors overlooked because they didn't have the vision or the right team members to see a potential opportunity.

Considering an Appraiser

Many real estate investors know appraisers solely in the role of providing the property valuation report required by lenders. And it is generally in this role that investors can find appraisers to be a source of aggravation, rather than a potential resource. However, an appraiser can be an effective team member if your real estate investment strategy involves buying and selling properties with somewhat hidden opportunities to add value. Appraisers sometimes possess insight into real estate opportunities that others miss.

Appraisers can help you by telling you the current value of a property, but they bring real value as part of your real estate investment team by:

- Providing insight into the factors that can lead to an increase in the market value of a property.
- Assisting you in maximizing the return on your investment in upgrades to distressed or fixer-upper properties.
- Giving you useful information on the demographics of the area and helping to identify those properties that are distressed but have plenty of upside potential (properties requiring work in good neighborhoods).

One of Robert's partners, a highly successful real estate investor in foreclosure properties, has even hired an appraiser as an in-house member of his real estate investment team. Virtually every property that appears on the weekly Notice of Default list from the title company is reviewed first by the appraiser, who looks for properties that are located in the path of progress and with some real upside potential if brought to marketable condition physically and aesthetically. (For more on Notice of Default, see Chapter 3; for information on getting in front of the path of progress, see Chapter 8.)

The appraiser is also able to assist in determining the as-is value and the cost of making the necessary repairs and upgrades to the property. This information helps the investor establish the maximum price she should pay for the property, based on comparable sales in the market.

Finding an Attorney

You may think that adding an attorney to your real estate investment team seems like an expensive luxury that you can't afford. Indeed, you may be able to purchase properties when you're just starting out as a real estate investor without consulting an attorney, because buying a small rental property is often not much different from purchasing your own home. The process is relatively simple with preprinted forms that seem so easy to complete. And you usually have an experienced real estate agent to guide you through the process. (See Chapter 11 for information on locating forms.)

For simple transactions, the retention of an attorney is strictly a function of whether attorneys are traditionally involved as the intermediary or closing agent. If you live in an area where attorneys aren't usually involved in real estate transactions, then an attorney may not be necessary. In some states, it's essential to have an attorney actually handle the transaction and closing.

But we strongly suggest that you consult with an experienced real estate attorney as your investments increase in size and complexity. With more complicated transactions, have the attorney review the documents — even in states where the title or escrow company handles the paperwork and serves as the independent intermediary or closing agent. A good real estate attorney can help you structure proposed transactions. Particularly if you're looking into a large transaction where you assume loans or you're attempting to secure special financing, a competent real estate attorney can be invaluable.

Robert's father is a real estate attorney and taught him early in his real estate investment career that the best time to consult with an attorney is before you finalize the proposed transaction. There is nothing your attorney can do to avoid legal snafus and expensive litigation if he isn't hired to draft, review, and negotiate the terms of your proposed transaction in advance. Although such a review may cost you some money up front, it's definitely much more economical than having to hire an attorney to get you out of a bind.

Seek an attorney who specializes in real estate purchasing and lease transactions. Ideally, you'll find one attorney or law firm that can assist you not only with your transactions, but also with the drafting and review of other documents as you operate the property. In particular, look for attorneys who have specialized knowledge of tenant-landlord laws and the complicated issues surrounding commercial leases.

Check references and find an attorney who has excellent communication skills and can explain complicated legal terms and documents in terms you understand. As with any professional, the old adage that "You get what you pay for" holds true more often than not. So remember that the lower hourly rate attorneys aren't necessarily your better option, because more expensive, yet more experienced, attorneys are your best bet when you're investing in large real estate transactions.

Part II

How to Get the Money: Raising Capital and Financing

"So ... how did our first stage financing go today?"

In this part . . .

In this important part, we detail the amount of money you need to have in hand for various real estate investments as well as where you can go to borrow the rest because few real estate investors buy property with 100 percent cash. In addition to discussing traditional lending sources, we also cover seller financing of properties. Last but not least, we explain how to save money and get the best loan for your situation.

Chapter 5
Sources of Capital

In This Chapter

- Moving beyond the no-money-down myth
- Knowing what you need to get going in real estate
- Locating cash

For many people, the trouble with real estate investing is that they lack the access to cash for the down payment. The old adage that "It takes money to make money" is generally true in our experience. Most real estate investing books make one of two assumptions. Some assume that you have plenty of money and just need to figure out how to buy, add value to a property, and then sell. Of course, it would be great if that were true, but not all of us are flush with cash. The other common assumption is that you have no money and must resort to scouring the real estate market in search of sellers so desperate to sell that they or their lenders don't require any down payment.

So how do you get started in real estate if you don't want to own distressed properties in the worst neighborhoods and you don't have a six-figure balance in your checking account to pay top dollar in the best neighborhoods? Successful real estate investing requires patience and a long-term vision. Our method of building real estate wealth over time is to create investment returns that are sustainable and provide generous returns on your investments.

Calculating the Costs of Entry

At some point in your life, you've surely had the experience of wanting to do something and then realizing that you don't have sufficient money to accomplish your goal. Perhaps it was as simple as lacking the pocket change to buy a chocolate bar as a child. Or maybe it happened on a vacation when you ran low on funds and tried to do business with a merchant who only took Visa when you only carried American Express. No matter — the world of real estate investing is no different. You can't play if you can't pay.

Forgetting the myth of no money down

The title of this chapter says it all: To invest in real estate, you need capital, and likewise you need a source from which to gather said capital. On late-night infomercials, at seminars, on audiotapes, and in books, you may hear many self-appointed real estate experts tell you that you can invest in real estate with literally no money. And if that's not enticing enough, you may hear that you can buy properties where the seller will put cash in your hands.

Have such no-money-down situations ever existed among the billions of completed real estate transactions in the history of the modern world? Why, yes they have. Realistically, can you find such opportunities among the best real estate investing options available to you? Why, no you can't.

Think of the people you know who still haven't found the perfect mate after decades of searching. Mr. and Ms. Perfect don't exist. Ditto the ideal real estate investment. If you use our sensible criteria when seeking out properties that'll be good real estate investments and then add the requirement that you can only make such investments with no money down, you'll probably waste years searching to no avail. We've never made a no-money-down real estate investment because the best properties simply aren't available on that basis.

Our experience is that the no-money-down properties we have seen aren't properties we want to own. And if you receive cash out of escrow upon closing on a property, you're either buying a severely distressed property that will soon require major cash infusions or you've overleveraged the property. If it sounds too good to be true, it *is* too good to be true! For a more complete discussion of no money down, please see Chapter 3.

Determining what you do need to get started

The fact that you're not likely to find good no-money-down real estate investments doesn't mean that you must be wealthy or have great savings to begin making attractive real estate investments. In this book, we present a wide range of investment options so there's something for virtually everyone's budget and personal situation.

Before we jump into that though, we must point out that most of the time, real estate investors make a down payment and borrow the majority of the money needed to complete a purchase. That is the "conventional way" to purchase real estate investment properties and will be the most successful method for you in the long run (as it has been for us).

Getting in the door with good credit

Lenders, property sellers, potential partners, and so on will all prefer to deal with you if you've established a reputation for paying your bills. Good to great credit is essential. Both of us began building our credit through the responsible use of credit cards in college, and to this day, our high FICO scores have allowed us to borrow at favorable rates and terms and save tens of thousands of dollars per year in financing costs.

Don't underestimate the importance of establishing good credit, because the best returns on real estate rely upon the use of credit to obtain the leverage of using OPM (other people's money). Why pay more for money when you can show the ability to handle it properly and be rewarded with a lower price? We cover the importance of good credit and ways to remove unsightly blemishes on your credit history that may keep you from getting solid interest rates in Chapter 7.

For most residential investment properties, such as single-family homes, attached housing such as condos and townhomes, and small apartment buildings of up to four units, you'll have access to the best financing terms by making at least a 20 to 25 percent down payment. You can make smaller down payments (as low as 10 percent or less) but you'll pay much higher interest rates and loan fees. (We cover the topic of financing in Chapter 6.)

You won't find such wonderful financing options for larger apartment buildings (five or more units), commercial real estate, and raw land. Compared with residential properties of up to four units, such investment property generally requires more money down and/or higher interest rates and loan fees. Please see Chapter 6 for more details.

Determining how much cash you need to close on a purchase is largely a function of the estimated purchase price. Suppose you're looking to buy some modest residential housing for $100,000. Your 25 percent down payment suggests you need $25,000, and adding in another 5 percent for closing costs brings you to $30,000. If you have your heart set on buying a property that costs three times as much ($300,000 sticker price), then you'll need to triple these amounts to a total of about $90,000 for the best financing options.

Overcoming down payment limitations

Most people, especially when they make their first real estate purchase, are strapped for cash. In order to qualify for the most attractive financing, lenders typically require that your down payment be at least 20 percent of the property's purchase price. The best investment property loans sometimes require

25 to 30 percent down for the most favorable terms. In addition, you need to reserve money to pay for other closing costs such as real estate commissions, title insurance, and loan fees.

If you don't have 20-plus percent of the purchase price, don't panic and don't get depressed — you can still own real estate. We've got some solutions:

- **Low money down loans with private mortgage insurance:** Some lenders may offer you a mortgage even though you may be able to put down only 3 to 10 percent of the purchase price. These lenders will likely require you to purchase private mortgage insurance (PMI) for your loan. This insurance generally costs several hundred dollars per year and protects the lender if you default on your loan. (When you do have at least 20 percent or higher equity in the property, you can generally eliminate the PMI.)
- **Dip into your retirement savings:** Some employers allow you to borrow against your retirement account balance, under the condition that you repay the loan within a set number of years. Subject to eligibility requirements, first-time homebuyers can make penalty-free withdrawals of up to $10,000 from IRA accounts. (***Note:*** You still must pay regular income tax on the withdrawal.)
- **Delayed gratification:** If you don't want the cost and strain of extra fees and bad mortgage terms, postpone your purchase. Go on a financial austerity program and boost your savings rate. Examine your current spending habits and plan to build up a nest egg to use to invest in your first rental. Often real estate investors get started by actually buying a new home and simply keeping their old home as a rental. For more information, see the section "Make saving a habit" later in the chapter.
- **Think smaller:** Consider lower-priced properties. Smaller properties and ones that need some work can help keep down the purchase price and the required down payment. For example, a duplex where you live in one unit and rent out the other is also a cost-effective way to get started.
- **Partner up:** If smaller, lower-priced properties don't satisfy your desires, you may be able to find a partner. For example, find a duplex and get a partner where you both initially occupy the property and make the payments, because duplexes are typically more cost-effective per unit than unattached properties. (More on this option later in this chapter.)
- **Seller financing:** Some property owners or developers may finance your purchase with as little as 10 percent or even less down. However, you can't be as picky about such seller-financed properties because a limited supply is available and many that are available need work or haven't yet sold for other reasons. Often these are reasons that only become apparent after you're the owner!

Turning to low entry cost options

For the ultimate in low entry costs, real estate investment trusts (REITs) are best. These stock exchange traded securities (which can also be bought through REIT-focused mutual funds) can be bought into for several thousand dollars or less. REIT mutual funds can often be purchased for $1000 or less inside retirement accounts. (See Chapter 2 for more on investing in REITs.)

Lease options represent another low cost (although more complicated) opportunity. With these, you begin by renting a property you may be interested in purchasing down the road. In the interim, a portion of your monthly rental payment goes toward the future purchase price. If you can find a seller willing to provide financing, you can keep your down payment to a minimum. Turn to Chapter 3 for more on lease options.

Rounding Up the Required Cash

Most successful real estate investors that we know, including ourselves, got started building their real estate investment portfolio the old fashioned way — through saving money and then gradually buying properties over the years. Many people have difficulty saving money because they don't know how to or are simply unwilling to limit their spending. Easy access to consumer debt (via credit cards and auto loans) creates huge obstacles to saving more and spending less. Consider that more than half of all Americans holding credit cards carry debt balances. Investing in real estate requires self-control, sacrifice, and discipline. Like most good things in life, you must be patient and plan ahead to be able to invest in real estate.

Make saving a habit

As young adults, some (but not most) people are good savers out of the gate. Those who save regularly are often folks who acquired good financial habits from their parents. Other good savers have a high level of motivation to accomplish goals such as retiring young, starting a business, buying a home, having the flexibility to spend time with their kids, and so on. Achieving such goals is much harder (if not impossible) when you're living paycheck to paycheck and worried about next month's pile of bills.

If you're not satisfied with how much of your monthly earnings you're able to save, you have two options (and you can take advantage of both):

- **Boost your income:** To increase your take-home pay, working more may be a possibility, or you may be able to take a more lucrative career path. Our main advice on this topic is to keep your priorities in order. Your personal health and relationships shouldn't be put on the back burner for a workaholic schedule. We also believe in investing in your education. A solid education is the path to greater financial rewards and will lead to all of the great goals we discuss here. Education isn't only key for your chosen profession, but also for real estate investing. Consider getting a real estate license or learn to be an appraiser or property manager — skills that not only help you with your property investing, but that also might allow you to take on part-time work to supplement your income.
- **Reduce your spending:** For most people, this is the path to increased savings. Start by analyzing how much you expend on different areas (for instance, food, clothing, insurance) each month. After you've got the data, decide where and how you'd like to cut back. Would you rather eat out less or have a maid come less often? How about driving a less expensive (but not less safe) car versus taking lower cost vacations? Although the possibilities to reduce your spending are many, you and only you can decide which options you're willing and able to implement. If you need more help with this vital financial topic, consult the latest edition of Eric's bestseller *Personal Finance For Dummies* (Wiley).

Tap into other common cash sources

Saving money from your monthly earnings will probably be the foundation for your real estate investing program. However, you may have access to other financial resources for down payments. Before we jump into these, we offer a friendly little reminder: Monitor how much of your overall investment portfolio you place into real estate and how diversified and appropriate your holdings are given your overall goals. (Please see Chapter 1).

Borrowing against home equity

Most real estate investors that we know began building their real estate portfolio after they bought their own home. Tapping into your home's equity may be a good down payment source for your property investments.

You can generally obtain mortgage money at a lower interest rate on your home than you can on investment property. The smaller the risk to the lender, the lower their required return — and thus, the better rates for you as the borrower. Lenders view rental property as a higher risk proposition and for good reason: They know that when finances go downhill and the going gets really tough, people pay their home mortgage to avoid losing the roof over their heads before they pay debts on a rental property.

Unless your current mortgage was locked in at lower rates than are available today, we generally recommend refinancing the first loan and freeing up equity that way versus taking out a home equity loan or line of credit.

A variation on the borrowing against home equity idea uses the keep-your-original-home-as-a-rental strategy. You build up significant equity in your owner-occupied home and then need or want a new home. Refinance the existing home (while you still live there for the best owner-occupied rates) and then convert it into a rental. Take the tax-free proceeds from the refinance and use that as the down payment on your new owner-occupied home.

Before you go running out to borrow to the maximum against your home, be sure that you:

- **Can handle the larger payments.** We don't recommend borrowing more than the value of your home, as you may be enticed to do with some of the loan programs that pitch borrowing upwards of 125 percent of the value of your home. We hear these programs being routinely touted as not only a way to free up equity and pay down consumer debt, but also encouraging people to borrow in excess of the current value of their home so they can invest in more real estate. This excessive leveraging is dangerous and could come back to haunt you! Please see Chapter 1 for the big picture on personal financial considerations.
- **Understand the tax ramifications of all your alternatives.** Borrowing more against your home at what appears to be a slightly lower rate may end up costing you more after taxes if some of the borrowing isn't tax deductible. Under current tax laws, interest paid on home mortgages (first and second homes) of up to $1 million is tax deductible. You may also deduct the interest on home equity loans of up to $100,000.

  Be careful to understand the tax deductibility issue when you refinance a home mortgage and borrow more than you originally had outstanding on the prior loan. If any of the extra amount borrowed isn't used to buy, build, or improve your primary or secondary residence, the deductibility of the interest on the excess amount borrowed is limited. Specifically, you may not deduct the interest on the extra amount borrowed that exceeds the $100,000 home equity limit.
- **Fully comprehend the risks of losing your home to foreclosure.** The more you borrow against your home, the greater the risk that you could lose the roof over your head to foreclosure should you not be able to make your mortgage payments.

Stocks, bonds, mutual funds, and other investments

As you gain more comfort and confidence as a real estate investor, you may wish to redirect some of your dollars from other investments like stocks, bonds, and mutual funds into property. If you do, be mindful of the following:

- **Diversification:** Real estate is one of the prime investments (the others being stocks and small business) for long-term appreciation potential. Be sure that you understand your portfolio's overall asset allocation and risk when making changes. Please see Chapter 1 for more details.
- **Tax issues:** If you've held other investments for more than one year, you can take advantage of the low long-term capital gains tax rates if you now wish to sell. The maximum federal tax rate for so-called long-term capital gains (investments sold for more than they were purchased for after more than 12 months) is now just 15 percent. Investors in the two lowest federal income tax brackets of 10 and 15 percent pay a mere 5 percent long-term capital gains tax rate. Try to avoid selling appreciated investments within the first year of ownership.

Cash value life insurance

You may own a *cash value* life insurance policy — one that combines a life insurance death benefit with a savings type account in which some money accumulates and on which interest is paid. In addition to being a costly cash drain with its relatively high premiums, cash value life insurance investment returns tend to be mediocre to dismal.

You're best off separating your life insurance purchases from your investing. If you need life insurance (because others are dependent upon your income), buy a *term life* policy, which is pure, unadulterated life insurance. But don't cancel your current cash value policies before replacing them with term if you do indeed need life insurance protection.

Robert had a $500,000 whole life policy that he was sold when he was much younger and more naive — and before he knew of Eric and his financial advice! He ultimately decided to cash out the policy, the proceeds from which he used to invest in an apartment deal. So rather than earning a meager few percent per year in a cash value life policy, Robert has since enjoyed double-digit annualized returns in a good real estate investment.

Advanced funding strategies

Sophisticated investors who develop an extensive real estate investment portfolio can employ more complicated strategies. In this section, we outline those along with our advice for how to make them work.

Leveraging existing real estate investments

Over time, if the initial properties that you buy do what they're supposed to do, they'll appreciate in value. Thus, you may be able to take extra tax-free cash from your successful investments to make more purchases. This is called *hypothecating* your real estate. As we discuss in the section "Borrowing against home equity" earlier in this chapter, many investors begin by employing this strategy with their owner-occupied home. They buy a home, it appreciates over the years, and then they tap that equity to fund other real estate purchases. By the same token, as you acquire more properties and they then appreciate, you can tap their equity for other purchases.

As you build a real estate empire, you must exercise care not to overextend yourself. The downside to continually pulling equity out of appreciated properties is that your fortunes may change. If the local real estate market or economy hit difficult times, you could find yourself with vacancies and falling rents. In the worst cases, excessively leveraged real estate investors have ended up bankrupt.

Partners and investors

Especially to accomplish larger deals, you may need or want to invest with a partner or other investors for the sake of diversification and risk reduction. Bringing in a partner can also provide additional financial resources for down payments and capital improvements as well as greater borrowing capability.

Partners can be either the best thing or the worst thing that ever happened to you. Although the additional financial resources are essential when you're starting out in real estate, attempt to find partners with complementary skills to really take advantage of the potential of real estate investment partnerships.

For example, Robert has focused on establishing partnerships where each partner brings a needed skill to the table. One partnership consisted of a top local real estate broker who identified properties along with a partner who was a real estate lender and who knew the ins and outs of lending. Robert's company provided the property and asset management to reposition the property and create value. This team used their complementary skills to successfully purchase, renovate, and later resell a 48-unit apartment building while providing cash distributions to the partners during the holding period.

With the assistance of a good attorney, prepare a legal contract to specify (among other issues) what happens if a partner wants out. A *buy/sell agreement* makes a lot of sense, because it outlines the terms and conditions in advance for how partnership assets can be redistributed. With life events (death, divorces, new marriages) constantly changing partnerships, having a buy/sell agreement in place at the time the partnership is initially established prevents bickering down the road. Partnership disputes often enrich attorneys and accountants, rather than the partners or their intended beneficiaries.

Family members sometimes make good partners. Parents, grandparents, and perhaps even siblings may have some extra cash they'd like to loan or invest. But some families aren't suited for partnering to buy and operate real estate. Disputes over management style, cash distributions versus reinvesting in the property, and how and when to sell are difficult in any partnership but particularly in families where there may be different goals based on the age or personal desires of the family members. If you don't get along real well at family gatherings, throw in a real estate partnership to really get the fireworks going! To minimize the potential problems, we strongly suggest documenting any real estate investment or lending relationship in writing just as diligently as you would with a non–family member. When working with family, you may be better off borrowing money with a promissory note, a repayment plan, and interest payments. Check out Chapter 12 for more on partnerships.

Seller financing

You may be able to find some properties that your research suggests offer potentially attractive investment returns and that the seller may be willing to extend financing for. This can be an extremely beneficial way to buy real estate when your cash position is limited. You can often set up the transaction as an installment sale so that the seller has the added benefit of stretching the reporting of income over a period of time and thus reducing her tax liability. You conserve your cash; the seller reduces her taxable income.

Avoid properties that are distressed. Don't get sucked in by great financing alone; only consider purchasing a property with seller financing that you would be willing to buy conventionally. The seller financing should just be an extra benefit, not the only benefit! Please see Chapter 6 for details.

Margin debt

In the section "Stocks, bonds, mutual funds, and other investments" earlier in this chapter, we cover selling some of your non–real estate investments in order to raise capital for property purchases. If you own stocks and other securities in a brokerage account, you can actually borrow funds against those investments. For example, if you're the proud owner of $100,000 worth of so-called marginable securities in a brokerage account, you may be able to borrow up to $50,000 at attractive interest rates, typically a little lower than on fixed rate mortgages for a home.

In addition to providing you with a relatively low-cost source of funds, utilizing margin debt for real estate purchases also enables you to hold onto more securities, which can better diversify your real estate holdings.

Be careful when using margin debt. Stocks, bonds, and other investments can drop in value, sometimes sharply. When that happens, you may face what is known as a *margin call,* whereby you'll be required to increase the equity in your brokerage account, either by adding cash to it directly or by selling some of your securities.

Chapter 6

Financing Your Property Purchases

In This Chapter

- Understanding lender financing options
- Selecting the best mortgage for your situation
- Looking at home equity loans
- Knowing which mortgages to avoid
- Seeking seller financing

You can't play if you can't pay. We know property investors who spent dozens to hundreds of hours finding the best locations and properties only to have their deals unravel when they were unable to gain approval for needed financing.

You probably also have questions about how to select the mortgage that is most appropriate for the property you're buying and your overall personal and financial situation. This chapter covers the financing options you should consider (and highlights those that you should avoid). In Chapter 7 we cover the actual process of applying for and locking up the specific loan you want.

Taking a Look at Mortgages

Although you can find thousands of different types of mortgages (thanks to all the various bells and whistles available), only two major categories of mortgages exist: fixed interest rate and adjustable rate. Technically speaking, some mortgages combine elements of both — they may remain fixed for a number of years and then have a variable interest rate after that. This section discusses these major loan types, what features they typically have, and how you can intelligently compare them with each other and select the one that best fits with your investment property purchases.

Fixed-rate mortgages

Fixed-rate mortgages, which are typically for a 15- or 30-year term for single-family properties, condos, and one- to four-unit apartments, have interest rates that remain constant over the life of the loan. Because the interest rate stays the same, your monthly mortgage payment stays the same.

Examining the pros and cons

For purposes of making future estimates of your property's cash flow, fixed-rate mortgages offer you certainty and some peace of mind, because you know precisely the size of your mortgage payment next month, next year, and ten years from now. (Of course, the other costs of owning investment property — such as property taxes, insurance, maintenance, and so on — will still escalate over the years.) But this piece of mind comes at a price:

- You generally pay a premium, in the form of a higher interest rate, compared with loans that have an adjustable interest rate over time. If you're buying a property and planning to improve it and sell it within five to ten years, you may be throwing money away by taking out a fixed-rate loan to lock in an interest rate for decades.
- If, like most investment property buyers, you're facing a tough time generating a healthy positive cash flow in the early years of owning a particular investment property, a fixed-rate mortgage is going to make it even more financially challenging. An adjustable-rate mortgage, by contrast, can lower your property's carrying costs in those early years. (We discuss adjustable-rate mortgages in the next section.)
- Fixed-rate loans carry the risk that if interest rates fall significantly after you obtain your mortgage and you're unable to refinance, you'll be stuck with a relatively higher-cost mortgage. You may be unable to refinance, for example, if you lose your job, your employment income declines, the value of your property decreases, or the property's rental income slides. Also remember that even if you're able to refinance, you'll probably have to spend significant time and money to get it done.

Making a point of comparing fixed rates

In addition to the ongoing, constant interest rate charged on a fixed-rate mortgage, lenders also typically levy an up-front fee, called points, which can be considered prepaid interest. *Points* are generally a percentage of the amount borrowed. To illustrate, 1.5 points are equal to 1.5 percent of the loan amount. So, for example, on a $200,000 mortgage, 1.5 points translate into a $3,000 up-front interest payment. Points can add significantly to the cost of borrowing money, particularly if you don't plan to keep the loan for long.

Generally speaking, the more points you pay on a given loan, the lower the ongoing interest rate that the lender charges on that loan. That's why you can't compare various lenders' fixed-rate loans to one another unless you know the exact points on each specific mortgage, in addition to that loan's ongoing interest rate.

The following are two approaches to dealing with points, given your financial situation and investment goals:

- **Minimize the points:** When you're running low on cash to close on a mortgage, or if you don't plan to hold the loan or property for long, you'll probably want to keep your points (and other loan fees discussed in the next section) to a minimum. You may want to take a higher interest rate on your mortgage.
- **Pay more points:** If you're more concerned with keeping your ongoing costs low, plan to hold the property for many years, and aren't cash constrained to close on the loan now, consider paying more points to lower your interest rate. This is known as *buying down the loan rate* and can be an excellent strategy to lower your overall costs of borrowing and increase the property's cash flow and equity buildup.

To make it easier to perform an apples-to-apples comparison of mortgages from different lenders, get interest rate quotes at the same point level. For example, ask each lender for the interest rate on a particular fixed-rate mortgage for which you pay one and two points. You might also compare the *annual percentage rate* (APR), which is a summary loan cost measure that includes all of a loan's fees and costs. However, please remember that the APR assumes that you hold the mortgage for its entire term — such as 15 or 30 years. If you end up keeping the loan for a shorter time period, either because you refinance or pay off the mortgage early, the APR isn't valid and accurate (unless you recalculate based on the changed term and payoff).

Adjustable-rate mortgages (ARMs)

Adjustable-rate mortgages (ARMs) carry an interest rate that varies over time. An ARM starts with a particular interest rate, usually a good deal lower than the going rate on comparable length (15- or 30-year) fixed-rate mortgages, and then you pay different rates for every year, possibly even every month, during a 30-year mortgage. Because the interest rate on an ARM changes over time, so too does the size of the loan's monthly payment. ARMs are often attractive for a number of reasons:

- You can start paying your mortgage with a relatively low initial interest rate compared with fixed-rate loans. Given the economics of a typical investment property purchase, ARMs better enable an investor to achieve a positive cash flow in the early years of property ownership.
- Should interest rates decline, you can realize most, if not all, of the benefits of lower rates without the cost and hassle of refinancing. With a fixed-rate mortgage, the only way to benefit from an overall decline in the market level of interest rates is to refinance.

ARMs come with many more features and options than do fixed-rate mortgages, including caps, indexes, margins, and adjustment periods. The following sections help you to understand these important ARM features.

Start rate

The *start rate* on an ARM is the interest rate the mortgage begins with. Don't be fooled though: You won't pay this tantalizingly low rate for too long. That is why it's often called a *teaser rate.* The start rate on most ARMs is set artificially low to entice you. In other words, even if the market level of interest rates doesn't change, your ARM is destined to increase as soon as the terms of the loan allow (more on this in a minute). An increase of one or two percentage points is common. The formula for determining the future interest rates on an ARM and rate caps is far more important in determining what a mortgage is going to cost you in the long run.

Future interest rate

The first important thing to ask a mortgage lender or broker about an ARM you're contemplating is the formula for determining the future interest rate on your loan. ARMs are based on the following formula:

Future Interest Rate = Index + Margin

The *index* is a designated measure of the market interest rate that the lender chooses to calculate the specific interest rate for your loan. Indexes are generally (but not always) widely quoted in the financial press. The *margin* is the amount added to the index to determine the interest rate that you pay on your mortgage.

For example, suppose that the loan you're considering uses a one-year Treasury bill index, which is currently 4 percent, and the loan you're considering has a margin of 2.75 percent (also often referred to as 275 basis points; 100 basis points equals 1 percent). Thus, the following formula would drive the rate of this mortgage:

One-Year Treasury Bill Rate (4.75 percent) + Margin (2.5 percent)

Do the math and you get 6.75 percent. This figure is known as the *fully indexed rate* (the rate the loan would have after the initial rate expires and if the index stays constant). If this loan starts out at just 4.75 percent, you know that if the one-year Treasury bill index remains at the same level, your loan can increase to 6.75 percent. If this index rises one percent to 5 percent during the period that you're covered by the ARM's start rate, that means the loan's fully indexed rate would go to 7.75 percent (5.00 + 2.75), which would be three percent higher than the loan's start rate.

Compare the fully indexed rate on an ARM you're considering to the current rate for a comparable term fixed-rate loan. You may see that the fixed-rate loan is at about the same interest rate, which may lead you to reconsider your choice of an ARM that carries the risk of rising to a higher future level.

Understanding ARM indexes

The different indexes used on ARMs vary mainly in how rapidly they respond to changes in interest rates. If you select an adjustable-rate mortgage tied to one of the faster-moving indexes, you take on more of a risk that the next adjustment may reflect interest rate increases. When you take on more of the risk that rates may increase, lenders cut you breaks in other ways, such as through lower *caps* (the maximum rate increase possible over a given time period; see "Future interest rate adjustments" later in the chapter) or points.

Should you want the security of an ARM tied to a slower-moving index, you'll pay for that security in one form or another, such as a higher start rate, caps, margin, or points. You may also pay in other, less-obvious ways. A slower-moving index, such as the 11th District Cost of Funds Index (COFI), lags behind general changes in market interest rates, so it continues to rise after interest rates peak and goes down slower after rates have turned down.

- **Treasury bills (T-bills)** are IOUs that the U.S. government issues. Most ARMs are tied to the interest rate on 6-month or 12-month T-bills (also referred to as the *one-year constant maturity Treasury index*). This is a relatively rapidly moving index. Some investment property mortgages are tied to the rate on ten-year Treasury Notes. Being a somewhat longer-term bond, a ten-year index doesn't generally move as rapidly as the shorter-term indexes.
- **Certificates of deposit (CDs)** are interest-bearing bank deposits that lock the depositor in at a set interest rate for a specific period of time. ARMs are usually tied to the average interest rate that banks are paying on six-month CDs. Like T-bills, CDs tend to respond quickly to changes in the market's level of interest rates.

- **London Interbank Offered Rate Index (LIBOR)** is an average of the rate of interest that major international banks charge each other to borrow large sums of U.S. dollars, which is commonly referred to by real estate lenders as an index for their adjustable loans. LIBOR tends to move and adjust quite rapidly to changes in interest rates and is at times even more volatile than the U.S. treasury or CD index rates.
- **Eleventh District Cost of Funds Index (COFI)** is a relatively slow-moving index. Adjustable-rate mortgages tied to the 11th District Cost of Funds Index tend to start out at a higher interest rate. A slower-moving index has the advantage of moving up less quickly when rates are on the rise. On the other hand, you have to be patient to benefit from falling interest rates.

In a relatively low-interest rate environment, such as in the early 2000s, few lenders were offering COFI loans. This illustrates the point that lenders don't always offer the same choice of indexes. Rather, each lender offers one or typically no more than two indexes, and borrowers should specifically look at the index as part of their overall decision on choosing a lender.

Future interest rate adjustments

After the initial interest rate ends, the interest rate on an ARM fluctuates based on the loan formula. Typically, ARM interest rates change every 6 or 12 months, but some adjust every month. In advance of each adjustment, the lender will send you a notice telling you your new rate. Be sure to check these notices because on rare occasions, lenders make mistakes.

Almost all ARMs come with a rate cap, which limits the maximum rate change (up or down) allowed at each adjustment. This limit is usually referred to as the *adjustment cap.* On most loans that adjust every six months, the adjustment cap is 1 percent — the interest rate charged on the mortgage can move up or down no more than one percentage point in an adjustment period.

Loans that adjust more than once per year usually limit the maximum rate change that's allowed over the entire year as well — known as the *annual rate cap.* On the vast majority of such loans, 2 percent is the annual rate cap. Likewise, almost all ARMs come with *lifetime caps,* which represent the highest rate allowed over the entire life of the loan. Lifetime caps of 5 to 6 percent higher than the initial start rate are common for adjustables.

Taking an ARM without rate caps is like heading out for a weeklong outdoor trek without appropriate rain gear. When you consider an adjustable-rate mortgage, you must identify the maximum payment that you can handle. If you can't handle the payment that comes with a 10 or 11 percent interest rate, for example, then don't look at ARMs that may go that high. As you crunch the numbers to see what your property's cash flow will look like under different circumstances (see Chapter 10), consider calculating how your mortgage payment will vary based on various higher interest rates.

Avoiding negative amortization ARMs

As you make mortgage payments over time, the loan balance you still owe is gradually reduced or *amortized. Negative amortization* (when your loan balance increases) is the reverse of this process. Some ARMs allow negative amortization. How can your outstanding loan balance grow when you continue to make mortgage payments? This phenomenon occurs when your mortgage payment is less than it really should be.

Some loans cap the increase of your monthly payment amount but don't cap the interest rate. Thus, the size of your mortgage payment may not reflect all the interest that you currently owe on your loan. So, rather than paying the interest that you owe and paying off some of your loan balance (or *principal*) every month, you end up paying off some, but not all, of the interest that you owe. Thus, lenders add the extra, unpaid interest that you still owe to your outstanding debt.

Negative amortization is similar to paying only the minimum payment that your credit card bill requires. You continue to rack up finance charges (in this case, greater interest) on the balance as long as you only make the artificially low payment. Taking a loan with negative amortization defeats the whole purpose of borrowing an amount that fits your overall financial goals.

Avoid ARMs with negative amortization. The only way to know whether a loan includes negative amortization is to explicitly ask. Some lenders and mortgage brokers aren't forthcoming about telling you. If you have trouble finding lenders that will deal with your financial situation, make sure that you're especially careful — you find negative amortization more frequently on loans that lenders consider risky.

Reviewing Other Common Fees

Whether the loan is fixed or adjustable, mortgage lenders typically assess other up-front fees and charges. These ancillary fees can really amount to quite a bundle with some lenders. Here's our take on the typical extra charges you're likely to encounter and what's reasonable and what's not:

- **Application fee:** Most lenders charge $200 to $300 to work with you to complete your paperwork and see it through their loan evaluation process. Should your loan be rejected, or if it's approved and you decide not to take it, the lender needs to cover its costs. Most lenders credit or return this fee to you upon closing with their loan.
- **Credit report charge:** Most lenders charge you for the cost of obtaining your credit report, which tells the lender whether you've repaid other loans on time. Your credit report should cost about $50 for each individual or entity that will be a borrower.

- **Appraisal fee:** The property for which you borrow money needs to be valued. If you default on your mortgage, a lender doesn't want to get stuck with a property that's worth less than you owe. The cost for appraisal typically ranges from several hundred dollars for most residential properties to as much as $1,000 or more for larger investment properties. (On particularly larger properties, this fee can be more significant — on a 30,000-square-foot office building, an appraisal may run around $5,000, and on a 300-plus-unit apartment building, it would be more in the $10,000 range.)
- **Environmental assessment or phase I:** Virtually all lenders making loans on residential properties with five or more units or, especially, commercial property, require a qualified engineering company to perform a site assessment and overview of the entire area in which the property is located to identify possible environmental issues. This type of report is commonly referred to as a phase I environmental report and the cost is directly correlated to the location, type of property, size, and even the prior use of the property and the surrounding area. Phase I reports can run from $300 to as much as tens of thousands of dollars. (We include more details in Chapter 12.)
- **Third-party physical inspection:** Depending on the property being financed, lenders often require third-party inspections by competent professionals. For example, an inspection report from a licensed pest control firm documenting the property condition and specifically the presence of termites and/or wood-destroying organisms is required in virtually all transactions, including single-family homes and commercial properties. Again, the cost of these reports varies depending on the property. (More details to come in Chapter 12.)

Request a detailing of other fees and charges in writing from all lenders that you're seriously considering. You need to know the total of all lender fees so that you can accurately compare different lenders' loans and determine how much closing on your loan will cost you. For residential and commercial income properties, the lender usually asks for a deposit that the lender uses to cover the types of fees and charges outlined here.

No-point mortgages aren't no-brainers

Some property buyers are attracted to *no-point* or *zero-cost mortgages* (which also sometimes have no other loan fees or costs either). Remember that if a loan has no points, it's sure to have a higher interest rate. That's not to say that no-point loans are better or worse than comparable loans from other lenders, but don't get duped into a loan because of a no-points sales pitch. The lenders who heavily promote these types of loans rarely have the best mortgage terms.

Consider a no-point/no-fee mortgage if you can't afford more out-of-pocket expenditures now or if you think that you'll only keep the loan a few years. But if you're that cash constrained, you may want to consider whether you can truly afford to buy investment property (see Chapter 1).

To reduce the possibility of wasting your time and money applying for a mortgage that you may not qualify for, ask the lender if there are any reasons they might not approve you. Disclose any problems on your credit report or with the property. Don't expect the lender to provide you with a list of credit or property problems that could conceivably put the kibosh on a mortgage.

Making Some Decisions

You can't (or at least shouldn't) spend months deciding which mortgage may be right for your situation. So, in this section, we help you zero in on which type is best for you.

Deciding between fixed and adjustable

Choosing between a fixed-rate or adjustable-rate loan is an important decision in the real estate investment process. Consider the advantages and disadvantages of each mortgage type and decide what's best for your situation prior to going out to refinance or purchase real estate. This section covers the key factors to consider.

Your ability and desire to accept financial risk

How much risk can you handle in regard to the size of your property's monthly mortgage payment? If you can take the financial risks that come with an ARM, you have a better chance of saving money and maximizing your property's cash flow with an adjustable-rate rather than a fixed-rate loan. Your interest rate starts lower and stays lower with an ARM, if the overall level of interest rates stays unchanged. Even if rates go up, they'll likely come back down over the life of your loan. If you can stick with your ARM for better and for worse, you should come out ahead in the long run.

ARMs make more sense if you borrow less than you're qualified for. If your income (and applicable investment property cash flow) significantly exceeds your spending, you may feel less anxiety about the fluctuating interest rate on an ARM. If you do choose an adjustable loan, you may feel more financially secure if you have a hefty financial cushion (at least six months' to as much as a year's worth of expenses reserved) that you can access if rates go up.

Some people take ARMs when they can't really afford them. When rates rise, property owners who can't afford higher payments face a financial crisis. If you don't have emergency savings that you can tap into to make the higher payments, how can you afford the monthly payments and the other expenses of your property?

If you can't afford the highest-allowed payment on an ARM, don't take one. You shouldn't take the chance that the rate may not rise that high — it can, and you could lose the property.

Ask your lender to calculate the highest possible monthly payment that your loan allows. The number that the lender comes up with is the payment that you face if the interest rate on your loan goes to the highest level allowed, or the *lifetime cap.* (For more on caps, see the "Future interest rate adjustments" section earlier in the chapter.)

Don't take an adjustable mortgage because the lower initial interest rate allows you to afford the property that you want to buy (unless you're absolutely certain that your income and property cash flow will enable you to meet future payment increases). Try setting your sights on a property that you can afford to buy with a fixed-rate mortgage.

Length of time you expect to keep the mortgage

Saving interest on most ARMs is usually a certainty in the first two or three years. An adjustable-rate mortgage starts at a lower interest rate than a fixed one. But, if rates rise, you can end up repaying the savings that you achieve in the early years of the mortgage.

If you aren't going to keep your mortgage for more than five to seven years, you'll pay more interest to carry a fixed-rate mortgage. A mortgage lender takes extra risk in committing to a fixed-interest rate for 15 to 30 years. Lenders don't know what may happen in the intervening years, so they charge you a premium in case interest rates move significantly higher in future years.

You might also consider a hybrid loan, which combines features of fixed- and adjustable-rate mortgages. For example, the initial rate may hold constant for three, five, seven, or ten years and then adjust once a year or every six months thereafter. Such loans may make sense for you if you foresee a high probability of keeping your loan seven to ten years or less but want some stability in your future monthly payments. The longer the initial rate stays locked in, the higher the interest rate. Don't confuse these loans with the often-unadvisable balloon mortgage (which we discuss in the "Mortgages That Should Make You Think Twice" section later in the chapter).

Deciding between short- and long-term

Most mortgage lenders offer you the option of 15-year or 30-year mortgages. You can also find 20-year and 40-year options, but these are unusual. So how do you decide whether a shorter- or longer-term mortgage is best for your investment property purchase?

To afford the monthly payments and have a positive cash flow, many investment property buyers need to spread their mortgage loan payments over a longer period of time, and a 30-year mortgage is the way to do it. A 15-year mortgage has higher monthly payments because you pay it off quicker. At a fixed-rate mortgage interest rate of 7 percent, for example, a 15-year mortgage comes with payments that are about 35 percent higher than those for a 30-year mortgage.

Locking yourself into higher monthly payments with a 15-year mortgage may actually put you at greater financial risk. If your finances worsen or your property declines in value, odds are you'll have trouble qualifying for a refinance. You *may* be able to refinance your way out of the predicament, but you can't count on it.

Don't consider a 15-year mortgage unless you can afford the higher payments that come with it. Even if you can afford these higher payments, taking the 15 year option isn't necessarily better. You may be able to find better uses for the money. If you can earn a higher rate of return investing your extra cash versus paying the interest on your mortgage, for instance, you may come out ahead investing your money instead of paying down your mortgage faster.

If you decide on a 30-year mortgage, you still maintain the flexibility to pay the mortgage off faster if you choose to. You can choose to make larger-than-necessary payments and create your own 15-year mortgage. However, you can fall back to making only the payments required on your 30-year schedule when the need arises. The only situation in which you can't pay off your 30-year mortgage faster is if the loan has a prepayment penalty. We dislike mortgages with *prepayment penalties* (penalties for paying off your loan before you're supposed to). Normally, prepayment penalties don't apply if you pay off a loan because you sell the property, but when you refinance a loan with prepayment penalties, you have to pay the penalty.

Borrowing Against Home Equity

Home equity loans (or a derivative called a *HELOC* — Home Equity Line of Credit) enable you to borrow against the equity in your home. Because such loans are in addition to the mortgage that you already have (known as the *first mortgage*), home equity loans are also known as *second mortgages.*

A home equity loan may provide a relatively low-cost source of funds for an investment property purchase, especially if you're seeking money for just a few years. You could refinance your first mortgage and pull cash out for an investment property purchase — but we don't advise doing that if your first mortgage is at a lower interest rate than you can obtain on a refinance.

Home equity loans generally have higher interest rates than comparable first mortgages because they're riskier to a lender. The reason: In the event that you default on the first mortgage or file for bankruptcy protection, the first mortgage lender gets first claim on your home.

Interest paid of up to $1 million on home mortgages for primary or secondary residences is tax deductible (on loans taken out after October 13, 1987). The tax deduction for home equity loans is limited to the interest paid on up to $100,000 of home equity debt. See Chapter 5 for a discussion of borrowing against home equity in the context of finding down payment money.

Mortgages That Should Make You Think Twice

You may come across other loans such as balloon loans and interest-only mortgages. We also want you to know the potential risks associated with recourse loans. The following section presents our thoughts on these.

Balloon loans

One type of loan that is sometimes confused with a hybrid loan is a balloon loan. *Balloon loans* start off just like traditional fixed-rate mortgages. You make level payments based on a long-term payment schedule, over 15 or 30 years, for example. But at a predetermined time, usually three to ten years from the loan's inception, the remaining loan balance becomes fully due.

Balloon loans may save you money because they have a lower interest rate than a longer-term fixed-rate mortgage. Sometimes, balloon loans may be the only option for the buyer (or so the buyer thinks). Buyers are more commonly backed into these loans during periods of high interest rates. When a buyer can't afford the payments on a conventional mortgage and really wants a particular property, a seller may offer a balloon loan.

Balloon loans are dangerous for the simple reason that your financial situation can change, and you may not be able to refinance when your balloon loan is due. What if you lose your job or your income drops? What if the value of your property drops and the appraisal comes in too low to qualify you for a new loan? What if interest rates rise and you can't qualify at the higher rate on a new loan? We recommend balloon loans only when the following conditions apply:

- Such a loan is your sole financing option.
- You've really done your homework to exhaust other financing options.
- You're certain that you can refinance when the balloon comes due.

If you take a balloon loan, get one with as much time as possible, preferably seven to ten years, before it becomes due.

Interest-only loans

Especially in higher cost housing markets where buyers are stretching to buy, we're seeing increased promotion of interest-only mortgages. In the early years of such mortgages, your monthly mortgage payment is used only to pay interest that is owed. Although this helps to keep your payments relatively low (because no money is going toward repaying principal), the downside is that you're not making any headway to pay down your loan balance.

Usually, after a preset time period, such as five or seven years, your mortgage payment jumps substantially so that you can begin to pay down or amortize your loan balance. We're finding that many people don't really understand or investigate this.

The main attraction that we see for interest-only mortgages for investment property purchases is that the low initial payments will help you to achieve more positive cash flow early on. Our concern, however, is in seeing some property buyers attracted to interest-only loans to afford purchasing high-cost property that is difficult to realize positive cash flow from.

If the only way for you to invest in an income property is to use an interest-only loan, then perhaps you shouldn't invest. Likewise, lenders are now aggressively promoting the 40-year fixed-rate loan, because the payments are lower than the conventional 30-year loans and not much more than the interest-only loans. If you only qualify to purchase a property by using an interest-only or 40-year amortized loan, this could be an indicator that properties are overpriced or you don't have sufficient financial resources. Investing in rental real estate is risky and you can lose your entire investment if the market turns and you don't have staying power to ride through the real estate cycles.

If you consider an interest-only mortgage, be sure that you understand exactly how high your payment will be after the loan moves out of the interest-only payment phase. And be sure that you've surveyed the mortgage marketplace and understand how the terms and conditions of interest-only loans stack up versus other types of mortgages.

Recourse financing

The goal of most real estate investors is to accumulate wealth over time while not taking any unreasonable risks. That's why we discourage using interest-only loans or loans with balloon payments. But there is another factor to explore before agreeing to any loan: Is the loan nonrecourse or recourse?

- **Nonrecourse financing:** In the event you fail to fulfill the terms of your loan, this type of loan limits the lender to only foreclosing on the underlying property. Foreclosure is the full and complete satisfaction of the loan, and the lender can't seek a deficiency judgment or go after your other assets.
- **Recourse loans:** These loans lower the lender's risk because they offer additional protection. The lender has the legal right to seek a deficiency judgment against you personally or pursue other assets to cover any shortfall should the property value not fully cover their outstanding debt balance. Remember that after a loan is in default, the interest penalties and legal fees can add up quickly. If you're already in default on the loan for your rental property, the last challenge you need is to have a lender looking to take your home or other viable rental properties to satisfy their deficiency judgment.

As long as you're not too aggressive and don't overleverage your rental properties, real estate investing can be relatively safe and the chances are you won't be faced with losing your property by defaulting on your loan. But there are limits to your ability to control all of the diverse factors that can affect your property. For example, your cash flow will definitely suffer if the major employer in your area suddenly leaves.

Nonrecourse financing has more stringent qualification standards, such as higher debt coverage ratios, and will generally result in a lower loan amount. But just as with borrowers who utilize 40-year mortgages or interest-only loans so that they can borrow as much money as possible, the closer you live to the edge, the more likely you'll regret it.

Many of the loans you'll consider will be nonrecourse, but if you're seeking financing for an *unstabilized property* (a property whose cash flow is uncertain due to vacancy or unusually high expenses) or a property requiring major renovation, you may find that lenders will only provide the funds you need if the loan is full recourse. So no matter what type of loan you use, we strongly recommend that you only use nonrecourse financing, and you will sleep better at night!

Typically you'll be evaluating different loan proposals with either full recourse or full nonrecourse financing. But lenders can also offer a partial recourse loan. A partial recourse loan allows the lender to seek a deficiency judgment up to a certain limit if you default. Again, there may be great real estate investment options where such a loan will make sense, but be very careful before agreeing to such terms, and include the consequences to your overall financial status in a worst-case scenario in your overall analysis.

Seller Financing

Not every seller needs or even wants to receive all cash as payment for his property, so you may be able to finance part or even all of an investment property purchase thanks to the property seller's financing. The use of seller financing is the cornerstone of most no-money-down strategies.

Seller financing is a transaction is which the seller accepts anything less than all cash at closing. One form of an all-cash transaction to the seller is the buyer literally paying all cash, but typically it's a transaction in which the buyer uses a *conventional loan* (money to purchase the property from a lender other than the seller) so that the seller effectively receives all cash at closing.

Some sellers are financially well off enough that they won't need all of the sales proceeds immediately for their next purchase or will be buying a property for less money — or maybe not buying a replacement property at all — and prefer to receive payments over time. They may be looking for the payments to replace their income in retirement or they may prefer to receive the funds over time so they can reduce their taxable income.

Any seller with equity can offer seller financing, but usually private individuals are the best sources. The best candidates for seller financing are sellers with significant equity or, best of all, folks who own their property free-and-clear (without any debt on the property at all).

Sometimes sellers will offer this option, but in other cases, you need to pop the question. We can think of two good reasons to ask for the seller to help finance an investment property purchase:

- **Better terms:** Mortgage lenders, which are typically banks or large monolithic financial institutions, aren't the most flexible businesses in the world. You may well be able to obtain a lower interest rate, lower or waived fees, and more flexible repayment conditions from a property seller. There are also many expenses with conventional loans that a property seller may not require: loan points, origination fees, and an appraisal. Some sellers may not even require a loan application or credit report, but they'd be wise to retain these requirements.
- **Loan approval:** Perhaps you've had prior financial problems that have caused mortgage lenders to routinely deny your mortgage application. Some property sellers may be more flexible, especially in a slow real estate market or with a property that's challenging to sell. A seller can also make a decision in a few days, whereas a conventional lender will often take weeks.

Be careful when considering a property where a seller is offering financing as part of the deal. This may be a sign of a hard-to-sell property. Investigate how long the property has been on the market and what specific flaws and problems it may have.

Some of the reasons why sellers may offer their own financing are listed below:

- **They're attracted to the potential returns of being a mortgage lender.** This is a reason that shouldn't concern the buyer as long as the terms of the seller financing are reasonable and avoid the issues raised earlier in the chapter about balloon payment or interest-only loans.
- **The seller has significant equity.** Another win-win opportunity for both the buyer and seller to use seller financing.
- **The current financing has prepayment issues.** This can be a problem for the buyer if the underlying financing has a *due-on-sale clause* and the lender becomes aware of the sale of the property and demands the full payment of the outstanding loan balance on short notice.
- **They're seeking a price that exceeds the normal conventional loan parameters, or the property doesn't qualify for a conventional loan for some reason.** Examples of qualification issues include a cracked slab, environmental issues, and so on. This is a risky scenario for the buyer and may be an indication that they're over-reaching or pursuing a property that's not a good investment.

Be sure that your seller financing agreement is nonrecourse (as discussed earlier in the chapter) and doesn't contain a due-on-sale clause. If the seller requires a due-on-sale clause, then you'll have to pay off the full balance owed to the seller at the time of your sale of the property. Most sellers will wisely ask for the due-on-sale clause so that the property can't be sold to another owner. The due-on-sale clause would prohibit you from selling the property without paying off the loan in full.

Chapter 7

Shopping for and Securing the Best Mortgage Terms

In This Chapter

- Understanding the best ways to shop for mortgages
- Solving common loan problems

In Chapter 6, we discuss how to choose among the many loan options available to select the one that best suits your personal and financial situation. In the process of delving into the different types of real estate investment financing, you may have already begun the process of speaking with different lenders and surfing Web sites.

In this chapter, we provide our top tips and advice for shopping for and ultimately securing the best financing that you can for your real estate investment purchases and refinances. We also cover common loan problems that may derail your plans.

Shopping for Mortgages

Financing costs of your real estate investment purchases are generally the single biggest expense by far, so it pays to shop around and know how to unearth the best deals. You will find that many, many lenders would love to have your business, especially if you have a strong credit rating. Although having numerous lenders competing for your business can save you money, it can also make mortgage shopping and selection difficult. This section should help you to simplify matters.

Relying on referrals

Many sources of real estate advice simply tell you to get referrals in your quest to find the best mortgage lenders. Sounds simple and straightforward — but it's not. For instance, loans for commercial investment properties and residential rental properties with five or more units have different lender underwriting requirements and terms compared with residential one- to four-unit loans (see Chapter 2 for explanations of these types of investments).

Good referrals can be a useful tool for locating the best lenders. Here are a few sources we recommend:

- Start with a bank or credit union that you have a relationship with currently and then seek referrals from them if they're not interested in making the specific loan you have in mind.
- Collect referrals from people who you know and trust and who have demonstrated some ability to select good service providers. Start with the best professional service providers (tax advisors, lawyers, financial planners, real estate agents, and so on) you know and respect, and ask them for their recommendations.
- Contact associations of real estate investors, especially those in your state. (You can find a comprehensive list organized by state at the Web site www.realestateassociations.com.) Networking with local investors is a great way to learn about the local real estate market and to benefit from other people's experiences.

Don't take anyone's referrals as gospel. Always be wary of business people who refer you to folks who have referred business to them over the years. Whenever you get a recommendation, ask the person doing the referring why they're making the referral and what they like and don't like about the service provider.

Mulling over mortgage brokers

You don't need to use a mortgage broker unless you're trying to get a loan for a property that has some challenges or you as the buyer have less than stellar credit or want to put the minimum down. Thus, we recommend going directly to lenders for simple deals (a relatively small price tag, a property that's in good condition and enjoys a good location, and so on) and using mortgage brokers for bigger, more complicated, or more difficult deals.

But many property buyers get a headache trying to shop among the enormous universe of mortgages and lenders. Check out the following sections when deciding on whether you want to use a broker.

Counting a broker's contributions

A good mortgage broker can make the following contributions to your real estate investing team:

- **Advice:** If you're like most people, you may have a difficult time deciding which type of mortgage is best for your situation. A good mortgage broker can take the time to listen to your financial and personal situation and goals and offer suggestions for specific loans that match your situation. Brokers do work on commission, which unfortunately can temper the objectivity of their advice, so tread carefully. Don't blindly accept a mortgage broker's advice, which may be nothing more than a commission driven sales pitch masquerading as counsel.
- **Shopping:** Even after you figure out the specific type of mortgage that you want, dozens (if not hundreds) of lenders may offer that type of loan. (You'll find fewer lender options for five-plus-unit residential properties and commercial properties.)

  Thoroughly shopping among the options to find the best mortgage takes time and knowledge you may well lack. A good mortgage broker can probably save you time and money by shopping for your best deal. Brokers can be especially helpful if you have a less than pristine credit report or you want to buy property with a low down payment — 10 percent or less of the value of a property. (It's quite difficult to purchase a multifamily residential property with five or more units or a commercial, industrial, or retail property with less than a 20 to 30 percent down payment.)

  Be careful, though, when selecting a broker, because the worst among them get in the habit of using the same lenders time and time again — perhaps because of the lofty commissions those lenders pay out. (More on understanding mortgage broker's commissions in the "Keeping up with commissions and other contingencies" section.)
- **Paperwork and presentation:** An organized and detail-oriented mortgage broker can assist you with completing the morass of forms most lenders demand. Mortgage brokers can assist you with preparing your loan package so that you put your best foot forward with lenders.

  The larger the loan, the more involved and complicated the paperwork. Have your personal financial statement prepared in advance so that it can be easily updated, because each time you seek a loan for an investment property, you'll be required to provide a current financial statement to the broker (and, actually, all potential loan sources).
- **Closing the deal:** After you sign a purchase agreement to buy a real estate investment property, you still have a lot to do before you're the proud new property owner (see Chapter 12 for all the details). A competent mortgage broker will make sure that you meet the important deadlines for closing the deal.

Keeping up with commissions and other contingencies

A mortgage broker typically gets paid a percentage, usually between 0.5 to 1.0 percent, of the loan amount. This commission is completely negotiable, especially on larger loans that are more lucrative. (In case you're interested, the commissions on larger deals — say, on a loan of $25 million or more — is 0.25 percent.)

Be sure to ask what the commission is on every alternative loan that a broker pitches. Some brokers may be indignant that you ask — that's their problem. You have every right to ask; after all, it's your money.

Even if you plan to shop on your own, talking to a mortgage broker may be worthwhile. At the very least, you can compare what you find with what brokers say they can get for you. Again, be careful. Some brokers tell you what you want to hear — that is, that they can beat your best find — and then aren't able to deliver when the time comes.

If your loan broker quotes you a really good deal, make sure you ask who the lender is. Most brokers refuse to reveal this information until you pay the necessary fee to cover the appraisal, credit report, and required environmental reports. But after taking care of those fees, you can check with the lender to verify the interest rate, the points, the amortization term, and the prepayment penalties (if any) that the broker quotes you, and make sure that you're eligible for the loan.

Web surfing for mortgages

You can shop for just about anything and everything online so why should mortgages be any different? Mortgage Web sites often claim that they save you lots of time and money.

In our experience, the Internet is better used for mortgage research than for securing a specific mortgage. That's not to say that some sites can't provide competitive loans in a timely fashion. However, we've seen some property purchases fall apart because the buyers relied upon a Web site that failed to deliver a loan in time.

Here's a short list of some of our favorite mortgage related Web sites that you may find helpful:

- **HSH Associates:** The folks at HSH Associates (www.hsh.com) publish mortgage information for most metropolitan areas. For $20, you can receive a list of dozens of lenders' rate quotes, but you need to be a real data junkie to wade through all the numbers on the multipage report that features lots of abbreviations in small print.

- **Government-related sites:** The Web sites of the U.S. Department of Housing and Urban Development (www.hud.gov) and the Veterans Administration (www.va.gov) provide information on government loan programs and feature foreclosed homes for sale.

  Fannie Mae, which stands for the Federal National Mortgage Association (www.fanniemae.com), and Freddie Mac, which is the Federal Home Loan Mortgage Corporation (www.freddiemac.com), are private companies that have worked over the years with the federal government to support the mortgage marketplace. Fannie Mae and Freddie Mac buy mortgages meeting their criteria from lenders, freeing up lender capital to make additional mortgages. They then package many of those loans and offer them to investors looking for stable, longer-term investments.

- **Mortgage Bankers Association:** The trade association for mortgage lenders, the Mortgage Bankers Association (www.mbaa.org), has tons of articles and data on the mortgage marketplace. Their Web resources page also includes links to state and local mortgage banker associations.

  TIP: This is an excellent source of information on loans for residential properties with five or more units and commercial, industrial, and retail properties.

- **E-LOAN:** One of the first major online lenders, E-LOAN has stood the test of time and continues to offer competitive loans (www.eloan.com). This well-organized site can give you a quick overview of competitive mortgage pricing. Of course, you're under no obligation to use one of their mortgages just because you survey the options available.

- **Journalist sites:** Numerous Web sites feature news and information about the real estate markets around the country. Several journalist sites worth perusing include www.bobbruss.com, www.deadlinenews.com, and www.inman.com.

- **Legal research sites:** Legal issues certainly raise their ugly head on many a real estate deal. The Web site of self-help legal publisher Nolo Press (www.nolo.com) offers some free resources as well as details on all of the company's legal books.

  Cornell Law School's Legal Information Institute (www.law.cornell.edu/topics/mortgages.html) includes legal information on mortgages, including hard-to-find links to federal- and state-specific statutes.

Solving Loan Predicaments

In Chapter 5, we discuss the different types of mortgages and how to select the one that best fits your situation. But remember that just because you want a particular mortgage doesn't mean that you're going to get approved for it.

The best defense against loan rejection is avoiding it in the first place. To head off potential rejection, disclose anything that may cause a problem *before* you apply for the loan. For example, if you already know that your credit report indicates some late payments from when you were out of the country for an extended period or your family was in turmoil over a medical problem, write a letter to your lender that explains this situation. Or perhaps you're self-employed and your income from two years ago on your tax return was artificially much lower due to a special tax write-off. If that's the case, explain that in writing to the lender.

Even if you're the ideal mortgage borrower in the eyes of every lender, you may encounter financing problems with some properties. And of course, not all real estate buyers have a perfect credit history, lots of spare cash, and no debt. If you're one of those borrowers who must jump through more hoops than others to get a loan, don't give up hope. Few borrowers are perfect from a lender's perspective, and many problems aren't that difficult to fix.

Polishing your credit report

Late payments, missed payments, or debts that you never bothered to pay can tarnish your credit report and squelch a lender's desire to offer you a mortgage loan. If you've been turned down for a loan because of your less-than-stellar credit history, request a free copy of your credit report from the lender that turned you down.

Getting a report before you even apply for a loan is advisable. Serious real estate investors should actually pay for a credit report, particularly one that includes your FICO scores. Getting turned down for a loan makes the "free" credit report much, much more expensive than paying $10 to $12 for a single report or about $40 for a special report with your FICO scores from all three major credit bureaus. One of many Web sites from which you can order your credit report and FICO scores is `www.myfico.com`. This site also offers a service to correct errors on your credit history plus tips on how you're able to get a loan the first time by improving your credit score.

If problems are accurately documented on your credit report, try to explain them to your lender. Getting the bum's rush? Call other lenders and tell them your credit problems up front and see whether you can find one willing to offer you a loan. Mortgage brokers may also be able to help you shop for lenders in these cases.

Sometimes you may feel that you're not in control when you apply for a loan. In reality, you can fix a number of credit problems yourself. And you can often explain those that you can't fix. Some lenders are more lenient and flexible than others. Just because one mortgage lender rejects your loan application doesn't mean that all the others will.

As for erroneous information listed on your credit report, get on the phone to the credit bureaus. If specific creditors are the culprits, call them too. They're required to submit any new information or correct any errors at once. Keep notes from your conversations and make sure that you put your case in writing and add your comments to your credit report. If the customer service representatives you talk with are no help, send a letter to the president of each company. Getting mistakes cleaned up on your credit report can take the tenacity of a bulldog — be persistent.

Another common credit problem is having too much consumer debt at the time you apply for a mortgage. The more credit card, auto loan, and other consumer debt you rack up, the less mortgage you qualify for. If you're turned down for the mortgage, consider it a wake-up call to get rid of this high-cost debt. Hang on to the dream of buying real estate and plug away at paying off your debts before you make another foray into real estate. (See Chapter 5 for more information.)

Conquering insufficient income

If you're self-employed or have changed jobs, your income may not resemble your past income, or more important, your income may not be what a mortgage lender likes to see in respect to the amount that you want to borrow. A simple (although not always feasible) way around this problem is to make a larger down payment. For example, if you put down 30 percent or more when you purchase a rental home or small one- to four-unit rental property, you may be able to get a no-income-verification loan. If you can make that large a down payment, lenders probably don't care what your income is — they'll simply repossess and then sell your property if you default on the loan.

If you can't make a large down payment, another option is to get a cosigner for the loan — your relatives may be willing. As long as they aren't overextended themselves, they may be able to help you qualify for a larger loan than you can get on your own. As with partnerships, make sure that you put your agreement in writing so that no misunderstandings occur.

Lenders who understand investment property

An investor who Robert knows, Al, had an interesting experience when a lender initially indicated that Al had insufficient income to support the purchase of four brand-new rental condos he was buying. (This situation is also a real-world example of a potential quick buy-and-flip scenario — the properties in question appreciated about 12 percent from a purchase agreement in six months.)

The lender had trouble understanding a basic concept of real estate ownership — it offers the benefits of depreciation to shelter other income for real estate professionals. So much of Al's income is sheltered through real estate holdings that his tax returns show only about 20 percent of his actual income, which wasn't sufficient to qualify for the loan. Al had to actually educate the loan underwriters by showing them the various real-estate limited-liability corporation tax returns with the significant amounts of depreciation and how they flowed through to his personal tax return.

Real estate investors need to be aware that when they're looking to purchase additional real estate, they need to work with a lender that understands that depreciation is a noncash item that allows real estate investors to actually keep more of their income. Al asked the mortgage broker who is a better risk — someone who makes $100,000 and has no tax benefits from depreciation and thus pays 40 percent in taxes with a net income of $60,000, or someone who makes several hundred thousand dollars but only reports $50,000 and thus pays taxes at a lower rate. Remember the old adage, "It is not what you make but what you keep that really counts."

Dealing with low property appraisals

Even if you have sufficient income, a clean credit report, and an adequate down payment, the lender may turn down your loan if the appraisal of the property that you want to buy comes in too low. This is a relatively rare situation (that happens more in rapidly appreciating markets): It's unusual for a property not to appraise for what a buyer agrees to pay.

Assuming that you still like the property, renegotiate a lower price with the seller using the low appraisal. If the appraisal is too low with a property that you already own and are refinancing, you obviously need to follow a different path. If you have the cash available, you can simply put more money down to get the loan balance to a level for which you qualify. If you don't have the cash, you may need to forgo the refinance until you save more money or until the property value rises.

Part III

Finding and Evaluating Properties

"OF COURSE I COULD NEVER AFFORD A SHOE THIS SIZE IF I WEREN'T COLLECTING RENTS FROM A TENNIS SHOE ACROSS TOWN AND TWO ESPADRILLES IN FLORIDA."

In this part . . .

Here's where the rubber hits the road. In this part, we discuss what, where, and how to buy a rental property. We cover the vital topic of how to value and evaluate real estate investment properties using a variety of financial tools and techniques. And, if you want the low down and advice for negotiating contracts, performing inspections, and closing of your purchase, this is the part for you.

Chapter 8

Location, Location, Value

In This Chapter

- Choosing your investment area
- Looking at what makes a good investment area
- Discovering what's in your own backyard
- Contrasting neighborhoods
- Getting to know seller's markets and buyer's markets

As the most well-known saying in real estate goes, "The three most important factors to success in real estate are location, location, and location!" There *is* a strong correlation between the location of your real estate investments and your financial success. And we firmly agree that the location of your real estate investment is critical in determining your success as a real estate investor. But we prefer the phrase coined by Eric: "Location, location, value." This revised adage clearly emphasizes location but also stresses the importance of finding good value for your investment dollar.

Merely owning real estate isn't the key to success in real estate investing; acquiring and owning the right real estate at the right price is how to build wealth! As you gain experience in real estate, you'll develop your own strategy, but to make any strategy succeed, you need to do your homework and diligently and fairly evaluate both the positive and negative aspects of your proposed real estate investment. That's where we come in.

In this chapter, we cover important aspects of regional and local demographics, how to analyze the economy, and which factors are most important to real estate investing. We also discuss barriers to entry and the supply/demand equation. Then we show you where to find this information and how to interpret the numbers to determine your local areas with the most potential. Finally, we discuss real estate cycles and timing.

Deciding Where to Invest

If you're going to invest in real estate, you need to decide on a location. Most real estate investors initially — and wisely — look in their local communities.

WARNING!

The dangers of investing out of your area

In many regions of the country, real estate prices have escalated to the point that it's difficult for entry-level real estate investors to buy. If you live in such an area, it can be tempting to go far afield in search of reasonably priced property.

Lately, we've noticed a proliferation of seminars that promise real estate investment opportunities in other areas of the country. In California and other high-priced real estate markets, seminar sponsors target owners and wannabe real estate investors, touting the great investments that can be found in other, often unnamed, parts of the country. They claim that you can buy rental real estate for a fraction of your local prices and achieve high returns on your investment. They even provide pictures of these properties — but there are always tiny little disclaimers somewhere on the page!

We strongly advise against investing blindly in areas that you don't know personally. And never consider these investments unless you have the proper local contacts such as a great property manager, contractors and suppliers, and competent legal and accounting advice.

Robert routinely serves as an expert witness and recently had a case where an out-of-state owner saw a great investment opportunity for an upscale four-bedroom executive home. Even though he worked over 3,000 miles away, what could go wrong with such a beautiful rental in a dynamic and prosperous suburb of San Diego? It looked like a good investment in a great neighborhood, and the property manager found a respectable renter in just a few days.

Unfortunately, what seemed so good suddenly turned south when the initial check for the security deposit and first month's rent was returned, marked, "account closed." Later that week, the owner got a long-distance call from a disgruntled neighbor complaining about the barking dog and that many more people were occupying the home than just one family. Six months later, after paying hefty legal bills for the eviction plus making several cross-country airline flights, the owner finally regained possession of his now trashed executive home. Aside from the lost rent for six months, the damage to the home was in excess of $50,000. In the subsequent lawsuit against the broker, it came out that the broker had recommended an unlicensed property manager who never did any screening of the tenant.

One experience like this, and you may stick to money market accounts. So when you read about great real estate opportunities in faraway places, remember that it is better to be safe than sorry. Our experience indicates that "If it sounds too good to be true, it *is* too good to be true!" Risk and return are truly related. It is better to have a more solid and easy-to-manage property in your own community than to try and hit a home run in a different time zone.

We give you the tools to evaluate properties anywhere, but you have an inherent advantage if you begin your search close to home. Unless you really know another real estate market and regularly find yourself there for other reasons anyway, we recommend that you stay close to home with your real estate investments — no more than one to two hours by your favorite mode of transportation.

Robert has had success with a real estate investment strategy that limits his potential markets to cities where he had personal management experience when he worked for a large real estate syndicator. He also limits himself to areas that are no farther than a one-hour, nonstop flight on Southwest Airlines.

Although we strongly advise that you cut your teeth on an income property or two in your local market, establish parameters that meet your specific needs. For example, maybe you have family responsibilities that limit the amount of time you can devote to overseeing and managing your real estate investments. The one-hour-flight rule that Robert uses would likely be too taxing in that situation, and could be replaced by something like a 30-minute-drive rule.

Although virtually everyone lives in an area with opportunities for real estate investing, not everyone lives in an area where the prospects are good for real estate in general. That's why it's important to broaden your geographic investment horizon as long as you don't compromise your ability to effectively manage and control your property.

Even if you decide to invest in real estate in your own locale, you still need to do tons of research to decide where and what to buy — extremely important decisions with long-term consequences. In the pages that follow, we explain what to look for in a region, a community, and even a neighborhood before you make that investment decision. Keep in mind, though, that you can spend the rest of your life looking for the *perfect* real estate investment, never find it, never invest, and miss out on lots of opportunities, profit, and even fun.

Evaluating a Region: The Big Picture

Though we advise you to think local, any decision about where to invest should start with an evaluation of the overall economic viability and trends of the surrounding region. If the region isn't economically sound, then the likelihood for successful real estate investments within that area is diminished. To buy right, you need to understand how to evaluate important economic data so that you can invest in the areas that are poised for growth.

We define a *region* as a concentrated population base (rather than an entire state or section of the country). Data for any larger geographic area would be difficult to use for the types of real estate investments you'll be making. For example, data for the state of Texas isn't as important as vital economic trends for your proposed investment in the Houston area.

Gathering and analyzing the relevant economic data has never been easier, thanks to the Internet. The most important data for population growth, job growth, and economic trends is available online, and there are numerous entities tracking this information. From the federal government, to state and local governments, to universities and business groups, information on regional economic trends is readily available.

In addition to the academic and governmental agencies that provide broader economic indicators, several private firms specialize in providing specific data on occupancy and rental rates for different types of real estate for many of the major cities throughout the country. For example, two of our favorites are the CoStar Group (`www.costar.com`) and Real Estate Research Corporation (`www.rerc.com`).

You can find the vital economic data you need for your evaluation through your local economic development department, chamber of commerce, or public library. Real estate lenders often have in-house economists that collect information concerning areas where they lend money, and these folks are often the first to detect weaknesses in the market. So if your lender isn't particularly enamored about the location for your proposed real estate investment, they probably know something that you should heed. Also, contact a professional appraiser in your area, because they routinely collect this information for their appraisals.

These sources collect, record, analyze, and report information according to specific geographic boundaries as established by the federal government. The U.S. government divides urbanized areas of the country into *Standardized Metropolitan Statistical Areas* (SMSA). SMSA's are large areas that consist of one or more major cities. For example, the entire San Francisco Bay Area, the combined areas of both Dallas and Fort Worth, greater Los Angeles, and greater New York City are each a single SMSA.

If your proposed investment isn't in an area tracked as part of an SMSA, much of the same information is available, but you'll have to do a little more digging.

You're looking for more than just numbers. Attitude and leadership are important as well. Many neighboring cities are working together with regional planning boards and economic development agencies. Their goal is job creation and they possess great powers to make important economic decisions regarding regional airports, mass transportation, and the reuse of surplus military installations. Clearly, such regional governance can have a major impact for better or worse on your real estate investments.

The problem with forecasting the future

No one can precisely predict the future. And with due respect to our friendly economists, forecasts of population and job growth can go awry. For example, the impact of 9/11 was widely predicted to present a crushing blow to local economies that relied heavily on tourism. A significant decrease in tourism would then ripple through the economy and result in the loss of employment for thousands and lead to lower real estate demand.

There was a short-term impact and some people were adversely affected. However, Robert saw an opportunity. He figured that everyone needs a vacation, and if folks can't feel safe traveling abroad, then they're going to travel domestically. So he invested in Las Vegas apartments at a time when the major hotels were still limiting their employees to part-time work in an effort to stem losses. Now, only three years later, most tourism-dependent cities have actually seen a record number of visitors — Americans have fundamentally shifted their travel patterns and habits and now prefer to travel domestically — where they feel safe.

You're looking for a region or area that is growing and has a diverse economic base with strong employment prospects. In the following sections, we cover some of the more significant factors that can impact real estate demand and values.

Population growth

Population growth is one of the cornerstones upon which demand for real estate is based. An area with a steady growth in population will soon need more residential and commercial rental properties. More people mean more demand for housing, higher demand for retail shopping, and increased demand for offices and service providers. In other words, people use real estate, so the demand for real estate is enhanced as the population increases.

Increases or decreases in population are the result of three activities: births, mortality, and people moving into or out of the area. In most areas, births exceed deaths (because our population base is clearly living longer), and thus most areas will experience moderate growth. So the real impact comes from our dynamic and mobile society. We've seen tremendous shifts in population from northern states to the more temperate climates of the Sunbelt. Immigration has also been a major factor in many parts of the country.

How does population growth affect your real estate decisions? Simply put, economists find that a new household is needed for every increase in population of three persons. Of course, these numbers can vary based on average household size. So if you're considering investments in rental homes or small apartment buildings in a certain area, the overall net population growth can be a factor in determining current and future demand for rental housing.

But knowing the increase in population for the entire SMSA or region isn't enough, because population growth isn't evenly spread and can vary. As you get down to the next level in your research (see the "Investigating Your Local Real Estate Market" section later in the chapter), you need to determine the communities and even neighborhoods where the increased population will want to live, work, and shop. Real estate developers, and their lenders, look closely at net population growth in specific submarkets to forecast the demand for their proposed developments.

Job growth and income levels

Job growth is another fundamental element in determining demand for real estate. Economists generally predict that a new household is needed for every 1.5 jobs created. So if a new employer moves into the area and brings 150 new jobs, then the local real estate housing market will need approximately 100 new dwelling units. Of course, these new jobs also positively impact the demand for commercial, industrial, and retail properties.

The U.S. Bureau of Labor Statistics compiles job growth and other economic data by SMSA as well as by county. This info is available at the Bureau's Web site (www.bls.gov). Other great sources for economic data are local colleges and universities and good local libraries.

But you need more information about the types of jobs before you can estimate their effect on the demand for each type of real estate. Although job growth is critical, so are the following factors:

- **Income levels:** Without stable, *well-paying* jobs, an area can stagnate. Even with positive growth in population and jobs, a lack of income can stifle the demand for additional residential and commercial properties. Many areas of the country have plenty of jobs, but they're lower- rather than higher-paying jobs. Ideally, look to invest in real estate in communities that maintain diverse job bases.

- **Level of employment diversification:** If the local economy is heavily reliant on jobs in a small number of industries, that dependence increases the risk of your real estate investments. One of the most notable examples historically has been the greater Seattle area where the job market, and hence real estate market, was tied to the rising and falling fortunes of the Boeing company.
- **Industries represented:** Consider which industries are more heavily represented in the local economy. If most of the jobs come from slow-growing or shrinking employment sectors, such as farming, small retail, shoe and apparel manufacturing, and government, real estate prices are unlikely

to rise quickly in the years ahead. On the other hand, areas with a greater preponderance of high-growth industries, such as technology, generally stand a greater chance of faster price appreciation.

- **Types of jobs:** The specific types of jobs available can be important depending on the target market for your income property. If you're buying a class A office building in an urban area, look for statistics on current and future employment levels for professional employment. For example, owning an office building across the street from the new regional courthouse gives you a real advantage in attracting law firms and legal support firms. Of course, you also want to make sure that the area boasts a good mix of nearby retail and food services to complement and support the tenants in your building.

In addition to job growth, other good signs to look for include the following:

- **Stable to increasing wages:** The demand for real estate is clearly correlated to income levels, so local jobs with strong underlying demand are key. With many jobs being outsourced to other parts of the country and world, it's important that the local jobs are not only secure, but are also unlikely to see an erosion in purchasing power.
- **A recession-resistant employment base:** Traditionally, jobs that enjoy stability are in the fields of education, government, and medical services. Even areas renowned for strong demand and limited supply of real estate can slow down if the economy is hit hard, as shown by the collapse of some technology firms in the early 2000s.
- **Employment that's highly unlikely to be outsourced:** Jobs can flow to another area of the country or overseas to the latest low-cost manufacturing base.
- **Declining unemployment:** Examine how the jobless rate has changed in recent years. You wouldn't want to invest your entire savings into a rental property located adjacent to the large typewriter factory!

Investigating Your Local Real Estate Market

Although everything starts at the regional level, you need to fine-tune your perspective and look at your local real estate market, too. All of the same types of economic data that you collect on a regional basis are important in evaluating your local real estate market.

With real estate investing, deciding where to invest is frequently more important than choosing the specific rental property. You can have a rental property that meets the needs of the market, but if it's located in a declining area where the demand is weak or an area with overbuilding and an excess of available properties, then your investment won't perform financially. (These are the properties that perform the worst over time but are typically the types of properties highly touted by the infomercial gurus who love to brag about how much real estate they control but rarely tell you about their long-term investment returns.)

Likewise, you need to determine the areas that may be too richly priced, because your cash flow and future appreciation will be hurt if you overpay for a property. Often properties in the best neighborhoods in town are so overpriced that there is little upside potential and thus we advise you to seek other properties unless you're content with low returns analogous to investing in safe and low yielding bonds.

In many local real estate markets, the demand for real estate is impacted more by the regional economy than by the local economy. For example, bedroom communities have high demand for rental homes and apartments even though they may only have service sector jobs in the immediate area, because the higher income professional and manufacturing jobs are concentrated in other areas of the region.

In the sections that follow, we help you research quantitative issues to consider when deciding where to invest in real estate. But you also must consider other factors, for instance, the weather or recreation and entertainment options — all key factors in the livability or quality of life for citizens. All of these criteria contribute to the overall desirability of a local market area and should be important considerations for the real estate investor. And don't underestimate the image or reputation of an area.

Supply and demand

The supply and demand for real estate in a given market has a direct impact on the financial performance of your income property. And although we firmly believe that the overall economic prospects for a region or community are vital, you must also find supply and demand information about the specific type of real estate that you plan to purchase.

Obviously, the best environment for investing in real estate is one with strong demand and limited supply. When the demand exceeds supply, there are shortages of available real estate.

Both sides of the equation — supply and demand — have indicators that you should evaluate in forming your consensus about the strength of the local real estate market. In the sections that follow, we take a close look at each indicator in detail. Supply-side indicators include building permits, the rate at which new properties have been rented or absorbed into the market, and the availability of alternatives for similar real estate. Demand indicators include occupancy and rent levels.

The overall relationship between supply and demand determines the market conditions for real estate. For example, a large number of pending or recently issued building permits, weak absorption or rental of new properties, and an excess of income property listings that have been on the market for an extended time are all indicators that the supply of a specific product type is greater than the demand. Such market conditions will soon result in lower occupancy, lower rents, and often, rental concessions like free rent or lower rental rates early in the lease, which mean lower cash flow and smaller appreciation potential. These aren't the markets you should be seeking.

When the demand for real estate is high, there are few vacancies and property owners will move to raise rents and eliminate or minimize any concessions. In commercial properties, landlords cut back on the tenant improvement (TI) allowance and require the tenants to take the space as-is and make any upgrades or changes to the space at their own expense.

Building permits and absorption

Building permits are often the first tangible step outlining the intent of a developer to build new real estate projects. Therefore, knowing about the issuance of building permits is an essential leading indicator to future supply of real estate.

The trend in the number of building permits tells you how the supply of real estate properties may soon change. A long and sustained rise in permits over several years can indicate that the supply of new property may dampen future price appreciation. Many areas experienced enormous increases in new building during the late 1980s, right before prices peaked due to excess inventory. Conversely, new building dried up in many areas in the late 1970s and early 1980s as onerous interest rates strangled builders and developers. The current real estate cycle has been unusual in that, despite the record low-interest-rate environment, most parts of the country aren't overbuilding.

Absorption, the rate at which new buildings are rented and occupied, can be useful to determine the potential for the market to become *saturated* or oversupplied with certain types of real estate. A healthy real estate market is one in which the available new properties have rented in a relatively short period of time — typically measured in months. Absorption is measured in housing units for residential properties and in square footage for all commercial types of properties.

Absorption can be either a positive or negative number and is usually tracked on a quarterly and annual basis.

- **Positive absorption:** More space is rented or occupied by owners/users during the measured time period than was built and brought online.
- **Negative absorption:** The new supply of a given type of real estate is being built faster than users can or want to use it.

You can obtain information on building permits from your local planning or building department. Absorption statistics aren't as easy to find, but absorption is tracked by local real estate appraisers and real estate brokers. For example, professional real estate brokers holding the CCIM (Certified Commercial Investment Member) designation specialize in the sale of income properties and often have that information. See Chapter 4 for many other reasons to have an appraiser on your real estate team.

Building permits and absorption are property-type specific and an oversupply in industrial properties generally has no bearing on other types of commercial income properties such as retail or office. The only exception is when the use of a property can be changed. For example, many industrial properties have been upgraded to add office space for manufacturing firms so they can have their administrative functions and operations in the same facility. This type of hybrid usage is more difficult to track — but extremely important to note if it's occurring in your proposed investment market.

Another noteworthy trend for residential real estate investors is that new construction favors single-family homes rather than multifamily apartments. This can have a significant impact on your decision whether to invest in single-family rental properties or multifamily properties, because multifamily properties will benefit from the reduced competition. There are several reasons for this phenomenon and we discuss some of them later in this chapter under "Considering barriers to entry."

Availability of alternatives – renting versus buying

When the cost of buying is relatively low compared with the cost of renting, more renters can afford to purchase, thus increasing the number of home sales and lowering demand for rentals. A key indicator you can use to gauge the market is the number of property listings:

- **Increase in property listings:** Increasing numbers of property listings is an indication of future trouble for real estate price appreciation. However, as property prices reach high levels, some investors decide that they can make more money cashing in and investing elsewhere. When the market is flooded with listings, prospective buyers can be choosier, exerting downward pressure on prices.

- **Decrease in property listings:** A sign of a healthy real estate market is a decreasing and low level of property listings, which indicates that the demand from buyers meets or exceeds the supply of property for sale from sellers. At high prices (relative to the cost of renting), more prospective buyers elect to rent and the number of sales relative to listings drops.

Although these guidelines are true for all types of real estate, the best example currently is in residential rental housing where low interest rates have led to record home purchases in many parts of the country. Landlords surveying their departing residents routinely hear that their tenants are moving because they just purchased a home. In some areas, builders and sellers of existing homes report that demand for single-family detached homes is so high that they have multiple offers within hours of their property being placed on the market. However, a rise in interest rates can have a negative effect on home sales with the average time on the market increasing significantly. That will mean an increase in the availability of purchase alternatives and lower demand for homes while the demand for rental housing rises.

Stepping in the path of progress

One of Robert's best real estate investments was a 30,000-square-foot two-story medical center complex on 3 acres in Santee, California, a suburban bedroom community of San Diego. The building had been a hub of activity before the large medical group that occupied the property disbanded. The building was foreclosed on by the lender and was virtually vacant for several years, because the area didn't easily attract new tenants due to the lack of nearby sit-down restaurants and shopping.

However, Robert found out that major redevelopment was planned around the new trolley and transportation center located within a half mile. Besides a multiscreen cinema as the anchor tenant, the brand-new center would include everything from clothing stores to bookstores, plus several new restaurants. Robert was confident that the new center would be a catalyst for the entire area, so he quickly purchased the rundown and neglected two-building center for less than the assessed value on the property tax rolls. His investment plans included significant renovation — including complete exterior painting, parking lot repairs, installation of a large monument sign for tenant promotion, plus cleaning and upgrading the vacant suites. He also renamed the center to Santee Professional Center to improve its image, build identity in the community, and attract nonmedical tenants.

Lest you think that Robert made the perfect investment that had no snags, soon after his purchase, the national cinema chain filed bankruptcy and the developer halted plans. But a new developer came in and signed the national department store Target as the anchor tenant, and within 18 months, they had built and fully leased the new 500,000-square-foot shopping center. Now there are several other new office buildings completed or planned and major upgrades to the other buildings in the area. The Santee Professional Center is now almost full and was recently appraised at nearly three times the acquisition price of just five years earlier!

Occupancy levels

The market occupancy rate is another way to gauge the supply and demand for a given property type in the local market. The *market occupancy* rate for a particular type of property is the percentage of that type of property available for occupancy that's currently rented. For example, you may find data telling you that there are 2,312 total rental units in a local market in apartment buildings and the occupancy rate is 97 percent (or 2,242 are occupied), which would mean that 3 percent (or approximately 70) of the units are vacant. For commercial, industrial, and retail properties, the occupancy level is calculated based on square footage.

Before you invest your hard earned money, determine the current occupancy levels for your proposed type of income property.

With commercial, industrial, and retail properties, determining the occupancy levels is relatively easy. A quick look at the directory or a walkthrough of the property can give you a lot of information.

The true occupancy rate is actually much more difficult to determine with apartment buildings. With apartments, the vacancies aren't as obvious, and obtaining accurate information can be challenging — most professionally managed properties don't advertise their occupancy levels or volunteer this info (nor do they post tenant directories any more due to safety and privacy concerns). But fear not, we have some suggestions:

- **Trade organizations and industry service providers:** Some of these groups track this data. For example, the local affiliates of the National Apartment Association (`www.naahq.org`) and the Building Owners and Managers Association (`www.boma.org`) often publish vacancy and rent surveys for apartments and office buildings, respectively.
- **The do-it-yourself approach:** You can contact owners of comparable properties and offer to collect this data and give them a copy of the results.

After you acquire the info, here's how to use it:

- **Low vacancy rates:** When combined with a low number of building permits, low vacancy rates generally foretell future real estate price appreciation. If you find minimal vacancy in your market, it's a landlord's market with higher demand from tenants for existing units, which is a good sign for real estate owners. And good for real estate investors if the market prices remain reasonable.
- **High vacancy rates:** High rates indicate an excess supply of real estate, which may put downward pressure on rental rates as many landlords compete to attract tenants.

Concessions, which typically include free rent, often indicate weakness in the rental market. However, some types of real estate and rental markets almost always have concessions, no matter how strong the rental market. This is very common in larger professionally managed apartment communities where a prospective tenant's first question when calling to inquire about a potential rental unit is inevitably, "What's your special?" Apartments in Phoenix and many other areas of the Sunbelt may be able to raise their rents and maintain occupancies at or above 95 percent, but can't eliminate the rental concessions or their rental traffic will simply evaporate. In commercial properties, the TI or tenant improvement allowance is similar — with many markets requiring certain levels of dollars per square foot in custom build-outs or upgrades when the rental rate is actually less negotiable. (Check out Chapter 10 for more information on concessions.)

Rental levels

The trend in *rent levels,* or *rental rates,* that renters are willing and able to pay over the years also gives a good indication as to the supply/demand relationship for income properties. When the demand for real estate just keeps up with the supply of housing and the local economy continues to grow, rents generally increase. This increase is a positive sign for continued real estate price appreciation.

Of course, you need to be careful to make sure that you're getting the true and complete story on rents. Owners and their property managers are very smooth and savvy and won't allow their quoted rental rates to fall when the market shows some signs of softening. This is logical because other tenants may have recently leased at a higher rate and would be upset to see the new tenants getting a better deal. So owners and property managers offer concessions or other perks to make sure that they are competitive in the current market while maintaining the perception of stable rents.

As a prospective rental property owner competing against these owners, you need to evaluate the current rent levels on a level playing field, so you want to calculate the *effective rental rate.* For example, if you see a comparable rental property available at $1,200 per month, but the owner is offering a concession of one month free rent on a 12-month lease, then the effective rent is really $1,100 per month.

An advantage of investing in commercial real estate is that there are few governmental regulations and controls and the relationship between tenants and landlords is essentially a free market. However, residential *rent control* or *rent stabilization* (local laws regulating how much rents may increase) is an issue in some cities and towns. Investing in markets with rent control, or even with a protenant environment where a landlord has difficulty terminating a lease, may not provide adequate returns on investment and appreciation will be more limited. Although occupancy levels are usually strong in such areas, your overall cash flow could be threatened because the property's expenses may rise faster than you can legally raise the rents. In these communities, landlords that invest in major upgrades or capital improvements to a rental unit may not be able to raise rents or recover their costs because any rent increases must be approved by the local rent control board. Then, even if allowed at all, the approved capital improvements are amortized or spread over many years. Don't put your real estate future in the hands of others!

Path of progress

Buying real estate in up-and-coming areas with new development or renovated properties greatly enhances not only the ease of finding and keeping good tenants, but leads to higher occupancy, lower turnover, and higher rates of appreciation.

In virtually all major cities, some areas are experiencing new construction and growth — and have the reputation of being *the* area to live in. But by the time most folks feel this way, you've lost an opportunity to get in when prices have more upside potential. So, here are a few indicators to use to stay ahead of the game:

- **Follow the retailers:** You can often take a clue about where you should invest by looking for major retailers who do extensive research before making a decision to open in a given neighborhood. For instance, maybe a new home improvement store like Home Depot or Lowe's is opening or a new Costco is anchoring the new shopping center.
- **Follow the highways:** One of the best and most obvious indicators of where new development is headed is transportation. But make sure that the roads or mass transit projects actually get built. With so many funding and environmental challenges today, it can be extremely risky to invest in real estate based on proposed transportation projects. But after they're built, you're sure to find real estate investment opportunities.

But the path of progress isn't limited to new development. Many cities have areas that have seen better days and local leaders are doing their best to revitalize these tired and even blighted sections of town. A key component can be redevelopment districts that are formed with the property tax revenues being diverted to a special redevelopment agency that promotes new projects through a streamlined approval process and financial assistance. Often, the traditional downtown areas are being redeveloped with many incentives for developers and owners willing to be among the first ones in.

The poster child for limited land supply

Upward pressure on real estate prices tends to be greatest in areas with little buildable land. This characteristic was one of the things that attracted Eric to invest in real estate in the San Francisco Bay Area when he moved there in the mid-1980s. If you look at a map of this area, you can see that the city of San Francisco and the communities to the south are on a peninsula. The ocean, bay inlets, and mountains bound the rest of the Bay Area. More than 80 percent of the land in the greater Bay Area isn't available for development because state and federal government parks, preserves, and other areas protect the land from development, or the land is impossible to develop. Of the land available for development in San Francisco and the vast majority of it in nearby counties, virtually all of it had already been developed.

Although redevelopment areas can be great opportunities, significant risk is associated with investing in areas that are dynamic and changing. Like transportation projects, sometimes the best intentions of local leaders and redevelopment agencies can hit a snag.

Considering barriers to entry

Investing in real estate in an area that has strong demand and limited supply is likely to enhance your profitably. One of the trends to follow is the creation of more roadblocks to new development and thus severe limitations on the construction of additional buildings to meet even the increasing demands for real estate from natural population growth.

For example, maybe your chosen area has inhabitants with strong antiapartment sentiments or concerns about the environment. If you currently own or quickly invest in existing apartments in such areas, these factors can actually work to your benefit, because they make the addition of more housing units (competition) more difficult.

We suggest that you look for markets where natural and even man-made barriers to entry exist.

The popular board game Monopoly taught most of us from an early age about the importance of location and barriers to entry. When you control the playing field and prime properties, you dramatically improve your odds of successfully building wealth. In the following sections, we cover some of the more prominent factors that limit the supply of real estate and enhance cash flow and future appreciation for those who already own existing properties.

But, in the long term, the lack of buildable land in an area can prove a problem. Real estate prices that are too high may cause employers and employees to relocate to less expensive areas. If you want to invest in real estate in an area with little buildable land and sky-high prices, run the numbers to see if the deal makes economic sense. (We explain how to do this in Chapters 9 and 10.)

Environmental issues

Individuals and organizations concerned about the environment aren't a new trend. Environmental issues are now a key factor in the potential development of real estate projects in just about every area of the country.

Those concerned about the environment are expressing their disapproval of new and proposed projects with more authority and success, because federal and state laws require excruciating investigative reports on all aspects of proposed land development. It is extremely difficult in most urban areas to find land suitable for development that doesn't have some limitations or require remediation, such as the relocation or preservation of endangered species or plants. (Remediation can also include the cleanup and removal of contaminants.)

Many of these laws or guidelines find universal support — no one wants to live in a concrete world or destroy our beautiful countryside. And nearly everyone wants clean air, clean water, and the highest quality of living possible.

But preserving and protecting our environment comes at a cost: A large portion of potential developable land is being taken out of production or even consideration for use. The land that isn't available for development is being broadened and now includes much of the government-owned lands and virtually all land that can be classified as a hillside, wetland, or *vernal pool* (seasonal or temporary wetland). In many areas, additional swaths of public and private land are being designated and set aside by governmental agencies to protect endangered plants and wildlife.

These man-made decisions to preserve land, combined with other factors, can lead to a shortage of buildable land.

Shortage of buildable land

We learned in Economics 101 that strong demand and a limited supply will lead to rationing through higher pricing. Well, that is exactly what's happening in many of our major metropolitan areas as we quickly exhaust the supply of buildable land.

Environmental concerns are a contributing factor, but the market itself can also contribute to the scarcity of buildable land. The strong job growth and relatively modest home prices in the Las Vegas area have led to record construction of new homes. The cities of Las Vegas, Henderson, and North Las

Vegas are three of the ten fastest growing cities in the country, based on increased population. This incredible level of demand for new homes has led to home builders bidding up the price of land to the point that the construction of multifamily apartments has been severely restricted because the land is so expensive only for-sale housing can be built.

This is good news for the current owners of rental apartments: The steady influx of several thousand new residents per month into the Las Vegas area, combined with new apartment construction at levels significantly below the demand, have led to higher occupancy, the reduction and even elimination of rent concessions at more desirable properties, and upward pressure on rents.

CANES: Citizens Against Nearly Everything

Many cities are now putting more authority into the hands of local and even neighborhood planning boards that exercise their influence and control over proposed new developments. Although many of the representatives on these local planning boards are just interested in maintaining the aesthetics or compatibility of proposed developments with the existing land uses, some are motivated by another agenda.

The term CANES — Citizens Against Nearly Everything — was coined by then San Diego Padres President Larry Lucchino, who Robert interviewed on his weekly radio show many times while the baseball team proposed and fought for the development of a new ballpark. Various groups claiming to represent taxpayers, citizens, and environmentalists objected at every opportunity. Ultimately, after years of delays and dozens of lawsuits, the ballpark finally opened in downtown San Diego at the start of the 2004 baseball season.

This trend isn't unique to San Diego. Across the country, those opposed to growth seek to avoid increased traffic, congestion, and overcrowding of their schools and parks. In many communities and neighborhoods, homeowners are expressing their disapproval of new multifamily development. (If you want a big turnout at city hall, just announce that 300 new low-income apartments are being built across the street from the new for-sale housing tract.)

Such resistance to new development or even redevelopment isn't new. But it does seem to be a trend that should be considered by even a real estate investor with a duplex or a couple of rental homes. Unbridled growth isn't the answer nor is stagnation and decline, but our point is that you need to evaluate the impact of such attitudes on your income properties. Barriers to entry are a reality that you shouldn't overlook.

For example, increased demand in a community opposed to growth will result in higher prices, so investing in these areas will certainly enhance your prospects for appreciation. However, well-planned or *smart* growth can also lead to higher quality of living and greater long-term returns on your investment.

Condo conversion and construction defect lawsuits

Carefully evaluate the impact of the condominium market in your area because it can have a material effect on the overall supply of rental housing. Apartments converted to condos often result in fewer rental units because condo conversion units are typically purchased by owner-occupants that find such housing to be a financially viable entry-level opportunity. The drastic reduction in the building of new condominiums is the result of the unavailability of insurance for developers and their subcontractors due to the proliferation of construction defect lawsuits. New condominiums are often purchased by investors to use as rentals that will compete for tenants. These are barriers to entry that can affect your real estate market and should be part of your real estate strategy.

Many apartment buildings in urban areas were originally built as condominiums, but market weakness or the threat of construction defect legislation (discussed later in this section) led to a business decision by the developers to operate these condos as rental units. There is not much controversy about the ultimate conversion of these rental condos to owner-occupied units.

However, a dilemma faced by many cities is the return of the conversion of apartment rental communities into condominiums. On one hand, the severe shortage of affordable entry-level housing in many cities makes the conversion of apartments to condominiums an excellent opportunity for first-time home buyers. The concern is that conversion of apartments to owner-occupied condos reduces the rental housing stock.

How are condo conversions typically handled? The most common game plan for a conversion of an existing apartment community to a condominium project will almost always consist of extensive exterior renovation, including painting, landscaping, and other cosmetic items. Occasionally, local ordinances will require some structural repairs or upgrades, but the exterior work is primarily limited to the cosmetic issues. In other words, rarely do developers spend a lot of money on a new roof!

The unit interiors also receive a complete overhaul and upgrade — new flooring, window treatments, new and often upgraded appliances, and solid countertops and other decorative touches to really make the unit shine. These converted condos can be quite attractive as reasonably priced investments that look great and are well located, many times in areas where new development is difficult because the area is completely built-out and the cost to acquire the land would be prohibitive. But you need to look deeper than the smoke and mirrors that create the attractive façade of quality construction.

The problem is that in most cases, the existing building systems, such as the roof, plumbing, electrical, and HVAC, haven't been upgraded or replaced. So you could have a brand-new interior that looks sharp, but the major structural systems are quite old. Also, properties built under the code requirements for apartments usually have lower standards for weatherproofing, insulation, and noise attenuation. If you buy one of these converted apartments as a rental property, you may not know that your tenants can hear everything, and we mean everything, that goes on in the adjacent unit. That is, until they call to complain!

This conversion of apartments to condominiums can impact the rental market in one of two ways.

- Many of the condos will be purchased by individuals that intend to live there personally. In this case, that reduces the rental housing stock, which means less competition for apartments.

  Further, a good balance of owner-occupied housing units with their inherent increased pride of ownership can be healthy for the overall rental market. We strongly advise real estate investors to purchase rental homes in areas that are predominantly owner-occupied.

- Other converted condos won't be owner occupied, with many investors snapping up the reasonably priced units speculating that they will enjoy good returns. These units will be rented so there is no reduction in the rental housing stock.

In the long run, we believe that investing in condominiums that began life as apartments isn't wise. In the early years, when everything is relatively new, there is not much to go wrong. But after the true age of the building begins to show through increased repairs and maintenance, the volunteer association board of directors will face a real challenge. Will they be willing and able to dramatically increase the monthly assessments to cover the increased costs and to accrue the funds necessary to handle major capital items? Robert has managed associations for over 25 years and his experience is that the assessments will be kept artificially low and the property condition will decline over time. You don't want to own a unit in an association with major physical problems and no reserves.

The construction of new, attached, for-sale housing (or condominiums) has been severely restricted since the 1990s in many parts of the country due to construction defect lawsuits. The building industry claims that such lawsuits are unnecessary and extremely wasteful and the attorneys representing homeowners insist that if the builders simply wouldn't build such shoddy and poorly constructed housing units there would be no need for litigation. At the end of the day, the reality is that construction defect lawsuits are reducing the number of attached housing projects that are being built, because insurance is virtually nonexistent for developers and subcontractors.

Government's effect on real estate

Our country offers many examples of the importance of state and local government on prospects for prosperity. The following are key governmental and quasi-governmental factors to consider when researching a prospective community in which to invest:

- **Tax considerations:** For decades, California had an unbeatable combination of great weather and job growth that attracted millions from around the world. In the early 2000s, California suffered from a declining economy and what some real estate investors and business owners felt was excessive government regulation and taxation.

  California real estate investors and others with means are establishing legal residency in Nevada, Texas, Washington, Florida, and other states without state income taxes in increasing numbers. It can make a significant improvement in a person's overall income tax liability and it may not even be that much of a sacrifice. For example, a California real estate syndicator that attended one of Robert's property management courses pointed out that they found living on the east side of beautiful Lake Tahoe (in the state of Nevada) was just as nice as the west (or California side) where the top income tax rate can add up to another 10 percent in addition to the federal income tax.

  You should also have a detailed understanding of the property taxation system and appeals process. Be sure to determine whether a proposed income property acquisition is in a special assessment district where additional taxes are assessed against properties. Such special assessment districts may offer some advantages of better schools, parks, fire and police services, and may be well worth the additional annual investment. But you should know in advance how much the additional costs will be, how long you'll be required to participate, and exactly what you're getting in return so that you can properly evaluate whether you'll be able to generate a commensurate increase in your rental income.

- **Economic development incentives:** The economic development groups for many of these states are advertising in business publications and major newspapers and aggressively encouraging employers to relocate with incredible real estate incentives such as virtually free land or lower property and/or income taxation. Besides lucrative offers of real estate and tax incentives, as the global economy becomes ever more competitive, businesses are being lured to locations that will reduce their costs of labor, energy, transportation, and energy.

- **Community's reputation:** Your local chamber of commerce, tourism bureau, and city hall all work very hard to establish the right reputation and attract the top employers. These organizations can have a real impact on the market environment for businesses and thus create more jobs in the long run, which leads to increased population and higher demand for all types of real estate.

- **Business-friendly environment:** We can't underestimate the importance of a probusiness attitude among state, regional, and local governments to help create a vibrant economy where your real estate investments will prosper.

Comparing Neighborhoods

The reputation of particular neighborhoods can be based on many factors, but certain key or essential elements differentiate the neighborhoods with good reputations and positive trends from the areas that are stagnant or trending the wrong direction.

Schools

If you don't have school-age children, you may not initially be concerned about the reputation and test scores of the local schools. Think again. Whether you're investing in residential or commercial income properties, schools matter. The demand for residential and commercial property (and the subsequent value of the property) is highly correlated to the quality of local schools.

Ask any real estate agent about the impact of schools on the demand and sales price for a home in a great school district. Likewise, employers use the quality of local schools in recruiting their key personnel — and sometimes even relocate company facilities to be near areas known for their schools.

The Internet can be a very useful tool in determining the quality of local schools. Most school districts have Web sites that include information on the test scores of their students for mandatory state and federal testing. Unfortunately, many people make snap judgments about school quality without doing their homework. Visit the schools and don't blindly rely on test scores. Talk to parents and teachers, and discover what goes on at the school.

Crime rates

Crime can have a significant and sobering effect on the demand and desirability of all types of income properties. No one wants to live in a high crime area, and commercial tenants and their customers will neither work at nor patronize unsafe businesses. No areas are going to be crime-free, but you don't want to find out after the close of escrow that you have purchased a rental property that is "claimed" by rival gangs. Before you make your investment decision, consult these sources:

- **Local law enforcement:** Contact local law enforcement and obtain the latest and historical crime statistics.
- **Local newspapers:** Newspapers often have a police-blotter section that provides information on major and even petty crimes in the community.
- **Sexual-offender databases:** Laws require certain convicted sexual offenders to register with local law enforcement. These databases allow you to identify the general locations of convicted sex offenders who have committed sexual offenses against minors and violent sexual offenses against anyone.

  These databases aren't foolproof. The states haven't been consistent in their efforts to maintain and make them available. Also, persons required to register don't always follow the requirements, but at least you can find out about the known ones.

  Be sure to advise your tenants to check the database as this information is dynamic and everyone needs to make their own decision about the safety of their family. You should always disclose any known registered individuals in the neighborhood (that doesn't mean that you need to do the research).

Pride of ownership

Pride of ownership is an intangible attitude that has tangible results. Pride of ownership also has no economic boundaries — even modest-income areas can really look sharp. Look for rental properties in neighborhoods that reflect pride of ownership — well kept, litter-free grounds, trimmed plants, beautiful flowers, fresh paint, and so on. This is the curb appeal that helps you attract and retain your tenants.

Although everyone may have a different perception of exactly what constitutes a well-maintained property, pride of ownership is readily apparent, and the effort made by business owners and homeowners to keep their properties looking sharp is important to real estate values.

You may find that some of the more aesthetically pleasing areas look that way for a reason. Homeowners associations and business parks typically have a board of directors and architectural review committees that routinely inspect the properties under their jurisdiction as well as review and restrict improvements to meet certain standards.

Other areas may have informal committees of neighbors who band together to keep their properties in tiptop condition. This is also true of multifamily residential and commercial properties, and these properties usually must submit to local laws and regulations enforced by the building or code enforcement departments.

You can control the appearance, condition, and maintenance of your own property, but your options are limited if the properties surrounding it fall into disrepair. Your purchase of a fixer-upper and the investment of time, money, and sweat equity won't be rewarded financially if the surrounding properties are in a state of disrepair and have owners that don't really care.

Property values, occupancy, and rental rates all sag when property owners no longer take pride in their property. Avoid declining neighborhoods that display the red flags of dispirited owners — poorly kept properties, junk-filled vacant lots, inoperative cars in the parking lot or street, graffiti, vandalism, and deferred maintenance. Neighborhood deterioration is a blight that spreads from one property to another.

Role play: What attracts you to the property?

One of the best ways to evaluate the prospects for a particular neighborhood is to play the role of a residential tenant looking for the best place to call home. Go back in time to when you made the decision to live in your neighborhood. What were the primary criteria you used to make that determination? You're probably typical of many of your potential tenants. They prefer rental properties in close proximity to employment centers, transportation, schools, childcare, places of worship, shopping, recreation, and medical facilities. These details can be captured in a *property knowledge sheet*.

Property knowledge sheets

One of the best ways to have the answers to the questions that may be raised by your rental prospect is to prepare a *property knowledge sheet* for each of your rental property locations. A property knowledge sheet contains all the basic information about your rental property, such as the size and type of the rental unit and the unit number (for multiple-unit properties), plus the age, type of construction, and other important details about the unit.

A thorough property knowledge sheet also contains important information about the local neighborhood and general area. Like the chamber of commerce or visitor's information bureau, you want to be able to answer questions about the area. Rental prospects are generally interested in knowing about employment centers, transportation, local schools, child care, places of worship, shopping, and medical facilities. You can really make a positive impression on your rental prospect if you can tell them where the nearest dry cleaner or Thai restaurant is located.

With all this vital information from your property knowledge sheet at your fingertips, you can be ready to answer your rental prospect's questions. The more you know about your property, the easier it is for you to offer important reasons for a prospect to select your rental over the competition.

Property knowledge sheets can definitely give you the edge over your competition. Because you'll often be competing with large multifamily rental properties, you need to be prepared to answer important questions about the area. Often, immediately knowing a detail such as whether a certain child-care center is in your area can make the difference between success and failure.

Check out Figure 8-1 for an example of a property knowledge sheet.

Property Knowledge Sheet

Property Information

Rental address ____________ Unit # _____ City ____________ Zip code _______
Office hours (if any) __________ Square footage of unit(s) ____________
Unit mix—Studios ____ 1 Bedroom ____ 2 Bedroom/1 Bath ____ 2Bedroom/2 Bath ____ Other ______
Rent—Studios _____ 1 Bedroom _____ 2 Bedroom/1 Bath _____ 2Bedroom/2 Bath _____ Other ______
Application fee _________ Security deposit ___________ Concessions ____________
Age of rental _________ Type of construction ___________ Parking ____________
Recreational facilities ____________ Laundry ____________ Pets ____________
Storage ____________ Utilities (who pays?) ____________ AC/Heat __________
Appliances ____________ Floor coverings ____________
Special features/comments ____________
____
____

Community Information

School district ____________ Grade school ____________ Jr. high ____________
High school ____________ Jr. college ____________ College ____________
Trade school ____________ Pre-school (s) ____________
Childcare ____________ Places of worship ____________
Police station ____________ Fire station ____________ Ambulance ____________
Electric ____________ Natural gas ____________ Telephone ____________ Cable ____________
Water ____________ Sewer ____________ Library ____________ Post office ____________
Hospital ____________ Pharmacy ____________ Vet ____________
Other medical facilities ____________
Nearby employment centers ____________
Transportation ____________
Groceries ____________ Other shopping ____________
Local services ____________
Restaurants ____________
Comments ____________
____

Rental Market Information

Rental competitors/rental rates/concessions ____________
____
____
Our competitive advantages ____________
____
Our disadvantages ____________
____

Figure 8-1: Property knowledge sheet.

Commercial property considerations

Looking at a property from a tenant's perspective is also useful if you're investing in commercial properties. Remember that your commercial tenants are in business to make money — and their location is often a key factor. Have you ever seen a small retail center that includes several vacant suites with butcher paper in the windows? That is the universal sign that a property is in financial trouble and in need of proactive ownership, management, and leasing — or the spiral toward foreclosure will continue.

Right down the street from a failing property, you may find another retail property with long-term leases and a waiting list, because successful retailers almost always flock together. That explains the success of many regional shopping malls that command high rents. Sometimes, just getting the right anchor or primary tenant in a commercial, industrial, or retail income property is all it takes to start the chain reaction toward the dream for any landlord — high occupancy, high rents, and low turnover!

Finding well-situated properties is easier when you're considering investing in an area where you've lived your entire life, but not as easy for investing in other locales. Nonetheless, every area has potential if you know what you're looking for and are willing to take the time to do the research.

Mastering Seller's Markets and Buyer's Markets

Some real estate investors make the mistake of not continuing to research the economics of their real estate markets after they've made their investments. Even if you plan to buy and hold, you need to pay attention to the market conditions. As we have seen, the criteria we advise you to consider in making decisions about which markets are the best for investing are dynamic and fluctuate.

Savvy real estate investors monitor their markets and look for the telltale signs of real estate cycles. These cycles present opportunities for expansion of your real estate portfolio or repositioning from weaker markets to stronger markets because not all areas experience peaks and troughs at the same time. That is why you need to know and track the timing of seller's and buyer's markets.

Real estate cycles

We believe that real estate is cyclical and that successful real estate investors always remain aware of the real estate cycles in their areas. First, let's define what we mean by saying seller's or buyer's market:

- A **buyer's market** occurs when the current owners of property are unable to sell their properties quickly and they must be more flexible on the price and terms. This is a great opportunity to seek seller financing.
- A **seller's market** is almost like the classic definition of inflation — "too much money chasing too few goods." In this case, the "goods" are real estate properties, which are in high demand with buyers lining up for the chance to purchase them. When sellers are receiving multiple offers within 24 to 48 hours of a listing or you see properties selling for more than the asking price, then you're in a strong seller's market.

Real estate traditionally experiences cycles as the demand for real estate leads to a shortage of supply and higher rents and appreciation. That leads to the building of additional properties, which, along with changes in demand due to economic cycles, usually results in overbuilding and a decline in rents and property valuation.

However, not everyone agrees that real estate cycles are relevant to residential real estate investors. Some of the real estate infomercial gurus claim that real estate investing in homes and apartments is recession-proof because people always need a place to live. Although that is partly true, we think that the economic base of the community where you invest does have a direct impact on all aspects of your operations — occupancy, turnover, rental rates, and even quality of tenant.

For example, when times are tough, residential tenants are the first to improvise with some finding that "doubling up" or even taking in roommates is palatable if it results in lower costs for housing. Some renters are even willing to move back in with Mom and Dad or another relative when their personal budgets don't allow them to have their own rental unit.

Robert has managed all types of income properties throughout the western states and has observed a broad cross-section of economic activity. He has seen how real estate cycles may be similar in a particular region but often vary from region to region. For example, when some areas of the country were setting records for rents in the mid '80s, landlords couldn't give away their apartments in Texas. Even venerable California was a miserable place to own real estate in the early '90s.

Can real estate investors who track these real estate cycles make investment decisions based on this information? Absolutely. That is where most successful and knowledgeable real estate investors see potential for increasing their real estate investment returns by timing the real estate market.

Timing the real estate market

Although the length and depth of the real estate cycles vary, there are clear highs and lows that real estate investors need to consider.

In some real estate markets, the double-digit appreciation over the last 5 to 10 years has brought record prices for homes and income properties. Lately, the most common question for Robert on his southern California radio show *Real Estate Today!* is "Should I buy income properties in southern California at these seemingly high price levels or should I invest elsewhere?"

There is no one-size-fits-all answer to this critical question. A key factor is the *investment horizon* or planned holding period for a particular investor and that specific investment. If the holding period is long enough, even purchasing income properties in today's overpriced markets will probably look good 15 to 20 year from now.

The alternatives are to identify those markets with excellent economic fundamentals where prices have remained low and invest there. The concept is similar to the "Buy low, sell high" truism for stocks except you sell in overpriced markets and reinvest in the lower priced markets. Such markets do exist but the question is whether the properties in the lower priced markets are going to provide the same or better investment returns in the long run versus alternative markets.

Unlike the stock market, real estate transactions entail significant transaction costs (as a percentage of the market value of the property). That's why selling and buying property too frequently undermines your returns.

It is our contention that even in the few markets where such "bargains" exist, they aren't really great opportunities. We are reminded of the business concept that in the long run you usually get what you pay for! There is so much more than just the projected rent and the selling price. Without going into a detailed analysis of property condition, expenses, and other invaluable criteria, you should simply consider whether these areas will pass muster after performing the economic analysis described earlier. Probably not.

Carleton Sheets, plus many other well-known infomercial gurus, have traditionally advised their followers that you should seek income properties where the projected gross monthly income is at least 1 percent of the purchase price. This would mean that if you acquire a rental property with a projected monthly income of $2,000, your acquisition costs should not exceed $200,000. The advice is sound, but there are fewer and fewer markets where such properties exist.

You may remember from your reading on investments that risk and return are generally related. That is, the lower the risk you take, the lower your expected return. (That is why short-term government-backed bonds and federally insured money market accounts offer nominal rates of interest or return on investment, and investments with higher risk, such as real estate, demand higher rates of return.)

So the real question is what are the risk-adjusted returns like for investing in these areas of the country with record high prices versus the risk-adjusted returns available in other lower priced real estate markets? You may find a rural property where the monthly rent exceeds 1 percent of the purchase price, but what about rent growth and appreciation? At the end of the day, you may find that your lower priced market with all of those "bargains" provided you with minimal cash flow and marginal appreciation.

Knowing when to sell and when to buy real estate is easier said than done. But if you follow the fundamentals of economic analysis, and remember that "location, location, value" is the key to successful real estate investing, you can do well.

Chapter 9

Examining Leases and Understanding Value

In This Chapter

- Looking at leases
- Comprehending valuation
- Developing value benchmarks

Location, as discussed in Chapter 8, is an important consideration when looking to invest in income property. But what you pay for the property and the cash flow it generates will make a significant difference in the success of your investment. In this chapter, you start your research, analysis, and evaluation of specific properties by analyzing the leases. Leases generate the income stream that's the foundation upon which your real estate investment strategy should be based. All the quantitative analysis we guide you through in Chapter 10 will be for naught if you don't have a handle on the leases.

We then introduce you to the concepts behind evaluating potential investment properties. We explain the key principles behind property valuation that you need to be familiar with. We then provide you with a few quantitative tools that you can use to size up prospective properties and determine whether you should move onto other properties or investigate further.

Evaluating Leases

A *lease* is a contractual obligation between a *lessor* (landlord) and a *lessee* (tenant) to transfer the right to exclusive possession and use of certain real property for a defined time period for an agreed consideration (money). A verbal lease can be enforceable, but it's much better to have a written lease that defines the rights and responsibilities of the landlord and the tenant.

Owning a nice property with attractive and well-maintained buildings may give you a sense of pride of ownership, but you're really investing in the leases. Successful real estate investors know that an excellent opportunity is to find properties with leases that offer *upside potential* in the form of higher income and/or stability of tenancy.

Regardless of the type of property you're considering as an investment, make sure that the seller provides all of the leases. And don't accept just the first page or a summary of the salient points of the lease — insist on the full and complete lease document along with any addendums or written modifications with the seller's written certification that the document is accurate and valid. (Verbal modifications to the written lease aren't generally enforceable.) Have your real estate legal advisor review the leases as well (see Chapter 4).

Lease transferability and analysis

Existing leases almost always *run with the property* upon transfer of ownership and thus are enforceable. The new owner of the property can't simply renegotiate or void the current leases they don't like. Because you'll be legally obligated for all terms and conditions of current leases if you buy a property, be sure that you thoroughly understand all aspects of the property's current leases.

You may find that you're presented with the opportunity to purchase properties with leases that are detriments to the property and actually bring down its current and future value. For example, the leases may be so far above the current market conditions that an investor should discount the likelihood that the leases will be in place and enforceable in the future.

Other common problems with leases include:

- Preprinted boilerplate forms (as opposed to a customized lease tailored to the specific tenant-landlord agreement) that may or may not comply with current laws or issues relevant for the specific tenant.
- The charges for late payments, returned checks, or other administrative fees may not be clearly defined or may be unenforceable.
- The rules and regulations may not be comprehensive or enforceable.
- There is no rent escalation clause or it isn't clearly defined.

We're not saying to bypass purchasing any properties with leases with the above problems. Just be aware and factor the effect, if any, into your decision making to determine whether you want to buy the property, or just simply note that you need to change the onerous terms upon renewal.

A seller should be honest and disclose all material facts about the property he's selling, but most states don't have the same written disclosure requirements that are mandated for residential transactions. So even though your broker or sales agent and other members of your due diligence investigation team (see Chapter 4) may be assisting you with inspecting the property and reviewing the books provided during the transaction, at the end of the day, you're the one who cares the most about your best interests.

Note the expiration dates of the leases, because any lease that's about to expire should be evaluated based on current market conditions. Future leases may not be at the same rent level, plus you must consider the concessions or tenant improvements that will be necessary to get the lease renewed.

- Residential lease renewals may require a monetary concession or possibly a perk for the tenants such as cleaning their carpets or installing microwaves or ceiling fans.
- Commercial lease renewals can require significant tenant improvements or rent concessions.

Factor these costs into your analysis because renewing a tenant, even with the associated costs, is typically much more cost effective than the turnover of a tenant.

Comprehending residential leases

The analysis of current leases for residential properties is usually fairly straightforward, but that doesn't mean you shouldn't do your homework! Review *each and every* residential lease to make sure that no hidden surprises are awaiting you, such as future free rent, limits to rent increases, or promises of new carpet or other expensive upgrades. Some sneaky sellers of residential properties know that some buyers don't thoroughly review each lease, so they load the leases with future rent concessions in exchange for higher rents up front, which they use to make the property's financial statements look more desirable. The *net effective rent* is what you're looking for to make your payments. An above-market lease isn't really above market if you're giving away free rent or promising to replace the carpet upon lease renewal.

Making sense of commercial leases

Residential leases tend to be fairly straightforward; however, evaluating commercial property leases is a whole different ballgame. Commercial leases are much more complicated than residential ones and therefore, the real estate investor must have a thorough understanding of the contractual obligations and duties of the lessor (landlord) and lessee (tenant).

The analysis of commercial leases is typically called *lease abstraction.* A *lease abstract* is a written summary of all the significant terms and conditions contained in the lease and is much more than a rent roll. Although a good *rent roll* covers the lease basics — rent, square footage, length of lease, and renewal date or options — a good abstract covers other key tenant issues such as signage, rights of expansion and contraction, and even restrictions or limitations on leasing to other tenants that offer similar products and services. Have written lease abstracts prepared for any commercial property you're considering, to ensure that you understand all the terms.

When obtaining financing for commercial properties, lenders typically require a certified or signed rent roll along with a written lease abstract for each tenant. However, because the income of the property is critical to the owner's ability to make the debt service obligations, most lenders don't simply rely on the buyer's numbers, but independently derive their own income projections based on information they require the purchaser to obtain from the tenants. This information will include:

- **Lease estoppel:** A *lease estoppel* certificate is a legal document completed by the tenant that outlines the basic terms of his lease agreement and certifies that the lease is valid without any breaches by either the tenant or the landlord at the time it is executed. These estoppel certificates are also very beneficial for the purchaser of the property and you should seriously consider requiring estoppels from all tenants when you purchase a commercial building — regardless of the requirements of any lender.

  Although tenant or lease estoppel certificates are rarely required by lenders or purchasers for residential transactions, there is a strong argument that the benefits of the estoppel certificate also apply in the residential setting because residential tenants are more likely to dispute the amount of the security deposit or claim that they were entitled to unwritten promises by the previous owner — free rent or new carpet or waiving late charges.

- **Financial statements:** The rent provided in the lease is a concern, but it is the amount you actually collect that determines the profitability of your real estate investment. Because of this, many leases require the commercial tenant to periodically provide (or present upon request) a recent financial statement.

- **Recent sales info:** Most retail leases have provisions for percentage rents in which the tenant pays a base rent plus additional rent based on a percentage of sales. The percentage rent is often on a sliding scale whereby the percentage paid by the tenant increases as their sales increase. Be sure that you receive and review recent sales information and ensure that the tenant is current on their percentage rent payments.

Reviewing the financial strength or sales figures for your commercial and retail tenants can be an excellent indicator of the future results of your property. Many of your best tenants in the future will be your small tenants that have successful businesses and need to expand. Also, look at the personal guarantees provided to see whether they're backed by sufficient resources. The compatibility of the tenant mix is also important.

One of the best ways to make money in real estate is to find commercial leases where the person in charge of the property isn't collecting the proper rent due under the terms of the lease. For example, you may find that the rent roll from the seller of a property you're considering for purchase hasn't implemented rent increases when due. Even more common is the failure of landlords and their property managers to correctly calculate and collect the common area maintenance charges or ancillary fees and reimbursements due from the tenant (see Chapter 10). Of course, you may also find that the landlords are actually overcharging the tenants and thus you would never want to purchase a property relying on phantom income that you don't have the legal right to collect.

Understanding Principles of Valuation

Knowing certain economic principles can be useful when seeking to evaluate the current and future value of potential real estate investments. In this section, we supply you with some background information to help you determine which properties are likely to have strong demand.

Have you ever traveled to a foreign country and observed miles of beautiful coastline that you know would be worth a fortune at home? Robert recently returned from Costa Rica where he saw dozens of faded "For Sale" signs on mile after mile of unimproved oceanfront property with spectacular water views. Local folks told him that these properties rarely sell and are available at very low prices. The weather is humid but not much different than similar weather along the Florida coast where property is cost prohibitive. So what are the factors behind such wide disparities in pricing and value?

Well, you need to consider several important economic principles when evaluating the potential value of a property. The basis of value for any piece of real estate is grounded in the following four concepts:

- **Demand:** The need or desire for possession or ownership backed by the financial means to satisfy that need.
- **Utility:** The property's ability to satisfy its intended purpose. For example, a very inaccessible location isn't suitable for a retail property.
- **Scarcity:** Similar properties are finite, and the economic concept of substitution doesn't indicate that other properties can meet the same needs. *Substitution* is the concept that an investor won't pay more for a property than the price of another similar property.
- **Transferability:** The relative ease with which ownership rights are transferred from one owner to another.

In the example above, the oceanfront land in Costa Rica wasn't in high demand, was relatively inaccessible (the closet major airport was in the capital city of San Jose — nearly 100 miles away), the availability of so many similar properties made the scarcity a nonissue, and the complications of the government requirements for foreign ownership could limit the ability to transfer the property to non–Costa Ricans.

An understanding of the current value and future potential of real estate investments is based on these four concepts. But there are also three other important economic principles that can affect the value of real estate now and in the future:

- **Regression:** A property's value is negatively impacted by surrounding properties that are inferior, of lower value, or in worse condition. In other words, don't buy the best property in a bad neighborhood.
- **Progression:** A property's value is positively impacted by surrounding properties that are superior, in better condition, and have a higher value.

  This concept is one of the most important for the real estate investor looking for long-term success. You want to buy a well-built but neglected and poorly maintained property located in a good neighborhood. You then add significant value by repositioning the property up to the level of the surrounding properties through proper maintenance, repairs, and upgrades.
- **Conformity:** Property values are optimized when a property generally conforms to the surrounding properties, and negatively impacted when they don't. Higher or optimized value through conformity is what you're seeking when you purchase the distressed property and renovate it to enhance its appearance and utility. This is also the economic principle that cautions against overimproving the property.

Determining highest and best use

All of these economic principles are based on the premise that the maximum value of real estate is achieved when a property is being utilized in its highest and best use. *Highest and best use* is the fundamental concept that there is one single use that will result in the maximum profitability by the best and most efficient use of the property. (This concept focuses solely on financial issues. For example, it says nothing about the impact that a significant, dense property development has on traffic and the local environment.)

The highest and best use of a specific property doesn't remain constant over time. Zoning of a property can eliminate certain possible uses of a property at the time of evaluation. However, particularly for properties in the path of progress, time can create new opportunities. For example, agricultural land in the middle of a rapidly expanding commercial and resort area isn't the highest and best use (financially speaking) of the property. (Check out Chapter 8 for more on zoning issues.)

This was the case for the strawberry fields that bordered the west side of Disneyland in Anaheim for several decades. The long-time owner of the property wasn't interested in selling at any price, so the property wasn't utilized to its highest and best use. However, after the owner passed away, his heirs quickly sold the property, and the Disney resort developed the property.

Comparing fair market value and investment value

When discussing real estate values, most people immediately think of fair market value — basically the price that the buyer and seller will agree to for a real estate transaction. Determining the fair market value of real estate often seems like an illusive concept much as the old adage "Beauty is in the eye of the beholder."

A bit more specifically, the *fair market value* is the most likely price a buyer would pay and a seller would accept for a property at a given time. This is based on three assumptions: The market for similar real estate is open and competitive; the buyer and seller are both motivated, acting prudently and with knowledge; and the buyer and seller aren't under any undue influence or affected by unusual circumstances.

However, real estate investors encounter another type of value — investment value. Although the market value is the value of a property to a typical investor, *investment value* is its value to a specific investor based on his particular requirements, such as the cost of capital, tax rate, or personal goals.

Some day, you may find yourself competing against another buyer for a prime investment property only to be surprised that she seems willing to pay much more. If you've carefully analyzed the property, and the seller provided the same information about the property to all potential purchasers, the other buyer is likely basing her offer on the property's investment value to her.

Maybe the other buyer needs a replacement property for a 1031 exchange and has the strong motivation of potentially losing the deferral of significant capital gains unless she buys property of equal or greater value within certain defined time periods (see Chapter 16). Such buyers are often willing to pay a premium or even dramatically overpay for a property to avoid losing the tax deferral benefits available under federal and many state tax codes.

You don't want to get into a bidding war for a property and overpay, so remember that market value and investment value are two different concepts. Investment value can be higher or lower than market value. For example, an investor who can't use the tax benefits of depreciation would be willing to pay less for a property that would generate large annual depreciation than would an investor that has other passive income and can use the deferral of taxation to reduce his current income tax obligations.

Reviewing the sources of information

As a prospective buyer, you'll find that quite a few folks have an idea of what a piece of property is worth:

- **Professional appraisers:** Owners and lenders hire these property valuation specialists to formulate the value of a property at a given point in time. Sellers rarely consult appraisers unless the sale is the result of litigation or probate, or a government entity is the buyer or seller.
- **Brokers and agents:** A Competitive Market Analysis (CMA) or a Broker Opinion of Value (BOV) is an estimate of market value that is generally available from brokers or agents active in the local area where the property is located. Because brokers and agents routinely track the listing and sale of comparable properties, they offer this information to owners with the goal of getting a listing on the property. Their valuation may be fair and reasonable; however, a buyer should remember that the real estate agent isn't a disinterested third party, but only paid if he's involved in a sales transaction — and then he's compensated more for a higher sales price.
- **Sellers:** Many sellers also do their own informal or anecdotal research by obtaining information about recent sales of properties they know in the area. Ultimately, the seller must make the final critical decision as to the asking price for a property. Because the valuation of real estate has many variables, inefficiencies in the pricing of income properties are common.

As a prospective buyer, the values these folks come up with are merely starting points for your analysis. Much more research is required. We spend the balance of this chapter, and Chapter 10, helping you get that research done.

Many real estate investors find that becoming real estate appraisers can be helpful to their success in investing in real estate. You may want to pursue a designation in real estate appraisal while making your real estate investments. Another benefit is that you qualify for the favorable tax treatments offered to real estate professionals (as described further in Chapter 16). Or you may just want to have a better understanding of the techniques used by appraisers for evaluating your own properties. For more information on professional appraisers and their education and training, please refer to www.appraisalfoundation.org or www.appraisalinstitute.org.

Establishing Value Benchmarks

The proper analysis of real estate requires due diligence and research, which starts with evaluating the existing leases (see the "Evaluating Leases" section earlier in this chapter) and continues with crunching the numbers (see Chapter 10). However, almost more than any other investment, the real estate industry has relied for years on value benchmarks to set prices and evaluate potential purchases.

One of the reasons value benchmarks are so widely used is that they can easily be calculated using basic information available on a property. Virtually all properties for sale that you encounter will have this information included in the listing brochures or offering packages provided by sellers or their brokers or sales agents.

These value benchmarks are general guidelines only and they can be misleading, especially to the novice real estate investor. When you first hear them, they sound impressive, but they're only quick and simple indicators of value and you shouldn't make investment decisions without calculating the Net Operating Income (NOI) (which we cover in detail in Chapter 10). The measures in this section shouldn't be *the* basis for the purchase of income-producing real estate.

Some professional appraisers may perform these calculations as a verification "test" to ensure that their results are in the ballpark and even include them in their appraisal. However, these numbers aren't as accurate at indicating value as the traditional methods of appraising the value of real estate (the cost approach, market approach, and income capitalization approach as discussed in Chapter 10). Neither are they formally recognized and mandated by the professional appraisal institutes or federal lending guidelines as approved methods of appraising real estate.

In the following sections, we cover the standard value benchmarks that apply to all types of real estate, as well as some that are unique to a specific sector.

Gross rent/income multiplier

Two important value benchmarks include:

- **Gross Rent Multiplier (GRM):** GRM is most commonly used for residential income properties, such as single-family rental homes and small apartment buildings, because virtually all of their income is in the form of rent payments from tenants.
- **Gross Income Multiplier (GIM):** GIM includes rent plus all other sources of income and therefore is more widely used to quickly evaluate commercial or industrial real estate investments.

The monthly rent or income is used in some areas of the country, but typically the GRM and GIM will be calculated using annual numbers. Both the GRM and GIM are calculated by dividing the proposed acquisition price by the annual rent or total income. For example, the GRM for a rental home that can be acquired for $100,000 with a monthly rent of $750 ($9,000 annualized):

$$GRM = \frac{\text{Proposed acquisition price}}{\text{Annual rent}}$$

$$= \frac{\$100{,}000}{\$9{,}000}$$

$$= 11.1$$

Likewise, an industrial building that sells for $250,000 with an annual gross income of $20,000 will have a GIM of 12.5.

These formulas require little information and are a simple way to quickly compare similar properties. Savvy real estate investors glance at the GRM or GIM on a listing sheet and may either eliminate some properties from, or earmark them for, further consideration, but they don't write an offer to purchase just because the ratio seems attractive. These investors know that much more analysis is needed because these formulas don't consider future appreciation, financial leverage, the risk of the investment, or operating expenses. They focus on income only.

Here's how relying on these formulas can be tricky: If the GRM and GIM ratios seem high, you need to check further to see if the price is too high — in which case you should pass on this property. Or maybe the rents are below market and the price is reasonable. Conversely, you may see a low GRM and think that you found your next investment prospect only to discover that the property is really overpriced because the seller has projected unrealistic rents based on seasonal rentals for dilapidated furnished studio apartments in a beach community.

Because both GRM and GIM only consider the income side of the investment, these formulas don't differentiate between the operating and capital expense levels of each property. The income is important, but what you're left with after paying the expenses makes your mortgage payment and provides you with cash flow. As we discuss in Chapter 10, the operating and capital expense levels can make a tremendous difference in the overall cash flow and the value of the property.

For example, compare two small apartment communities — both available for $1,000,000 and each with an annual gross income of $100,000. On each, the GRM is 10. But which is the better investment? The GRM doesn't give any indication, but further analysis gives you the answer because expenses for each property probably differ.

One apartment building is over 40 years old and has only month-to-month rental agreements with a high turnover of tenants. The property has interior hallways, is poorly maintained, and has an elevator that has never been modernized. This property suffers from above-average annual operating expenses of $85,000. The other potential investment is also an older property but caters to seniors on long-term leases who rarely move and do very little damage. The building is a two-story, garden-style walk-up with annual expenses of $45,000. Clearly, assuming the same financing is used for each property, the second property (with $40,000 less in expenses) will result in greater cash flow to the owner.

Price per unit and square foot

For apartment investors, the asking *price per unit* can provide a general feel for the reasonableness of the seller's demands. Price per unit is calculated by simply dividing the asking price by the number of units. For example, a six-unit building priced at $240,000 works out to $40,000 per unit.

Like the GRM calculation, the price per unit does have its limitations. The calculation doesn't account for the location or age of the property or the unit size and condition. It should only be used as a quick indicator of relative value when comparing similar properties in the same market area.

The *price per square foot* is a widely used yet simple calculation most often associated with commercial, industrial, and retail properties. (Although sometimes used for residential properties too.) To find this number, take the asking or sales price of a property and divide it by the square footage of the buildings. It's only a ballpark gauge of relative value and can be limited because it doesn't factor in the location or quality of the improvements or other important issues like the parking ratio or the occupancy level and rent collections.

For example, a 5,000-square-foot building going for $250,000 may seem like a good value at $50 per square foot in your market until you find that it's in a distressed area of town and hasn't been occupied for years. Or a 10,000-square-foot building for $1,250,000 may seem overpriced at $125 per square foot until you discover that the U.S. Postal Service just signed a 20-year net lease at full market rent with generous annual cost-of-living increases.

Replacement cost

Replacement cost is another factor that real estate investors should consider prior to making a real estate investment. The *replacement cost* is the current cost to construct a comparable property that serves the same purpose or function as the original property. The calculation of replacement cost is usually done by comparing the price per square foot to an estimate of the cost per square foot to build a similar new property, including the cost of the land.

If you buy an investment property below its replacement cost, then you can generally know that a prudent builder probably won't construct a similar new product. This minimizes the chance that overbuilding will result in excess supply. It isn't until resale value (minus depreciation) of existing properties equals the cost to construct new properties that a builder will find it financially feasible to build an additional product.

If you're considering investing in a real estate market that seems overpriced, try to avoid buying investment properties where the cost for new construction is equal to or lower than the replacement cost of a similar building. When prices rise to the point that it is more economical to build a new product rather than buy existing investment properties, builders know that they can build an additional product and sell it at a profit. And you will then have additional properties to compete with.

Chapter 10

Crunching the Numbers: How Much Should I Pay?

In This Chapter

- Getting a return on your investment
- Understanding the mysteries of Net Operating Income
- Delving into cash flow
- Looking at three basic approaches to valuation
- Determining what you should pay for a property

With the help of your real estate team, you need to narrow your real estate investment opportunities down to just those properties that seem to have the best chance to produce financially in the long run. In Chapter 9, we cover the basics of property valuation and provide you with the information you need to examine the leases of prospective properties.

In this chapter, we get down to the business of running the numbers. We cover the essential elements of understanding and arriving at a property's income and expenses and Net Operating Income — and we explain what that is! We then take these important numbers a step further and show you the best valuation tools traditionally used by appraisers and commonly used by lenders to determine what a property is "worth."

But after you've done all of your research and analysis, the reality is that you still need to establish whether a proposed property has the potential to be a good investment opportunity. Overpaying for a good property isn't any better than getting a deal on a bad property. Neither will meet your goals. So we close the chapter by putting it all together to help you decide how much you should consider paying.

Producing a Return on Your Investment

The purchase of an investment property is really the purchase of a future income stream or cash flow. Although pride of ownership or the satisfaction of being the owner of a rental property may be an important issue for some people, most real estate investors focus primarily on the investment returns that they can generate from a given property.

Four elements determine the return you'll see on your investment:

- **Net cash flow:** Net cash flow is money generated by the property after deducting all costs and debt service from the income. See the "Calculating Cash Flow" section later in this chapter.
- **Tax benefits of depreciation:** Many investors are able to use these tax benefits to shelter other sources of income (we cover this subject in Chapter 16).
- **Buildup of equity:** If you acquired the property with debt, the equity buildup from paying down the debt over time is a factor.
- **Appreciation:** True wealth is created through buying property and selling it for much more, years down the road. Significant estates and generational wealth are created through appreciation.

The key to generating a profitable real estate portfolio is finding and purchasing properties that exhibit the potential for high occupancy and growth in income while keeping expenses and turnover reasonable. Success in real estate investing depends on purchasing a property for the right price so that you have the ability to use your management skills to increase the value over time. Don't base your investment decision on emotions. Falling in love with a property can lead to overpaying.

You also need to determine what work needs to be done to the property to correct any deferred maintenance or functional obsolescence. Even if you simply hold the property and look for cash flow and appreciation, you want to be able to evaluate the holding costs during your ownership period.

Then you need to determine the future value of the property to calculate the likely disposition price and determine your return on investment.

Figuring Net Operating Income

Knowledgeable real estate investors begin a serious analysis of a potential property acquisition by deriving the projected Net Operating Income, commonly abbreviated as NOI. We find it surprising how many real estate investors don't make the effort to calculate the NOI before buying a property. Instead, the quick-and-easy nature of the benchmarks we cover in the previous chapter seduces unwitting investors into a false sense of security.

The calculation of Net Operating Income is simply: Income – Expenses.

NOI is the most critical factor in determining the potential for return on your investment in real estate. Determining the NOI of a property is one of the fundamental building blocks to analyzing real estate investments. Any decision — to buy, hold, or sell — should only be made after a careful analysis of the *actual current* and *projected future* NOI for a given real estate investment. Arriving at a reasonable estimate for future NOI is the key to determining the value parameters for your real estate investment. We recommend that you value a property based on the projected NOI for the next year, or preferably next few years.

The current NOI is fairly easy to obtain and is often provided by the seller. Deriving the projected NOI is a more time-consuming and in-depth process. The forecasting of a property's NOI is typically more of an art than a science. Many times, the estimation of NOI is based on a number of assumptions or projections about future events that are anything but certain. Will your tenants renew their leases and at what rates? Will the tenants make their rent payments and other contractual requirements as agreed in their leases? Will expenses stay within the expected range or will there be significant world or local events that lead to a spike in costs (like the availability and cost of property insurance after 9/11)?

Whether you receive current or projected NOI estimates from a seller, be careful to verify the numbers. Some sellers, and many real estate brokers and agents, prefer to provide a *proforma NOI* (a projection of future financial performance of the property) that uses higher rents and lower expenses. These fictitious numbers are based on the theory that the new owner will raise the rents to market level and simultaneously lower the costs of operating the property. These assumptions are rarely valid. Unless the property has leases that renew at higher rates or below-market leases that are expiring while the demand is high, you seldom find a professionally managed property with below-market rents. If it were that easy to increase income, wouldn't the current owner do it? Expenses are also unlikely to decrease significantly.

Have you ever seen a projection from a seller, her broker, or her sales agent that projects a lower NOI for an investment property on the market? They act as if the only way for NOI to go is up. Although you want to invest in properties where that is the likely result, the reality is that real estate is a cyclical business and supply and demand factors have a major impact.

"Garbage in, garbage out" holds true for your projections of your future NOI. Therefore, make a careful and detailed analysis of the property you're considering. Real estate investing isn't something you should do by the seat of your pants. Develop your own operating proforma prior to purchasing any property. And any evaluation or projection of the income stream for a property should begin with an analysis of each lease or rental agreement (which we cover in Chapter 9).

Evaluating income: Moving from fiction to useful figures

To evaluate the income side of your budget, we advise that you painstakingly record and verify all income using a zero-based budget concept. A *zero-based budget* is where you start with a blank piece of paper (or spreadsheet if you enjoy computer software) and individually, tenant by tenant, create the projected rents and income stream for the property. (A similar zero-based budget concept is useful for determining your likely or expected expenses and is discussed in further detail later in the chapter.)

Sellers may provide or be asked to sign a certified rent roll or similar document verifying the accuracy of the tenants and rents listed. Although this document may be a great exhibit in your lawsuit against the seller for fraud, we advise that you use this document as a tool in developing your own analysis of the current and future rent payments due under the terms of the existing leases. Don't just gather static data and numbers on your current tenants; you must be able to interpret the data. Evaluate the strength of each tenant. The lease may give you the legal right to future rent payments, however, a tenant who is unable or unwilling to meet his lease obligations won't be good for your rental collections.

You want a property that not only has tenants with the current financial strength to meet their obligations under the lease, but also tenants who will enhance or increase your income in future years. For example, you may determine that one of your commercial office building tenants will be looking to expand and will probably replace a tenant that is barely surviving — and unlikely to renew their lease.

It's truly amazing how little some commercial landlords know about the needs of their current tenants. Be sure to actually talk to your prospective tenants (in addition to getting the estoppel certificates discussed in Chapter 9). Tenants are the key to your future success, and you want to make sure that you can provide the proper environment so their businesses can grow and prosper while you benefit from their rental payments that ultimately pay for the building you plan to own free-and-clear in the future.

But the income side of the equation involves more than just estimating rents. The typical income and expense statements for reporting in real estate include standard terminology that all real estate investors should know:

- **Gross potential income** or GPI is the maximum gross income that would be generated from the rent if the property were at 100 percent occupancy and all money owed were collected in full. (This is sometimes referred to as *gross possible income.*)
- The **effective gross income** or EGI is essentially the money that is actually collected. EGI is calculated by taking the GPI and then subtracting the vacancies, concessions, delinquencies, and collection losses and then adding the other income from late charges, returned checks, and all other ancillary sources.

In the sections that follow, we provide the details on what to subtract and add to work your way from GPI to EGI.

Accounting for vacancies

The real estate investment community seems to be locked on using 5 percent as the vacancy factor. You will typically see a 5 percent vacancy factor used by brokers and even lenders without any regard for the actual market conditions. This number may or may not be the right number to use; we advise that you carefully determine the most accurate estimate of future vacancy, rather than use a standard figure such as 5 percent.

The issue of vacancies is particularly applicable to many new real estate investors who begin either by retaining their current homes as investment properties when they move up to larger homes or by purchasing rental properties as investments. Novice investors often simply compare the monthly rental rate that they plan on charging to the monthly costs for paying the mortgage and any other recurring expenses (property taxes, utilities, homeowners dues, and so on). This can be dangerous if you don't have sufficient cash reserves for the unexpected — like being unable to find or retain tenants.

If you have a single-family rental home, the property is either occupied or vacant. With the average length of residential tenancies in many parts of the country at less than one year, it would be unrealistic to use a 0 percent vacancy factor. Our suggestion for your proforma for a single-family rental home is to anticipate a loss of income equivalent to one month per every 12 months, which reflects an 8.3 percent vacancy rate. This may be a vacancy or a delinquency or a concession (see the following sections), but our experience indicates that, one way or another, you're likely to lose at least one month's income every year and you should allow for this in preparing your proforma to determine the potential income before making your investment decision.

Calculating concessions

A *concession* is any benefit or deal sweetener offered by the landlord to entice the tenant to enter into a lease or rental agreement. Concessions can be anything of value that motivates the tenant, but most commonly include free or reduced rent or additional features (a ceiling fan, microwave, upgraded finishes, and so on). In many areas, concessions are a significant factor in estimating future income. Remember that a concession of one month's free rent is essentially an 8.3 percent discount of the annual rent. A free month's rent for a simple residential tenancy with a monthly rent of $1,000 means that you'll only collect $11,000 in the first year, or an effective rental rate of $916.66 or a concession rate of 8.3 percent. This is a significant factor when added to your expected vacancy rate and an allowance for collection loss.

Deducting delinquencies and collection losses

The industry standard for *collection loss* (rent or other charges that the landlord must write off as uncollectible) is typically one half of one percent of rental income. This is another number that seems to be acceptable as a general rule; however, savvy real estate investors make their own analysis of the actual collection loss they may experience based on the strength of the tenant, the strength and depth of the local job market, the transiency of the area overall, the amount of security deposit they hold, and the nature of local tenant/landlord laws. For example, collection losses for residential properties in the Las Vegas area will often exceed 2 to 4 percent, and the continued advent of protenant legislation in California and other major metropolitan areas foretells increased losses to landlords as a result of the inability to evict nonpaying or disruptive tenants.

Adding in additional income streams

In addition to rent, other types of payments are essential elements to your income stream. Other income items can consist of late charges, returned check charges, and various ancillary income items. The ancillary items depend on the type of investment property, but for residential properties, they can consist of laundry, parking, vending, Internet services, storage, concierge service, and so on. Examples for commercial properties can include sources similar to those for residential properties, plus items like common area maintenance charges (CAM), supplemental HVAC (heating, ventilation, and air conditioning) charges, special security requirements, and telecommunications.

Tallying operating expenses

Just as you did with your income, use a zero-based budget concept to forecast the projected operating expenses for your property. Although historical expenses are worth reviewing and sometimes can be quite accurate in forecasting future expenses, we recommend that you question every expense. Who knows, you may find that the current landscaper is actually willing to charge you less just to keep the account.

The income and expense information presented by most owners or their real estate agents doesn't accurately reflect the current financial results. Inevitably, they'll claim that the rents are too low and they'll underestimate the operating expenses to show the maximum NOI. As the potential purchaser of this property, you want to deal with reality, so be sure to require the seller to provide you with a copy of her federal tax return Schedule E for each year of her ownership — or at least the last several years. Rarely will the tax return overstate the income or understate the expenses of a rental property — and you want to base your decisions on fact, not fiction.

Utilities

Evaluate your utility costs as soon as you can, because this expense is typically one of the larger costs of operating your property and is also subject to significant increases. Determine the current and projected rates for the utilities by contacting the service providers for electricity, natural gas, water and sewer, telephone, cable, waste removal, and any other utilities that are provided at the property. Virtually all of these utilities are regulated locally or at the state level and must file future rates well in advance.

Thus, it is relatively easy to determine the future cost for utilities if your usage remains the same. But seriously consider any energy and resource efficiency improvements that you can make, such as lighting, low-flow toilets, automated sprinkler systems, and other ways to dramatically reduce the consumption and provide incentives for your tenants to conserve.

One sure way to get tenants to conserve is to make them responsible for their utility usage. This approach can dramatically improve your NOI, and it's often a win/win situation because many tenants make long-delayed energy-efficient changes to improve conservation practices. You can make these changes in a number of areas:

- **Electric usage:** In the '70s, the rates for electricity led to master-metered residential and commercial buildings being submetered so that each tenant paid for his own electric usage. Recently, Robert dramatically improved the NOI for one of his client's commercial office buildings by over $100,000 per year — simply by installing separate electric meters and requiring the tenant to pay for its own electricity. The significant improvement in NOI occurred even after the tenant was given a reduction in the rental rate based on the utility company's estimate of a reasonable monthly expense for electricity for that suite. The tenant was a food broker and had 12 large, inefficient freezers that helped to generate a monthly electric bill of over $15,000 — paid by the landlord. Surprise, surprise — when the tenant began paying for its own electricity, it quickly cut the number of freezers in half and invested in new energy-efficient models.

- **Water usage:** Across the country, individual water meters are being retrofitted for each residential tenant. An EPA-sponsored three-year study recently concluded that billing residents for their water usage by direct metering could reduce annual water consumption by an average of 15 percent.
- **Waste collection and disposal:** This category will be the next major cost item that landlords will want to pass on to tenants because these costs are rising rapidly in most areas of the country.

We recommend you limit your investments to those residential buildings with separate meters for water, sewer, and electricity (see the "Accounting for Commercial Property Lease Options" section later in the chapter).

Management fees

A common mistake made by many investors is failing to incorporate the value of their time if they self-manage their property. Your estimate of operating costs should include a management fee even if you self-manage. Your time is worth something and there is an *opportunity cost* (what else productive you could be doing with that time) as well. Also, you may decide in the future to hire a property manager so that you can focus on the acquisition, improvement, and disposition of your real estate holdings. Including a comparable management fee now saves your projections from taking a hit later. See Chapter 13 for more on hiring a property management firm.

Insurance

Like utilities, property-casualty insurance is another major operating expense for which you need to get a specific quote for future projections rather than relying on historical data provided by the seller. Insurance coverage and rates can vary widely from one insurance company to another and there are also many opportunities to benefit from package or volume purchases of insurance. See Chapter 14 for the scoop on risk management.

Other operating costs

Don't forget all of the other operating costs for your property, including your outside vendors that provide services. You may have landscaping, pest control, parking lot sweeping, cleaning and janitorial, and other services. Contact each firm for pricing — and put these services out for competitive bids when you feel that the pricing and services offered aren't the best values.

Be sure to get current bids for all of the other expenses of owning and maintaining your property. For maintenance, you can look at historic numbers, but you want to keep the age and condition of the building in mind when setting your budget for maintenance.

Almost every real estate investor will at some point consider purchasing a property that the seller claims has been fully renovated. The seller implies that the required maintenance expenditures will be nominal and your expenses will be lower. Our experience is that even properties that have been recently renovated still have ongoing maintenance needs. Don't cut back on, or fail to allow sufficient funds for, ongoing maintenance and repairs when you crunch the numbers.

Calculating Cash Flow

As you begin to look at various properties that you may want to acquire, you will discover that the real estate investment community always refers to the NOI of a given property and that is the number commonly used to set the value or asking price of a property. The NOI is the number that tells you what you can afford to pay for the property. We show you the calculations in the "Figuring Net Operating Income" section earlier in this chapter.

However, don't confuse the NOI with *cash flow* — which is NOI minus debt service and capital expenditures. In the example in Table 10-1, the Net Operating Income is $600,000 but the actual cash flow before taxes to the investor is $150,000.

Table 10-1 Sample Investment Property Cash Flow

Annual gross potential rental income	$1,000,000
Plus other income	20,000
Plus CAM reimbursement	30,000
Minus vacancy and collection loss	(50,000)
Effective gross income	1,000,000
Operating expenses	(400,000)
Annual Net Operating Income	**$600,000**
Annual debt service	(400,000)
Capital improvements	(50,000)
Annual Cash Flow Before Taxes	**$150,000**

After you have your NOI, you can project your annual cash flow. The formula is straightforward:

NOI – Debt Service – Capital Improvements = Pretax Cash Flow

Servicing debt

Although a *broker information sheet* (or sales flyer) on an available property may provide proposed financing, make sure that the debt service projection in your income and expense proforma relies on a firm financing commitment that you have received.

Although the annual debt-service payments are a direct result of the amount of the purchase price borrowed, for most conventionally financed properties, the debt service will be 80 to 90 percent of the NOI. If you have fixed-rate financing, the debt service is going to be an easy number to plug into your income and expense proforma.

Making capital improvements

In developing their estimates or proformas of projected financial results for a proposed investment property, many investors neglect to account for, or seriously underestimate the need for, capital improvements to the property. *Capital improvements* are the replacement of major building components or systems such as the roof, driveways, HVAC, windows, appliances, elevators, and floor coverings. Real estate investing requires planning and the allocation of funds to protect and preserve the asset in the long run.

Often sellers indicate that the property had been fully renovated and imply that the purchaser won't incur any capital improvements for many years to come. But buildings age and things break — especially in rental properties where you can be assured that tenants break things! Just as homeowners associations are required to put aside funds each year in a reserve account for capital improvements, you should allocate a portion of your income to reflect the fact that certain components of your property are deteriorating over time and will need to be replaced. Otherwise, you may find that your roof needs to be replaced and you don't have the funds to cover the expense.

Capital improvements are also an essential component of the repositioning or renovation plans that will lead to improved financial performance for investment real estate. As an investor, always look for those properties where owners have neglected to properly maintain and upgrade the properties. This is one of the best target markets for investing and your proforma income and expenses should contain a realistic capital improvement budget.

Your due diligence should include a detailed walk-through of the property by a qualified contractor who can identify health and safety issues that should be addressed immediately — either during escrow by the seller or by you as the new owner. A leasing broker or someone knowledgeable about the competitive properties in the market should also be part of your due diligence team. This person should compile a prioritized list of needed work and cost-effective upgrades that will position your property to outperform the rental market.

This important feedback should by documented with written summaries by suite or unit number, plus a detailed evaluation of all common areas to bring the property into conformance with your overall marketing plan. Then contact the appropriate suppliers and contractors to formulate a capital improvements budget by month or year. Even with the most diligent walk-throughs and cost estimates, the reality of property renovation and repositioning is that the costs will always exceed your expectations and the timelines will rarely be met.

The capital improvements or reserves for replacement vary based on the age, location, and condition of the property, as well as the tenant profile. The higher the turnover of tenants and the less the prior owner has invested in properly maintaining the property over the years, the higher the capital expenses. A location impacted by climatic conditions can also be a significant factor in the lifespan of building components. Properties located in a marine climate require more frequent painting, and replacement of items affected by moisture and corrosion.

Capital expenses are very subjective. Our advice is to be very conservative and estimate toward the high side of a range. If you don't have to spend the funds, your real estate investment results will be enhanced. But you don't want to plan on scrimping by not addressing needed repairs and replacements. Deferred maintenance will be more costly to address in the future, plus you will ultimately have a negative impact on your income if your property doesn't attract financially strong and stable tenants.

Accounting for Commercial Property Lease Options

Leases for rental properties come in three basic forms. In some leases, the tenant may be responsible for paying certain costs (like janitorial); therefore, the cost of such services shouldn't be included as an expense of the property.

- **Gross lease:** In a gross lease, the landlord pays for almost all of the operating expenses of the property.
- **Modified gross lease:** Some of the expenses of owning and operating the building are passed through directly to the tenants. Examples of modified gross leases include leases where the landlord pays all operating expenses except for certain items such as utilities, parking, or janitorial expenses.
- **Net lease:** These provide for the tenant to pay for the majority of the costs of operating the building, including property taxes, insurance, and maintenance costs. Those leases in which the tenant pays virtually all costs associated with operating the building are called *triple net leases*.

The leases for a commercial property can be gross leases, modified gross leases, or net leases, but residential properties are almost always leased on a gross basis, except utilities.

Counting on CAM

Costs in multitenant commercial buildings that are passed on to the tenant are called *common area maintenance charges* or *CAM charges.* CAM charges are paid proportionately by each tenant for the upkeep of areas designated for the use and benefit of all tenants, and include items such as parking lot maintenance, security, snow removal, and common area utilities. Some tenants negotiate that they won't have CAM charges. But, for those tenants whose rent includes CAM, they're handled pursuant to the lease in a variety of ways and can be due in advance or paid in arrears. For accounting purposes, CAM charges are typically reflected in the cash flow as "CAM reimbursement" (refer to Table 10-1). Although they're indicated as an income item, they're essentially offsetting the corresponding expense items included in the operating expenses for the property.

The most common method is to use an estimated annual budget for the property as a basis for the collection of a monthly CAM charge. At the end of a previously agreed upon time period (usually annually), the actual expenses incurred for the items are calculated and reconciled against the sum total of the estimates paid during that time period. Then either a billing is generated to collect the shortfall that the tenant hasn't paid or a refund of any excess funds collected is provided to the tenant.

Handle the CAM reconciliation as soon as possible after the accounting is complete for the relevant time period in order to quickly collect any funds that are due as well as to provide feedback in case the future estimates need to be increased or decreased.

As the potential purchaser of a commercial property, carefully evaluate the leases and determine what operating expenses, if any, are paid by the tenants. You need to understand whether the property is using gross or net leases. Otherwise, you may be deceived regarding the actual NOI and cash flow that you will receive for the property.

Clearly, the rent charged for commercial properties with net leases, where the tenants are directly responsible for making the property tax and insurance payments and where they handle their own maintenance, will be lower than a similar property with a gross lease. But the end result may be similar because the higher rents received on the gross lease property will go toward those same expenses and costs that the tenant is paying at the net leased property.

Balancing things out

There are different thoughts about which is better: gross leases, modified gross leases, or net leases. Many investors believe that the management of the property is reduced if the tenant is on a net lease, but this isn't necessarily true. The owner must still ensure that the property is properly maintained. One argument against net leases is that the tenant may skimp on the maintenance of the property. That is why you typically don't see net leases in residential properties. Can you imagine a residential tenant being responsible for all of the maintenance of his rental home?

We find that modified gross leases in which the tenant pays for expenses that she can control are a good balance for all types of properties. This is essentially how the relationship is structured in most apartment buildings:

- The landlord retains control of the property maintenance and makes the necessary repairs and upgrades inside and out to ensure the long-term integrity of the building rather than allowing the building integrity to be compromised by a thrifty tenant. The landlord is also be able to ensure that the assessed value is kept low and the property taxes are paid on time, plus make sure that proper insurance coverage is in place.
- However, the landlord doesn't control certain expenses that are better suited to be paid directly by the tenant. For example, tenants have a direct impact on the utility usage and will be more careful to conserve if they pay that expense. This is why we recommend you limit your investments in residential property to those buildings with separate meters for water, sewer, and electricity. Likewise, some commercial tenants will be able to live with weekly janitorial service rather than daily if they're paying the cost directly.

Three Basic Approaches to Value

Professional real estate appraisers traditionally use three basic valuation techniques to arrive at an accurate estimate of current value: the market data (or sales comparison) approach, the cost approach, and the income capitalization approach.

Typically, each valuation method arrives at a slightly different estimate of value, and the appraiser reconciles or weighs the different results based on the applicability or reliability in determining the final estimate of value. The appraiser's derived estimate of value may be greater or lower than the price a particular investor is willing to pay — the investment value. But lenders require appraisals to protect their position and show that there is sufficient equity so that if they're suddenly forced to foreclose and sell, they're less likely to suffer a loss. In the following sections, we guide you through each process and then show you how to reconcile the different results.

Market data (sales comparison) approach

The market data, or sales comparison, approach takes the economic concept of substitution and applies it to real estate. In real estate, the *substitution principle* essentially states that the value of a given property should be approximately the same as a similar or comparable property that provides the same benefits. This method is very much like what you may do yourself when purchasing a major item for your home — you compare similar items at various stores to assist you in determining what price to pay. Likewise, you don't want to pay more for one property than a similar property would cost.

You've seen this concept at work in housing tracts in your area. When you see two similar homes built by the same builder at the same time on comparable lots, you expect them to sell for approximately the same price. (Of course, no two homes are identical and adjustments in the price may need to be made for deferred maintenance, upgrades, terms of sale, and the specific supply and demand at the time of the proposed sale.)

The accuracy of the market data approach relies on a sufficient number of recent sales of comparable properties. This approach to valuation is primarily used for single-family homes, condos, and small apartment buildings because they're typically more plentiful and offer many recent sales.

If there is a shortage of completed sales, an appraiser may look at current listings and pending sales, but they typically discount such potential transactions because they're not a finalized transaction and many things can happen before the sale.

Typically, appraisers look for at least three comparable properties in close proximity to the subject property. Of course, the usage and type of real estate should be the same and a *good comp* is similar in age, size, amenities, and condition of the property. The timing of the sale is also important.

Appraisers strive to find several comparable properties, but the reality is that every property is unique, and there are no *truly* comparable sales or listings. So appraisers need to make either positive or negative adjustments to account for the differences. They then factor all of these variances into an adjustment to the price then calculate an indicated value for the subject property.

For example, you want to buy a duplex in your own neighborhood, which you can rent as an investment property. You see one listed for $205,000 that is 2,500 square feet with two three-bedroom, two-bath units that are 1,250 square feet each. The property is about ten years old, in good condition, and has a great location on a corner lot. Using the sales comparison method, you want to know the value of this property, so you contact a local broker and gather the recent sales data for comparable properties sold on the open market in your neighborhood. Table 10-2 contains the information you've collected for recent sales of duplexes.

Table 10-2 Market Data Summary

Category	*Proposed Subject Property*	*Property A*	*Property B*	*Property C*
Price	$205,000	$170,000	$200,000	$220,000
Age	10 years	9 years	14 years	New
Location	Corner lot	Midblock	Corner lot	Midblock
Condition	Good	Fair	Good	Excellent
Features	Pool	N/A	N/A	Pool
Sale Date	On market	10 months ago	Last month	2 months ago

Because there are differences in the properties, you need to make some adjustments to formulate a price for the proposed property. The adjustments are made for items or features that typical buyers and sellers in that area feel have a material impact on value either positively or negatively. For example, in the Phoenix area, a rental home with a swimming pool is more desirable than one without, and property condition and corner lots tend to be important in all markets.

After researching the local market to figure out what factors are important to buyers and sellers, you determine that adjustments should be made for the subject property based on its age, location on a corner lot, its condition, and the fact that it offers a swimming pool (see Table 10-3).

- **Property A** is comparable in age to the subject property but is clearly inferior — it doesn't have the corner lot or the swimming pool and is only in fair condition. The property sold ten months ago and your research shows that prices for comparable properties in the neighborhood have risen 5 to 6 percent over the last year. So overall, you expect that if this property was being sold today in good condition, and had the corner lot and the swimming pool, it would've sold for approximately $30,000 more than the actual sale ten months ago or an adjusted sales price of $200,000. You made adjustments for the corner lot ($5,000), condition ($5,000), the swimming pool ($15,000), and market timing ($5,000) for a total of $30,000 in adjustments to bring the property in line for comparison to the subject property.

- **Property B** is a little older, but because it's been well-maintained and is in good condition, no adjustment is necessary for that factor. It's also on a corner lot and sold just last month, so no adjustments are necessary for these factors. However, it doesn't have a swimming pool, which you have determined is worth at least $15,000 in value. With the swimming pool, this property would have likely sold now for $215,000.
- **Property C** is brand new, has a swimming pool, and sold within the last two months. The only disadvantage when compared to your proposed investment is this property's location in the middle of the block. Overall, your research indicates that the price difference for brand-new properties is $15,000 higher than a ten-year old property like the subject property. But comparable properties located in the middle of the block sell for $5,000 less. Therefore, you need to adjust the Property C price lower by $15,000 for age and higher by $5,000 for the inferior location, which is a net downward adjustment of $10,000 and leads you to an adjusted value of $210,000.

In reviewing the results of your analysis and adjustments in Table 10-3, you feel that the asking price is right in line with (if not slightly below) the current market price for comparable properties in the neighborhood. You decide that if you can purchase the property for $205,000 or less that you have a good investment.

Table 10-3 Adjusting Sales Price to Determine Value

	Proposed Property	*Property A*	*Property B*	*Property C*
Price	$205,000	$170,000	$200,000	$220,000
Adjustment	0	30,000	15,000	(10,000)
Value	**$205,000**	**$200,000**	**$215,000**	**$210,000**

Cost approach

The cost approach to real estate valuation also relies on the concept of substitution, whereby an informed buyer would not pay more for a property than what it would cost to build a comparable property. This approach to real estate valuation can be used when there is a lack of data on comparable sales, but it is more commonly used, and even the preferred method, for proposed construction or brand-new properties. Also, the cost approach is the best method for unique properties that typically don't generate an income (including schools, hospitals, public buildings, or places of worship).

Real estate investors find that this method can be useful for establishing replacement cost. As we cover in Chapter 9, the replacement cost of a property can often be an indicator of barriers to entry that exist in the market. Owning real estate in high demand with high barriers to entry for competing properties is one of the best ways to ensure the success of your real estate investments.

In determining valuation using the cost approach, the property is divided between the land and improvements (buildings) and each segment is valued separately. Here are the steps an appraiser follows in applying the cost approach:

1. **Estimate the value of the land if vacant and being used in its highest and best use (see Chapter 9).**

   The appraiser looks for sales of comparable vacant land in the area.

2. **Estimate the current cost to reproduce the existing building as new, before depreciation.**

3. **Estimate all forms of accrued depreciation and deduct that amount from the calculation in Step 2 to arrive at the approximate cost to reproduce the building in its current condition.**

   Accrued depreciation can be caused by three sources:

   - **Physical deterioration:** Normal wear and tear that occurs from use over time. For example, a 12-year-old roof that can normally be expected to last 20 years.
   - **Functional obsolescence:** Decline in the usefulness of a property due to changes in preferences by consumers. For example, a rental home with three bedrooms and only one bathroom.
   - **External obsolescence:** Loss in value resulting from external forces. For example, the major employer in town closes down the factory and the closest comparable jobs are in a city 25 miles away.

4. **Combine the value of the land and the value of the depreciated improvements to arrive at the total value of the property.**

Using the duplex example from the previous section, you determine that the cost of a comparable vacant lot would be $40,000. Checking with local builders in your market indicates that the cost to build a new property would be $80 per square foot; however, because the building is ten years old, there is some wear and tear. You therefore estimate that the cost to rebuild the property in its current condition is $70 per square foot (this isn't an exact science). The property is 2,500 square feet, so the total value of the depreciated improvements is $175,000.

Adding the land value of $40,000 to the $175,000 value for the depreciated improvements, gives an overall value of the property of $215,000 using the cost method of valuation.

Income capitalization approach

This method of valuation is primarily used for larger income-producing properties but can be useful for small income properties as well. (It's not used for valuing owner-occupied properties or properties whose primary purpose isn't income producing.)

The income capitalization method is based on the principle that the greater the income generated, the more an investor is willing and able to pay for the property. *Capitalization* is the process of converting an income stream to a value using a capitalization rate or overall rate.

Our discussion of the income capitalization approach to valuation must start with the fundamental building block of determining value for this method — the direct capitalization or IRV formula. Here are the players in this formula:

- **Value (V):** With this method, you're looking to determine the value of a given property by examining the relationship between Net Operating Income (NOI) and the capitalization rate (R).
- **Net operating income (NOI):** Yes, it's back. Check out the "Figuring Net Operating Income" section earlier in this chapter, to determine this piece of the puzzle.
- **Capitalization rate (R):** Also called the *cap rate* and *overall rate,* this number is derived from the market or the buyer's objectives. It is the required rate of return commonly sought in the real estate investment market for similar properties in a similar market at a given time.

Put it all into equation form and you get:

$$\text{V (value)} = \frac{\text{NOI (Net operating income)}}{\text{R (Capitalization rate)}}$$

To illustrate, take the example of the proposed acquisition of a duplex in your neighborhood. The seller provides you with financial information on the property for the past two years and after a careful analysis using the techniques discussed earlier in this chapter, you determine that the projected NOI for this property in the next 12 months will be $19,500 per year.

Based on discussions with real estate brokers and your local county assessor, an analysis of recent comparable sales indicates that conventional sales of similar properties in the same area have sold for a cap rate of 10 percent.

$$V = \frac{NOI}{R} = \frac{\$19{,}500}{.10} = \$195{,}000$$

Therefore, you calculate the as-is value of this property at $195,000.

The cap rate can be subjective but is a measure of the risk-adjusted return a particular investor would expect to receive if he purchased a similar property at a similar price. Real estate brokers and agents often have information on current cap rates in the local market and you can actually derive the cap rate yourself by examining recent sales prices for similar properties as long as you have reliable info on the Net Operating Income. The formula is simply:

$$R\ (\text{Capitalization rate}) = \frac{NOI\ (\text{Net operating income})}{V\ (\text{value})}$$

You can use this formula to determine the capitalization rate or investment performance based on a given NOI and a purchase price. If the property could be acquired for $190,000, what would the rate be?

$$R = \frac{NOI}{V} = \frac{\$19{,}500}{\$190{,}000} = 10.26\%$$

You've increased your return by just over a quarter percent.

The direct capitalization method has some distinct advantages over the value benchmarks like the GRM or GIM because it includes operating expenses, but it still doesn't objectively consider potential appreciation, financial leverage, or the risk of the investment. These important variables or investment criteria need to be considered by each investor and factored into the derivation of the proper capitalization rate to determine the investment value of a given property. For example, properties with high appreciation potential, the ability to use positive leverage to increase overall return on invested capital, and low risk, will require a lower capitalization rate or expected rate of return.

Games sellers play to inflate NOI

The NOI used in the IRV calculation should be the projected Net Operating Income. However, sellers often price the property based on the historic or most recent NOI for the past 12 months because they can support that number with their financial records. As a buyer, you should be aware that some sellers plan the sale of their property only after operating it in a soon-to-be-for-sale mode for at least 12 months — making sure that they maximize income and minimize operating expenses. Although this basic concept or business strategy to maximize the Net Operating Income is common sense and something that all owners should do all the time, some owners can be very sneaky about the numbers they report in the 12 months or more before they make the property available for sale. For example, they may defer income or collect lump sum payments that artificially inflate the income; they may make considerable improvements to the physical aspects of the property in preparation for a lean-and-mean 12-month operating cycle in which they essentially defer all normal ongoing maintenance in order to report abnormally low operating expenses. Or they may claim that many of the normal operating expenses of the property are capital items and not part of the NOI calculation.

Our advice is to use the zero-based budget method of projecting the income and operating expenses to arrive at a realistic Net Operating Income for your first year of ownership. Developing your own numbers minimizes the possibility that you will make your investment decision on artificial numbers. And don't stop with the NOI. Especially if the property operations have been manipulated by deferring maintenance and repairs, you want to formulate a detailed and thorough capital expense budget from what you observe during your due diligence walk-through(s). Remember that the only numbers you should trust are the ones that you have independently verified yourself.

The proper calculation of value using income capitalization is to use future NOI projections, because the historic numbers aren't relevant to your potential ownership except for financing. However, most lenders are sophisticated and will discount unusually positive financial results or give you the benefit of a proforma income-and-expense projection when determining the terms of your loan.

A *proforma budget* is one in which the budget for next year or a given period of time is projected based on an analysis of the current data available for the building. For example, the historic operating reports for a commercial office building don't include the new lease with a major anchor tenant but a proforma operating budget does.

Reconciliation

An appraiser takes the numbers derived from the market data approach, the cost approach, and the income capitalization approach and *reconciles* them to determine a single estimate of market value at a specific time. However, the appraiser doesn't simply take an average of the three estimates of value, because all three methods may not be equally valid or reliable for the subject property.

Rather, the reconciliation process takes into consideration the relative merits of each approach, with more weight given to the most applicable approach. For appraisals of income-producing real estate, appraisers and real estate investors generally rely the most on the income capitalization approach, because the property is being acquired as an investment.

In the proposed investment in the duplex, we have determined the following values:

- Sales comparison: $205,000
- Cost: $215,000
- Income capitalization: $195,000

You're pursuing this property as a real estate investment rather than an owner-occupied property, so give the most weight to the value suggested by the income capitalization method. The next most relevant valuation method is the market data approach, which indicates a value of $205,000. The indicated value based on the cost approach is considered but not given that much emphasis since the building is existing and is not going to be rebuilt. Thus, by placing the most weight on the income capitalization indicated value of $195,000 and also factoring in the $205,000 from the market approach, you determine that $198,000 sounds about right for an offer.

You can then compare this value to the asking price for the property of $205,000. Although the seller may not be willing to accept an offer at $198,000, remember that you won't become wealthy in real estate by paying retail for properties. You're looking for a property that is available at a below-market price, such as a motivated seller might offer, or a property where you have the opportunity to add value.

Remember that the appraisal process isn't an exact science, but the principles of valuation are important for real estate investors and the concepts should be understood. You will want to be able to estimate value so you don't overpay for a property. Your lender will require an appraisal to determine how much you will be able to borrow, and these same appraisal techniques can help you determine the appropriate asking price when you look to sell your real estate investment.

More sophisticated valuation techniques

Although the traditional valuation methods used by appraisers are important for real estate investors to understand, additional investment analysis tools used by professional real estate brokers and investors analyze the cash flow generated by a property over several years to estimate the value. These methods don't take just a single year's NOI and estimate value based on an overall capitalization rate. Rather they use the following methods:

- **Discounted cash flow (DCF):** The discounted cash flow technique takes the annual projected cash flows for the proposed investment property and uses a discount rate to determine the present value. This method acknowledges the concept of time value of money in which cash received in the future isn't as valuable as cash received today.
- **Net present value (NPV):** A commonly used measure of value that uses discounted cash flows to evaluate an investment considering the time value of money, plus the size and risk of an investment. Easily handled by software programs or a financial calculator, NPV is a calculation where each estimated future cash flow is discounted back to the present value using the appropriate discount rate or target yield. This discount rate for individual investors is typically their opportunity cost — or the interest rate they could earn in a comparable investment that is similar in size, risk, and duration. Corporate investors generally use their cost of capital (the weighted sum of their cost of equity and their cost of debt).

  The NPV can be a positive number, a negative number, or precisely zero. An NPV of zero means that the proposed investment exactly met the discount rate whereas a positive NPV indicates that if the investment performs as anticipated, the return will exceed the target yield. A positive NPV is also an indicator of how much more the investor can pay to acquire and improve the property, or it can be considered as a cushion or safety factor against shortfalls in future cash flows while still achieving investment goals. Conversely, a negative NPV reflects that the property will fall short of the target yield by the amount of the NPV. The investor should lower her offer to purchase by the amount of the negative NPV or she'll need to increase the net projected cash flows or simply accept a lower than desired rate of return for this particular investment.
- **Internal rate of return (IRR):** The most popular of the advanced valuation techniques for evaluating and comparing investment returns, which is widely quoted by real estate brokers in the marketing of investment properties. The IRR is the percentage rate earned on all dollars invested for the specific periods each is invested. IRR doesn't measure the return of the equity dollars invested but only those additional dollars earned on the invested capital, so an IRR requires that the total dollars received must exceed the dollars spent on the investment. The return on invested dollars is dependent on both the amount of the excess and when the excess is received. The IRR and NPV are related because the IRR is simply the interest rate at which the NPV for an investment is equal to zero (0). The IRR is useful to compare real estate opportunities with alternative investments such as money market accounts, mutual funds, stocks, bonds, and commodities.

Figuring the results for each of these methods has been simplified by the advent of software programs that can perform complicated calculations.

Putting It All Together: Deciding How Much to Pay

After you've done all of your research and exhausted every possible calculation, the reality is that you still need to determine whether a proposed property is a good opportunity — and at what price? You don't want to pay retail, but the typical properties you see are based on unrealistic representations by most sellers.

You want to buy when you project that the property has a strong likelihood of producing future increases in NOI and cash flow. So you should look for properties where your analysis shows that the income for the property can be increased or the expenses reduced.

Mastering valuation techniques

In this chapter, we've covered NOI, cash flow, and the valuation techniques used by the professionals. Using those techniques can help you to determine the maximum price that you should pay for a property.

But sellers are also using similar techniques to set the maximum price they think they can squeeze out of the most generous buyer in the market. You need to understand how the game works and how they may bend and twist the facts to present their property in the best light. The following examples demonstrate how being able to properly value investment real estate before making a purchase offer is essential.

Examining the seller's rental rate and expense claims

For example, virtually every seller of an investment property claims that the rents are below market. Sellers imply that instantly, and almost magically, upon purchasing the building the buyer will be able to enhance the value of her new investment property and improve her cash flow by merely (yet significantly) increasing rents.

Of course, you may be wondering: If I can make money by simply raising the rents, why doesn't the current owner increase the rents and then sell the building at a much higher price? After all, sellers know that buyers will base their offer on NOI. The answer is that they usually do raise rents before putting the property on the market. But sellers (and their real estate agents) still go ahead and claim that the buyer can raise the rents even more. And if a buyer hasn't done her homework and carefully evaluated the current rental market, she may well fall for the seller's tricks.

The same scenario is found with expenses. The seller typically cuts back on spending to show artificially low expenses or claims that the buyer can cut expenses through an energy conservation program or some other seemingly sensible method. This assumes that the current owner hasn't taken advantage of legitimate ways to cut down on expenses.

Of course, you can find exceptions where an owner has truly been too nice or lazy to keep the rents at market level or conduct an energy conversion to lower expenses. But we suggest that even if these claims are true, the buyer should receive the benefit (and not pay an inflated price based on the assumption of being able to make these changes) because the buyer will have to go through the process. If you've ever given out a rent increase to full market value, then you know that it's generally unpleasant and *you* should be compensated for your efforts — not the seller (who lacked the fortitude to implement the rent increase).

Deciding which set of numbers to use

When you look at listings of properties for sale, you'll find that many sellers and their brokers or agents develop a proforma or future estimate of the NOI. From this artificially high NOI, they then derive an above-market asking price for the property. They also use the unrealistic proforma NOI to show all of the various value indicators such as GRM and cap rate. In reality, the NOI could even drop if you were to unexpectedly lose some of your key tenants or be faced with a major unanticipated expense. So remember that this proforma is an *estimate* of future operations of the property. The future is uncertain, so none of the numbers are truly right or wrong. And you'll be amazed by how universally optimistic sellers are about how much more money you'll make than they did when you buy their property!

Although the IRV formula uses the future NOI and the value of the building is determined based on those numbers, we suggest that you find a seller who will calculate his asking price based on actual historical operating income and expenses. You want to anticipate the future and pay for the present. You need to set your offering price based on your own calculations as to the NOI you truly expect to earn in the year after your purchase. (For more on IRV, see the "Income capitalization approach" section earlier in this chapter.)

The other key component to the IRV formula is the capitalization rate. We demonstrate that if you lower the capitalization rate or required return, you can dramatically increase the value of the property. A lower rate of return is required when the risk associated with the cash flow of a property is lower. The risk is lower when the property is competitive with or superior to other comparable properties, has minimal deferred maintenance, and has solid tenants with leases in place that are at market.

Finding properties where you can add value

So you're looking for properties that will allow you to lower the cap rate, which is essentially lowering the required rate of return. You want to buy when you determine that the property has a strong likelihood of producing future increases in NOI and cash flow. So you should look for properties where your analysis shows that the income for the property can be increased or the expenses reduced.

However, there are certain clues to look for when evaluating whether a property really has rents that are below market. Properties with no vacancies and a waiting list are prime candidates. Other telltale signs are properties that have low turnover and then have multiple applicants for those rare vacancies. Economics 101 says that if demand exceeds supply, our price is too low.

Some owners will actually market their real estate investment properties at a below-market price. These sellers are the typical motivated sellers and there can be a variety of personal reasons for their need to sell the investment property quickly and for less than the actual market value they could derive if they had more time and patience. Health reasons, family dissolutions, financial issues, and so on are all likely reasons that a seller will agree to a quick sale at a below-market price.

However, some sellers don't achieve the top value in the market for other reasons. For example, some owners despise the whole process of selling their rental properties so much that they knowingly underprice the property to ensure a quick and clean transaction and retain the ability to reject any and all contingencies that a buyer would typically require in a "market deal." The elimination of hassling and haggling is paramount to these sellers and they just want to get the sale done, so they're willing to give the buyer such a good deal that the buyer will take the property essentially as is.

Some sellers are truly ignorant of the actual market value of the property they're selling. There really is no excuse for a seller in a major metropolitan area to not know the true value of the property he owns because there are many real estate professionals who can inexpensively assist sellers in determining the estimated value of their property. Simply ask a real estate broker for a comparative market analysis (CMA) or hire an appraiser and they'll give you a detailed report determining the current as-is value of the investment property.

The most common question Robert hears from real estate investor callers to his radio show is "How do I find these underpriced properties?" Our experience indicates that you're more likely to find these characteristics of underpricing of investment properties with owners who are older and have no mortgage and typically have exhausted the possibility of taking depreciation deductions on their tax return.

Look for properties where you can increase value. These *value-added properties* are properties that allow you to either increase the NOI or decrease the rate and thus create value. As we point out in the "Income capitalization approach" section, earlier in this chapter, the value of a property is increased with an increase in NOI or a decrease in the capitalization rate. The capitalization rate is directly correlated to the anticipated risk of the investment, so stabilizing properties through long-term leases and more financially viable tenants can reduce risk and lead to a lower cap rate.

A simple example of how to increase the value of a building is to find a residential rental property in a high demand area where all rental rates are the same for similar floor plans. Typically, there are differences, because not all two-bedroom units have the same location benefits. For example, a unit overlooking the pool is often more desirable than a unit on the main street. So raising the rents for the more desirable units increases rental income.

Chapter 11

Preparing to Make an Offer

In This Chapter

- Honing your negotiating skills
- Understanding how to make an offer

You and your real estate team will log many hours in locating and valuing property. Then comes the moment when you must decide whether you wish to try and buy a property or keep looking for a more attractive opportunity. In this chapter, we discuss how to negotiate a deal that meets your needs as well as the seller's. Finally, we cover the all-important details of real estate investment contracts.

Negotiating 101

You make money in real estate when you purchase your investment property. If you buy a well-located and physically sound property below market value and replacement cost, the property will provide you with excellent returns for many years. Superior knowledge combined with superior negotiating leads to superior returns. This section explains how to be a champion negotiator.

Selecting negotiating styles

Although everyone approaches negotiating from their own perspective, we think that it's important to understand that the real estate community in most areas is actually a close-knit group of professionals who network. Thus, word of mouth referrals and a reputation for honesty and integrity are critical elements to your long-term success. Hard driving, one-sided transactions may make you some extra money in the short-run, but word travels fast.

We are reminded of the university study that indicated that people who have a favorable experience will share their positive feelings with an average of four others. However, those who've had a negative experience will go out of their way to tell over 20 people how they feel about you. Human nature also indicates that they'll likely embellish the story with each conversation.

Here's what we don't recommend:

- **Take it or leave:** Even in a weak market with few buyers and many potential sellers, the my-way-or-the-highway style is a short-term, dangerous strategy. It may work if you plan to purchase only a single property in a geographic area, but we believe you need to be active in the same market for many years and build a positive reputation. And this bare knuckles strategy doesn't always work even just once, because even the weakest sellers sometimes have alternatives and choices. They may decide life is better if they don't sell their property to an unethical jerk.
- **Lowballing:** Making patently frivolous offers, trying to get lucky, is another technique recommended by some real estate gurus. Our experience is that sellers aren't stupid and they'll quickly eliminate further offers, even reasonable ones, from such greedy bottom-fishers.

The problem with many aggressive negotiating techniques is that you can get so wrapped up in just "making the deal" that you forget what you're doing. You can make some serious mistakes and buy properties that you should've eliminated during your pre-offer due diligence. Don't get emotionally involved in any potential property. You're buying investment real estate and not your dream house. You simply want to have someone else pay rent and make your mortgage payments so that you can build wealth and cash flow.

Building your knowledge base

The most important negotiating tool in an investment property purchase is superior knowledge. You need to know more about your proposed property acquisition than anyone else, especially the seller. You need to know about the property, neighboring properties, local and state laws, and all of the economic data we discuss in Chapter 8 that can help foretell which properties are in the path of progress versus those that have already seen their best days. You need to set the maximum price that you can pay and still receive a solid return on your investment in light of the associated risks.

Do your homework

We don't suggest that you mislead anyone, but it's amazing how many current owners of property just don't pay attention to even the most basic publicly available information. There's nothing immoral or illegal about having vision to upgrade and renovate a property to achieve its full value because your research with the local chamber of commerce or economic development agency indicates that a major new employer is moving into the area and demand will dramatically increase for half-vacant and tired commercial properties — like the one you're considering for purchase.

BEWARE

Infomercial negotiating strategies don't pan out

We hate to be the bearers of bad news, but all of those late-night TV infomercial gurus don't tell the full story when they and their testimonials say how easy it was for them to start with nothing and suddenly own vast real estate holdings that all seem to magically be worth millions and provide great cash flow. If it were really that easy, the gurus wouldn't be telling you about it — they would be busy making great deals just for themselves.

There *are* times when you buy just before the market takes off and you can't lose. But those infomercials claim that the buyers who follow their advice can leave the closing table with checks (you can buy a property with no money down and actually have the seller pay you at closing). They're not telling the full story that the funds are proceeds from a loan or other debt that was assumed or placed on the property. Or maybe the funds represent the seller's prorated share of the large property tax installment that you'll have the pleasure of paying in full next month!

Do you get excited and think you've "found" money when you withdraw cash from your bank account at an ATM? Of course not, and so you won't be fooled by receiving cash at a close of escrow if you're really just borrowing more against the property. Being able to borrow against real estate is one of its greatest benefits, but one that should never be confused with receiving free money!

The old adage "If it sounds too good to be true, it *is* too good to be true" applies to real estate and particularly the thought that the best real estate is available to the average person at unbelievably favorable terms. There's so much capital available to owners of real estate that even truly desperate sellers have the ability to borrow against the value of the real estate. The interest rates and terms may be horrendous, but money is almost always available for any property that isn't a toxic waste dump, so there's no need for an owner to give their property away unless it has no equity. If you're buying a property with no equity, then there's little room to make a good deal. If there's no equity, you indeed may be able to pay little or nothing down to the current owner, but that doesn't mean you're getting a great deal. Rather you're simply stepping into the shoes of the seller and either assuming or placing new debt on the property for the full value and don't have any equity yourself. Remember, there's no free lunch — you usually get what you pay for.

The only way you can get these unbelievable terms as a buyer purchasing property dramatically below its market value is if the seller has a lot of equity and they're overwhelmed, extremely motivated, and out of time. But if the seller has a lot of equity in a truly great property, then he could simply borrow money against that equity and continue to own the property and use the cash flow from the property to pay off the loan. He wouldn't sell it to someone who listened to a tape in her car and made a ridiculously low offer.

With real estate investing, you'll be extremely successful in negotiating great real estate deals if you not only know the right people and have a good real estate investment team, but also know the important factors that affect supply and demand in the local market.

Maybe you're seeing local companies growing rapidly and hiring lots of new workers. You know that because of a local housing shortage, the many new families moving into the area will be unable to afford a new home and will need to rent instead. That's a good sign that rents will increase and the demand will be high for nice three- to four-bedroom rental homes located in quiet cul-de-sacs near the best schools. Clearly, you can use this information to properly negotiate the purchase of prime rental homes in such a market.

Or the final approval by the local transit district to extend a new light rail line into and through a rundown area of the community could really be a catalyst for positive change. So you do your homework and find an older couple who has lost interest in their commercial property in that area. You purchase and renovate this small retail strip center across from the new station, because you know it'll be an attractive location for retail tenants targeting commuters.

This is the reason that negotiating is so important to being successful with your real estate investments: You want to pay the seller only for the current value of the property as-is and not the future potential that your skill and expertise will create. Patience, vision, and perseverance are also great virtues when it comes to making the best real estate deals. If you're unwilling to do the homework necessary to justify the right price, you're almost guaranteed to overpay for real estate. Although an occasional seller dramatically underestimates the true market value of the real estate, the vast majority of properties you see offered for sale are overpriced.

Determine the current supply and demand in the marketplace so you know whether it's a buyer's or seller's market. That doesn't mean you can't still make some great real estate investments, but you need to be realistic. Buying in a seller's market at prices above replacement cost can be dangerous. Don't even consider it if your goal is a short-term hold on the property.

As the potential purchaser, you must discover as much as you can about the property and the owner before making an offer. How long has the property been on the market? What are its flaws? Why is the owner selling? The more you know about the property you want to buy and the seller's motivations, the better your ability to make an offer that meets everyone's needs.

Most real estate investors utilize the services of a real estate agent and the agent usually carries the burden of the negotiation process. Even if you delegate responsibility for negotiating to your agent, you still need to have a plan and strategy in mind. Otherwise, you may overpay for real estate.

Figure out the seller's motivations

Some listing agents love to talk and will tell you the life history of the seller. Encourage this free flow of information. The goal for you and your agent is to get the seller or his agent to reveal helpful information (without sharing any pertinent or strategic information about yourself). Always seek the answer to the most important question: "Why are you selling?" The answer tells you a lot about the seller's motivation and give you a reason to either move on or be calm and patient and make your offer the one that best meets the needs of the seller while still providing you with a great investment opportunity.

Also, the more you know about the seller's needs and motivation, the better you can structure your offer. You can also avoid wasting your time negotiating with a fake seller who isn't motivated to sell. Some sellers are really just testing the market or only willing to sell if they can get a price well over the market value.

Figure out how to spot these fake sellers early on. Look for the warning signs such as unexplained delays in responding to offers or questions, a reluctance to answer questions or give you access to the property, and a generally uncooperative attitude across the board. If you see these signs, then you don't even want to make an offer on the property.

Information is a two-way street. Don't give out any information about your motivations that will give the seller added negotiating leverage. The less you say about how much you like the property or your reasons for making the offer, the better. For example, many sellers are able to stick to their full price terms and as-is condition of the property if they know that the buyer is in a 1031 tax-deferred exchange with its tight time restrictions. A buyer facing the possibility of paying significant capital gains taxes if she doesn't close the transaction within 180 days may suddenly be agreeable to almost any reasonable condition requested by a seller if she's down to her last week

Bring your data to the table

Bring facts to the bargaining table. Get comparable sales data to support your price. Too often, investors and their agents pick a number out of the air when they make an offer. If you were the seller, would you be persuaded to lower your asking price? Pointing to recent and comparable investment property sales to justify your offer price strengthens your case. Rarely will you find a seller of investment grade real estate who doesn't have access to plenty of market data. But sellers often don't select the right comparable properties — preferring to creatively use just those comps that will provide for the highest possible asking price. This is the heart of negotiating: information.

If the property needs repairs, never rely on bids provided by the seller. You must independently verify the numbers with licensed professional contractors. You can also use these written proposals to support your position regarding the true cost to make needed repairs rather than just making verbal representations that a prudent buyer should take with some skepticism. However, you should always leave yourself a little cushion or wiggle room. We have found that even with the most comprehensive bids from the top industry professionals, any significant renovation or remodeling project is likely to take longer and cost more than is estimated.

Assembling attractive and realistic offers

We have covered and hopefully dispelled many of the negotiating theories or fallacies of the get-rich-quick gurus. We don't want to just tell you what not to do, so here are some examples of realistic and creative ways to negotiate and structure a real estate offer that accurately reflects the value of the property but also provides you with a reasonable return on your investment.

Factoring in fix-up costs

Say you come across an opportunity to buy a great three-bedroom, two-bath house. You live close by, and you know the area is terrific. The house would be an ideal rental because it's two blocks from a new school. You estimate that the property will rent for $1,750 per month, and there's strong demand for rental homes. The seller is asking $200,000, which appears to be its market value — based on the home having no deferred maintenance. But there's no such thing as a rental property with *no* deferred maintenance, so you call your home inspection contractor. His report indicates that overall, the property is in decent condition and the big-ticket items of appliances and flooring have recently been replaced. But there's also some bad news: The roof needs to be replaced before the next winter. You contact three reputable roofing contractors, and the best value bid for a roof replacement that'll last 20 years is $8,000. You also estimate that you'll need about $2,000 in minor repairs and upgrades to the landscaping and the irrigation system.

What should you pay? If you said $190,000, you aren't necessarily wrong, but you're not providing any room for contingencies — or any compensation or reimbursement for your time and the risk involved in overseeing and coordinating this work. We suggest that you take your actual conservative estimates for all repairs and add at least 50 percent. Cover those surprises that are likely to occur plus compensate yourself for the time, effort, and risk associated with renovations. Contractors and other professionals always allow for contingencies, overhead, and profit when they present their bids, so why should a real estate investor who invests her sweat equity utilizing her own handyman or contracting skills not be equally compensated? This is one of the biggest mistakes that novice real estate investors make and can avoid.

Creatively meeting the seller's price

Price is only one of several negotiable items, but it's the first clause the seller will review in a purchase offer. Because many sellers are fixated on the price they'll receive for the property (perhaps they want to get at least what they paid for it themselves several years ago), you can offer the full price, but seek other concessions in order to reduce the effective cost of buying the property. These creative offers allow you to pay what the property is worth and the seller can feel satisfied that he held firm and received his full asking price:

- **Get the seller to pay for certain repairs or improvements.** The buyer should always look for the seller to correct all health and safety items and required pest control repairs before closing escrow. But other items can also be negotiated. For example, you can often entice the seller to provide a credit in escrow for the replacement of old worn-out carpeting, window coverings, or appliances. Likewise, rather than have the seller patch that 30-year-old roof that you'll be replacing anyway, have them take the cost of the repairs off the purchase price.
- **Seek attractive seller financing.** For example, you may find a small well-maintained commercial property on the market for $200,000 that you believe is really worth no more than $195,000. But the seller is determined not to sell for less than his asking price. You could structure your offer at $200,000 with the seller agreeing to lend you some money at a below-market interest rate for ten years that essentially saves you much more than $5,000.

The time that you need to close on your purchase is also a bargaining chip. Some sellers may need cash soon and may concede other points if you can close quickly. And the real estate agent's commission may be negotiable too. Finally, try as best you can to leave your emotions out of any property purchase. This is easier said than done, but try not to fall in love with a property. Keep searching for other properties even when you make an offer — you may be negotiating with an unmotivated seller.

Making Your Offer

The purchase and sale of real estate is always done in writing. The most critical document in any transaction is the sales contract, which is referred to as the *purchase agreement* in real estate transactions. After you have found a property that meets your investment goals, have your real estate agent prepare a real estate contract for presentation to the seller or her agent.

Understanding the basics of contracts

A real estate contract is a legally binding written agreement between two or more persons regarding an exchange of some sort. These contracts are legally enforceable sets of promises that must be performed and that rely on the basics of contract law. (Contracts may also be oral, but as we discuss later in the section "Elements of a contract," oral contracts should be avoided.)

Taking two to tango: Bilateral versus unilateral contracts

Real estate contracts can be either bilateral or unilateral:

- **Bilateral:** Most real estate contracts are *bilateral,* meaning that each party to the contract promises to provide some *consideration* (something of value) and each promises performance of the terms of the contract. For example, the seller will give the buyer title to the property in exchange for cash and/or a promissory note.
- **Unilateral:** A unilateral contract is a one-sided agreement in which only one party promises to do something. An example is an *option agreement* in which the seller (optionor) gives a potential buyer (optionee) an unconditional purchase option for a certain period of time. The option is enforceable only by the optionee. If the option isn't properly exercised, the optionor's obligation and the optionee's rights expire.

Elements of a contract

A legally binding contract must include consideration passing between the parties, an intention on the part of all parties to be bound to the contract, a meeting of the minds of the parties as to the contents of the contract, and an element of clarity such that the terms of the contract may be interpreted, understood, and enforced by a court. Such a contract is valid because it contains all of the necessary elements that make it legally enforceable. In the following list, we outline the basic elements of a legally binding and enforceable real estate contract. The terms may sound a bit technical, but you need to be familiar with them.

- **Legally competent parties:** Every party to the transaction must have *legal capacity,* which is defined as being of legal age (usually 18 in most states) and having the mental capacity to understand the consequences of their actions. Convicted criminals and certain mentally ill persons may not have legal capacity. Be careful when dealing with older persons if they seem to have any difficulty understanding or communicating. Politely inquire if they have anyone who is acting on their behalf in a representative capacity.
- **An offer:** An offer to purchase real estate is a written communication to the current owner of the buyer's willingness to purchase a specific property at the terms indicated. The seller can continue to market the property while considering the offer. Unless an expiration clause is included, an offer may be accepted by the seller at any time before it is rescinded by the buyer.

  Virtually all offers have a specific expiration time. ("This offer is valid until Friday, June 19th at 5 p.m. EST only.") Follow suit to prevent the seller from using the offer as a negotiating tool with other interested parties, shopping your offer around, trying to entice another buyer to raise her offer. Also, if the offer is open-ended, then the buyer has to affirmatively rescind the offer, which is more work and trouble than simply having the offer expire after some passage of time.

- **Acceptance:** Acceptance is a positive written response in a timely manner to the exact terms of an offer. A legal requirement to have acceptance is that the buyer must be given legal notice of the acceptance. Commonly, the seller will not accept the offer as presented, but will propose changes in the terms or conditions — which is a counteroffer.
- **Counteroffer:** This is legally a new offer; the original offer is rejected and is void. Counteroffers can go back and forth until both buyer and seller have agreed and the final accepted offer becomes the binding agreement between the parties. Just like offers, counteroffers must be in writing and can also be rescinded at any time prior to acceptance.
- **Consideration:** Payment of money or something of value, or the agreement to not do something, which is typically offered by the buyer to the seller in exchange for the seller to enter into the real estate contract for purchase of real estate. A real estate contract isn't binding if each party doesn't offer at least some consideration to the other party.
- **Clearly and uniquely identified property:** A requirement so there's no uncertainty about precisely which property is being sold and transferred to the buyer. Typically, a legal description of the property is used.
- **Legal purpose:** The real estate contract must be for a legal purpose and can't be for an illegal act or an act so immoral that it's against public policy. An example of a potential transaction where a buyer would want to cancel the purchase would be if they were purchasing a single-family home with the intent to run their property management company there but discover during the due diligence process that such use violates local prohibitions against operating a business in a residentially zoned area.
- **Written contract:** A written contract is required for all enforceable transfers of real estate. All terms and conditions of the purchase agreement or sales contract must be set forth in writing, even for minor items that may not seem consequential. Generally, the written contract helps ensure that there is no confusion about what is included in the sale. For example, if you want to make sure that the supplies in the maintenance shop for a commercial or apartment building are included and not taken before the sale, you must specify it in the contract. Remember that if something isn't in writing, you won't prevail.

Agreements for the sale of real estate must be in writing or they're unenforceable. *Never* make an oral agreement of any type regarding real estate no matter how convenient or expedient or reasonable it may seem at the time. The Statute of Frauds is a legal concept that requires all transfers of real estate to be in writing to be enforceable in a court of law. Real estate–related contracts that must be in writing include sales contracts or purchase agreements, leases for more than one year, real estate loans secured by a mortgage or note, listing contracts and commission agreements with agents, and an employment agreement with an agent to locate property.

A failure to meet all of these essential elements could lead to the contract being declared void. A void contract would have no legal force or effect and would be unenforceable in a court of law. A *voidable real estate contract* is one that may be treated as legally unenforceable at the option of a party (usually the injured party) but remains enforceable until that party exercises her option. An example is a real estate contract with a minor that is voidable only by the minor.

Besides all the legal elements, real estate sales contracts specify the sale price and the terms and conditions as well as any contingencies (see the "Using contingencies effectively" section later in the chapter). The contract must be signed and will include a standard statement that "time is of the essence," which ensures that all dates and times of day noted in the contract are important and can't be ignored by any of the parties without the written consent of the other party; otherwise, there is a breach of the contract. If the contract is breached, the other party may be entitled to monetary damages.

Completing the purchase agreement

The *purchase agreement* is the legal document that outlines the details of the transaction for your proposed purchase of the subject property. Depending on where you live, there are other terms for a contract for the purchase of real estate, such as a *sales contract,* an *offer to purchase,* a *contract of purchase and sale,* an *earnest money agreement,* and a *deposit receipt.*

No matter what it's called, the purchase agreement is the most important document in the sale of real estate. It indicates how much you pay, when you pay, the terms and conditions that must be met to close the transaction, and the conditions under which the agreement can be canceled and the buyer's deposit returned. It starts out with the basics of the names of the sellers and buyers and a description of the property and the proposed financing terms.

Don't let a real estate agent tell you that your offer must be on a certain form, because there are many purchase agreement forms available to real estate investors but none that are required. Which form you use is up to you — we recommend that you use a purchase agreement form that's easy to read and understand. The more complicated the language, the more likely it is that the parties get confused or disagree on the meaning of the terms of the offer.

To find forms to use in your real estate investment activities, look to local title and escrow companies and your local association of realtors. However, most of these firms and realtor boards don't offer their proprietary forms to the public. California real estate attorney James McKenney is a frequent guest on Robert's radio show and he owns a company that specializes in plain-language forms that are used throughout the country by real estate investors and property managers. The sample purchase agreement in the appendix was provided by Professional Publishing Company, 365 Bel Marin Keys Boulevard, Suite 100, Novato, CA 94949; 415-884-2164; `www.profpub.com` or `www.trueforms.com`.

Go over the form in detail with your real estate broker or agent and carefully consider the terms that you will offer in each paragraph. Don't leave any blank spaces and have your attorney mark through any clauses that you feel aren't appropriate. Just because a certain clause is preprinted doesn't mean that you can't cross it out or modify the language to suit your needs. Just make sure that you clearly initial any changes that you make and require the other party to also initial every single change and the bottom of each page to ensure that you agreed on the specific terms.

Some of the terms are at your discretion, but your real estate agent can advise you as to the local custom and practice concerning issues such as the standard for earnest money deposits or the length of contingency periods for inspections of the property, books, and records. Your agent can also inform you about local standards for prorating the closing agent costs and the other miscellaneous costs of the transaction.

The following sections cover other key provisions that should be carefully evaluated, as there are many decisions to make about your offer before the purchase agreement is ready for your signature.

Earnest money deposit

Right after the purchase price, one of the most important terms that can set the emotional tone for further negotiations is the amount of the earnest money deposit you're willing to submit with your purchase offer. The *earnest money deposit* is usually fully refundable for a defined time period. Your deposit will be held in trust by either the seller's agent or by a title or escrow company. Never make an earnest money deposit payable directly to the seller.

The purpose of the deposit is to show good faith by the buyer and the intention to follow through with the terms of the purchase agreement. The amount of the deposit varies in different areas depending upon local custom or the specific needs of a particular transaction. Also, depending on state law, the earnest money deposit may or may not pay interest. If she can, a prudent buyer always insists that her earnest money be placed in an insured trust account that bears interest and that the purchase agreement clearly spells out that the buyer is credited with all interest earned.

Some psychology is involved because the size of the deposit has an effect on the desirability of the offer. An offer with no earnest money or a nominal amount may be interpreted by the seller as coming from a buyer who isn't serious about the transaction or lacks the cash to make a meaningful deposit.

A lousy recommendation suggested by some real estate investment gurus is for the buyer to offer a *promissory note* (a written document promising to pay the holder of the note a certain sum of money at some given time in the future) with their offer. That's a sure way for a seller to identify that you're not a serious buyer. Such no-money-down seminar graduates could be classified as bottom-feeders or opportunists who are really only interested in properties with desperate and uneducated sellers.

When determining the earnest money deposit, buyers should remember that if they don't live up to the agreement or don't cancel it within the allowed time frames, the deposit shall be forfeited to the seller. The forfeiture of the earnest money deposit for nonperformance is called *liquidated damages,* which is essentially the payment for any and all damages incurred by the seller as a result of the buyer not completing the purchase as proposed. Under the terms of most purchase agreements, a seller who keeps the earnest money deposit can't sue for any further damages.

To avoid any expensive lessons about earnest money, follow this advice:

- As a buyer, make sure you know the exact date upon which your earnest money *goes hard,* which is the real estate industry term meaning that your earnest money is nonrefundable and passes to the seller regardless of whether you complete the purchase of the property.
- Don't wait until the last few days to cancel your purchase agreement. If you're still unsure of your interest or ability to complete the transaction as proposed, send a written cancellation of the purchase agreement and then try to renegotiate additional time.
- Both buyer and seller must agree to any changes in writing. Never rely on any verbal representations as to any extensions or changes of terms or conditions.

Assigning your rights

Many purchase agreements specifically include a clause giving the buyer the ability to assign his interests to another party. *Assignment* is the transfer of the right or duties under a real estate contract by the buyer to a third party. This is an extremely important clause for buyers and we strongly encourage you to include the right to assign the contract as a term of your purchase offer. In the contract, simply include the language "or assignee" after the name of the legal entity indicated as the purchaser. Of course, if the preprinted purchase offer has a clause that prohibits assignment, then you need to cross out that language and have both parties initial the change.

Leaving the buy-and-flip door open

Even though we're not ardent promoters of the buy-and-flip strategy, the ability to assign or transfer your purchase agreement to another real estate investor gives you the opportunity to realize a profit without ever having to close on the deal yourself. When the real estate market is appreciating rapidly, some real estate investors have found that the property has increased in value so significantly that they can sell their contractual position.

In really hot housing markets, some real estate investors (they should really be called real estate speculators), go to new housing tracts and sign contracts with builders — up to a year or more before the property is built. If, during the extended contract and escrow period, the value of the property being built goes up, the buyer can merely transfer their contractual rights to buy the property at the locked in price and terms to another buyer for a profit.

The reality is that profiting from speculating on new housing tracts isn't guaranteed or easy. Builders aren't naïve and many don't allow the assignment of the purchase agreement — so the buyer must actually complete the sale and then resell the property to earn their profit, if they actually turn a profit after deducting the costs of two transactions. Also, many builders specify that they don't sell to buyers who won't occupy the homes. Some simply require larger earnest money deposits for speculators. If housing prices fall instead of rise, the buyer may have to complete the purchase or lose his earnest money deposit. These facts haven't stopped many of the late-night infomercial kings from promoting the idea that fantastic returns can be achieved by simply placing nominal deposits on homes to be constructed. We've even heard of some charlatans who hold seminars to attract investors willing to fund these speculative ventures. Often they're a form of Ponzi scheme and should be avoided. Our advice is to never invest in real estate with "partners" that you just met at a real estate seminar!

Installing an emergency exit

There's another scenario where the ability to assign your interests in a purchase agreement can be a lifesaver. Many savvy investors have gotten into a real estate transaction in which the due diligence time frames have passed and their earnest money is at risk — and they're unable or unwilling to complete the transaction. This typically happens because the buyer has second thoughts, not enough money to close, finds a better deal, or doesn't have the capability to handle the problems with the property. In this scenario, an assignment would allow the buyer to potentially recover his earnest money deposit or even his due diligence costs from another interested buyer rather than walk away and let the seller take the earnest money and then turn around and sell the property to another party. The buyer who has the property under contract controls the property and can make a deal with other parties.

Setting the closing date

An important term of your purchase offer is the proposed closing date for the transaction, which determines the anticipated escrow period (see Chapter 12 for escrow information). The length of the escrow period is a matter of negotiation between the buyer and seller with consideration given to the length of time needed to obtain financing and the amount and complexity of due diligence necessary to complete the sale. A complicated financing transaction, a property in need of a zoning change, or possible environmental issues require a much longer escrow period than a simple transaction.

Of course, the seller is usually interested in selling the property as soon as possible and wants a short escrow period and a fixed closing date while the buyer generally wants as much time as the seller will allow and some flexibility on the closing date. The buyer also would like the unilateral right to close the transaction earlier if they have completed their work. But the lack of a specific time line can create problems for the seller, particularly if they are trying to buy another investment in a tax-deferred exchange (see Chapter 16), or if they have tenants in place who need to be vacated.

The more time for the buyer, the better opportunity they have to make sure they're not making a mistake — and the seller knows that. But, the seller also knows that there are many buyers who aren't serious about purchasing the property and use an extended due diligence period to find problems with the property and try to wear down the seller into granting concessions or lowering the purchase price.

Some buyers will also use a long escrow period to tie up the property hoping to find another investor who will pay more for the property. If they find one, they can then close escrow and immediately flip the property in a *double escrow,* which is actually two separate transactions done at the same time. The investor purchases the property from the original owner and simultaneously sells the property to a new buyer usually at a profit without really even taking possession of the property other than for possibly a matter of seconds or minutes between the recording of the two transactions.

Ultimately, what you agree on in the purchase agreement is legally binding, but is really just an estimated closing date as there are so many different moving parts to close the sale. But the closing date should be met unless both parties agree to an extension per a written addendum or escrow instruction (see "Other issues to iron out" later in the chapter).

Using contingencies effectively

A *contingency* in a real estate purchase agreement is simply a condition that must be fulfilled or an event that may or may not happen in the future before a contract becomes firm and binding. Contingencies can be for the benefit of either the seller or the buyer. The seller of an estate property, for example, may require a contingency that the probate court approves the sale. Buyers often have contingencies for financing, physical inspections, and other items.

Contingencies are escape clauses that can protect the buyer from purchasing a property that doesn't meet his needs. Without contingencies, purchasing a property would be extremely risky, because the buyer would have to be sure that he had all of the financing in place and that the property was in good condition, met his needs, and the terms and conditions were acceptable before making an offer. Few buyers would be willing to do this, or they'd discount their offer to account for the additional risk of buying a property without the protection of a contingency. So sellers wanting to sell their property and receive the maximum value would be required to open up their property to any and all potential purchasers, which would be inefficient and chaotic.

Although legally different from an option, contingencies can have a similar effect by allowing a prospective buyer the exclusive opportunity to buy the property for a limited time frame but not obligating the buyer to complete the transaction if any issues arise that can't be satisfactorily resolved within the time limits of the purchase agreement. Naturally, sellers attempt to eliminate unreasonable contingencies. For instance, most purchase agreements include contingencies that ask for 10 to 30 days to conduct the physical inspection and/or approve the books and records. If you request 60 days to conduct these items, the seller may reject your offer as unreasonable.

The terms of most purchase agreements provide that by certain defined dates, all of the contingencies must be resolved one way or another by the beneficiary or party that stands to gain from the contingency. Once in place, a contingency will have one of three outcomes:

- **Contingencies can be satisfied.** This means that the pending sale is no longer subject to cancellation or modification for that particular item. For example, the buyer could comply with the financing contingency upon receiving a written loan commitment at acceptable terms.
- **The beneficiary of the contingency can unilaterally agree to waive or remove the contingency.** For example, the seller may have asked for a contingency to identify a replacement property as part of an IRS section 1031 tax deferred exchange. If the seller decides not to do an exchange, then she may simply notify the buyer in writing that she's waiving that condition or contingency.
- **A contingency can be rejected or fail.** The beneficiary of the contingency is then no longer obligated to perform under the contract. For example, the buyer may receive a termite inspection report indicating that there's extensive damage and infestation and then decide that he's no longer interested in completing the purchase. Under this scenario, the buyer will typically receive the return of his earnest money deposit and be glad that he diligently conducted a physical inspection.

Although the list will vary depending on the property type, size, and location, here are contingency clauses that we recommend:

- **Marketable title:** Obtain a preliminary title report with full and complete copies of each and every exception and have your attorney review these documents.
- **Financing:** Outline the specific terms (type of loan and maximum acceptable interest rate) of a new loan that will be required in order to complete the purchase. Require copies of the current loan documents and the most recent loan statement if you're assuming existing financing.

- **Appraisal:** This condition demands that an independent professional appraisal of the property arrives at a value equal to or greater than the proposed purchase price. This could be a function of the financing or simply because the buyer doesn't want to overpay for the property.
- **Physical inspection:** Most purchase agreements include an inspection clause that mandates that the buyer has unlimited access to the property for a certain amount of time to inspect the interior and exterior of the property. The buyer should retain qualified property inspectors, including specialists in key areas such as roofing, plumbing, and electrical systems, to conduct a thorough inspection of all rental units or suites. The results of the inspection can be used to negotiate with the seller by giving her the opportunity to make the necessary repairs, adjust the purchase price, or simply terminate the purchase agreement.
- **Books and records inspection:** Another important contingency for the real estate investor purchasing a large residential or commercial property is the opportunity to review and inspect the income and expense statements and the leases. Ask for a copy of the seller's Schedule E (filed with the IRS) to ensure that the income and expenses for the property are consistent with what the seller has been reporting. If the seller refuses to provide these tax documents, there is nothing you can do — but simply making the request sends a signal that they better not be misrepresenting the actual numbers. If litigation were ever to ensue, these documents could be subpoenaed and used as a basis to prove fraud and misrepresentation. A review of the leases should also include estoppel agreements. (These are covered in Chapter 8.)
- **ALTA property survey:** This survey shows the property boundaries or parcel map along with the site plan for all existing improvements, plus any easements and restrictions. It may be required by the lender, particularly if the loan is from an institution.
- **Contracts:** The buyer should make sure that she receives copies of all service agreements and contracts currently in place at the property. Ideally, the seller should be required to cancel or terminate all nonessential contracts (unless they are especially attractive in the current market conditions) at the close of escrow so the buyer has the option of bringing in her own preferred vendors.

Other issues to iron out

In addition to the contingency clauses, many buyers negotiate a separate clause giving them the unilateral right to extend the closing date under certain conditions. For instance, the lender may require an environmental report, which when received indicates that further investigation is necessary before they can make a loan commitment. Or possibly the occupant of the property will not allow access to the property and legal action is necessary to gain their cooperation. A well-written purchase agreement will provide for an extension of the closing date under such circumstances. Be sure that any such extension is clearly agreed to in writing prior to the closing date indicated in the purchase agreement to avoid any potential disputes.

Unequal "standardized" contracts

Some real estate seminar promoters, infomercial mavens, and authors, such as Robert Shemin, recommend that you create your own "standardized" contracts — one for buying a property and a different form for selling a property. A quick review of his sample contracts reveals why he makes this recommendation: The terms and conditions of each contract are clearly one-sided. For example, in the "standardized" contract that he suggests you use for buying a property, there is a provision for a 120-day escrow, a litany of contingencies that give you essentially an unlimited ability to cancel the escrow without penalty, a broad assignment clause, a stipulation that the seller pays all costs, and no mention of an earnest money deposit.

Then the "standardized" contract that you are to use when you sell your property requires a ten-day escrow, provides the buyer no contingencies and no access to the property, states that the buyer pays all the costs, and demands a nonrefundable earnest deposit. Further, this author advises that the key to pulling this off is that you actually have these forms printed with the words "Standardized Contract" typeset. Then, if the other party questions any of the terms, you simply tell them that this is a standardized contract — and you can't make any changes.

This is the type of advice that has given the late-night real estate investment information gurus such a questionable reputation. Of course, many of these items are negotiable and there is absolutely nothing wrong with demanding different terms based on legitimate market factors. Maybe you need to close on another property so you require a 60-day escrow instead of 90 days. That is fine and a justifiable business reason, but we strongly encourage you to treat everyone you deal with in an equitable manner. If you plan on having a long and successful career investing in real estate in your local community, your reputation as a straight shooter is extremely valuable to you and you should never engage in such practices.

The buyer should also be sure that his purchase agreement clearly indicates what personal property is included. The personal property can be a significant factor in large apartment buildings because it can include the appliances and window coverings, plus common area furnishings and fixtures.

Depending on her plans for the property, the buyer may want the property conveyed with or without tenants. If the tenants aren't on valid and enforceable long-term leases, and the property value will be increased by renovation and gaining new tenants, requiring the seller to deliver the property vacant and "broom clean" at the close of escrow can be prudent. This is also true if you buy a seller-occupied property. Either include a clause requiring that they vacate prior to the close of escrow or negotiate a lease with them for continued tenancy at mutually agreeable terms.

Presenting the purchase agreement

After you and your agent are comfortable with the purchase agreement you've prepared, insist that the offer be presented by your agent in person. Although much business today is transacted electronically, the best negotiation is done eyeball-to-eyeball and your agent can get a much better sense of the other party's personality and needs and wants through an in-person meeting.

Your offer should include a set time limit for response. Depending on the type of property and the size of the transaction, give the seller 24 to 72 hours to respond to the offer. The larger and more complicated the transaction, the more time the seller will need to evaluate your offer. As we discuss in the section "Understanding the basics of contracts" earlier in this chapter, the seller can accept your offer as presented, respond with a counteroffer, or even outright reject the offer or simply let it expire. After your offer for the property is accepted, you control the property and you have it "under contract." Now the real work begins.

Chapter 12

Due Diligence, Property Inspections, and Closing

In This Chapter

- Opening escrow
- Formal due diligence
- Property inspections
- Renegotiating the deal or seeking credits in escrow
- Determining how to hold title
- Closing the transaction

Your work is just beginning when you have an accepted offer for your proposed acquisition, the property is under contract, and an escrow account has been opened. You control the property and can begin to determine whether the property has been accurately represented by the seller.

In Chapters 9 and 10, we cover the pre-offer due diligence, which is essential in weeding out properties that clearly fail to meet your investment goals. Now the formal due diligence period begins. *Due diligence* is the investigation and confirmation of information performed prior to the close of escrow on behalf of the buyer to verify material facts as to the physical and fiscal condition of the proposed property purchase.

Only complete the transaction if the property physically and fiscally meets your needs and the financing is satisfactory. But the property may still be worth pursuing if the seller is willing to correct deficiencies or give you a monetary credit to cover your costs to complete the necessary work yourself.

In this chapter, we focus on some of the important issues in opening an escrow, conducting formal due diligence, performing property inspections, handling credits in escrow, the various methods of taking title, and ultimately closing the transaction and taking over your new property.

Opening Escrow

Escrow is a method of completing a real estate transaction in which a disinterested third party acts as the intermediary to coordinate the closing activities. The first step after the buyer and the seller sign the purchase agreement is for the earnest money funds to be deposited with the escrow holder and an escrow account to be opened in the name of the buyer.

A real estate transaction for even small investment properties can be complicated, because the buyer and seller have different interests that need to be fairly represented. The escrow holder acts as a neutral third party who handles the details of the transaction and often serves as the referee when disagreements develop between buyer and seller. In some parts of the country, the role of the escrow officer is much more limited. Your real estate agent can guide you as to the custom and practice in your area.

An escrow officer at an escrow company or a title company can handle escrow. Although escrow officers handle most escrows, in some areas of the country, attorneys act as the intermediary throughout the transaction. We refer to escrow officers, escrow agents, and real estate attorneys who handle the closing simply as escrow officers throughout this chapter.

Our good friend Ray Brown (and co-author of *Home Buying For Dummies* with Eric) recommends that you remember that the escrow officer is a human being and you can gain an advantage by simply picking up the phone and introducing yourself. Ask if she has everything she needs for the transaction to progress efficiently. Also let her know how she can reach you at various times of the day or week. Although the professional escrow officer will remain an unbiased and fair intermediary, this personal touch never hurts and may make things easier if your escrow doesn't proceed smoothly.

Escrow instructions

The escrow officer prepares the escrow instructions that guide the transaction between the parties. The escrow instructions are derived from the specific terms found in the purchase agreement and in any other written documents mutually agreed upon by both the buyer and seller.

The escrow instructions are critical. To minimize surprises, carefully review the instructions because that's the document that the escrow holder will rely upon exclusively to determine what to do in the event of a dispute. Unless allowed in the escrow instructions, the escrow officer can't make any changes or respond to any requests without a written agreement signed by all parties.

The escrow officer only performs items that are mutually agreed upon, in writing, by both the buyer and the seller. If the escrow officer receives conflicting information or requests, nothing happens until all parties reach an agreement or obtain a court order instructing the escrow officer. You'll be asked to review and sign these instructions, and they'll serve as the official document during the remainder of the transaction. If something isn't allowed in the escrow instructions, both the seller and the buyer must present a fully executed change order to the escrow officer modifying the agreement. In other words, make sure that the escrow instructions meet your expectations.

Preliminary title report

Soon after the escrow instructions have been signed, your title company should send you a copy of the preliminary title report (or *prelim*). Have this extremely important document reviewed by an attorney unless you have a lot of personal experience and the prelim contains relatively few indicated items.

The preliminary title report indicates the current legal owner of the property and any mortgage liens, unpaid income, property tax liens, judgment liens, or other recorded encumbrances against the property. It also shows any easements or restrictions or third-party interests that will limit your use of the property such as the Covenants, Conditions, and Restrictions (C, C, & Rs) commonly found with planned unit developments or condominiums.

Obtain and review copies of the detailed backup materials for each item so that you know exactly what's encumbering the property. The approval of the preliminary title report by the buyer is one of the basic contingencies in most real estate transactions that give the buyer the right to cancel the purchase if the preliminary title report contains unacceptable items. Of course, the buyer can also require the seller to have unacceptable items removed or renegotiate the price and terms in order to continue with the transaction.

The preliminary title report gives you a good idea as to whether the seller can provide you with marketable title to the property, but it isn't the same thing as title insurance, which we cover later in this chapter.

Removing contingencies

As we discuss in Chapter 11, the purchase agreement should contain a number of contingencies that allow the buyer and seller the opportunity to cancel the transaction if certain items aren't satisfactory. It's the escrow officer's job to track these contingencies and receive and follow the instructions from the buyer and seller. One of three things happens with contingencies:

- Contingencies can be approved or satisfied.
- The beneficiary of the contingency can unilaterally agree to waive or remove the contingency.
- A contingency can be rejected or fail.

Contingencies create a sort of option and are critical elements that can make or break a transaction. The purchase agreement and escrow instructions usually contain deadlines — the parties have certain rights pertaining to contingencies for a limited period of time. For example, the physical inspection contingency may provide only ten days to make the inspection; after that the contingency is considered approved (or satisfied) and the seller has the legal right to refuse access for a physical inspection.

The holder of the contingency option must notify the escrow officer at once if the contingency is rejected or fails. Also, it isn't the escrow officer's responsibility to attempt to negotiate or mediate a resolution of any rejected contingencies or other deal threatening issues that arise during the escrow. It's up to the buyer and seller and their respective agents to come up with solutions and keep the deal alive.

Estimating the closing date

After all of the buyer's and seller's contingencies pertaining to items such as the financing, appraisal, books and records, and the physical inspection have been met or waived, then the escrow officer will advise the parties of the estimated closing date for the transaction.

Our experience is that when buying real estate, the process generally takes longer than planned. Therefore, if you're intent on keeping your efforts to purchase your investment property from going awry because of unanticipated delays, make provisions up front that will provide the additional time to properly close the transaction.

This doesn't mean that the escrow should be allowed to drag on indefinitely, but the more costly the property in escrow, the more likely that you'll encounter unexpected challenges in satisfying or removing contingencies. For example, lenders, with their layers of approvals and particular requirements, often cause unforeseen delays. Also, when the real estate market is active, appraisers can be backlogged and your appraisal delayed; and your loan application won't go far toward approval before the appraisal is complete.

No matter the size of your deal, negotiate the right to extend escrow. Some local Realtor boards have even developed a separate addendum that provides for extensions under certain conditions in order to enhance the likelihood of the transaction's completion. These extensions usually provide for an initial 14-day extension at no cost if the closing is delayed due to issues beyond the buyer's control. However, additional extensions will typically only be allowed if the buyer compensates the seller for the equivalent of the seller's mortgage payment and/or her lost rental income if the property is vacant.

Conducting Formal Due Diligence

The formal *due diligence period* (the time period between the acceptance of the offer and the close of escrow or completion of the sale), is the time to ask those tough questions. Don't be shy. Talk to the tenants, the neighbors, and the contractors or suppliers to the property, and be sure that you know what you're getting. Communicate regularly and work closely with the seller and his representatives, but only rely upon information provided in writing. This time period may be your best or only opportunity to seek adjustments, if important issues have been misrepresented. After the property sale is completed, it's too late to ask the seller to fix the leaky roof.

Practical examples of due diligence include collecting economic data about the region and neighborhood, calling competitive properties for current market rental rates and concessions, verifying the accuracy of the financial information and leases presented by the seller, and conducting a thorough physical inspection of the property by a licensed general contractor or property inspector. Although you may have completed some of these items before presenting your initial offer (see Chapter 10), some of the information may have only become apparent from a review of the seller's actual books and records plus the unlimited access to the property that's generally only available during the formal due diligence.

Don't underestimate the importance of this step — this review of the books and records, along with the physical inspection, reveals the actual operations of the property and allows you to determine whether the property is suitable, fairly priced, and meets your financial goals. The due diligence period is your last chance to decide whether you should complete the transaction or cancel the escrow, get your money back, and search for a new possible acquisition.

Reviewing the books and records

Although savvy real estate investors conduct pre-offer due diligence and often receive a copy of a pro forma operating statement, you likely won't have an opportunity to review the actual books and records until you're formally under contract and in the due diligence period. Here are some things to make sure you have on hand *before* the deal is final:

- **Seller-verified income and expense statement for at least the past 12 months:** The actual income and expense history will reveal any surprises that may not have been obvious from the pro forma statement you received from the seller. The best source will be the seller's Schedule E from their federal tax return — you can be fairly comfortable that the seller is unlikely to overstate income or understate expenses to the IRS! After you have the most accurate numbers, you may find that the property has a serious problem with collections or your anchor tenant's suite has several large refrigerator units tied to your common electric house meter. This will also give you a good idea of where to look for opportunities to improve on the financial performance of the property.
- **Seller-verified rent roll:** A *rent roll* is a list of all rental units with the tenant name, move-in date, lease expiration date, current and market rent, and the security deposit. Also, get a seller statement that no undisclosed verbal agreements, concessions, or side agreements have been made with any tenant regarding the rent or security deposits.
- **Seller-verified list of all tenant security deposits on hand:** When acquiring a new rental property, follow state or local laws in properly handling the tenant's security deposit. Many state laws require the seller and/or purchaser of a rental property to advise the tenants in writing of the status of their deposit. The law usually gives the seller the right to either return the deposit to the tenant or transfer it to the new owner.

  If the seller refunds the security deposits, you will have the challenge of collecting deposits from tenants already in possession of the rental unit or suite, which is never easy. For this reason, strongly urge the seller to provide you a credit for the full amount of the security deposits on hand in escrow and have each tenant agree in writing to the amount of the security deposit transferred during the sale. This streamlines the process and prevents you from having to recollect security deposits from current tenants. To avoid problems at the time of move-out, send your tenant a letter confirming the security deposit amount.
- **Copies of the entire tenant file of each current tenant:** Make sure you have the rental application, current and past leases or rental agreements, all legal notices, maintenance work orders, and correspondence for every tenant. Also, insist that the seller advise you in writing about any pending legal action involving your tenant's occupancy.
- **Copies of every service agreement or contract:** Review all current contractors and service providers the current owner uses (maintenance, landscaping, pest control, boiler maintenance, and so on). If you plan to terminate the services of a contractor or service provider, the seller may be willing to send a written conditional notice of termination indicating that, if the property sells as planned, their services will no longer be needed as of the close of escrow. You can then find new contractors or maybe even renegotiate better terms with the current company.

- **Copies of all required governmental licenses and permits:** In many areas, rental property owners are now required to have business licenses, certificates, or permits. Contact the appropriate governmental office in writing and make sure that they're properly notified of the change in ownership and/or billing address. Often these governmental entities have stiff penalties if you fail to notify them of a change in ownership in a timely manner. And they'll eventually discover the change in ownership, because they usually monitor the local recording of deeds and receive notification of changes in billing responsibility from local utility companies. Make sure that you have current copies of all state and local rental laws and ordinances that affect your rental property.
- **Comprehensive list of all personal property included in the purchase:** This may include appliances, equipment, and supplies owned by the current property owner. ***Remember:*** Don't assume anything is included in the sale unless you have it in writing.
- **Copies of the latest utility billing:** Get all of the account and payment information for every utility provider, which may include electricity, natural gas, water/sewer, trash collection, telephone, cable, and Internet access. Prior to the close of escrow, contact each company and arrange for the transfer of utilities or a change in the billing responsibility as of the estimated escrow closing date. If provided with sufficient advance notice, many utility companies can have the meters read and/or the billing cutoff coincide with the close of escrow, preventing the need to prorate any of the utility billings between the owners.

  Also find out if the seller has any deposits on hand with the utility company and if the buyer will be required to place a deposit for service. You may be able to simply handle the transfer of the deposit through escrow with a written deposit transfer acknowledgment from the utility.

  If a review of the property expenses indicates that utility costs are unusually high, you may want to insist on reviewing copies of the actual historical bills in order to determine if there was a one-time variance or if the property may benefit from conservation efforts.
- **Copy of the seller's current insurance policy (if available) and the loss history:** One of the most important steps in the takeover of your new rental property is securing insurance coverage. Make sure that you have the proper insurance policy in place at the time that you legally become the new owner. Most lenders won't fund your loan until they have written evidence that the property is adequately insured with policy limits in excess of their loan amount. Although the seller's policy can't protect you, request a copy of their policy or declaration of coverage, because this information can be helpful to your insurance broker or agent when analyzing the property to determine the proper coverage.

When you receive this information, verify the accuracy of all records. Most sellers are honest and don't intentionally withhold information or fail to disclose important facts; but the old adage "buyer beware" is particularly true in the purchase of rental real estate. Questions and issues that are resolved at this time can eliminate unpleasant and contentious disagreements with your tenants in the future. The takeover of your new rental property can be chaotic, but don't fall into the trap of just verbally verifying the facts. Verify all information in writing and set up a detailed filing system for your new property. Ultimately, the best proof of the expenses is to insist on receiving copies of last year's invoices to verify operating costs such as utilities.

With experience, you'll be able to evaluate a property with surprising accuracy just by looking at the actual income and expenses. Look for discrepancies between the pro forma operating statement given to you during pre-offer due diligence and the actual income and expense numbers provided by the seller during escrow due diligence. There are many tricks that sellers and their brokers try to get past the unwary buyer. For example, watch for property tax numbers that will significantly increase upon a sale of the property if such taxes are based on the market value of a property or sales price. Also, be careful if the rent roll lists vacant units at higher market-rent rates that exceed the actual rental rate for the occupied units.

Inspecting the property

The condition of a property directly affects its value. The prudent real estate investor always insists on a thorough physical inspection before purchasing an investment property even if the property is brand new.

Your new investment property may look good on paper and your pre-offer due diligence may reveal no legal or financial issues or concerns. But your investment is only as good as the weakest link, and a physically troubled property is never a good investment (unless you're buying the property for the land and plan to scrap the current buildings).

You're probably making one of the biggest financial purchases and commitments of your life. Though real estate investors by nature tend to be frugal, never try to save money by foregoing a proper physical inspection by qualified experts. Unless you have extensive experience as a builder and contractor, you probably have no idea what you're getting into when it comes to evaluating the condition of most building systems. But even if you have experience, never rely on your own inspection entirely or try to "save" money by cutting corners. Even experienced and fully qualified real estate investors can find their judgment tainted by an emotional attachment to the property.

Our experience shows that an inspection usually pays for itself. Inevitably you're going to find items that the seller needs to correct that are greater in value or cost to repair than the nominal sum you spend on the inspection. This isn't just a marketing ploy by inspection firms. But it also isn't a game that the buyer "wins" if he can offset the inspection cost by finding enough items that the seller must correct or provide credit in escrow for — as some real estate gurus seem to believe. Instead, the inspection is a serious matter and not just a way to squeeze more from the seller.

The best result is if the inspection reveals no problems. Although you've spent money, what a great relief to know that your property (at least at the time of the inspection) is in good condition. That doesn't mean there won't be items in the future, possibly the very near future, that need attention. In Robert's early days in real estate investing, he worked for an apartment developer whose favorite saying was "To own is to maintain!"

Virtually all real estate purchase contracts provide that the transaction can be canceled without penalty or loss of the earnest money deposit if the buyer's physical inspection isn't satisfactory. But often, additional negotiations between the buyer and seller result. It is this competently prepared written inspection report that will provide the information you need and serve as the basis to go back and ask the property seller to fix the problems or reduce the property's purchase price (see the "Negotiating Credits in Escrow" section later in the chapter).

Savvy real estate investors actually have a two-step inspection process with their initial pre-offer walkthrough of the property as a prelude to even making the offer. If the offer is made and accepted, the professional inspection is to identify any deal-killer problems with the property or any items that warrant renegotiation. You are looking for two types of defects:

- **Patent defects:** Defects that are readily visible by simply looking at the property. Patent defects could be a broken window or a leaking faucet.
- **Latent defects:** Hidden and not readily visible defects that require intrusive or even destructive testing. Examples include corroding copper pipes underneath the slab or ceiling or window leaks that the owner has cosmetically repaired through patching and painting to hide from potential buyers. That is why disclosures are so important.

Disclosure requirements

With purchases of a residential rental property with four or fewer units, many states have seller *disclosure requirements:* Sellers must provide the buyer with a written transfer-disclosure statement that outlines all known structural and mechanical deficiencies, plus in many areas, sellers must complete a comprehensive information questionnaire. The agents, if any, for both parties also complete a written disclosure indicating that they've made a reasonably diligent visual inspection of the interior and exterior of the property.

However, investors purchasing residential investment properties with five or more units or any type of commercial property typically don't have the same legislative protections. This is based on the premise that the buyers and sellers and their respective agents are more sophisticated and don't need the mandatory protections of a formal written *transfer disclosure statement* (real estate brokers and other industry professionals commonly abbreviated it as a *TDS form*).

Whether the transfer disclosure statement form is legally required or not, sellers in some states will still have a legal duty to disclose any and all material facts that could impact the value or intended use of the property. For example, if the property had severe roof leaks last winter and the roof hasn't been competently repaired, the seller must disclose this fact. Even if the roof had major leaks and was professionally repaired, an ethical seller will disclose this fact and provide the buyer with a copy of the invoice outlining the specific work done and the individual or firm that performed the repairs.

The as-is gambit

Some sellers attempt to avoid any disclosures by proposing that their property is being sold to you strictly on an as-is and where-is basis. The theory (which is supported by many late-night real estate gurus when they're the seller) is that an as-is sale means that the seller isn't required to correct any deficiencies in the property before the completion of the sale and they're not responsible for any issues that arise after the sale. They erroneously believe that such terms are legally enforceable under all conditions and act as a blanket disclaimer against claims of misrepresentation, fraud, or negligence. However, in most areas of the country, the as-is strategy only offers minimal protection to the seller.

Be extremely careful if considering the purchase of a property offered on an as-is basis. An as-is property is a major red flag; buyers should sincerely consider whether it is worth the increased risk. Although the seller may simply be following the ill-advised recommendations of their broker or seminar speaker, some sellers are dishonest and hide significant issues that reduce the property's true value. A property offered on an as-is basis significantly below the expected market value is rarely a good deal.

Likewise, when you're selling your investment property, don't attempt to hide behind the as-is language. This technique isn't effective and will hurt your reputation as a real estate investor. Our advice, regardless of any legal requirements, is to *disclose, disclose, and disclose again.* Fully document all disclosures in writing, with copies of any invoices or reports, because failure to disclose material facts that affect the value or use of the property is a serious issue and one that often finds its way to the courthouse for resolution.

Types of inspections

If you can get full access to the property, go ahead and conduct your own brief physical inspection before making your offer. This initial overview doesn't cost anything other than your time and will keep you from wasting further time on properties that can't even pass your smell test. But this is no substitute for a professional inspection.

Tactics sellers use to avoid inspections

Unscrupulous sellers use several tricks to avoid the scrutiny of a thorough and detailed property inspection. One angle is to offer the buyer a warranty or property protection plan that provides repair services for the major systems and appliances of the property. These are typically only offered for rental homes and condos or small residential properties and aren't acceptable in lieu of an inspection. Actually, these plans don't make much sense at all, because even for a single rental unit or home they cost several hundred dollars up front, plus there is a deductible of $25 to $100 every time you make a claim.

Or some sellers tell you that they've already had an inspection report prepared — so you don't need to take this step. This is the seller's attempt to control the inspection process while claiming to be interested in saving you time and money by providing you with a copy of an inspection report that they authorized through an inspector of their choice. It doesn't hurt to review this report and give a copy to your inspection team, but never accept a seller's inspection report as your only source of information. When a seller hires an inspector, she may hire someone who isn't diligent or critical of the property. Also, beware of inspectors who are popular with real estate agents. They may be popular because they fail to document all the problems.

Don't rush the inspection process. The seller must give you complete and unfettered access to the entire property. Don't agree to any unreasonable time or access limitations. We've seen sneaky sellers who unrealistically limit access to the property, particularly if it's occupied. Make sure that the tenants have been properly notified, as required by law and/or their lease agreements, with a liberal access time period so that you can thoroughly conduct all of your inspections without interference or interruptions.

There are generally three types of professional inspections performed during the due diligence period while your property is in escrow, and we just happen to cover them in the following sections.

Physical or structural inspection

Naturally, you, as the buyer, want to have all of the physical aspects of the structures on your property inspected. However, your lender may also require you to pay for a separate physical inspection report by a firm of their choice. This is typical only for large residential and commercial types of properties.

You can also have your architect inspect the property and determine any changes of use or modernization that will enhance the property. Because the key to success in real estate is in creating value, a professional architect can be an invaluable team member who can offer many suggestions. Of course, she can also quickly tell you that your plans aren't structurally or fiscally feasible as well and you can move on to another candidate for acquisition.

Areas that you want to hire people to help you inspect include

- Overall condition of property
- Structural integrity
- Foundation, crawl space, basements, subflooring, and decks
- Roof and attic
- Plumbing systems, including fixtures, supply lines, drains, and water heating devices
- Electrical systems, including all service panels and ground-fault circuit-interrupters (GFCI)
- Heating and air conditioning
- Landscaping, irrigation, and drainage
- Doorways, walls, and windows
- Moisture intrusion
- Seismic, land movement, or subsidence and flood risk
- Illegal construction or additions and zoning violations

Some specific telltale signs indicate the property may have serious structural issues and require further investigation:

- **Cracks:** Look at the entire property, including foundation, walls, ceilings, window and door frames, chimney, and any retaining walls, for cracks. Don't let the seller or her agent tell you these cracks are merely settlement cracks; let your qualified property inspector or other qualified professional make that determination. A few isolated hairline cracks may be naturally occurring settlement of the structure over time, but if you can stick a screwdriver into the crack, something else is going on.
- **Unleveled or squishy floors:** As you walk through the property, pay attention to any slant or sloping of the floors. Also watch for any soft spots in the flooring on upper levels, including the ground floor if the property has a raised foundation with a crawl space or basement.
- **Misaligned structure:** Buy one of those handy laser levels and walk through the property looking for floors, walls, and ceilings that are uneven or out of plumb. Another sign is when doors or windows stick and don't open or close easily.
- **Grounds:** Excess groundwater, poor drainage, or cracked/bulging retaining walls or concrete hardscape can be signs of soil issues such as slope failure or ground subsidence that requires inspection by a civil or soils engineer. Be sure that the property properly drains and that all drains are properly installed and maintained.

- **Moisture intrusion:** Look for current and historical indications of leaks such as discoloration and stains on ceilings, walls, and particularly around window and door frames. Musty odors or the smell of mold may be merely stale air or poor housekeeping; or they could indicate ongoing moisture issues. Sump pumps anywhere on the property are a red flag that should be explored in detail.
- **Plumbing leaks:** Have a qualified plumbing contractor or other expert check all possible sources of leaks or moisture — under sinks, supply lines for faucets, toilets, dishwashers, and washing machines, plus roofs, windows, sprinklers, and drainage away from the building.

Don't buy a property with the polybutylene domestic water supply systems (Qest was the most widely known brand). The track record for these products hasn't been acceptable. Many properties experienced an extremely high rate of failure that resulted in class-action lawsuits and settlement funds for redoing these plumbing-affected properties.

TIP

Carefully inspect for any signs of water intrusion. Allegations of property damage and serious negative health effects from resulting environmental toxins and mold are creating a real problem for both residential and commercial rental property owners throughout the country.

And to minimize the chance of having to deal with unpleasant calls in the middle of the night, we strongly advise that you immediately install steel-braided supply lines on all water sources — including sinks, toilets, and washing machines. Also, make sure to check that sink and bathtub overflows are properly connected.

Pest control and property damage

Pest control firms are the natural choice for this type of inspection, but what they inspect is actually more than just infestations by termites, carpenter ants, powder post beetles, and other wood-destroying insects. A thorough pest control and property damage inspection also looks at property damage caused by organisms that infect and incessantly break down and destroy wood and other building materials. These conditions are commonly referred to as *dry rot,* but ironically they're actually a fungus that requires moisture to flourish.

The report you receive from your pest control and property damage inspector will usually include a simple diagram of the property with notations as to the location of certain conditions noted. Some require attention immediately; others are simply areas to watch in the future:

- **Part I items:** The most serious problems are infestations or infections that must be dealt with at once to protect the structure from serious damage. These recommendations may also include the repair and replacement of compromised structural elements. Unless otherwise agreed, the seller is virtually always required to pay for this work. Your lender will not fund the property loan until a professional pest control firm and/or licensed contractor completes such required work.

- **Part II items:** These items are recommended but not required work, which the prudent real estate investor will address herself right after the close of escrow or will require the seller to complete before completing the purchase. These items may not be a current structural deficiency that endangers the property or occupants, but if not corrected, they may cost substantially more to repair in the future. If not resolved now, these conditions will continue to fester and will develop into required items that must be addressed when you sell the property in the future.

Environmental issues

For commercial and residential rental investment properties with five or more units, the lender will usually require a *phase I environmental report,* which reviews the property records for the site, including all prior uses of the property and aerial photographs.

Review the report prepared for the lender at your expense, and make sure that there are no surprises. Only purchase properties, regardless of the price, if they have a clear environmental report. The downside of environmentally challenged properties is so significant that you should obtain the phase I environmental report even if you're purchasing the property for cash.

Most properties don't have problems, and the phase I report will be all that is required. But Robert has had clients whose purchase ground to a complete halt over something as simple as crank case oil in the dumpster area of an apartment building. Such a condition results in a negative phase I report, making further investigation and remediation necessary. Problems found in the phase I report can be ridiculously expensive and cause delays of several weeks or even months while additional testing and analysis takes place, a phase II report is prepared, and contractors complete the required work per the specifications outlined by the environmental engineers.

Buyers should also be extremely careful when purchasing commercial, retail, and industrial properties, particularly if they have certain types of tenants, such as dry cleaners, photographers, and any industrial tenants that use petroleum solvents. Watch out for any property, and especially vacant spaces, sporting the ubiquitous 55-gallon drums.

Have an environmental engineer check drains that connect to the storm drain system or sewer to ensure that toxic or hazardous materials haven't been disposed of through your proposed property. If the EPA or comparable state agency later determines that the source of the contaminants was your property, you could face a budget-busting cleanup bill. The governmental agencies don't care that these violations occurred under prior ownership.

Lenders are extremely concerned about making a loan on a property with the potential for environmental hazards. They know that many buyers would simply walk away from the property and leave them with the devastating cost of cleaning up the property. That's why most lenders now require buyers to remain personally responsible for environmental issues even if the loan is *nonrecourse* (the lender can only foreclose on the underlying property in the event of a default). This is commonly referred to as a *carve-out* and is designed to protect the lender from owners who may be tempted to bail out and leave the lender on the hook for a contaminated property.

Qualifying the inspectors

Just like selecting the closing agent, many real estate investors pick inspectors as an afterthought or simply take the recommendation of their real estate agent. But inspect the property inspectors before you hire one. As with other service professionals, interview a few inspectors before making your selection. You may find that they don't all share the same experience, qualifications, and ethical standards. For example, don't hire an inspector that hesitates or refuses to allow you to accompany her during the inspection.

The inspection is actually a unique opportunity for most property owners and, because you're paying, we strongly recommend that you join the inspector while he's assessing your proposed purchase. What you learn can be invaluable and may pay dividends throughout your entire ownership. When an unscrupulous contractor later tries to tell you that you need to completely replumb your property, you can tell him to get lost if your property inspection revealed only isolated problems that can be resolved inexpensively.

The field of property inspections is still relatively new and, just like during the days of the Wild West, there is virtually no governmental licensing or supervision of the inspectors. Every real estate investor needs to look out for her own interests and look for telltale signs of potential problems. Red flags include inspectors that are affiliated with a contractor, offer a special discount if you call who they recommend, or credit their inspection fee toward work.

Only consider full-time, professional inspectors. Hire an inspector who performs at least 100 comprehensive inspections per year and carries errors and omissions insurance. Such coverage isn't cheap and is another key indicator that the person is working full-time in the field and is participating in ongoing continuing education.

Many inspectors are licensed general contractors, but not all home inspectors have designations or credentials specifically relating to inspecting real estate. One of the best certifying trade associations for professional property inspectors is the American Society of Home Inspectors (ASHI). In addition to home inspections, many ASHI members are qualified and experienced enough to assist you with your due diligence physical or structural exterior and interior inspection of multifamily residential properties and all types of commercial properties. You can find certified inspectors and more info about the inspection process including tips and checklists at `www.ashi.org`.

Some individuals or companies adopt names that at first glance may indicate adherence to certain professional practices. For example, a fictitious but potentially misleading name is "Professional Property Inspection Association." Do some research to find the best state or regional association and one whose qualified members adopt a code of ethics. For example, in California, the California Real Estate Inspection Association (CREIA) is the group that offers education and designations for real estate inspectors.

Review a copy of inspectors' resumes to see what certifications and licenses they hold. A general contractor's license and certification as a property inspector are important, but also find out whether they've had any specialized training and whether they hold any specific sublicenses in areas such as roofing, electrical, or plumbing. These can be particularly important if your proposed property has evidence of potential problems in any of these areas. For example, if a property has a history of roofing or moisture intrusion problems, an inspector who's a general contractor and roofer is an extra plus.

The inspection report must be written, and to avoid surprises, request a sample of one of the recent inspection reports that have been prepared for a comparable property. This simple request may eliminate several potential inspectors but is essential so that you can see whether an inspector is qualified and how detailed a report he will prepare for you. A simple check-the-box form may suffice for a single-family rental home or condo, but for larger properties, the more detail, the better. Check out Figures 12-1 and 12-2 for a sample interior inspection checklist.

The advent of digital photography is a boon to property inspectors and makes their sometimes mundane and difficult-to-understand reports come to life. Select a technologically savvy inspector and require her to electronically send you her report, including digital photos documenting all of the conditions noted. With the report in the electronic realm, it is a simple process to e-mail this information as needed.

Although the cost of the inspection should be set and determined in advance, the price should be a secondary concern because inspection fees often pay for themselves. Just like many other professional services, there is a direct correlation between the pricing of your inspection and the amount of time the inspector takes to conduct the inspection and then prepare the report. If the inspector only spends a couple of hours at your new 20-unit apartment building, whatever you pay her is too much.

Finally, require the finalists to provide the names and phone numbers of three people who used the company's services within the past six months. Make sure that these clients were satisfied and the inspector acted professionally and ethically.

Unit Inspection Checklist

____ Mold — **General condition of rental units** — ____ Plastic Supply Lines

Tenant Name(s) ____________ Unit Number ________ Date ________

Kitchen	Condition:					Appliances	Condition:				
Floors/floor covering	E	G	F	P	N/A	**Gas stove/oven**					
Walls & ceiling	E	G	F	P	N/A	Outside	E	G	F	P	N/A
Windows/locks/screens	E	G	F	P	N/A	Burners	E	G	F	P	N/A
Window coverings	E	G	F	P	N/A	Drip pans	E	G	F	P	N/A
Doors/knobs	E	G	F	P	N/A	Hood vent/microwave	E	G	F	P	N/A
Light fixtures/bulbs	E	G	F	P	N/A	Timer/controls	E	G	F	P	N/A
Cabinets/cupboards	E	G	F	P	N/A	Broiler pan	E	G	F	P	N/A
Drawers/countertops	E	G	F	P	N/A	Light	E	G	F	P	N/A
Shelves/drawers	E	G	F	P	N/A	Other ________	E	G	F	P	N/A
Sinks/stoppers/faucets	E	G	F	P	N/A	**Refrigerator (Size ______)**					
Drains/plumbing	E	G	F	P	N/A	Outside	E	G	F	P	N/A
Other ________	E	G	F	P	N/A	Inside	E	G	F	P	N/A
Dishwasher						Ice trays	E	G	F	P	N/A
Outside	E	G	F	P	N/A	Other ________	E	G	F	P	N/A
Rack	E	G	F	P	N/A	**Garbage disposal**	E	G	F	P	N/A
Other ________	E	G	F	P	N/A	**Angle stops/supply lines**	E	G	F	P	N/A

General comments, including specific notes for all health & safety issues: ________________

Living Room						Dining Room					
Floors/floor covering	E	G	F	P	N/A	Floors/floor covering	E	G	F	P	N/A
Walls & ceiling	E	G	F	P	N/A	Walls & ceiling	E	G	F	P	N/A
Windows/locks/screens	E	G	F	P	N/A	Windows/locks/screens	E	G	F	P	N/A
Window coverings	E	G	F	P	N/A	Doors/locks	E	G	F	P	N/A
Doors/locks	E	G	F	P	N/A	Ceiling fans/bulbs	E	G	F	P	N/A
Light fixtures/bulbs	E	G	F	P	N/A	Closet/shelves	E	G	F	P	N/A
Closet/shelves	E	G	F	P	N/A	Other ________	E	G	F	P	N/A
Fireplace	E	G	F	P	N/A	Other ________	E	G	F	P	N/A

General comments, including specific notes for all health & safety issues: ________________

Hall						Bedroom 1 (smallest)					
Floors/floor covering	E	G	F	P	N/A	Floors/floor covering	E	G	F	P	N/A
Walls & ceiling	E	G	F	P	N/A	Walls & ceiling	E	G	F	P	N/A
Windows/locks/screens	E	G	F	P	N/A	Windows/locks/screens	E	G	F	P	N/A
Window coverings	E	G	F	P	N/A	Window coverings	E	G	F	P	N/A
Doors/knobs/locks	E	G	F	P	N/A	Doors/knobs/locks	E	G	F	P	N/A
Light fixtures/bulbs	E	G	F	P	N/A	Light fixtures/bulbs	E	G	F	P	N/A
Closet/shelves	E	G	F	P	N/A	Closet/shelves	E	G	F	P	N/A
Doorbell	E	G	F	P	N/A	Other ________	E	G	F	P	N/A

Guest or 2nd Bedroom						Master Bedroom					
Floors/floor covering	E	G	F	P	N/A	Floors/floor covering	E	G	F	P	N/A
Walls & ceiling	E	G	F	P	N/A	Walls & ceiling	E	G	F	P	N/A
Windows/locks/screens	E	G	F	P	N/A	Windows/locks/screens	E	G	F	P	N/A
Window coverings	E	G	F	P	N/A	Window coverings	E	G	F	P	N/A
Doors/knobs/locks	E	G	F	P	N/A	Doors/knobs/locks	E	G	F	P	N/A
Closets/shelves	E	G	F	P	N/A	Closets/shelves	E	G	F	P	N/A
Light fixtures/bulbs	E	G	F	P	N/A	Light fixtures/bulbs	E	G	F	P	N/A
Other ________	E	G	F	P	N/A	Other ________	E	G	F	P	N/A

General comments, including specific notes for all health & safety issues: ________________

Figure 12-1: Sample interior unit inspection checklist Robert uses for large multifamily apartment communities (page 1 of 2).

Unit Inspection Checklist (Side 2)
General condition of rental units

Master Bath	Condition:				
Floors/floor covering	E	G	F	P	N/A
Walls/tile/grout/ceiling	E	G	F	P	N/A
Windows/locks/screens	E	G	F	P	N/A
Window coverings	E	G	F	P	N/A
Doors/knobs/locks	E	G	F	P	N/A
Light fixtures/bulbs	E	G	F	P	N/A
Exhaust fan/heater	E	G	F	P	N/A
Counters/shelves	E	G	F	P	N/A
Mirrors/cabinets	E	G	F	P	N/A
Sink/basin/faucets	E	G	F	P	N/A
Angle stops/supply lines	E	G	F	P	N/A
Drains/plumbing	E	G	F	P	N/A
Tub/shower/caulking	E	G	F	P	N/A
Shower head/tub faucet	E	G	F	P	N/A
Shower door/curtains	E	G	F	P	N/A
Shower tracks	E	G	F	P	N/A
Towel racks	E	G	F	P	N/A
Toilet bowl/seat	E	G	F	P	N/A
Toilet paper holder	E	G	F	P	N/A
Other ____________	E	G	F	P	N/A

Bathroom 2	Condition:				
Floors/floor covering	E	G	F	P	N/A
Walls/tile/grout/ceiling	E	G	F	P	N/A
Windows/locks/screens	E	G	F	P	N/A
Window coverings	E	G	F	P	N/A
Doors/knobs/locks	E	G	F	P	N/A
Light fixtures/bulbs	E	G	F	P	N/A
Exhaust fan/heater	E	G	F	P	N/A
Counters/shelves	E	G	F	P	N/A
Mirrors/cabinets	E	G	F	P	N/A
Sink/basin/faucets	E	G	F	P	N/A
Angle stops/supply lines	E	G	F	P	N/A
Drains/plumbing	E	G	F	P	N/A
Tub/shower/caulking	E	G	F	P	N/A
Shower head/tub faucet	E	G	F	P	N/A
Shower door/curtains	E	G	F	P	N/A
Shower tracks	E	G	F	P	N/A
Towel racks	E	G	F	P	N/A
Toilet bowl/seat	E	G	F	P	N/A
Toilet paper holder	E	G	F	P	N/A
Other ____________	E	G	F	P	N/A

General comments, including specific notes for all health & safety issues: ____________________

Other Items					
Gas hot water heater	E	G	F	P	N/A
Heating/thermostat	E	G	F	P	N/A
Heat pump; A/C	E	G	F	P	N/A
A/C filters & vents	E	G	F	P	N/A
Cable TV/antenna	E	G	F	P	N/A
Electrical system	E	G	F	P	N/A
Telephone	E	G	F	P	N/A
Other ____________	E	G	F	P	N/A

Smoke Detectors			Date, if replaced
Hallway	OK	Inoperative	________
1st bedroom	OK	Inoperative	________
Guest or 2nd bedroom	OK	Inoperative	________
Master bedroom	OK	Inoperative	________

Laundry Equipment					
Washer	E	G	F	P	N/A
Gas dryer	E	G	F	P	N/A

General comments, including specific notes for all health & safety issues: ____________________

Moisture Intrusion/Mold/Mildew (record location and detailed description, including possible source)

____

Tenant Profile

Health/Safety/Housekeeping issues: Y N Describe: ____________________

Other potential lease violations : Y N Describe: ____________________

Pet? Y N Type ____________ Problems: ____________________

Additional Items/Comments

____

Figure 12-2: Sample interior unit inspection checklist (page 2 of 2).

Negotiating Credits in Escrow

Most purchase agreements require the seller to deliver the property in good physical condition with all basic systems in operational order unless otherwise indicated. But the inspection process often reveals deficiencies that need to be corrected. For example, the physical and structural inspection by the property inspector may indicate the need to repair a defective ground-fault circuit-interrupter (GFCI), or the pest control and property damage report may show evidence of drywood termites that need to be eradicated.

So with your inspection reports in hand, preferably with digital photos, you're prepared to contact the seller's representative(s) and arrange for the seller to correct the noted items at his expense. The seller may debate some of the items and claim that the property is being sold as-is even if he didn't previously indicate any such thing. Be prepared to refer him to the warranty of condition clause in your copy of the purchase agreement; hopefully he'll take care of the problems without any further grumbling or delay.

Some sellers and buyers actually prefer to handle deficiencies through a monetary credit in escrow in favor of the buyer so that the buyer can make the needed repairs on her own. This is particularly beneficial if the buyer plans on making significant renovations to the property or the item is one of a personal nature — like the type and color of replacement carpet for a rental house. In that case, giving the buyer a credit that she can use to pick the type, grade, and color of carpeting or even an entirely different type of floor covering that suits her needs is a sensible approach. The seller shouldn't be concerned as long as the amount is equal or less than his cost to do the work; plus, the seller doesn't have the hassle of coordinating the work or making payments.

Negotiating for repairs or monetary credits can be challenging, and knowing where to draw the line can be difficult. Requiring the seller to make needed repairs or give a credit in escrow is common in most transactions and fully accepted in the industry. But some buyers use the due diligence period to completely renegotiate the purchase agreement. They make a virtually full-price offer with long contingency time frames for the physical inspection so they can keep the property off the market for an extended period. Then they have their inspection team scour the property looking for every single item that's wrong so they can demand that the seller significantly lower the price. Because the buyer has the property tied up, the seller is unable to cancel escrow and move on to another more reasonable buyer. This strategy may work once or twice, but will quickly earn you a negative reputation among sellers and agents. You may soon find it difficult to buy additional properties.

A buyer who receives a credit in escrow is often anxious to get started on making improvements to get the property in rent-ready condition immediately upon the close of escrow. Although tempting, buyers should be wary of making significant renovation or repairs to the property before the close of escrow. If the sale of the property doesn't go through, you may have spent considerable sums to upgrade the seller's property without any recourse.

As a buyer, use the escrow time period to your advantage and obtain all of your bids and proposals so that you're ready to begin as soon as the escrow closes. We recommend that you formulate your renovations and marketing plan in advance, but only sign contracts that contain a contingency clause that the proposal is null and void if your transaction doesn't go through, and only begin the actual work after you legally have title to the property.

Determining How to Hold Title

You must bear many issues in mind when deciding how to take title to your new investment property. Maintaining your privacy, minimizing your tax burden, and protecting your assets from claims and creditors are critical elements to most real estate investors. Take the time to evaluate and decide the most opportune way to take title to your property.

Don't allow the form of ownership to be made as an afterthought! Many real estate investors don't take this decision seriously and by default take title upon the advice of their real estate agent or the closing agent. Sometimes the first discussion about how title will be taken is when it is time to sign the documents and close escrow.

Of course, there's no one single right answer to the question of how to hold title, because each real estate investor or investment group has different perspectives and needs. The legal forms of ownership vary from state to state, so check your options with the assistance of legal, accounting, and tax advisors. To make the best decision, you need the assistance of your real estate team (see Chapter 4). Consult with your accountant, tax advisor, and attorney to understand the current ramifications as well as consider the impact on your estate planning needs and goals.

After reviewing the options of taking title and deciding which one is best for your proposed real estate investment, make sure that you inform your escrow officer of the exact title so that the deed is properly prepared for your signature just before closing your escrow.

In the following sections, we review some of the basics of each form of ownership — including privacy, taxation, and protection considerations — so you can build a working understanding of the pros and cons of each of the primary alternatives available.

Sole proprietorship

A sole proprietorship is certainly the easiest and cheapest form of ownership and requires no special prerequisites. Simply have title to the property vested in the name of an individual person on the deed and you have a sole proprietor. Other advantages include the following:

- **Exclusive rights of ownership:** You have sole discretion over the use of the property, and the right to sell, bequeath, or encumber the property any way you see fit.
- **Simple record keeping:** That can be a negative if you aren't disciplined.

However, sole proprietorship also has its downsides, including the following:

- **Unlimited liabilities:** You have absolutely no protections against lawsuits or other claims and your name is easily obtained through public records. Other forms of ownership can create a barrier between you and claimants and creditors.
- **No real tax advantages:** Sole proprietorships offer no real advantages in the area of death and taxes! All income and expenses are reported directly on your personal tax return and there is no preferential tax treatment or avoidance of the probate courts in the event of your death.
- **Possible marriage complications:** Married persons using the sole proprietorship form of ownership should be very careful. A sole proprietorship can become complicated if you're married or later get married and intend to keep your investment property as a separately held asset. Check with your tax advisor before making any significant changes in your marital status because you need to keep detailed accounting records to avoid any commingling of funds from community property that could create an interest for a spouse in the real property.

Joint tenancy

Joint tenancy is a way in which two or more individuals may hold title to a property together where they own equal shares of the property. Joint tenancy is only available to individuals (not legal corporate entities) because a unique feature of holding title in a joint tenancy is the *right of survivorship.* Upon the death of one of the joint tenants, the entire ownership automatically vests in equal shares to the surviving individual or individuals without going through the probate process.

In order to form a joint tenancy, there must be unity of time, title, interest, and possession. Unity of time means that all joint tenants must take title by the same deed at the same time. Another requirement is that each joint tenant own an equal interest or percentage of the property — so if you have two joint tenants, they each own 50 percent, whereas four joint tenants would each own 25 percent of the entire property. Any ownership of a property in disproportionate shares can't be a joint tenancy.

Each joint tenant is legally entitled to the right of possession and can't be excluded by the others. Some states specifically require the joint tenancy deed to include the wording "joint tenants with right of survivorship."

One concern is that joint tenants can sell, bequeath, or encumber their portion of the property without the consent of the other owners. It's possible for the joint tenancy to be terminated in the event of a judgment lien or bankruptcy. Likewise, a new joint tenant can only be added by executing a new deed. Income and expenses from operations of the property are reported on the individual's tax return.

Another unique advantage to joint tenancy, besides the right of survivorship, is that you get a stepped up basis on your deceased joint tenant's portion of the property. Receiving a *stepped up basis* means that the taxable basis is increased for the portion of the property owned by the deceased joint tenant to the current market value at the time of death. This can be a tremendous benefit for the surviving joint tenants and allows them to sell the property with significantly lower taxes.

Community property and tenancy by the entireties

Some states offer married couples an additional way to take title. The main advantage with *community property* is that both halves of your rental property receive a stepped up basis upon the death of one spouse. Also, because each community property spouse owns 50 percent of the asset, they have the right to transfer their interest, by will or otherwise, to whomever they wish. Community property is available in Arizona, California, Idaho, Louisiana, Nevada, New Mexico, Texas, Washington, and Wisconsin. Several of these states (Arizona, California, Nevada, Wisconsin) are now offering a modified form called "community property with right of survivorship," which adds the benefit of avoiding probate upon the death of a spouse.

Noted real estate columnist Bob Bruss has written in his monthly *Real Estate Newsletter* about the benefits of another form of ownership that applies only to husband and wife — *tenancy by the entireties.* It's essentially the same as joint tenancy with rights of survivorship but can't be terminated by one spouse alone and isn't subject to a partition action. Tenancy by the entireties must be specified on the deed and is only allowed in Alaska, Arkansas, Delaware, District of Columbia, Florida, Hawaii, Indiana, Kentucky, Maryland, Massachusetts, Michigan, Mississippi, Missouri, New Jersey, New York, North Carolina, Ohio, Oklahoma, Oregon, Pennsylvania, Tennessee, Vermont, Virginia, and Wyoming

For example, suppose two joint tenants buy a property for $200,000. One of the joint tenants dies and the property is appraised at $300,000. The new adjusted basis for the surviving joint tenant is $250,000 representing the original basis of $100,000 plus $150,000 (one half of $300,000) for the deceased joint tenant's interest. This basis is important when calculating the gain or loss upon sale of the property, so having the basis increase can dramatically lower your taxable capital gain (see Chapter 16 for details).

Although marriage isn't a requirement to use this method of holding title, traditionally, joint tenancy has been the most common way for married couples to hold title to investment properties. One of the primary advantages of joint tenancy is that the death of one spouse can result in a complete step up in basis to the fair market value at the time of death rather than just a step up for the portion owned by the deceased joint tenant. Depending where you reside, states have additional options for married couples, such as community property or tenants by the entireties. See the "Community property and tenancy by entireties" sidebar in this chapter.

Tenancy in common

One of the most common forms of co-ownership is *tenancy in common* (also known as *tenants in common*). A tenancy in common is the ownership of real property in which several owners each own a stated portion or share of the entire property. In most states, if the deed is silent as to the form of ownership, tenancy in common is the presumed method of holding title.

Unlike joint tenancy, in a tenancy in common, each owner can own a different percentage, can take title at any time, and can sell his interest at any time. Another distinguishing characteristic is that each owner has complete control over her portion of the property and can sell, bequeath, or mortgage her interest as she personally decides without any feedback from or recourse for the other owners. Further, upon her death, her share becomes part of her estate and can be willed as she sees fit.

Tenants in common products are now being aggressively touted by financial advisors as an investment product of choice for the owners of appreciated real estate who are looking for a more passive investment without the challenges of property management. These investments offer the investor a way to own fractionalized interests in real estate and can be structured as direct ownership of property with a deed for their interest, or many are actually security interests. The sponsored tenants in common products usually have a management agreement or governing document to address issues of control and avoid the problems discussed later.

Tenancy in common is a popular way to hold title for real estate investors but can be a problem unless there are clear understandings, preferably in writing, as to the asset and property management decisions of operating the property. But even then, problems and challenges are possible:

- **Death of an owner:** You may find that a co-owner has left his interest in a property you partially own to someone that you don't get along with.
- **Sale by an owner:** Because each owner has equal rights of control over the property, serious conflicts may arise when one owner wants to sell or borrow against the property. Or an owner may decide to sell to an individual or entity, which disrupts the spirit of cooperation among the various owners.
- **Financial problems of an owner:** You're financially tied to your co-owners for better or worse even in their activities other than the jointly owned property. A judgment against one of the co-owners could lead to the creditor foreclosing on that co-owner's interest in the property to satisfy a monetary judgment. Or a bankruptcy by one co-owner could lead to the bankruptcy court ordering a forced sale of the property to satisfy the bankruptcy creditors unless the other co-owners were willing to pay off the creditors and buy out the financially challenged co-owner.
- **Different plans:** Each co-owner may have a different plan for the property or the way it should be managed. With tenancy in common ownership, absent a written governing document, there's no majority rule or simple way to arbitrate differences in opinions and goals. Because a single owner can thwart the plans of all the others, disagreements about whether to borrow money using the property as collateral or whether to sell the property can result in a legal action. Robert has served as a referee in several of these actions (called *partitions*), and they can be quite stressful for the parties — who can't seem to agree on anything!

Income and expenses from operations of the property are reported on the individual's tax return, but a problem with tenants in common is that new investors acquiring a TIC interest may not qualify for the tax-deferral benefits generally associated with a 1031 like-kind exchange. The promoters and sponsors of the TIC programs often portray these investments as the answer to all your needs, but in reality, they don't always give you the full story. *Buyer beware* — before making any move, consult your tax advisor about the tax ramifications of selling appreciated real estate and investing the proceeds into a tenants in common or fractionized interest. Liquidity (ability to sell your interest) is also a concern because there are currently no public secondary markets for tenants in common interests. See our comments in Chapter 3, and remember: If it seems too good to be true, it probably is!

Partnerships

A real estate partnership is a form of business enterprise in which two or more persons join together to pool their capital and talent to purchase, manage, and ultimately sell real estate. Investors in a real estate partnership don't have actual title or ownership interest directly in the property, but actually own a partnership interest.

Although a partnership interest technically is transferable, a partner seeking to sell will find few, if any, ready buyers and will likely have to severely discount their asking price below its intrinsic value. The best option is to negotiate a buy/sell agreement in which the terms are thoroughly discussed and each partner has the ability to leave at any time based on predetermined criteria. Often, such agreements call for the other partners to purchase the outgoing partner's share.

A partnership isn't a corporation, and generally takes one of two forms:

- In a **general partnership,** each partner has the right to fully participate in the management and operations of the property and each partner is fully responsible for the debt, legal obligations, and any business losses incurred. General partnerships are easy to establish, but a serious concern is that each individual partner is able to contract on behalf of the partnership and all partners are then legally liable for these actions. Another disadvantage of a general partnership is that the death, bankruptcy, or withdrawal of one of the general partners may require the dissolution and complete reorganization of the general partnership.
- A **limited partnership** consists of one or more general partners along with one or more limited partners. The general partner (which can be an individual or a corporation) handles management and operations and has unlimited liabilities; the limited partners are restricted from participating in management and operations of the property and only have their actual cash investment at risk. Limited partnerships have been popular because they allow folks to invest relatively small amounts into larger real estate deals. Also, a limited partnership can continue on even if one of the partners dies, files bankruptcy, withdraws, or sells his partnership share.

Partnerships have been a common and successful way for individuals to work together to purchase larger real estate investment properties. Often, they bring together individuals with complementary resources and skills. For example, a good partnership could include a real estate broker, a property manager, a real estate financial analyst, and a real estate lender. The complementary skills of this partnership offer insight into each phase of the investment. Often, one of the partners doesn't have any real estate expertise or acumen, but instead provides a significant portion of the investment capital.

Examining private placement partnerships

Then there are partnerships that seek a broader participation. Most of these real estate partnerships abide by the Securities and Exchange Commission (SEC) regulations, which outline and control the process of raising capital through solicitation. In order to avoid the stringent public disclosure regulations required of public offerings, real estate partnerships are often organized under the simpler Private Placement rules, and are thus known as *private placement partnerships.*

An offering to invest in a real estate partnership would qualify as a private placement as long as the organizers follow the requirements of the SEC's Regulation D. Each state also has specific legal requirements about raising money from investors located in that state with detailed provisions to qualify for a "Blue Sky" exemption that allows the sponsor of the private placement to avoid the strict formation requirements and ongoing reporting of public offerings. One example is that there may be limits to the total number of investors, or requirements that the sponsor have a preexisting relationship with the investor. Also, there are different rules for each of the proposed participants who meet the criteria to qualify as an *accredited investor,* which means that they have significant net worth. The SEC wants to make sure that the individuals being solicited for these private partnerships have the experience and skills available to evaluate these complicated and essentially illiquid investments. When raising money from multiple investors, consult with legal counsel and tax advisors who are familiar with both federal and state laws concerning private and public offerings.

We strongly advise novice real estate investors to avoid any attempt at forming private placement partnerships for investing in real estate. Should you be successful investing at a smaller scale, you may find such investment alternatives attractive. But there are many pitfalls for the inexperienced and you should only consider larger partnerships when you're able to make the full-time commitment to real estate investing, and then you should consult with experienced real estate and legal experts at every step.

The expertise of the general partner can be an advantage of real estate partnerships over TICs, where the TIC governing documents typically provide that each owner can vote their proportionate share and the majority makes the decisions. The problem is that a collective majority in a TIC may not have the real estate acumen to make the best decision. In a real estate partnership, the owners of minority interests will find they have very little input into the major decisions of the partnership (such as refinancing and selling or exchanging the property). But this can actually be a benefit and a lot less stressful if the general partner is competent and knows what they are doing.

From a taxation standpoint, real estate partnerships must prepare an IRS form 1065 tax return and pass through the respective share of all profits and losses and depreciation to each individual partner. Each partner then reports these numbers on her personal tax returns. At the time of death of a partner, there are several tax related issues concerning the handling of the partnership interest, so a tax advisor should be consulted.

Limited Liability Company

Now available in all 50 states, the *Limited Liability Company* (LLC) is a relatively new hybrid form of doing business that combines characteristics of a partnership and a corporation. This is an unbeatable combination for many real estate investors and a great way to hold title to real estate holdings. LLCs have essentially replaced corporations and partnerships as the most common way to hold title to real estate because they offer the advantages of allowing each member to have a say in the management while extending limited liability to all members, without the burden of double taxation.

An LLC is a separate entity like a corporation and therefore carries liability protection for all of its members, but can be structured like a partnership so that the taxation flows through to each member individually. This feature simply requires the LLC to make a "joint venture" election with the IRS indicating the preferred flow-through taxation treatment of income and expenses. Like a partnership, an LLC is required to prepare and file an IRS form 1065 Partnership tax return unless they make the joint venture election.

Check with your own tax advisor, but many advisors recommend that their clients use a Limited Liability Company because it offers the best of both worlds — limited liability plus favorable and simplified tax treatment. Every state has its own requirements. Contact an attorney to have her prepare the Articles of Organization and an Operating Agreement (which are usually filed with the Secretary of State).

The owners are called *members* and can be virtually any entity including individuals, partnerships, trusts, corporations, pension plans, or even other LLCs. Typically, LLCs have multiple members that can own different percentages; however, virtually all states permit single-member LLCs, but not without some potential issues with the IRS that should be discussed with your tax advisor in advance. Fortunately, a husband and wife are considered two members when forming an LLC.

Despite all these advantages, seek the counsel of an attorney who specializes in the formation of LLCs to give you help with the following issues:

- **IRS limitations:** IRS regulations have some limitations on the characteristics of the LLC. An attorney can advise you on the best structure to establish — one that emphasizes the importance of limited liability and centralized management while foregoing continuity of life and easy transferability of interests. In addition to filing a partnership tax return with the IRS, most states also require an annual report of activity along with filing fees, withholding, or even franchise fees; however, most states don't have any minimum charges.

- **Costs:** The costs can be much greater than for other forms of ownership. Be sure to consult with a local tax advisor for details on the typical costs for operating an LLC in your state. Currently, the highest base cost for an LLC is found in California with a minimum franchise fee of $800 per year plus additional taxes based on gross receipts.

Corporations

A partnership consists of people, but a *corporation* is a legal entity owned by one or more shareholders. The most well-known form that corporations take is that of public corporations like General Electric and Microsoft, which have shares traded on a stock exchange. Real estate investors can also create their own private or closely held corporations to own real estate.

A real estate investor can establish a corporation by filing articles of incorporation and bylaws with the appropriate state agency, usually the Secretary of State's office. Corporate requirements vary from state to state, so consult your accounting and legal advisors prior to implementing a corporate form of ownership for real estate assets. Nevada and Delaware are two of the more popular states in which to incorporate, but your legal and accounting advisors can tell you if there are any advantages for your personal situation, as typically you'll find it best to incorporate in your state of residence.

The appeal for real estate investors is that there is limited liability for shareholders. The owners of a corporation actually own stock, which is personal property. Thus, when corporations own real estate, the shareholders don't actually own the real estate. They own shares of stock in the entity that legally owns the property. Therefore, the most a shareholder can lose is her equity investment.

A disadvantage for many real estate investors is the initial expense to have an attorney draft the organizational documents. Then there are the costs to cover the rather extensive reporting requirements at both the state and federal level to maintain their corporate status. If the corporation isn't sufficiently capitalized or fails to meet all of the detailed organizational and reporting requirements, creditors or lien holders can "pierce the corporate veil" and seek personal liability for individual shareholders.

There are two types of corporations available:

- **C Corporation:** Although C Corporations (the most well-known and popular type of corporation) have the advantage of continuity of life in the event a shareholder dies, their downside is the double taxation of profits. *Double taxation* is when the profits of the corporation are first taxed at the corporate level and then the profits distributed by the corporation to individual shareholders are taxed again on their personal returns.

Another negative is that if the corporation has losses, the corporation has to carry them over to the next tax year because the shareholders can't use C Corporation losses on their personal returns.

- **S Corporation:** A primary benefit of this type of corporation is the ability to avoid double taxation by passing through the profits and losses directly to the individual shareholders. But S Corporations are rarely used in the ownership of real estate because their primary disadvantage is that a liquidation of the S Corporation is a taxable event. So even if the shareholders of the S Corporation can agree to an equitable distribution of the assets, the IRS will deem the liquidation as taxable, and the shareholders will be forced to pay capital gains taxes and may be forced to sell some of the assets. (Note that in a liquidation of an LLC, the assets may be distributed to the members without a taxable event occurring.) There is also difficulty for shareholders that aren't involved in the day-to-day operations. The IRS requires *material participation* (an IRS term that indicates whether an investor worked and was involved in a business activity on a regular basis) for the realization of tax benefits.

Only consider using a corporation to hold your real estate assets if you're willing to pay for the professional, legal, and accounting advice up front and on a continuing basis to make sure that the protections of limited liability can't be violated. Although corporations have some inherent advantages, the drawback of double taxation and the ongoing technical requirements and expense to maintain the corporate status make corporations unsuitable for the average real estate investor.

Closing the Transaction

The closing of escrow is the consummation of the real estate transaction and the goal of the buyer, seller, the brokers, and all the other professionals who were part of the effort. It is the culmination of numerous individual acts and often constant negotiation right up until the last moment. The closing of escrow occurs only when all conditions of the escrow instructions and purchase agreement are fulfilled, including the funding of the loan, if any. There are quite a few details that must be resolved and come together before the escrow officer can actually close the transaction and record the deed.

The actual process or formalities of closing the escrow are handled in different ways throughout the country. Some areas bring all of the parties together and an attorney acts as the closing agent and funds are transferred among the parties after all of the documents have been signed and notarized. Your escrow officer will be at the center of activity as the essential elements come together to make your goal of purchasing an investment property a reality. Your team of inspectors, appraisers, lenders, and attorney all have roles in completing the due diligence required to ensure that there are no surprises with your potential new property acquisition.

However, there are still a few more fundamental items and details that need to be addressed as you wind down the escrow before you can call the property your own. Snags are still possible, so keep an eye out for the following:

- **Lender requests:** You need to make sure that you're in contact with your lender to avoid any last minute snags. Lenders are notorious for needing just one more signature or asking questions at the last minute about the source of your down payment. These questions aren't as random as they may seem and are usually brought up by the loan committee or final signatory that must sign off on your loan.
- **Document errors:** Don't assume the documents are correct. Robert recently completed a large refinance loan of a commercial property, and while proofreading the lender-prepared documents, he noted that they contained several mistakes including an incorrect loan amortization term.
- **Availability of parties and busy periods:** You need to be available to review and sign the loan documents, so let the lender or your mortgage broker know if you're planning any trips around closing time. But during certain times of the year, things just take a lot longer. The December holidays are the worst, but spring break and major three- or four-day weekends can also be times when your favorite property inspector, loan officer, or escrow officer may be planning to be out of the office.

Eleventh-hour issues are bound to arise, so don't leave important details to the last minute or you may have your back to the wall, particularly if there is a penalty clause to extend your escrow. You can almost guarantee lost documents and other unexplained communication breakdowns that occur any time you have so many moving parts. Anticipate logistical delays and allow time for anything and everything to take twice as long as it should.

Estimated closing statement

Several days before the projected date for the close of your escrow, both the buyer and the seller receive a copy of the estimated closing statement with the various charges. You may receive this statement at the time you sign some or all of the documents or it may be sent to you separately. This is an extremely important document because this is the best time to raise any issues or concerns if you feel that an error has been made.

The estimated amounts can, and usually will, change slightly. Often the escrow officer or closing agent will estimate these expenses a little on the high side because any shortage of funds will prevent the escrow from closing but any overage can easily be credited or refunded back to the buyer or seller.

The buyer should pay particular attention to the estimated closing statement because it indicates the funds expected to be received from the lender or credited from the seller if there's seller financing. It also indicates the amount of additional cash funds that the buyer needs to deposit in the form of a wire transfer, cashier's check, or other certified funds. The buyer must provide "good funds" in plenty of time for the escrow to close — your personal check will take up to a week to clear and credit cards and PayPal aren't accepted! ***Remember:*** If you have a large sum of money deposited in escrow, arrange for the escrow company to place the funds in an interest bearing account.

Title insurance

Title insurance has evolved to become a vital element in most real estate transactions. Title insurance companies track all recorded documents and transfers of interests in real estate so that they can issue *title insurance* — policies that insure the purchaser that the title to the property being transferred is legally valid and unblemished. This is commonly referred to as a *clean and marketable title.* Title insurance is like any form of insurance in that it defends and pays the claims made against the insured. There are two types of title insurance policies issued in most transactions:

- The seller provides one to the buyer to protect herself against claims that the purchase of the property wasn't a marketable title. For example, maybe the heir to a former owner may suddenly claim that there was a fraudulent transfer of the property years ago. If you bought title insurance when you purchased the property, the title company would defend any legal action or would compensate you in the event that the claim is valid and you lost the property.
- Mortgage lenders require title insurance to protect against someone else claiming legal title to your property. The lender provides funds toward the purchase of the property and wouldn't be protected if the property ownership were to change based on a claim of an improper transfer of title. There are many ways that a title can be transferred improperly. For instance, when a husband and wife split up, and the one who remains in the home decides to sell and take off with the money. If the title lists both spouses as owners, the spouse who sells the property (possibly by forging the other's signature) has violated the law. The short-changed spouse can reclaim rights to the home even after it has been sold. In this event, both you and the lender can get stuck holding the bag.

Most state insurance departments monitor and regulate title insurance companies because a company's ability to pay claims is always important. Although title insurers rarely fail, and most states do a good job shutting down financially unstable ones, check with your state's department if you're concerned. Title insurance companies receive ratings from insurance-rating companies, so you can ask the insurer for copies of the latest report.

Don't simply use the company that your real estate agent or lender suggests — shop around. Because many title companies provide escrow services, you need to watch out for companies that quote very low prices on one service and make up for it by overcharging in other areas. When you call around for title insurance and escrow fee quotes, get a handle on all the charges because there may be miscellaneous or hidden administrative fees that can sneak up on you and become major items — such as document preparation, courier fees, and express mail. If you find a company with lower prices, consider asking for an itemization in writing so that you don't run into any surprises.

Check with your title insurance company for special riders that will save you money if you're buying a distressed investment property with the intention of quickly renovating and selling the property in less than 24 months. These special policies will typically cost you 10 to 20 percent more up front but can be a real bargain if you can avoid having to purchase a brand-new title policy for a short holding period.

Property insurance

You must have insurance, often one of the larger expenses for investment properties. Unless you purchase the property entirely for cash, you won't be able to close the transaction and take over the property until you have a certificate of insurance in place. Your lender, or even the seller if he's providing any financing of your purchase, will prudently insist that you have adequate insurance coverage with policy limits that will effectively protect your financer's collateral or financial interest in the property.

In accounting terms, property insurance is a *fixed expense* (like your property taxes), which means that although you may be able to turn off the natural gas (a *variable expense*) when your property is unoccupied, you must have insurance coverage — even if your property is vacant. In fact, insurance is likely more important if your property is vacant for an extended time frame.

In order to avoid surprises in your cash flow, determine the cost of insurance while you're still in your due diligence phase of the transaction. At this point, you retain the ability to cancel without penalty if you find that proper insurance coverage is either not available or priced way too high.

Another benefit of getting your insurance early in the due diligence process is that your insurance agent or an underwriter from the insurance company may even inspect the property before providing you with a quote. Of course, any inspection by the insurance company will be limited in scope and is never a substitute for your own inspection or the detailed written inspections you need from your property inspector and other industry professionals or experts (see "Inspecting the property" earlier in the chapter). But it can be important to know if the insurance company is going to require any upgrades or changes to the property as a condition of offering insurance.

For example, many companies no longer write policies for multifamily residential properties that have balcony- or pool-fence wrought-iron railings with pickets spaced greater than 4 inches apart, due to the potential hazards to small children. The cost to correct this condition can be expensive and you would want to include such costs in your negotiations with the seller or at least include the amount in your capital budget. (We discuss the role of insurance in an effective risk management program in Chapter 14.)

You may trust your insurance broker or agent, but don't allow your escrow to close until you have written documentation confirming that your coverage is in force. It may seem improbable, but many properties have suffered a catastrophic loss or liability claim *in a matter of hours* after the property changed hands and the new owner's insurance coverage wasn't yet in place. Robert was an expert witness in a case where an owner thought his insurance agent had placed earthquake coverage on his new apartment purchase only to discover a few days after a devastating earthquake had substantially destroyed his building, that the request for coverage was never sent in!

Final closing statement

Just before your transaction is complete and escrow is closed, you'll receive a closing statement from the escrow officer. Besides the actual purchase price, there are several expenses incurred in the process of purchasing real estate that must be worked out between the buyer and the seller. For example, the seller may have paid the property taxes for the balance of the year and the buyer should reimburse him for the amount attributable to his ownership period after the close of escrow.

There are also expenses that the buyer and seller need to pay such as escrow and recording fees. Who pays what is usually outlined in the escrow instructions, and is determined by a combination of the purchase agreement negotiations between the parties, and custom and practice in the local real estate market. Table 12-1 contains a breakdown of the allocation of expenses that are typical in the purchase of investment properties.

Table 12-1 Typical Allocation of Expenses

Item	*Paid by Seller*	*Paid by Buyer*
Broker's commission	X	
Escrow fees	Split 50-50	Split 50-50
Recording fees: Loan payoff	X	
Recording fees: Transfer		X

(continued)

Table 12-1 (continued)

Item	*Paid by Seller*	*Paid by Buyer*
Transfer tax	X	
State or local revenue stamps	X	
Seller's title policy	X	
Lender's title policy		X
Loan origination fee		X
Loan commitment fee		X
Appraisal		X
Credit report		X
Loan prepayment penalty, if any	X	

In addition to the allocation of expenses between the buyer and seller, the final closing statement will contain credits (items that accrue to the benefit of the party receiving the credit) and debits (items that are paid out of escrow on behalf of the party being debited). Table 12-2 has a breakdown of the usual accounting of the debits and credits on the closing or settlement statement.

Table 12-2 Usual Accounting on Closing Statement

Item	*Buyer Credit*	*Buyer Debit*	*Seller Credit*	*Seller Debit*	*Prorated*
Selling price		X	X		
Buyer's loan principal	X				
Buyer's loan points/fees		X			
Prepaid interest		X			
Property inspection fees/appraisal		X			
Payoff seller's loan				X	
Tenant's security deposits	X			X	
Buyer's earnest money deposit	X			X	
Additional cash down payment	X			X	

Item	*Buyer Credit*	*Buyer Debit*	*Seller Credit*	*Seller Debit*	*Prorated*
Unpaid bills (for example, utility charges)	X			X	X
Prepaid property taxes		X	X		X
Prepaid insurance		X	X		X
Prepaid expenses (for example, utility deposit)		X	X		X
Supplies left by seller for buyer's use		X	X		X

The day before you close on the property, take a brief walk-through to make sure that everything is still in the condition it was before and that all the fixtures, appliances, window coverings, and other items the contract lists are still there. Sometimes, sellers don't recall or ignore these things, and consequently don't leave what they agreed to in the sales contract.

The escrow officer or closing agent will usually process the mandatory reporting of the real estate transaction to the Internal Revenue Service and the state tax authorities, if required. If they don't file the required 1099-S form, then the brokers or the buyer and seller may be required to handle the reporting, which includes the identity of the property transferred, the sales price, and the social security numbers of the buyer and seller.

Be sure to keep a copy of the closing statement, because this document will be used to establish your initial cost basis when you go to sell the property and need to determine your capital gain. Also, some of the expenses paid at the close of escrow may be deductible on your tax return, such as prepaid interest or points on your loan and property taxes and insurance.

Deed recording and property takeover

Although the escrow officer may have all of the signed documents, and funds have been transferred to the proper accounts, you aren't the proud owner of your investment property until the deed is recorded. The procedure for recording the documents varies throughout the country but is becoming more standardized. Nearly every county utilizes a county recorder to record documents like real estate deeds, mortgages, deeds of trust, and other real estate documents as a public notice. Typically, there is an office of the county clerk and recorder, or the county courthouse in smaller jurisdictions.

Electronic document processing technology has made great strides in improving the efficiency in recording and retrieving documents at virtually all recorders' offices. Now documents can be retrieved by computers in a matter of seconds and are usually indexed by grantor and grantee.

After you receive word that the deed has been recorded, the transaction is finalized, and you're the new owner, you begin the property takeover process. There are several steps that should be taken in the first few days of bringing your new investment property online, including:

- Conduct a final walk-through to make sure that the property hasn't been damaged prior to the close of escrow.
- Verify that all items indicated on the personal property inventory list are present.
- Make sure that all keys were received (you can change locks as an added precaution, if necessary).
- Check the utility meters to make sure that the utility company has switched the billing as of the close of escrow so you don't get billed for the former owner's usage.
- Meet with tenants and assure them that you're a responsive and concerned property owner who wants to cooperatively resolve issues.

Another issue to address right after the closing is the possession and control by the former owner. Because the escrow closing and recording can often happen during the day without any specific notice, it is best to wait until the following calendar day and personally verify that only the tenants that should be there are occupying the property. If the owner is still residing on the premises or is using some of the property for his own use, you need to immediately ask that he turn over full possession unless you've made other formal written arrangements in advance. To minimize this prospect, we suggest that you include significant daily monetary damages in the purchase contract for any unauthorized holdover usage by the seller.

Congratulations! You're now ready to begin managing your property and increasing value as you build the foundation of your real estate portfolio.

Part IV
Operating the Property

"In going over your figures, you calculated your rental property has depreciated 9 percent over the year. However, by trying to do your own taxes, we've calculated your brain has depreciated by nearly 72 percent."

In this part . . .

Being a good landlord requires knowledge, training, and experience. Although we can't guarantee you that this part provides everything you need, it can help you learn from the mistakes of the many who have come before you. In addition to attracting and retaining good tenants, being a wise landlord also boosts the value of your property — if you follow our time-tested strategies of property management. But should the unexpected or unfortunate occur, all your hard work can go for not, if you don't have the proper insurance and risk management plans in place. So, we help you square these issues away. We also discuss how to account for all the income and expenses on your investment properties and how to reduce your tax bill (legally, of course) when it comes time to sell.

Chapter 13

Landlording 101

In This Chapter

- Deciding between a property manager and managing yourself
- Making sense of discrimination laws and requirements
- Getting along with existing tenants while making desired changes
- Understanding the keys to filling vacancies
- Dealing with leases and other contracts and money collection like a pro

At the moment that you close the deal on buying a rental property, you've probably already put in dozens, if not hundreds, of hours. Now, however, the real work begins. To maximize the value of your investment, you've got to attract and retain excellent tenants, stay on top of government regulations, keep your eyes open for ways to cost effectively improve your property, and handle contracts and money flowing in and going out. This chapter shows you how to be the best landlord that you can be.

Managing Yourself or Hiring Help?

A *property manager* can be responsible for all operations of a property, including marketing, tenant selection, rent collection, maintenance, and accounting. To fill the position, you have to possess the corresponding basic skills. But you don't need a degree or a lot of experience to get started, and you're sure to pick up ideas of ways to do things better along the way.

Use the following questions to examine your own personality and skills to see whether you're cut out to be your own property manager:

- **Are you a people person?** Serving as a landlord is a labor of love. You must enjoy people and solving problems — while often being unappreciated yourself.
- **Do you have the temperament to handle problems?** Responding to complaints and service requests in a positive and rational manner is key.

- **Are you comfortable with numbers and basic accounting skills?** And meticulous with paperwork?
- **Do you have maintenance and repair abilities?** Being able to work with your hands goes a long way, but if you're adept at finding and managing good contractors, you're still in the game.
- **Are you willing to work and take phone calls in the evenings and on weekends?** Who needs a weekend, right?
- **Do you have sales and negotiation skills?** You need to sell the space.
- **Are you willing to commit the time and effort?** Other important tasks, such as determining the right rent and becoming familiar with property management laws, take even more time.

If you're impatient or easily manipulated, you aren't suited to being a property manager. You need to convey a professional demeanor to your tenants. They must see you as someone who will take responsibility for the condition of the property and operational systems of the unit. You must also insist that tenants live up to their part of the bargain, pay their rent regularly, and refrain from causing unreasonable damage to your property.

A rental property manager must be fair, firm, and friendly to all rental prospects and tenants. You need to treat everyone impartially and remain patient and calm under stress. You must be determined and unemotional in enforcing rent collection and your policies and rules. And you must maintain a positive attitude through it all. Not as simple as it looks, is it?

When you manage a rental property, you don't just have to deal with your current tenants. You also have to interact with rental prospects, contractors, suppliers, neighbors, and government employees. People, not the property, create most rental management problems. Be prepared to be flexible and learn from your property management experiences. The really good property managers may have credentials, but they have also graduated from the school of hard knocks. Practice makes perfect.

Being your own property manager

Many beginning real estate investors do all the work themselves — painting, cleaning, making repairs, collecting rent, paying bills, and showing the rental units. However, after a while, most investors delegate jobs that they don't enjoy or aren't suited for. Some new owners, of course, do just fine managing their own rental units. But others discover firsthand that on-the-job property management training can backfire with some costly lessons.

If you have the right traits for managing property, have the time, and live close to your property, consider doing it yourself. Among the advantages of self-management are:

- **You save the monthly property management fee.** Property managers' fees can be significant, so a potential advantage for the do-it-yourself approach is that you can save yourself a good deal of money. However, as we discuss in a moment, you must examine the bigger picture of the value of your time and realistically assess how much of your time property management will take up.
- **You can save on maintenance costs.** By keeping direct control of the management, you decide who does the repair work and mows the lawn. If you're qualified and have the time, doing your own maintenance or yard work is usually a good idea; if you hire someone else to do it for you, the cost can devour your monthly cash flow in a hurry — especially in the early years of ownership when cash flow is often tight. Develop a list of reliable fix-it and landscape personnel who are licensed, do good work, and charge fair rates.

Some owners who self-manage can tell you exactly how much money they "saved" by not hiring a property manager, but the one factor that many real estate investors overlook is the value of their own time in dealing with management issues.

If you earn your living regularly from something other than managing rentals, managing your investment property may not be worth your valuable time. If you're a higher-income, full-time professional, rushing off on weekdays to handle some minor crisis at your rental unit isn't only impractical, it could be downright damaging to your career.

As a jobholder, look at your annual income and figure out approximately what you earn per hour. Do the same for the cash savings you generate by managing your own property. Unless your management efforts produce significant cash savings compared to your job, you may be better off hiring a property manager for your rental units.

The same guidelines hold true even if you're an independent business owner or self-employed. Your schedule may be more flexible than that of a nine-to-five employee. But if you're earning $50 an hour, it doesn't make sense to devote hours of your productive work time to managing rental units, which may only amount to cash savings of $25 an hour.

Hiring professional management

Management companies accept the responsibility for all operations of the property. The right property manager can make a big difference in the cash flow your rental unit generates by finding good replacement tenants quickly or making sure that maintenance is done in a timely manner without breaking your budget. You need a property manager who is committed to helping you get the optimum results from your rentals. Try to find property managers familiar with your kind of investment property. With a little research, you can find the right fit for your property.

A poor management company will cut into your profits, not only with their fees, but also by providing improper maintenance and leasing to poor-quality tenants who will run your property into the ground. A bad property manager can leave you in worse shape than if you had managed the property yourself.

Doing the research

Visit the office of your management company and spend time interviewing the specific property manager that will have hands-on management of your rental property. Make a few extra phone calls to check references and don't sign a management contract until you feel confident that the company you hire has a sound track record. Checking with the property management company's chosen referrals isn't enough. Ask for a list of all their clients and contact the ones with rental properties similar in size and type to your own. Make sure the rental owners you contact have been with the property management company long enough to have a meaningful opinion.

Make sure that the firm you hire manages property exclusively, particularly when selecting a management company for a single-family home, condo, or small rental property. Many real estate sales offices (as opposed to property management firms) offer property management services; however, this service is often more about obtaining the listing to sell the property later on. Many property managers in real estate sales offices don't have the same credentials, experience, and expertise that an employee of a property management firm has. The skills required to represent clients in *selling* property are quite different than the skills required to *manage* property.

Also, be sure to investigate these issues:

- **Licenses:** Most states require property managers to have either a real estate license or a property manager's license or both. Call or use the Internet to verify that the property manager and the management company have a current license in good standing.
- **Credentials:** Also examine the property manager's credentials. The Institute of Real Estate Management (IREM), an organization of professional property managers, provides professional designations, including the Certified Property Manager (CPM) and Accredited Residential Manager (ARM) designations. A select group of management firms have earned the Accredited Management Organization (AMO) designation.

- **Insurance:** The company should carry insurance for general liability, automobile liability, worker's compensation, and professional liability (errors and omissions). The management company is your agent and will be collecting your rents and security deposits, so they should also have a large fidelity bond to protect you in case an employee embezzles or mishandles your money.
- **Accounting:** Look for a management company that keeps a separate accounting for each property managed rather than a master trust account where multiple clients' funds are commingled.

Talking money

In most management contracts, property management companies have the ability and right to perform emergency repairs without advance approval from the owner. Of course, this allows the property management company to take care of problems that occur unexpectedly. Most management contracts contain clauses that allow property managers to undertake repairs up to a specified dollar amount without the owner's advance approval. The limit should be commensurate with the type and size of the property. Commercial properties and larger residential properties may have a $2,500 limit, whereas a small duplex may have a limit of $250.

When you're in the early stages of working with a new management company, make sure you closely monitor their expenses. Even though they may have the legal right to use funds up to a certain amount, they should always keep you informed. Many management companies have in-house maintenance crews and keeping these workers busy making repairs at properties they manage can be a lucrative profit center. They may offer low management fees knowing that they will make it up by markups on repairs — and often the repairs aren't even necessary. Look for a property management firm that doesn't mark up materials, supplies, or maintenance labor.

Typically, management companies receive a percentage of the collected income for managing a property while some management firms offer a flat fee per month or a dollar amount per unit per month for the entire property. Try to find a company that has a management fee that is a percentage of the collected income; this kind of fee is a strong motivator to the management company to ensure that the rents are collected and kept at market rate. Generally, the larger the rental property, the lower the management fee percentage. Management fees for single-family homes, condos, and small rental properties typically run 9 to 10 percent; medium size properties 6 to 8 percent; and large residential properties of 200 or more units around 3 to 5 percent. Fees for commercial type properties have a similar scale.

Additional fees for the leasing of vacant space are often justified, because the most time-intensive portion of property management is tenant turnover. When one tenant leaves, the rental unit or the commercial, industrial, or retail suite must be made rent-ready; then the property manager must show the property and screen the tenants. Charges for residential rentals can vary but are often either a flat fee of a few hundred dollars or a percentage of the rent, such as half of the monthly rental rate. Leasing commissions for commercial, industrial, or retail properties are almost always a percentage of the gross rent with a declining scale where the longer the lease, the lower the percentage in the later years.

Avoiding Discrimination Complaints

If you're in the rental housing business for long, you'll hear about six-figure or larger legal awards against rental property owners for violating fair-housing laws. Problems often arise when investment property owners are unaware that their policies or practices are discriminatory. Families, children, and folks with disabilities often suffer from this lack of knowledge. Federal and state laws prohibit discrimination, and these laws impact your advertising, tenant screening, and selection process.

The Federal Fair Housing Act prohibits discrimination on the basis of race, color, religion, national origin, sex, age, familial status, and disability. Check the state and local fair-housing laws in your area; some additional state and local protected classes include sexual preference, gender identity, occupation, source of income (government assistance, Section 8), educational status, medical status, and even physical body size.

Discrimination is a major issue for investment property owners and has serious legal consequences. If you don't know the law, you may be guilty of various forms of discrimination and not even realize it until you've been charged with discrimination. That's why knowing the law is so important.

With residential rental properties, another form of illegal discrimination is *steering* — guiding a rental applicant toward living where you think he should live based on race, color, religion, national origin, sex, age, familial status, disability or handicap, or any other protected class. Not showing or renting certain living units to minorities is one form of steering; however, so is the "assigning of any person to a particular section or floor of a building, because of race, color, religion, sex, handicap, familial status, or national origin." Advertising or promotion that indicates or implies a preference is also discriminatory.

All commercial and residential rental applicants should receive information on the full range of vacant space or rental units available and be able to decide which suites or units they want to see.

Residential rental property owners often have good intentions when they suggest that a rental prospect with children see only rental units on the ground floor or near the playground, but such practices are a clear violation of current federal fair housing laws as they restrict housing options and can be used by some unscrupulous landlords as an excuse or justification to cover up their intentional discriminatory actions.

Being fair to families and children

All residential rental properties must be offered to all applicants, including those with children, as federal and state legislation has virtually eliminated "adult only" residential housing except for certain HUD-certified seniors properties. However, because there's less regulation of nonresidential properties, some commercial property owners may be within their legal rights to use their business judgment to refuse or discourage an applicant with plans to use the leased space as a daycare or other business that caters to children.

Some rental property owners are concerned about renting to families with children because of hazards on the property that may be dangerous for kids. For example, the property may not have any safe areas for the children to play. Although you may truly only have children's best interests in mind, it is the parent's right to decide whether the property is safe for their children. Of course, you do need to take reasonable steps to make your property safe.

Charging rental applicants with children higher rents or higher security deposits than applicants without children is also illegal, as is offering different rental terms, such as shorter lease terms, fewer unit amenities, or different payment options. The property facilities must also be fully available for all tenants, regardless of age, unless there is a clear safety issue involved. For example, some states have laws allowing a policy that an adult must accompany children under 14 when using the swimming pool.

As a rental property owner, you should welcome renters with children. Families tend to be more stable, and they look for safe, crime-free, and drug-free environments in which to raise their kids. Along with responsible pet owners, who also have difficulty finding suitable rental properties, families with children can be excellent, long-term renters. And typically, the longer your tenants stay, the better your cash flow.

Dealing with tenants with disabilities

The federal fair housing regulations state that property owners must

- Make reasonable accommodations at the owner's expense for tenants with disabilities, so they can enjoy the rental property on an equal basis.
- Make reasonable adjustments to their rules, procedures, or services upon request. A common example would be providing a wider and more convenient parking space, when practical.

- Allow disabled tenants the right to modify their living space at their own expense, under the following conditions:
  - The modifications can only extend to what is necessary to make the space safe and comfortable.
  - The modifications don't make the unit unacceptable to the next tenant, or if they do, the tenant agrees to return the rental unit to its original condition upon vacating the property.
  - The tenant must obtain your prior approval and ensure that the work will be done in a professional manner, including obtaining any necessary government approvals or permits.
  - The tenants must pay the funds necessary to perform the needed restoration into an interest-bearing escrow account to ensure that the work is actually completed and there will be no liens against the property.

The Americans with Disabilities Act (ADA), passed in 1992, affects most commercial and retail real estate but has limited requirements for many residential rental property owners, because it doesn't apply to private residential properties built prior to 1991. (See the more significant requirements for newer properties at the Department of Justice ADA Web site at `www.usdoj.gov/crt/ada/adahom1.htm`). The ADA addresses the accessibility of public areas. For example, a rental property with a pool area must be accessible to the handicapped and the removal of existing physical barriers at the rental property owner's reasonable expense is required.

Many local municipalities work closely with HUD to investigate ADA complaints and handle enforcement. Also, local jurisdictions oversee and enforce handicapped parking requirements for multiunit rental properties. Check with your local building and code enforcement office for details.

Service animals that assist tenants with daily life activities must be allowed in all rental properties, regardless of any no-pet policies. You must also allow a tenant to have a pet if requested under the "necessary and reasonable accommodation" provisions of the Americans with Disabilities Act (ADA). Some tenants do seek a companion animal based on their need for comfort or companionship, and federal law requires owners and managers to consider the tenant's claim and grant the request if it is reasonable.

Working with Existing Tenants

If you're like most investment property owners, you're acquiring property that's already occupied. Tenants are typically full of apprehension when their rental unit ownership is changing, so it's extremely important to begin your relationship with your tenants on a positive note.

Meeting tenants and inspecting units

When you first acquire a residential rental property, contact your tenants and reassure them that you intend to treat them with respect and have a cordial yet businesslike relationship. Deal with tenants' questions honestly and directly. The most common concerns usually include the following:

- Potential for a rent increase
- Status of their security deposit
- Proper maintenance or condition of their rental unit
- Continuation of certain policies, such as allowing pets

Just as you're evaluating your tenant, your tenant is evaluating you during these initial contacts. Be open and honest. Failing to do so can result in a loss of credibility should you later implement changes that you didn't acknowledge up front. And don't make any promises that you won't keep.

If you're investing in commercial investment properties, you should also meet with your tenants and listen to their concerns about the property. Although they typically aren't as concerned about sudden rent increases (because they're likely on a long-term lease), they are interested in hearing about your plans to maintain and upgrade the property or make any other improvements that may increase their business. Also, it is never too soon to begin courting your commercial tenants for a lease renewal.

Provide your tenants with a letter of introduction during this brief in-person meeting. This letter provides your tenant with your contact information, explains your rent collection policies, the status of their security deposit, and the proper procedures for requesting maintenance.

Although you most likely had a brief chance to view the interior of the rental unit or suite during the due diligence period before escrow closed, walking through again with the tenant now that you're the owner can be helpful. Pay special attention to the proper use of the space, particularly for commercial tenants where illegal activities such as the use or storage of hazardous materials could be a serious liability issue.

Don't just knock on the door and expect to walk through your tenant's rental unit or suite. But if you're at your investment property delivering the letter of introduction, you can schedule a mutually convenient time to meet. Some tenants will be glad to meet with you right then, but others won't. Giving your tenants time to think about any issues that they'd like to discuss is beneficial for both of you. In most states, tenants don't have to let you enter their rental unit unless you have a legal reason and have given proper advance notice.

The former owner of the investment property may have had a policy of documenting the condition of the rental unit or suite at the time the tenant took possession. If so, compare the noted condition when you actually walk through the rental unit or suite. If proper documentation of the move-in condition wasn't made, consider preparing such information during your walk-through. This will allow you to establish some sort of baseline for the condition of the unit to use upon the tenant's move-out, which will help you determine the amount of the security deposit to be returned to the tenant.

Entering into a new rental agreement

Although you may want to make some changes in the terms or policies, when you acquire an occupied rental property, your legal and business relationship is already established by whatever agreement the tenants had with the former owner. Therefore, you need to wait until the expiration of the lease to change the terms — or provide the tenant with proper written notice of proposed changes as required by state or local law.

Most new owners convert existing tenants to their own lease or rental agreement as soon as possible.

- **Single-family home, condo, or a small residential rental property:** Implementing your own rental agreement as soon as legally allowed is relatively easy and can be done upon the expiration of the lease and upon 30 days written notice if the tenant is on a month-to-month rental agreement.
- **Larger residential rental properties:** You may want to gradually transition to a new agreement upon tenant turnover rather than require current tenants to sign a new lease. It's quite a significant project at a larger property to generate all the new leases and then meet with each tenant one-by-one to go over the new lease.
- **Commercial properties:** You really have no choice but to implement new leases upon tenant lease renewal or turnover as the existing leases are valid and binding until their expiration.

Consider the potential impact of making significant changes in the rental rates or policies immediately after you acquire the property. For example, although you may have strong feelings against allowing pets on your residential rental property, your new tenants may have pets already. Although you legally have the right to implement a no-pet policy upon lease renewal or upon giving proper legal notice, you are almost guaranteed a vacant rental unit if you do so. Impose your policies over a reasonable time frame, but be sure you're aware of the potential financial consequences in the short run.

For residential investment properties, the tenant information the seller provided you during escrow (see Chapter 12) may be outdated. One quick way to update your records is to have the tenants voluntarily complete your rental application form. In many states, you may not have a strong legal argument for requiring existing tenants to provide this information; however, many tenants will understand your reasoning and not mind. Other tenants may be reluctant to complete an entirely new rental application, in which case you may not require them to complete all sections of the form. However, even if you receive initial resistance, seek this updated information prior to renewing any lease. You need to assess the financial qualifications of your tenants, particularly if you anticipate future rent increases.

Increasing rents

When you acquire an investment property, part of your research is to establish the fair market rental value of your new property. If the tenant's current rent is below market value and he's on a month-to-month rental agreement, one of your toughest decisions as the new owner of a rental property is how to handle rent increases.

As the new owner, you will likely have much higher mortgage payments and expenses to make necessary repairs and upgrades to the property than the last owner did. Some tenants will be upset and antagonistic about rent increases, however, and there is little you will be able to do to appease them.

The majority of tenants will reluctantly accept a rent increase as long as the rent isn't raised beyond the current market rent for a comparable rental unit or suite in the area and you're willing to make needed repairs or upgrades to their rental units or suites. Providing the tenants with information on comparable rentals in your area should aid your increased rent request.

Renting Vacancies

Vacant rental units or suites don't generate rental income, so fill your vacancies with good, stable, rent paying tenants quickly. Verifying information on prospective tenants' rental applications takes a while, but it's time well spent. Relying on your instincts is inaccurate, arbitrary, and illegal.

Establishing tenant selection criteria

In order to increase your chances of finding a long-term, stable tenant — and avoiding charges of discrimination — your tenant selection criteria and screening process should be clear, systematic, and objective. Tenant selection criteria are *written* standards that you use to evaluate each prospective tenant's qualifications as a tenant for your property. Determine your minimum qualifications and adhere to them, applying them *consistently* and *fairly* to *all* rental applicants. Of course, your written criteria can't be discriminatory or violate any federal, state, or local fair-housing laws.

Setting up a systematic screening process is particularly critical if you only own a single-family rental, rental condo, or a small, multiunit rental property. Deadbeat tenants who go from property to property causing damage and not paying rent are experienced and shrewd. They know that the novice property owner is more likely to be fooled and that the large, professionally managed properties have screening procedures to verify every single item on their rental applications. If certain items don't check out, the professional property manager doesn't just trust her feelings on the prospective tenant.

Sometimes the mere mention of the tenant screening process is enough to make the rental prospect fidget and then shift into the classic "I'm just looking" mode. Don't rush or allow a prospect to hurry you through the tenant screening and selection process. The wrong decision can be financially devastating, particularly if you own just one or two rental units or a small commercial investment property.

In order to establish your selection criteria, review what you're looking for in a tenant. At a minimum, we suggest that you seek tenants who are financially responsible, pay their rent on time, and are likely to renew their leases, treat rental property with care, and be good neighbors. With commercial properties, you're also looking for tenants with complementary businesses that enhance rather than compete with your current tenants.

You aren't required to provide your rental prospects with a copy of your written tenant selection criteria, but there are potential benefits. Although you must offer all prospects a rental application and process each one received, there is an advantage to prospects making their own decision not to apply for your rental based on the criteria you've set up. The key is to follow the criteria without exception and have the information available if you're challenged. Decide when you're most comfortable discussing the criteria — from the first inquiry call, when you actually receive the application, and so on — and once again, be consistent.

Always be thorough when you screen tenants, and use the same process with all applicants. You run the risk of a charge of illegal discrimination if you deviate from your written standards for certain applicants. There are many legally acceptable reasons to deny a rental application. Be sure that your requirements are clearly understood and followed.

The fact that you carefully prescreen all prospects is a positive factor not only for you, but also for your rental applicants, your current tenants, and even the neighbors. In fact, you have a responsibility to your current tenants to weed out the unqualified tenants with a track record of disrupting neighbors everywhere they go. The good rental prospects will appreciate the fact that their neighbors had to meet your high standards, too.

Over 90 percent of your residential rental applicants will be good tenants, pay their rent on time, take good care of their homes, and treat you and their neighbors with respect. You just need to carefully guard against those few bad apples; don't hesitate to deny prospects who can't meet your standards.

Determining lease length

The *lease* or *rental agreement* is the legal document that specifies the terms and conditions of the agreement binding the property owner and the tenant. It is a contract between the owner of the property and the tenant for the possession and use of the property in exchange for the payment of rent. Residential rental property owners commonly use one of two types of agreements (for information on other aspects of leases, check out Chapter 9):

- **Month-to-month agreement:** More common with residential properties than commercial, industrial, or retail, a month-to-month rental agreement is automatically renewed each month unless the owner or tenant gives the other proper written notice (usually 30 days) to terminate the tenancy. Month-to-month agreements give you much more flexibility than leases, because you can increase the rent or change other terms of the tenancy on 30 days' notice.

  You or the tenant may terminate or end the tenancy at any time by giving the required amount of written notice, again usually 30 days. Some owners prefer the flexibility offered by a month-to-month rental agreement to a lease. Although the month-to-month rental agreement does allow your tenants the right to move at any time merely by giving a 30-day written notice, the reality is that most tenants don't like to move and often stay long-term. The majority of tenants only move because of a job transfer or another significant reason, or because the rental owner doesn't properly maintain the property.

- **Fixed-term lease:** Commercial, industrial, and retail investment property owners almost always use long-term leases exclusively. Fixed-term contracts obligate you and the tenant for a set period of time and some owners like the commitment required from the tenant. The most common residential lease terms are for 6, 9, or 12 months and rarely exceed two years. With such a lease, you can't increase the rent or change other terms of the tenancy until the lease expires. You can't terminate or end the tenancy before the lease expires, unless the tenant doesn't pay his rent or violates another term of the lease. And in court, you have the *burden of proof,* which means you're the one who has to prove that the tenant didn't live up to his part of the contract.

Setting the rent

Setting the rent is one of the most important yet difficult tasks for most investment property owners. If you set your rent too high, you will have a vacant rental unit. And if you set your rent too low, your profits will suffer or, worse, you won't even cover your expenses. You can use two common methods for determining how much rent you should charge for your rental property — return on investment (which examines your costs) and market analysis (which examines a comparable property's rent).

Examining the return on your investment

The first step in determining your rent based on the return on your investment is to calculate your costs of owning and operating your rental property. You need to estimate costs for your mortgage, property taxes, insurance, maintenance, leasing, management, and a profit on your invested funds (for the details on this topic, please see Chapter 10).

Suppose that for a residential rental unit your monthly mortgage, tax payments, and operating expenses come to $800, plus you want a $200 monthly return (10 percent per year) on your original cash investment of $24,000 in this rental property. Thus, you need to generate a monthly rent of $1,000. (This simple calculation doesn't take appreciation, increasing equity, or tax advantages of real estate into account.)

Although you may have calculated that you need $1,000 per month for your rental unit, if the rental market is such that comparable units are readily available for $900, you may not be able to fully achieve your financial goals at this time. With most real estate investments, the initial returns may not match your original projections; in the long run, rents will often increase at a greater rate than your expenses, your debt service will remain constant, and your return on your initial investment will improve.

Many new investment property owners make the mistake of overestimating the potential income from their rental property while allowing for no rental discounts or concessions, and anticipating virtually no vacancy or bad debt. When reality strikes, they can be faced with negative cash flow, and ultimately, they may even lose their rental property.

Setting the rent is particularly critical if you own single-family or condo rental units or other small residential or commercial rental properties, because the rent loss from an extended vacancy or one bad tenant can seriously jeopardize your investment. Be conservative in setting your rents (along with being cautious in tenant screening and aggressive in maintaining your properties) to attract good, long-term tenants who pay on time. To avoid surprises, use a conservative budget for your rental property that anticipates rental income at 92 percent of the market rent for a comparable rental unit or suite and assumes one month's vacancy each year.

Surveying comparable rents

Knowing how much money you need to break even is important for evaluating the potential return on your real estate investment. And setting your rents properly is an independent decision based on current market conditions. Unfortunately, the realities of the rental market may put limits on what rent you can reasonably charge for your rental unit or suite, regardless of your costs of owning and maintaining the investment property.

Evaluating the rental rates being charged for similar rental units or suites in comparable locations is a great way to gather information before setting your own rent. Make minor adjustments in your rent because of variations in the location, age, size, and features of the properties you're comparing.

For example, if you own a residential investment property and one of your competitors has an available rental unit that is nearly identical to yours, your rent should be slightly higher if you also have a swimming pool. Of course, be honest and make downward adjustments for aspects of your rental property that aren't as desirable as alternatives.

In order to determine the market rents in your area, do your homework and locate comparable rental properties, which are those properties that your tenants are most likely to also consider when looking for a rental unit or suite. They may be located right in the neighborhood or in other areas.

Deciding on security deposits

Rental property owners are permitted to collect a security deposit from tenants upon move-in and hold it until the tenant leaves. The *security deposit* provides financial protection for the property owner in the event that the tenant falls behind in his rental payments or damages his rental unit or suite.

For residential properties, state laws often limit the amount of the security deposit, require interest to be paid on the deposit, and detail what are lawful deductions. Check with the local affiliate of the National Apartment Association for your state's security deposit laws. (Certain rental owners may be exempt from the rules.)

In most rental markets, typical security deposits are well below the maximum allowed by law. We recommend that you collect as large of a security deposit as the market will bear (staying within the legal limits). Don't lower or waive the security deposit. If the required funds to move in are too high for a desired tenant, collect a reasonable portion of the deposit prior to move in and allow the tenant to pay the balance in installments.

Because the funds don't belong to you, several states require that residential security deposits be held in a separate trust bank account. Some states require that owners provide tenants with a written notice indicating the location of this bank trust account at the beginning of the tenancy.

Adding value through renovations and upgrades

For residential properties, almost every rental unit has the potential for renovation or upgrades. Often this is where the real value can be created in rental units: When you have a rental unit that is dated, you can renovate it and increase the rent. Pay particular attention to those items that would be quick, easy, and inexpensive to replace but that can really improve the overall look of your rental unit.

If you have an older investment property, renovating or making tenant improvements may be more difficult due to some of the hazardous materials used in your building's original construction. Asbestos and lead-based paint was commonly used in construction of many older properties, and these materials can be quite costly to remove. Often, you're better off just leaving them in place as long as they haven't been disturbed. Consult with experts in these issues before doing any work. Also, check with your local building, code enforcement, or health department for its requirements regarding the proper handling and disposal of hazardous materials.

Again, if your chosen investment properties are residential, then keep in mind what features and strengths your prospective renters will find in competitive rental units. For example, if most of your competition offers dishwashers but your unit doesn't have one, you may want to install a dishwasher so that you remain competitive. Another simple upgrade is to replace your old electrical switches and outlets to create a more modern look.

Enhancing external appearances

Make sure that your rental prospects' first impression of your residential or commercial rental property is a positive one, because if it isn't, they'll most likely never take the time to see the interior. Start at the street and carefully critique your property as if you were entering a contest for the best-looking property in your area.

To attract tenants who will treat your property properly and stay for a long time, be sure that your grounds and exterior areas are sparkling clean and the landscaping is well maintained. Renovating the grounds by removing trash, junk, and weeds is an inexpensive task. A nice green lawn, healthy shrubs, and shade trees will enhance any investment property. Make sure that the building structure is presentable and inviting. Some specific exterior improvements to consider are ground level or hanging planters, brass address numbers, awnings, fresh paint, landscaping, and cleanup.

First impressions are critical and one of the key areas seen by all prospective tenants is the front entry. Make sure the entryway is clean, well kept, and well lighted. The entry door should be cleaned or freshly painted or stained. Buy a new welcome mat. Remove or replace a broken screen door.

Improving what's inside

The most qualified renters always have choices. You are in competition for these excellent tenants, and you need to ensure that your rental unit stands out from the rest. The positive first impression of your rental property's exterior won't matter if the rental unit's interior is poorly maintained.

Don't show your rental unit until it's completely rent-ready. Although you may lose a couple of potential showing days by taking the time to get the unit ready to rent, you will benefit in the long run with a more conscientious tenant. Here's a list of things to check:

- All plumbing and appliances are operating properly.
- Locks have been changed and are operational. Pay attention to all latches and catches, doorknobs and pulls, doorstops, and sliding doors.
- Windows, window locks, screens, and window coverings should be clean, unbroken, secure, and operating properly.
- Paint and/or wall coverings should provide proper coverage, without holes, cuts, scratches, nails, or bad seams.
- Floor coverings should be clean and in good condition.
- Thoroughly clean the toilet, tub, shower, sink, mirrors, and cabinets.
- Check all closets and storage areas. Rods, closet dowels, hooks, shelves, lights, floors, and walls should be clean.
- Counters, cabinets, doors, molding, thresholds, and metal strips should be clean and fully operational, presenting no hazards.
- Check smoke detectors, all lighting, and electrical outlets, including ground-fault circuit-interrupters (GFCI) and circuit breakers for proper operation.
- Patios, balconies, and entryways should be clean and the railings secure.
- Check the heating and air-conditioning for proper operation. Be sure the thermostat, filters, vents, and registers are all in working order.

Using contractors

Particular maintenance and improvements are best handled by outside contractors. Use outside contractors for those trades that require specialized licensing or training. For example, it would be unwise for you to act as an exterminator or a contractor dealing with environmental hazards, or to attempt to recharge the coolant in an air-conditioning unit. Specific regulations are in place and unique knowledge is required in these areas.

Your skill level, time constraints, and opportunity cost may help determine whether you do some chores yourself or hire a pro. For example, cleaning, painting, and light maintenance may be items that you feel qualified to handle and can complete promptly.

Every day your residential rental unit sits vacant is costing you rental income that you can never recover. If you decide to paint your own rental unit, it may take you six days working in the evenings and weekends to completely paint a single-family rental home. If the rental market is strong and the daily rental rate is $50 per day, you're actually losing money if you could have had the rental home professionally painted in one day for $200.

Regardless of how much work you choose to handle yourself, have on hand a list of competent and competitively priced service companies and suppliers for those times when you need a quick response. Your local affiliate of the National Apartment Association (NAA), the Institute of Real Estate Management (IREM), or the Building and Owners Managers Association (BOMA) can often provide names of service companies. Carefully check the references and the status of any bonds or licenses with the appropriate governmental agency, and ensure that they have the proper insurance in place before you allow them to commence any work on your property.

Advertising for tenants

Advertising is how you let people know that you have a vacant rental property available. Money intelligently spent on advertising is money extremely well spent. But when it's done poorly, advertising can be another black hole for your precious resources.

Determine the most desirable features of your rental property for your target market by asking your current renters what they like about where they live or work. You can also ask people who look at your property — whether or not they agree to rent — what aspects of your property they found of interest. Incorporate these selling points into your marketing efforts.

The best advertisement for your rental property is curb appeal — the exterior appearance. Properties that have well-kept grounds with green grass, trimmed shrubs, beautiful flowers, and fresh paint are much more appealing to your rental prospects. A well-maintained property often attracts a tenant who will pay more rent and treat your rental property with care.

Creating interest in your rental property used to be as simple as putting up a sign or placing an ad in the local newspaper. Although these tried-and-true methods of informing potential renters still often work, other options are available for you to consider. The target market for your rental property has a lot to do with which method of advertising works best for your rental unit. Referrals and property signs often give you good exposure to renters in your local area, whereas newspaper and Internet ads may let people or businesses relocating to your area know about your rental property as well.

Showing your rental

One of the most time-consuming aspects of owning and managing rental property is the time spent filling vacancies. Real estate investors with commercial properties often use professional leasing brokers, and owners of large residential properties have onsite managers and leasing agents. But residential rental property owners with small properties usually take this on individually and it can be a huge time trap.

Efficiently scheduling showings

The most efficient approach to showing your small residential rental is to hold an open house — which enables you to show your property to several interested rental prospects within a couple of hours. Select a two to three hour period for your open house that is convenient for you and most working people (preferably during daylight hours). Combining a weekday early evening open house with one on the weekend enables virtually all prospects to fit the rental showing into their busy schedules.

Another benefit of an open house is that many folks feel more comfortable touring a rental property when other prospects are around. They don't have to be concerned about meeting someone they don't know in a vacant rental property. This approach also helps ensure your own personal safety.

A newspaper ad simply indicating the time of your open house isn't a good idea, because you may end up with many unqualified renters walking through your property. But an open house where you invite all qualified prospects whom you have spoken with in response to your advertising is a good way to create a sense of urgency and competition, which often generates multiple applicants for your rental.

In a depressed rental market or if you find that you need to fill a vacancy during the holidays, you may not be able to generate enough interest for an open house for multiple prospects. If you have to schedule individual appointments, keep these points in mind:

- Be prepared to show your rental units in the evenings and on weekends, when most of your prospects are available.
- Try to consolidate your appointments to a certain time frame, but don't push this too far. Asking prospects to conform to your schedule may turn them off.
- Call each person to verify the rental showing before making a special trip to the property. By calling, you're also reassuring the prospect that you'll be there and aren't going to be delayed. Exchanging cellphone numbers can be helpful here.

Showing vacant versus occupied rentals

When showing a vacant residential rental, be a tour guide but don't be too controlling. Allow the prospects to view the rental in the manner that suits them. Some prospects go right to a certain room, which gives you a clue about the importance that they place on that aspect of your property. If the prospects hesitate or are reluctant to tour on their own, casually guide them through the rental property yourself.

As you begin to show the interior of your residential rental, avoid making obvious statements such as "This is the living room" or "Here's the bathroom!" Instead, listen and observe the body language and expressions of your prospects as they walk through the property. Don't oversell if they seem pleased, but feel free to point out the benefits of your rental.

Commercial properties are typically shown vacant after the prior tenant has vacated although you may be able to obtain the cooperation of the vacating tenant to show prospects through the suite while occupied. Because commercial tenants almost always require some specialized tenant improvements, it can be more useful to work off of drawings of the space — rather than conduct a physical tour — and have a space planner show the prospect how the space will meet their needs. If you do show an occupied commercial space, just be sure not to disrupt the tenant's business activities.

In most states, if the current residential tenants are at the end of their lease or have given a notice to vacate, the owner is specifically allowed to enter the unit to show it to a prospective tenant. Of course, you must comply with state laws that require you to give tenants advance written notice of entry prior to showing the rental unit. Your tenant may agree to waive this requirement, but make sure that you have that agreement in writing.

Cooperate with the current tenants when scheduling mutually convenient times to show the rental — and respect their privacy by avoiding excessive intrusions. Although the current tenant may legally be required to allow you and your prospects to enter the rental unit for a showing, he doesn't have to make any efforts to ensure that the property is clean and neat.

Showing a vacant rental unit is generally much easier, but touring your prospect through an occupied rental property does have some advantages. Your current tenants can be a real asset if they're friendly and cooperative and take care of the property. The rental prospects may want to ask the current tenant questions about their living experience at your property.

If you can, get copies of recent utility bills from your current tenant, in case your prospective renters have any questions about utility costs. Utility costs for electric, natural gas, water and sewer, and trash are becoming significant items in the budgets of many renters. You don't want your tenants to be unable to financially handle the typical monthly utility costs, because that may impact their ability to pay your rent. Plus, you may also be able to use low utility costs as a marketing tool.

If your current residential tenant is being evicted, isn't leaving on good terms, or has an antagonistic attitude for any reason, don't show the rental unit until the property is vacated. Also consider this strategy if your current tenants haven't taken care of the rental property or if their lifestyle or furnishings may be objectionable to some rental prospects.

Selling prospects

After you've qualified your residential rental prospect (see the "Establishing tenant selection criteria" section earlier in the chapter), convince her that you have the best rental unit available. People want more than just a place to live. Tenants want to feel they can communicate with you if a problem arises. They also appreciate it when someone shows an interest in their lives. By showing an interest, you set yourself apart from other property managers. Some prospects will take a rental unit that isn't exactly what they're looking for if they have a positive feeling about the rental property owner.

No matter how closely your rental unit meets the stated needs and wants of your prospects, they often hesitate and doubt their own judgment. Don't be pushy, but convince the prospects that your property is right for them. After you succeed in this regard, you have to close the sale. This is one area where many rental property owners and managers suddenly get cold feet. They may do a great job handling the initial telephone rental inquiry, the preparation and showing of the rental property, and even objections, but become shy to ask the prospect to sign and commit money.

Your goal at the end of the showing is to receive a commitment from the prospect to rent by having him complete your rental application and pay the credit screening fee, first month's rent, and security deposit. But don't forget that you still need to thoroughly screen the prospect and confirm that he meets your rental criteria before you sign a lease or rental agreement.

If, despite your best efforts, the prospect is still undecided, make sure that he gives you a holding deposit. Remind him that you may make a deal with the next prospect and he'll be out of luck. If you have a lot of demand for your rental units or suites, you should develop a waiting list. (Many applicants may be an indication that you set your rent too low.)

Accepting applications and deposits

You must offer every interested prospect (age 18 and older) the opportunity to complete a written rental application. You want to avoid having a prospect accuse you of discriminating against him by not permitting him to fill out the rental application. And, information provided on the application enables you to begin the screening process and select the best tenant for your rental property using objective criteria and your rental requirements.

Handling environmental disclosures

Take precautions to ensure that your rentals are a safe and healthy environment. Although legal implications and substantial liability for failing to meet required state and federal disclosures exist, most owners don't want to see their tenants get sick or injured.

Lead: Some older buildings may still contain lead paint (which was banned in 1978). A lead test is the only way to verify the existence of lead. Often, the best solution is to manage the lead rather than remove it, because the removal processes can release large amounts of lead dust. As a residential rental owner, know the dangers of lead and the federally required disclosures for residential properties only (providing a lead paint pamphlet that you can get at `www.epa.gov`). Most states have lead hazard reduction laws, some of which require testing and maintenance in addition to the federal disclosure requirements.

Asbestos: Although there are currently no federal disclosure rules for asbestos in rental housing and no federal requirements to investigate or remove asbestos, check with local and state officials for possible disclosure requirements. Asbestos was added to a variety of products to provide strength, heat insulation, and fire resistance. In most products, asbestos is combined with a binding material so that it's not released into the air. As long as fibers aren't released, there are no known health risks. Asbestos is dangerous if disturbed. Studies of people exposed to asbestos clearly show that breathing high levels of the fibers can lead to an increased risk of lung and other cancers. Don't test for asbestos on your own. Hire a professional environmental testing firm because the act of breaking open potentially asbestos-containing material to obtain samples could release asbestos into the air and create a dangerous situation.

Radon: Radon is an invisible, odorless, radioactive gas, and a known cancer-causing agent, found in soil and rock in all parts of the U.S. Inside some buildings, high levels of radon gas have been found to cause lung cancer. But most radon found in buildings poses no direct threat because the concentration is generally within the safe level. No federal requirements to disclose or test for radon currently exist, but it's potentially a serious issue and one that's receiving more attention. Conduct tests, which are cheap and simple to do, to determine radon levels in your rentals, and check with local authorities for more information about the prevalence and precautions to take. Visit the EPA Web site at `www.epa.gov` for more information.

Mold: Recently much has been made of alleged health problems caused by exposure to mold spores. Mold has been with us since biblical times and is found everywhere, but allegations that exposure to certain types can be hazardous are rather recent with several well-publicized lawsuits. The city of New York developed guidelines and a protocol for remediating mold in the early 1990s, but the EPA didn't generate any materials until March 2001. The EPA documents generally follow the New York City protocol, which has several levels of recommended responses depending on the size of the area where mold is found. Although a common claim is respiratory illness by some individuals while in direct contact with elevated mold levels, there are still no conclusive scientific guidelines as to acceptable limits for exposure. But rental owners should take claims of mold exposure seriously. Minimize the possibility of mold in your building by identifying and quickly repairing moisture intrusion. If there's a claim of mold by your tenant, follow the EPA guidelines and protocol and consult with experts if the problem is severe and persistent. Use qualified professionals and carefully document all communication to minimize the prospect of being sued by your tenants.

Rental property owners are legally allowed to choose among rental applicants as long as their decisions comply with all fair-housing laws and are based on legitimate business criteria.

Prior to accepting the rental application, carefully review the entire form to make sure that each prospective tenant has legibly provided all requested information. Pay particular attention to all names and addresses, employment information, driver's license numbers, and emergency contacts. Make sure that the prospect has signed the rental application authorizing you to verify the provided information and to run a credit report. Finally, ask each prospective tenant to show you her current driver's license or other similar photo identification so that you can confirm that she provided you with her correct name and current address.

If you go over the application with the prospect, only ask questions that are part of the form. Don't ask the rental applicant about his birthplace, religion, marital status, children, or about a physical or mental condition — such questions could lead to accusations of discrimination. You can ask him if he has ever been convicted of a crime and whether he's at least 18 years old.

After you approve the rental prospect, you should have her sign the rental agreement. If the prospect still insists she needs additional time, she should agree to pay the daily rental rate or you should refund her holding deposit and continue your leasing efforts.

If you use a holding deposit, you must have a written agreement or you're likely to encounter a misunderstanding or even legal action. State laws regarding holding deposits vary throughout the country, yet they're almost uniformly vague and can easily lead to disputes.

Verifying rental applications

Keep copies of all rental applications and corresponding verification forms, credit reports, and all other documents for both accepted and rejected applicants for at least three years. That way, if anyone ever makes a claim that you discriminated against him, your best defense will be your own records, which will clearly indicate that you consistently applied legal rental criteria. Here are the key items to review on renters' applications.

Adults' identity

Require each prospective adult tenant to show you his or her current driver's license or other similar (and official) photo ID so that you can confirm that the applicant is providing you with the correct name and current address. Advise each rental applicant that if his application is approved, you will need a photocopy of his ID to be kept in his tenant file. Ask about any discrepancies between the application and the ID provided. Even if the explanation seems reasonable, be sure to write down the new information. Maybe an old address appears on the photo ID, which you can check out further through a credit-reporting agency. Having a photocopy of the ID for each adult tenant is vital if a dispute about the tenant's identity arises in the future. In these situations, you need to be able to clearly show that you positively identified the tenant at move-in.

Rental history

When you first contact the rental applicant's current landlord, listen to his initial reaction and let him tell you about the applicant. Some landlords will welcome the opportunity to tell you all about your rental applicant, but some current and prior landlords may be

- **Dishonest:** A landlord may be upset with the tenant for leaving his property or unwilling to say anything bad about a problem tenant so that he can get the tenant out of his property and into yours.
- **Unforthcoming:** Many landlords are concerned that they will have some liability if they provide any negative or subjective information.

When a current or prior landlord isn't overly cooperative, try to gain his confidence by providing him with some information about yourself and your rental property. If you're still unable to build rapport, try to get him to at least answer the most important question of all: "Would you rent to this applicant again?" He can simply give you a yes or a no without any details. Of course, silence can also tell you everything that you need to know.

Some applicants will provide you with letters of reference from their prior landlords or even copies of their credit reports. Verify the authenticity of any documents provided by the rental applicant. Another useful screening tool is to request all tenants to provide copies of their water and utility bills for the past year. This will verify the tenant's prior address and also give you an idea whether they pay their bills on time.

Employment and income

Independently verify the company information and phone number the applicant puts on her application if you have any doubts about the authenticity of it. For example, you may have reason for concern if the employer is a major corporation and the telephone isn't answered in a typical and customary business manner.

You also need to be careful that you confirm the sensitive compensation and stability of employment questions only with an appropriate representative of the employer. Be prepared to send letters requesting the pertinent information and include a self-addressed, stamped envelope. Be sure to tell your rental prospect that you may have a delay in providing her with the results of your tenant screening process.

In addition to the results of your verification calls, the applicant should provide you with proof of her employment and income such as recent pay stubs. But no matter how strong the information is, verify it directly with the employer or the source of the income. For prospective commercial tenants, a copy of the most recent tax return is your best method of verifying income.

Credit history

Obtain a credit report on each applicant. A credit report shows all current and previous credit cards and loans, timeliness of making payments when due, plus all public record entries such as bankruptcy and judgment. You can figure out whether an applicant has been late or delinquent in paying his rent or other living expenses. The three major credit reporting agencies are Experian (`www.experian.com`; 888-397-3742), Equifax (`www.equifax.com`; 800-997-2493), and Trans Union (`www.tuc.com`; 800-888-4213). Credit information for commercial tenants can be found in the D&B database (`www.dnb.com`; 800-234-3867).

Carefully compare the addresses contained on the credit report to the information provided on the rental application. If there is an inconsistency, ask the rental prospect for an explanation. Maybe the person was temporarily staying with a family member or simply forgot about one of her residences. Of course, be sure to contact prior landlords and ask all the questions on the rental application verification form just to make sure that the applicant didn't neglect to tell you about that residence for a reason.

Information obtained in credit reports must be kept strictly confidential and can't be given to any third parties. In some states, the rental applicant is entitled to a copy of his own credit report upon request, and federal law allows anyone denied credit or housing on the basis of his credit report to obtain a free copy of the report.

Make sure that you're reviewing the credit report of your actual applicant. People with poor credit or tenant histories have been known to steal the identity of others — particularly their own children — by using the child's social security number. Many landlords no longer even ask for social security numbers, but if you do, one solution is to make sure that your credit reporting service provides a social security search, which will clearly indicate if there are any inconsistencies in the use of the number provided.

All personal references

You will occasionally find someone who will tell you that the rental applicant is her best friend but she would never loan the applicant money or let him borrow her car. Plus, if you call the references given and find that the information is bogus, you can use this information as part of your overall screening of the applicant.

Dealing with rental cosigners

If your rental prospect doesn't meet the criteria outlined in your statement of rental policy, you may consider approving his application if he provides a cosigner or *guarantor.* A guarantor must be financially qualified and screened or the guarantee is worthless.

Require your guarantor to complete a rental application, pay the application fee, and go through the same tenant screening process as the applicant. Keep in mind that the guarantor won't actually be occupying the commercial suite or living at your rental unit and thus will have his own housing costs. To ensure that the guarantor can meet all of his own obligations and cover your tenant's rent in case of a default, deduct the guarantor's cost of housing from his income before comparing it to your income requirements.

Although a lease guarantor can be very important and can give you the extra resources in the event of a rent default by your tenant, out-of-state lease guarantors aren't as valuable as in-state ones. Enforcing the lease guarantee against an out-of-state party can be difficult or even financially unfeasible.

Notifying applicants of your decision

Regardless of whether your rental applicant is accepted or rejected, be sure to notify the applicant promptly when the decision is made. If you have approved the applicant, contact him and arrange for a meeting and a walk-through of the rental unit prior to the move-in date.

Don't notify the other qualified applicants that you have already rented the rental property until all legal documents have been signed and all funds due upon move-in have been collected in full.

One of the most difficult tasks for the rental property owner is informing a rental applicant that you've denied his application. You obviously want to avoid an argument over the rejection, but even more importantly, you want to avoid a fair-housing complaint based on the applicant's misunderstanding about the reasons for the denial.

Notify your denied rental applicant in writing, and keep a copy of all rejection letters for at least three years. If you notify the applicant only by phone, you may have difficulty giving all of the details and required disclosures. The written notice-of-denial-to-rent form avoids a situation in which the applicant may form the opinion that you're denying his application in a discriminatory manner, in which case he could file a complaint with HUD or a state or local fair-housing agency.

Using a notice-of-denial-to-rent form to inform the applicant in writing of your decision as well as outline the valid reasons is an excellent idea. This form helps you to document the various legal reasons for your rejection of the applicant. It is a simple checklist that also allows you to provide the applicant with the required information per the federal Fair Credit Reporting Act.

If you reject an applicant based on his credit report, you're required by the federal Fair Credit Reporting Act to notify the applicant of his rights. Although it is not *required* to be in writing, provide the denied applicant with a letter containing the mandatory disclosures so that you have proof that you complied with the law. You must also provide this information even if you have approved the applicant but have required him to pay a higher security deposit, higher rent, or provide a cosigner.

Signing Leases and Collecting Money

Many owners of small investment property don't worry about setting detailed policies and guidelines (often called house rules) because they think the lease or rental agreement covers it all. But setting up some basic rules in writing that can be modified as necessary upon proper written notice to the tenants is a good idea because it ensures that you and your tenants are on the same page and it gives you flexibility as you manage your property. The rules you draft should be more informal and conversational in tone than your lease. Be clear, direct, and firm, yet not condescending. Make sure your policies and rules are reasonable and enforceable. They must not discriminate against anyone because of race, gender, ethnicity, religion, and so on. Be particularly careful to review your house rules to avoid any reference to children unless related to health and safety issues.

Reviewing and signing documents

Tenants and property owners alike are usually aware of all the legal paperwork involved in renting a property. And although sifting through all that legalese isn't fun for anyone, it is important. Rental property owners and tenants each have specific legal rights and responsibilities that are outlined in these documents, and being aware of what you're agreeing to — and being sure that your tenants know what they're agreeing to — is crucial.

After you approve the rental prospect, you should have her sign the rental agreement. If the prospect still insists she needs additional time, she should agree to pay the daily rental rate or you should refund her holding deposit and continue your leasing efforts.

Be sure that your tenant understands that when he signs your rental agreement, he's entering into a business contract that has significant rights and responsibilities for both parties. Be sure to have all adult occupants review and sign *all documents* — including any lease or rental agreement addendums — before taking possession of the rental unit. After the tenant has been given the keys and taken possession of the rental property, getting him to sign your required legal documents can be difficult, and regaining possession of your rental unit can be a long and expensive process. (Even if the tenant failed to sign the lease or rental agreement, an oral tenant/landlord relationship is established when you give the tenant the keys, but oral agreements often foster *dis*agreements, so avoid the situation altogether.)

In addition to the lease, take care of these issues:

- Give your residential tenants a copy of the required environmental disclosure form and the EPA pamphlet for lead-based paint and lead-based paint hazards, which is required under federal law.
- Inform your new tenant of the importance of smoke detectors. You may even want to create a separate smoke detector agreement to be sure your tenants fully understand the importance of this vital safety equipment and that they must take an active role in ensuring that the smoke detectors remain in place, operate properly, and have electrical or battery power in order to protect the tenant in case of smoke or fire.
- Have pet owning residential tenants complete and sign an animal agreement, which outlines pet-specific policies and rules at your property. Retain control over the number, type, and size of the animals on your property. You can meet and photograph the animal so there's no doubt as to what you have approved.

Collecting the money

In your meeting prior to move-in, be sure to collect the first month's rent and the security deposit *before* you give the tenants the keys to the rental unit. Payment may be in the form of cash, a cashier's check, or a money order. But don't accept a personal check (because you have no way of knowing whether the check will clear). Provide a receipt for the payments.

Accept cash for the move-in or the monthly rent payment only when absolutely necessary. Regularly collecting cash for your rents can make you a crime target. Most convenience stores offer money orders for a nominal cost and are open at all hours, so let your tenant take the risk of carrying the cash to the bank or convenience store to get a money order. Tell your new tenant that your policy is to accept only a bank cashier's check or money order upon move-in. Also, let him know whether your rent collection policy will allow him to pay his future monthly rent payments with a personal check.

Prior to giving the keys to your new tenant and allowing him to take possession, insist on having the cash in hand through *good funds* (as opposed to *insufficient funds,* where a person writes a check and doesn't have the money to cover it). Most owners do this by requiring cash, a bank cashier's check, or a money order. But many rental owners aren't aware that both bank cashier's checks and money orders can be stopped because they can be lost or stolen. However, the bank cashier's check and money orders are superior to personal checks because they do represent good funds and will at the least not be returned to you because there was no money to cover them.

If, despite our strong advice, you accept a personal check, at least don't give the tenant access to the property until you've called and verified with the tenant's bank that the check will be honored. Your best bet is to physically take the check to the tenant's bank and cash it or at least have it certified. If the bank will certify the check, they are guaranteeing that there are sufficient funds available and the bank will actually put a hold on the funds. Of course, cashing the check is the only sure way to collect your funds, because a devious tenant could always stop payment on even a certified personal check.

Inspecting the property with your tenant

The number one source of residential tenant/landlord disputes is the disposition of the tenant's security deposit. Many of these potential problems can be resolved with proper procedures before the tenant takes possession of the rental unit by using a move-in/move-out inspection checklist.

When properly completed, the inspection form clearly documents the condition of the rental property upon move-in by the tenants and serves as a baseline for the entire tenancy. If the tenant withholds rent or tries to break the lease claiming the unit needs substantial repairs, you may need to be able to prove the condition of the rental unit upon move-in. When the tenants move out, you'll be able to clearly note the items that were damaged or were not left clean by the vacating tenants.

Complete the inspection form *with the tenants* prior to or at the time of move-in. Walk through the premises with the tenants and agree that all items are clean and undamaged *before* they move in their stuff. Note the condition of the carpets and floor coverings — one of the most common areas of dispute upon move-out. Although tenants shouldn't be charged for ordinary wear and tear, if they destroy the carpet, they should pay for the damage. Indicate the age of the carpet and whether it has been professionally cleaned as part of your rental turnover process. You can also take photos or videotape the unit before the tenant moves in for additional material to refresh the tenant's memory or show the court if the matter ends up there.

Chapter 14

Protecting Your Investment: Insurance and Risk Management

In This Chapter

- Creating your risk management plan
- Looking into insurance options

After years of accumulating resources, every investment property owner needs to be concerned about protecting her assets through insurance and risk management programs. You have worked and sacrificed to build your wealth through real estate, so you don't want to be careless and lose it.

The concept of risk management includes much more than simply having an insurance policy. You need to take care to practice proper maintenance and recordkeeping and require that others provide you with coverage for their activities. That's what this chapter is all about.

Developing a Risk Management Plan

Many people get into the world of rental real estate without knowing how much risk they're exposed to just by owning real estate. You may read stories in the newspaper about lawsuits against deep-pocket defendants without much personal concern, but it is a reality shock when you're suddenly considered to be the one with those deep pockets.

Real estate investment property owners need a plan to minimize risks because they're frequent targets of those who suffer a personal injury or whose property is damaged. Many studies have shown that real estate rental property owners are sued more than any other single type of business entity.

But you can take steps to reduce and control your risk. Consider the following suggestions as preventative actions to minimize the potential of being named in a lawsuit:

- **Regularly inspect the property as part of a thorough maintenance program:** One of the easiest ways to minimize the potential of being named in a lawsuit is to routinely inspect your property and correct any noted deficiencies, such as health or safety problems. Make and retain copies of your inspections and document that all items were promptly and professionally addressed.
- **Listen to and address tenant complaints:** Don't just count on your own inspections, but be open and responsive to feedback from your tenants and others expressing concerns. Once again, a track record of a quick response to complaints is the best defense if you find yourself defending a claim or lawsuit alleging an injury or property damage due to your failure to properly maintain your investment property.
- **Transfer the risk to others:** The transfer of risk from the owner and property manager to the vendor or supplier is sound policy for managing and minimizing the risk. This can be done contractually by only using licensed and qualified contractors and suppliers who provide their own insurance coverage. Require that they provide written evidence that they have proper insurance coverage in place naming you individually and the legal entity that actually holds title to your investment property as an additional insured prior to performing work or providing materials.

  If you use a management company to handle the property management for you, then make sure that they have the proper internal controls in place requiring insurance declaration forms from all vendors and suppliers documenting $1 million minimum coverage limits prior to doing any work or even making deliveries to your property.
- **Remove certain risks or never allow them in the first place:** For example, many owners and managers of residential properties have removed diving boards and pool slides. Commercial property owners have restricted access to the roofs of their buildings with emergency door hardware.

Although you can minimize your risks by taking some of these steps, you can't eliminate all risks completely, and that's why you need proper insurance coverage. Insurance is an important element in a risk-management program.

Getting the Insurance You Need

As the owner of investment real estate, insurance coverage is one of your best protections and an essential risk management technique to ensure that you hold on to the wealth that you create.

If you've ever sat down with a sharp and assertive insurance agent, you may know that some insurance companies will sell you coverage against any possible danger or loss in the world. Experienced insurance agents seem to have mastered the art of describing all sorts of horrible problems that could befall your investment property. But you need to sift through the sales pitch, do further research, and decide which coverage is right for you — and make sure you're covered at a reasonable cost.

Your goal is to pay only for coverage for events and losses that could occur at your property. The right insurance coverage is worth a lot, but use resources wisely — hurricane insurance in Minnesota may not be your best bet.

You need to be concerned about lawsuits and having the proper insurance coverage to defend yourself and protect your assets. Insurance not only provides protection against actual losses, but is even more beneficial in that it provides a legal defense against the claims made against you as the owner of real estate. The expense of retaining competent legal counsel is what makes the threat of a lawsuit so devastating to many real estate investors.

Don't assume that all potential losses are covered by your insurance coverage. Your best defense against losses is to properly manage your rentals and assertively eliminate, transfer, or control the inherent risks of owning and managing rental property.

Understanding insurance options

The proper insurance coverage can protect you from losses caused by many dangers, including fire, storms, burglary, and vandalism. A comprehensive policy also includes *liability insurance,* covering injuries or losses suffered by others as the result of defective or dangerous conditions on the property. Liability insurance also covers the legal costs of defending personal injury lawsuits; a valuable feature because the legal defense costs of these cases are commonly much greater than the ultimate award of damages, if any.

Common coverages

The following list describes the three levels of coverage available for *primary policies,* all of which include liability coverage. Many insurance companies offer competitive insurance packages especially designed to meet the needs of rental property owners, so remember to shop around.

- **Basic coverage:** Most companies offer a basic coverage package that insures your investment rental property against loss from fire, lightning, explosion, windstorm or hail, smoke, aircraft or vehicles, riot or civil commotion, vandalism, sprinkler leakage, and even volcanic action.

This coverage often doesn't include certain contents, such as boilers, equipment, and machinery unless specifically added as an endorsement. Based on the type of property you have, you may need to consult with your insurance agent about additional coverage that may be beneficial.

But just because you own a small retail strip center with a couple of plate glass windows doesn't mean you need to have the special coverage that is offered. Insurance companies often have minimum policy premiums, so certain insurable items and acts aren't worth insuring as the potential for a claim is minimal and the costs are high.

- **Broad-form coverage:** You get the basic package, plus protection against losses of glass breakage, falling objects, weight of snow or ice, water damage associated with plumbing problems, and collapse from certain specific causes.
- **Special form:** This coverage is the broadest available and covers your property against all losses, except those specifically excluded from the policy. It offers the highest level of protection but is typically more expensive.

An insurance company can pay owners for losses in two ways:

- **Actual cash value:** The coverage pays the cost of replacing property less physical depreciation. The standard policies most insurance companies offer provide for actual cash value coverage only.
- **Replacement cost:** This coverage pays the cost of replacing the property without subtracting for physical depreciation. You must specifically have an endorsement and pay extra for replacement cost coverage. We encourage you to purchase replacement cost coverage.

As with homeowners' insurance policies, the location, age, type, and quality of construction of your property are significant factors in determining your insurance premiums. Be sure to get an insurance estimate before you buy your property to avoid unpleasant surprises (older properties with wood shake shingles located away from fire protection may not even be insurable, for example) and account for premium reductions (newer commercial buildings, and even some residential properties, were constructed with fire sprinklers and alarms that will reduce your insurance premiums, as will monitored intrusion alarms).

Some insurance companies have a *coinsurance clause* that requires rental property owners to carry a minimum amount of coverage. If you carry less than the minimum amount of coverage, the insurance company will impose a coinsurance penalty that reduces the payment on the loss by the same percentage of the insurance shortfall. For example, if you carry only $1 million in coverage when you should have $2 million, you're only carrying 50 percent of the minimum required insured value. If the building suffers a loss, the insurance company will only pay 50 percent of the loss.

Many rental property owners first become investors by renting out their former personal residences when they buy new homes. They may not realize they should immediately contact their insurance agent and have their homeowners policy converted to a landlord's policy, which contains special coverage riders that aren't in the typical homeowner's policy. Because of the increased liability risk for rental properties, some insurance companies may not even offer this coverage whereas others specialize in this business. Either way, obtain proper landlord's coverage for your rental property, or you could face the possibility of having your claim denied.

If you own multiple investment or rental properties, you may benefit on the insurance front if

- **You have a single insurance policy that covers all locations:** Rather than have separate policies for each rental property, you will also be able to get better coverage. For example, if you currently have three properties each with a $1 million policy, you could get a single policy with a $3 million limit at a more competitive cost.
- **You have an aggregate deductible:** An aggregate deductible is the portion of your loss that you essentially self-insure, because the losses at any of your three properties could be used toward meeting the aggregate deductible.

Excess liability (umbrella) coverage

Excess liability (umbrella) coverage can be a cost-effective way to dramatically increase your liability protection and is designed to supplement your main or basic policies. An umbrella policy provides both additional and broader coverage beyond the limits of the basic commercial general liability insurance and other liability coverage and this coverage is only available after the primary policy limits have been exhausted.

Your primary policy may have liability limits of $500,000 or $1 million, but an umbrella policy can provide an additional $1 million in vital coverage at a cost of $2,000 to $4,000 per year. Depending on the value of your property and the value of the assets you're seeking to protect, buying an umbrella liability policy with higher limits may make sense. Umbrella policies are available in increments of $1 million with even lower rates per dollar of coverage as the limits go higher. The most common umbrella coverage amount for the owners of large investment properties now is $5 million at an annual cost of approximately $7,500 to $12,000.

Purchase your umbrella policy from the same company that handles your underlying primary liability insurance package. The reason: If you have two different insurers instead of just one, the companies may have different agendas if legal problems arise.

Additional insurance options

A variety of other insurance coverages also make sense for most rental property owners:

- **Loss-of-rents coverage** provides income if your property is severely damaged by fire or another calamity and allows you to continue making your mortgage and other payments.
- **Workers' compensation** insurance pays employees and covers their medical expenses if they're injured or become ill as a result of their job. There are workers' compensation laws in all states; be sure to fully comply with them. This insurance coverage is often available through a government agency, whereas private insurance companies also offer coverage in other areas.

  Although some states may not require you to carry this coverage unless you have a minimum number of employees, we advise carrying workers' compensation coverage even if you don't have *any* employees. For example, any contractor you hire to perform work on your rental property should have his own workers' compensation insurance policy to cover all of his employees. However, if someone gets hurt and the contractor has limited or even no coverage, his injured employee may target you for compensation. Don't take chances; this coverage can often be added to your standard insurance policy for little cost.
- **Non-owned auto liability coverage** protects you from liability for accidents and injuries caused by your employees while working and using their own vehicle. Also, require them to provide proof of a valid driver's license (with a clean driving record) and proof that they currently have their own auto and liability coverage.
- **Fidelity bonds** provide reimbursement if you have a dishonest employee who steals your rents.
- **Endorsement for money and securities** covers losses caused by dishonest acts of nonemployees.
- **Building ordinance insurance** covers the costs of demolition and cleanup, plus the increased costs to rebuild if your rental property is partially or fully destroyed and the property needs to meet new or stricter building code requirements. This coverage is extremely important if your property is built at a *higher density* (more units or square footage) than current zoning allows and will compensate you for the lost property value if you can't rebuild the same size building.

- **Flood, hurricane, and earthquake insurance** are examples of coverage available for a separate cost. This coverage can be critical in the event of a natural disaster. However, these policies often are expensive with extremely high deductibles, making them unattractive for the average small rental property owner. Get quotes nonetheless, and see whether it's something you think you can afford.

Mold: The heir-apparent to asbestos

One coverage that is becoming much more difficult to obtain is a type of *environmental* insurance that specifically covers mold, fungus, and related issues. The number and magnitude of mold claims by tenants of both residential and commercial type properties have become a real challenge to the insurance industry with some highly publicized lawsuits claiming huge property damage and severe personal injury claims. Although certain insurance companies still offer limited coverage for mold and related causes, specifically inquire as to the exact protection included in your policy. Some policies don't cover actual damages for property and personal injury but they will offer a legal defense.

The best way to avoid claims of property damage and personal injury from mold is to properly maintain your property and only turn over possession to the rental unit or suite in good condition that is documented in writing. The challenge with most mold claims is that water intrusion and the subsequent concerns about mold typically occur within the tenant's space in areas where the owner has no access or control. Or the tenant can even be the cause of the source of moisture through negligence or inadequate cleaning.

Thus, the rental property owner must rely on the tenant to minimize the likelihood of mold as well as report any concerns immediately. A lease addendum is now beginning to be used by many owners advising tenants of their responsibilities in this area. Rental property owners should respond to all tenant concerns promptly and professionally while routinely inspecting accessible areas.

Determining the right deductible

The *deductible* is the amount of money that you must pay out-of-pocket before your insurance coverage kicks in and is a form of *self-insurance* (covering the potential loss yourself). Typically, deductibles for small rental property owners range from $500 to $1,000 while larger real estate portfolios will have much higher deductibles of $5,000 to $10,000. The higher the deductible, the lower your insurance premium. As your financial ability to self-insure grows, evaluate the possibility of having a higher deductible and using your savings to purchase other important coverage.

Selecting potential insurers

The coverage you can get as a rental property owner varies among insurers, with some firms specializing in real estate. Be sure to interview and select a qualified insurance broker or agent who understands your unique needs. The insurance professional can then provide you with information on the kinds of coverage worth considering. Insurance professionals are either independent brokers or exclusive agents that just write policies for one company.

As with any competitive product or service, speak with multiple independent insurance brokers and a couple of exclusive company agents to ensure that you receive the insurance coverage you need at the best value. Keep in mind that the lowest premium is often not the best policy or value for your specific needs.

In addition to the price of a policy and the insurer's reputation and track record for paying claims, an insurer's financial health is an important consideration when you choose a company. Insurers can go belly up. Major rating agencies that research and evaluate the financial health of insurance companies include A. M. Best, Moody's, Standard & Poor's, Duff & Phelps, and Weiss. The rating agencies use a letter-grade system and each company uses a different scale. Some companies use AAA as their highest rating, and then AA, A, BBB, BB, and so on. Others use A, A–, B+, B, B–, and so on.

Just as it is a good idea to get more than one medical opinion, two or three financial ratings can give you a better sense of the safety of an insurance company. Stick with companies that are in the top two — or, at worst, three — levels on the different rating scales. You can obtain current rating information about insurance companies by asking your agent for a listing of the current ratings.

After you've made your decision of which policies and insurers you wish to do business with, be sure that the premium is paid and insist on evidence that the insurance company has provided coverage. Typically, you'll receive a written binder as soon as you have coverage, however, your best proof of coverage is a formal certificate of insurance. The certificate of insurance is essential — prudent real estate owners never rely on verbal representations that they're covered.

Talking with tenants about renter's insurance

Renter's insurance is secured by and paid for by your tenants and covers losses to the tenant's personal or business property as a result of fire, theft, water damage, or other loss. As a rental property owner, you benefit from renter's insurance because it covers any claims in the event that the tenant starts a fire or flood. The tenant's premiums go up instead of yours.

Most commercial tenants have this coverage but residential tenants often think they don't need renter's insurance because they have few valuables. But renter's insurance covers much more than just their personal possessions, as protection against liability claims made by injured guests or visitors is also covered. The insurance also offers supplemental living expenses if the rental unit becomes uninhabitable due to fire or smoke damage. And it protects the tenant in the event that the tenant causes damage to another tenant's property. You can suggest that your tenants carry rental insurance, but because the majority of renters choose not to, you'd have trouble keeping your rentals occupied if you insisted that your tenants carry renter's insurance.

Dealing with claims

Record all the facts as soon as an incident occurs on your rental property, particularly if it involves injury. Because one of the primary issues in contention is the property condition at the time of the incident, a digital camera is extremely helpful to document facts and minimize extensive disagreements or discussions at a later date or during litigation. You can also use a recording device if you have obtained permission in advance from those involved (preferably in writing).

Be sure to immediately contact your insurance company or your insurance agent. Follow up with a written letter to ensure they were notified and have the information on file.

Put a reliable filing system in place to keep documents handy because litigation may not occur until years after the incident. For example, if a young child is hurt on your property, the statute of limitations doesn't begin until the child has reached 18 years of age. In these cases, the tenancy records and maintenance records could be subpoenaed and be critical to defending your actions of up to 20 years ago.

Chapter 15

Recordkeeping and Accounting

In This Chapter

- Putting your files in order
- Tracking the income and expenses for your rental activities

Recordkeeping and accounting may not be the most exciting aspects of real estate investment property ownership — but they're among the most rewarding. Every real estate owner should be interested in knowing how much money she's making on her properties and how much she's spending. She should also know how she could potentially reduce her taxes.

Traditionally, the least favored aspect of owning real estate is keeping all of the required paperwork and doing the accounting. More property managers have gained clients because of these essential, but tedious, requirements than any other. But recordkeeping has roles in maintaining your assets as well as documenting performance. And the accounting is the report card or feedback that will tell you just how well you are doing.

Now, we can't turn you into an accountant in the course of one chapter. Whole books are written on the subject! But what we can do is provide you with practical and useful information that you can use to organize your recordkeeping and accounting practices, and we can provide you with additional sources of information.

Organizing Your Records

If you have an aversion to details and keeping track of things, then managing your own investment rental properties may not be for you. If you own rental property, you need to prepare many important written records and keep them ready for prompt retrieval.

Maintaining property records

Maintaining complete and accurate records of all transactions is extremely important in the world of property management. Having your records squared away is necessary on three fronts:

- **Taxation:** You have to report your income and expenses for each rental property on IRS Form 1040 Schedule E to determine whether you have a taxable profit (or loss). The IRS requires rental property owners to substantiate all income and expenses by maintaining proper records, including detailed receipts of all transactions. Never get into a situation where you can't support the accuracy of your tax returns.
- **Financial management:** If you don't accurately document all the income streams coming in and the expense payments going out, you won't be a real estate investor for long. Check out the "Accounting for Your Rental Activities" section later in the chapter, for tips and information on this key aspect of your rental property.
- **Litigation:** Courts typically take the stance that residential tenants (and even small commercial tenants) are merely consumers, so the burden is primarily on the owner to provide any documents outlining the relationship or understanding between the parties. If the owner can't provide the required records, the tenant almost always prevails.

Here are a few documentation tips (check out the "Filing made easy" section, later in the chapter, for ideas on how to store this info):

- **Document your income on income journals:** Income journals are also called *cash receipt journals* and consist of the master rental income data collection sheet and ledgers for each individual rental unit or suite.
- **Keep all bank deposit slips:** Although your bank may require a deposit slip with your transaction, make a duplicate to keep for your records in case there's a discrepancy between your recordkeeping and the bank's records.
- **Get a written receipt for all expenses:** Rental property expenses, even if you write a business check, must have a written receipt to fully document the expenditure. The IRS may not accept a check as proof of a deductible property expense unless you have a detailed receipt as well.

  If you have multiple rental properties, develop and assign a one- or two-character code for each property and mark each receipt accordingly. (Indicate the unit or suite number, if appropriate.) When you have information for multiple properties on a single receipt, make photocopies and store the receipts in the folders you've set up for your respective properties. This way, you can provide evidence of the expense for each property instead of having to wade through all your folders looking for the information you need.

If you use your vehicle for your rental property activities, be sure to keep a detailed written log of all your mileage. Your mileage is a deductible business expense as long as it's directly related to your rental property and you have accurate records to document the mileage. This simple log should indicate the date, destination, purpose, and total number of miles traveled. You may be surprised at the number of miles you travel each year in your rental activities — the deductible expense can be substantial.

Here's a general guide of how long to retain your records:

- Keep all records pertaining to your rental property for a minimum of three to five years. (The time period depends on the legal requirements of the state regulatory commission or department of real estate where you live and/or own property.)
- For tax purposes, records regarding the purchase and capital improvements made during your ownership need to be maintained for as long as you own the property.
- Certain property records such as those concerning injuries to minors should be maintained essentially forever. Although even the IRS has a statute of limitations (except in the case of fraud), the statute of limitations for injuries to minors typically doesn't begin to run until the minor reaches the age of majority (usually 18).

Filing made easy

Every rental property owner should have a basic filing system with separate records kept for each rental property. Your filing system can be a simple accordion filing box with dividers, which you can find at any office supply store. If you own more properties and outgrow the accordion filing box, moving up to a lockable fireproof filing cabinet makes sense.

Organize your records at the property level and the unit level. You'll have some documentation overlap, but the benefit of having complete, easily retrievable records at your fingertips greatly outweighs the effort involved in making some photocopies. You may opt to keep many of the accounting records and files on your computer, but for owners of one to several rental units, a manual system works just fine. Start at the property level, and construct the following:

- **Ownership file:** From the moment you take your first steps toward purchasing an investment property, begin storing your paperwork in a property ownership file. Keep all the important documents of this transaction, including purchase offers and contracts, the closing statement, appraisals, loan documents, insurance policies, due diligence inspection and pest control reports, and correspondence. Also keep a photocopy of your deed in the property file, and place the original in a fireproof safe or bank safety-deposit box.

- **Income and expense files:** Each of your rental properties should have its own file section with separate folders for income reports like rent rolls, as well as a separate folder for each of the major property expense categories. Keep copies of all receipts in the expense folders, so that when tax time rolls around, you can easily locate the information you need.
- **Master maintenance file:** We recommend keeping a master property maintenance file for the records and receipts for all maintenance and capital improvements for the common areas. This one-stop source will give you the records you need for all repairs and maintenance during your ownership and can be helpful for your accountant in calculating your basis in the property when you ultimately sell or exchange the property.

Moving on to the unit level, put these files together:

- **Tenant file:** Create a separate file for each tenant that contains all the important documents for each tenant, including her rental application, lease agreement, the tenant ledger showing all charges and payments, all legal notices, tenant maintenance requests, and correspondence. Always keep the original of each document and provide the tenant with a photocopy. You'll need the signed originals of all pertinent documents should legal action ever become necessary. This tenant file is closed out and a new tenant file established upon turnover.

  When your tenants vacate, attach a copy of any paperwork from the termination of their tenancy and bind the entire tenant file together. Transfer it to a separate file for all former tenants, filed alphabetically by rental property.

- **Unit maintenance file:** We recommend keeping a separate maintenance file for each individual rental unit or suite with the records and receipts for all maintenance and capital improvements. This gives you a history of the physical condition of each rental unit or suite throughout your ownership. This file remains open even when the tenants change.

Use a system for recording all significant tenant complaints and maintenance requests. This will provide a valuable paper trail if a dispute ever arises regarding your conduct as an owner in properly maintaining the premises. Failing to have good records could well hurt your case should a dispute escalate and end up in court.

Accounting for Your Rental Activities

The financial management aspects of accounting for all the funds you receive and expend are critical elements of running your real estate rental property activities. After all, the ownership and management of even a single rental property is a business, and the government expects you to have proper financial records in order to prepare your tax returns.

But proper financial management isn't just for the benefit of the government. With accurate and timely information, you can manage your rental investment more efficiently and effectively. And when you decide to sell or exchange your rental property, your property will often generate a higher price if you have complete and accurate records, because buyers feel more comfortable knowing exactly what they're purchasing.

New technology in banking is particularly helpful to the rental housing industry and is simplifying and expediting the rental collection and reporting procedures.

- Some rental property owners now offer their residential and especially their commercial tenants the ability to make rent and other payments via credit card, automatic draft (automated clearing house, or ACH), or increasingly by electronic fund transfers to the property owner's account on a predetermined date.
- Even the traditional payment by check is enhanced with the advent of electronic check truncation where check readers or data entry software at larger residential properties can capture the salient information from the tenant's check and immediately debit their account. This electronic processing shortens the collection time and eliminates checks or money orders being returned for nonpayment.
- Online banking can also provide rental property owners the ability to make their own payments to vendors and suppliers electronically. Additionally, online banking provides access to records that immediately reflect all receipts (deposits or credits) and disbursements (payments or debits) and minimizes the chance of fraud by employees handling cash by making the tracking of daily activity easier.

Documenting income and expenses

If your tenants pay by check, you can always let the cancelled check serve as the tenant's receipt, but the best policy is to provide a receipt whenever possible, regardless of the method of payment. Likewise, track your expenses using checks or credit accounts rather than making cash purchases for which you receive generic receipts, because the legitimacy of generic receipts can be challenged.

Keep your rental property activities separate from your personal transactions. Although the IRS doesn't require you to keep a separate checking account for each rental property that you own, you need to be able to track the income and expenses for each property individually.

As you add rental units or commercial properties, the accounting becomes much more complex and the recordkeeping more critical. That's when you must seriously consider hiring a property manager with good recordkeeping and accounting procedures, who will create detailed monthly reporting that can be given to your accountant for tax planning and reporting.

Hiring a good tax advisor is a wise investment for even small rental property owners because tax rules are various and complex. For example, certain expenses can be classified as operating expenses and deducted in the current year to reduce your taxable income, but some expenses are considered capital items and must be depreciated or amortized over the estimated useful life of the improvement.

- One of the advantages to owning real estate is that you can deduct all operating expenses from your rental income. These operating expenses include payroll, maintenance and repair costs, management fees, utilities, advertising costs, insurance, property taxes, and interest paid on mortgage debt. You also benefit from *depreciation,* which is a noncash deduction that reduces your taxable income in the current year but is recaptured in the future. Depreciation is discussed in more detail in Chapter 16.
- Capital items typically include your building equipment or components that extend the useful life of the building and have a longer life span or are brand new, rather than routine maintenance or a repair. Your accountant is usually instrumental in providing guidance as to which items can be expensed versus the items that must be capitalized.

  Rental property expenditures for capital items must be accounted for separately and are capitalized when their cost basis is depreciated or amortized over multiple years rather than deducted as an operating expense in the current year. This means that you aren't able to reduce your taxable income by the full cost incurred but by a prorated amount over several years. Your accountant will generate depreciation or cost recovery schedules indicating the amount that can be deducted each year. Also, your accountant can keep you informed about changes in the federal tax code that affect depreciation deductions of certain capital expense items.
- Some costs of financing, such as loan fees or points paid at the time of the loan, can't be taken as an operating expense and must be amortized or taken incrementally over the life of the loan. However, if you refinance or sell the property and pay off the loan, then you can take a full deduction of remaining unamortized loan fees in that tax year.

Be sure you accurately record the payment of a tenant's security deposit. These funds aren't typically considered income; instead, they're considered a future liability that is owed back to the tenant if the tenant honors the terms of the rental agreement. The security deposit may become income at a later date if you apply any portion of it to cover delinquent rent, cleaning, repairs, or other charges.

Creating a budget and managing your cash flow

Every rental property should have a *budget,* which is simply a detailed estimate of the future income and expenses of a property for a certain time period, usually one year. A budget allows you to anticipate and track the expected income and expenses for your rental property.

Many rental owners neglect to allocate and hold back enough money for projected expenses, so when it comes time to make a repair, for example, they don't have the money set aside to cover it. If you set up a budget, you're better able to anticipate your expenses.

Although the budget for a single-family or rental condo is fairly simple, a proper budget for a newly acquired multi-unit apartment or commercial building can require some careful planning. That planning will include a thorough review of past expenses and the current condition of the property. Trends in expenses, such as utilities, can also be important when estimating the future cash flow of a rental property, so be sure you don't overlook them. Check out the income and expense categories we cover in Chapter 10 — the process is essentially the same whether you're formulating a prepurchase income/expense pro forma or the annual budget for ongoing operation of the property.

Many owners rely on cash flow from their rental properties not only to cover their expenses but also to supplement their personal income. But particularly if you're a small rental property owner, you need to have a built-in reserve fund set aside before you start taking out any rental income funds for personal reasons. Maintain a reserve balance large enough to pay your mortgage and all the basic property expenses for at least one month without relying on any rental income. Also, remember to allocate funds to cover semiannual and annual expenses such as your property taxes and potential income tax due on your rental property net income.

Set up a bank account where you set aside money for anticipated major capital improvements. For example, you may own a rental property that will need a new roof in the next five years. Rather than see your cash flow wiped out for several months when it comes time to pay for that new roof, you can begin setting aside small amounts of money into a capital reserve account over several years. Lenders on large residential and commercial type properties often require the monthly funding of a capital item reserve and replacement account. For large apartment projects, this expense can be from $150 to $250 per unit per year. The owner can periodically submit requests (with copies of paid invoices) for reimbursement of qualified expenditures such as appliances, floor coverings, and other capital items.

Doing your accounting manually

Most rental property owners begin their real estate investing with a single rental home or condo. At this level, the accounting is extremely simple and can be done manually with pencil and paper in a simple spiral notebook or using an accountant's columnar pad. But when you expand to multiple rental units or commercial properties, you need to look for better and more efficient systems that are geared to the specific needs of rental property accounting.

The classic manual accounting system for rental properties is a peg board set up for a one-write system (each transaction is entered once using stacked carbon documents). A single entry records information needed for a consecutively numbered rental receipt, the tenant's individual ledger card, a bank deposit ticket, and the daily cash receipt journal that provides a master record of all transactions. This popular rental accounting system is available from Peachtree Business Products (800-241-4623 or `www.property.pbp1.com`).

Using software

When you own several properties, consider using a computer with a spreadsheet or general accounting software program. Many basic software spreadsheet programs (such as Microsoft Excel) can handle a few rental properties. Somewhat better are the general business accounting packages, such as the entry-level Quicken, and the more advanced QuickBooks or Peachtree Accounting. These programs can handle and streamline all the basic accounting requirements of managing a handful of rental properties.

However, as good as these programs are, they lack the specific rental property features and reporting that are invaluable to effective property management. If you have more than five rental properties, we strongly recommend purchasing a professional rental accounting software program. These programs typically offer the following:

- Complete accounting (general ledger, accounts receivable, accounts payable with check writing, budgeting, and financial reporting)
- Tenant and lease management, including many standard rental management forms
- Tenant service requests, maintenance scheduling, and reminder notes
- Additional services such as tenant screening, payroll, and utility billing

Another advantage to using the computerized rental property accounting software packages is the ability to have your mortgage and other bills deducted electronically. Or you can work with these software packages to pay your bills online. If your tenants pay their rent electronically as well, you can decrease the time you spend handling rent collection and accounting.

Two programs that we recommend are

- **TenantPro for Windows:** If you have a small residential and commercial property portfolio, we recommend TenantPro, a rental accounting software package from Property Automation Software Corporation based in Richardson, Texas (www.tenantpro.com). This is an excellent accounting package for rental owners who want to have the benefits of efficient accounting and recordkeeping. You can combine the rental property accounting software with optional modules for tenant screening, electronic payment processing, payroll, and maintenance requests as well. Another great feature available is their module for common area maintenance (CAM) allocation (including utility metering and billing) that simplifies charging tenants for their individual charges based on square footage or other common predetermined reimbursement methods.
- **Yardi:** Robert recommends Yardi Voyager (www.yardi.com) for rental property owners or property management companies with significant portfolios of commercial and residential properties. Although Yardi offers software packages for all levels, the Voyager software (which Robert's company uses) actually stores property records on the software company's remote central server and permits the owner and your property manager access to real-time information via the Internet from anywhere in the world. These software solutions have all the basics features of prospect and tenant management, fully integrated accounts receivable and accounts payable, general ledger, and cash management, but they allow ready access to information, elimination of duplicate entries, and spontaneous delivery of reporting. They also offer electronic payments, maintenance, and other modules. Currently used by owners and managers of medium and large real estate holdings, the pricing is becoming reasonable even for owners with small rental property portfolios, so keep an eye out for them in the future.

When you use a management company, you'll typically receive several important accounting reports within a couple of weeks after the end of each accounting month. If you review these reports regularly, they can provide you with a good understanding of your rental investments and give you the opportunity to inquire about or suggest changes in the operations. But if you manage your own property and do your own accounting, it's important to actually review and analyze the financial reports in the same manner as you would if you had entrusted your investment to a property manager. You may think that you know everything you need to know about your rental property, and setting aside those monthly reports until tax time may seem harmless, but they're great tools for improving your management results if you use them properly.

You can customize the financial reporting offered by software programs to meet your needs. Monthly reports often contain income and expense information compared to the monthly budget as well as year-to-date numbers.

Chapter 16

Tax Considerations and Exit Strategies

In This Chapter

- Mastering the tax advantages of real estate investing
- Looking into exiting

Real estate is a great investment that offers you the opportunity to leverage a small cash investment to own and control large holdings that generate cash flow and can appreciate significantly over time. But cash flow, leverage, and appreciation aren't the only advantages of real estate. Utilizing current real estate tax laws has always been a key benefit for real estate investors.

Applying tax strategies properly allows rental real estate investors the ability to shelter income and even to eliminate — or at least defer — capital gains. Success in real estate, like all investments, is generally determined by how much money you keep on an *after*-tax basis. Real estate offers the potential to minimize taxation, so real estate investors need a thorough understanding of the best techniques to optimize their financial positions.

We discuss tax advantages in this chapter, but don't let tax considerations drive your decisions. Purchasing real estate should always be an economic decision. Only after a deal makes economic sense (both at time of purchase and after sale), should you consider the tax aspects. Also, real estate taxation is a constantly changing, complicated area. Although this chapter covers the key concepts, it isn't a substitute for professional tax advice. Every real estate investor needs a competent accountant or tax advisor (who specializes in real estate) on her investment team. Meet with your tax advisors regularly throughout the year, rather than only before the tax filing due date.

Because the subject is so entwined in tax considerations, we also cover real estate sales — also known as exit strategies. The tax implications of various exit strategies are important to understand so that the real estate investor can minimize the tax consequences of selling real estate holdings.

Understanding the Tax Angles

The tax laws regarding investment real estate are unique and far more complex than those regarding homeownership. For example, a homeowner can't deduct his costs of operating and the repairs and maintenance of his home — but as the owner of a rental property, you can deduct such costs. Also, the benefits of depreciation apply only to rental real estate and aren't available for property held as a personal residence.

Tax laws change frequently, so check with your tax advisor before taking any action. Use a certified public accountant (CPA), an enrolled agent (EA), or a tax specialist to prepare your tax returns if you have investment real estate. In the sections that follow, we discuss some important rental real estate tax concepts that you should understand if you want to make the most of your property investments.

Sheltering income with depreciation

Cost recovery (formerly called *depreciation* in the tax code) is an accounting concept that allows you to claim a deduction for a certain portion of the value of a rental property because the building "wears out" over time.

Depreciation is an "expense," but it doesn't actually take cash money out of your bank account. Instead, you treat the depreciation amount as an expense or deduction when tallying your income, which decreases your taxable income, allowing you to shelter positive cash flow from taxation. Depreciation lowers your income taxes in the current year by essentially providing a government interest-free loan until the property is sold.

The use of depreciation by real estate investors can be used to defer, but not permanently eliminate, income taxes. The annual deduction for depreciation is a reduction in the *basis* (calculated as your original cost in the property plus capital improvements) of the rental property, which is *recaptured* (added to your taxable profit) in full and taxed upon disposition or sale. Currently, all deductions taken for cost recovery are recaptured and taxed at a rate not to exceed 25 percent when you get rid of the property.

Depreciation is only allowed for the value of the buildings and other improvements because the underlying land isn't depreciable. The theory is that the buildings and other improvements ultimately wear out over time but the land will always be there. Because the amount of your depreciation deduction depends on the highest portion of the overall property value being attributable to the buildings, it's advantageous to allocate the highest fair market value of your rental property value to the improvements to increase your potential deduction for depreciation.

To determine the appropriate basis for calculating depreciation, many real estate investors have traditionally used the property tax assessor's allocation between the value of the buildings and land. But the IRS doesn't allow the assessor's allocation. They do accept an appraisal, which can be quite expensive unless you have a recent one available. But a more cost-effective method that the IRS accepts is the Comparative Market Analysis (CMA) that most brokers offer at a nominal charge or even for free.

Before 1993, depreciation could be accelerated in the early years of rental property ownership. This led to poor decision making on real estate deals that were motivated by the significant tax shelter offered by real estate, with only a secondary concern about return on investment or appreciation. See the "How depreciation and tax shelters have changed" sidebar in this chapter for more information.

But under current tax laws, recently acquired rental properties can only use straight-line depreciation. *Straight-line depreciation* reduces the value of the rental property by set equal amounts each year over its established depreciable life. The period of time during which depreciation is taken is called the *recovery period*. For properties placed in service or purchased on or after May 13, 1993, the IRS requires straight-line depreciation with the following recovery periods:

- **Residential rental property:** The recovery period is 27.5 years (or a cost recovery factor of 3.636 percent each year). A property qualifies as residential if the tenants stay a minimum of 30 days or more and no substantial services are provided, such as medical or health care.
- **Commercial properties:** The recovery period is 39 years (or an annual cost recovery of 2.564 percent). Mixed-use properties are classified as commercial unless the income from the residential portion is 80 percent or more of the gross rental income.

The cost recovery deductions for both the year of acquisition and the year of sale must use the *midmonth convention requirement* which means that regardless of the actual day of sale, the transaction is presumed to have been completed on the 15th of the month. Thus, the depreciation deduction is prorated based on the number of full months of ownership plus ½ month for the month of purchase or sale.

Commercial property owners typically modify vacant spaces to get potential tenants to sign a lease. The IRS requires that the cost of those improvements be depreciated over 39 years even though the lease and the actual useful life of the improvements are much shorter. This is a constant source of lobbying by commercial real estate interests seeking depreciation schedules that more closely coincide with the actual length of lease. The good news is that you can take a deduction in the current year for the full remaining undepreciated portion of the tenant improvements that was torn out as a result of one tenant vacating and new tenant improvements being installed for the next tenant. For example, if you replace carpet that hasn't been fully depreciated, you can deduct the remaining unamortized value in that tax year.

Minimizing income taxes

Taxpayers generally have two types of income:

- **Ordinary income:** This includes wages, bonuses and commissions, rents, and interest and is taxed at the federal level at various rates up to 35 percent. The taxable income you receive from your rental property is subject to taxation as ordinary income.
- **Capital gains:** These are generated when investments (such as real estate and stock) are sold for a profit. The income you realize upon the sale of your investment property is subject to taxation as a capital gain. Capital gains are classified as:
  - **Short-term:** For property held for 12 months or less, capital gains are taxed at the same rate as ordinary income.
  - **Long-term:** For property held for longer than 12 months, gains are taxed at lower rates than ordinary income with a current rate of 5 percent or 15 percent depending on your overall tax bracket.

But you can't pay taxes until you figure out exactly what part of your income will be taxed. To do that, you need to perform a cash-flow analysis. The cash flow from a property — positive or negative — is determined by deducting all operating expenses, debt service interest, capital improvement expenses, damages, theft, and depreciation from rental income.

Calculating the cash flow of a property follows the format shown in Table 16-1. We provide the details for most of these items in Chapter 10. Here, we provide a quick summary, and then factor in the taxman.

1. Start with the *Gross Potential Rental Income* (GPI) for the property, which is the hypothetical maximum rent collections if the property were 100 percent occupied at market rents and all rents were collected.
2. Add the other income affected by occupancy (laundry income at an apartment building would be one example). Then deduct the rent that isn't collected due to vacancy or the failure of tenants to pay to arrive at the *Effective Gross Income* (EGI).
3. Add the other income not affected by occupancy (for instance, the income from the rental of a cell tower on the roof) to the EGI to establish the *Gross Operating Income* (GOI).
4. Subtract the operating expenses from the GOI to calculate the *Net Operating Income* (NOI). (As we discuss in Chapter 10, the NOI is the essential number used in the income capitalization method of determining the value of the property.)

5. Subtract the capital improvements and interest paid on the debt service from the NOI to arrive at the before-tax cash flow.
6. Subtract the straight-line cost recovery (which is merely a noncash accounting deduction that reduces your tax liability without requiring an actual cash expenditure) from the before-tax cash flow. The result is the *taxable income.*
7. Multiply this year's taxable income or reportable loss by your ordinary marginal income rate to determine your tax liability or savings.
8. Deduct the tax liability (or savings, if the taxable income is negative and the loss can be used in the current tax year) and the annual debt service principal payments from the net taxable income and then add the non-cash deduction for the straight-line cost recovery. You now have the after-tax cash flow.

Table 16-1 Calculating After-Tax Cash Flow

Gross potential rental income	$100,000
Plus other income affected by vacancy	4,000
Minus vacancy and collection losses	(8,500)
Effective gross income	95,500
Plus other income not affected by vacancy	2,500
Plus CAM reimbursement (if any)	2,000
Gross operating income	100,000
Minus operating expenses	(40,000)
Net operating income	60,000
Minus capital improvements	(5,000)
Minus annual debt service interest	(35,000)
Before-tax cash flow without principal payments	20,000
Minus the straight-line cost recovery	(12,000)
Net taxable income	8,000
Minus tax liability (or savings)*	(1,950)
Minus annual debt service principal payments	(4,000)
Plus the cost recovery	12,000
After-tax cash flow	**14,050**

* Calculation of Tax Liability	
Net operating income	**$60,000**
Minus annual debt service interest	($35,000)
Minus the straight-line cost recovery	($12,000)
Net taxable income	**13,000**
Times investor's tax rate	15%
Tax liability	**$1,950**

Understanding passive and active activity

In 1986, Congress enacted passive income and loss provisions to eliminate the abuse of real estate tax shelters that were structured primarily to provide considerable tax benefits for investors.

Rental owners often start out with their real estate activities serving as second incomes. The majority of their income often comes from professions and sources totally unrelated to real estate. The taxation rules that apply to these part-time real estate investors are different than the ones that apply to real estate professionals. Unless you qualify as a real estate professional (discussed later in this chapter), the IRS classifies all real estate activities as *passive* and sets limits on your ability to claim real estate loss deductions.

A special IRS relief provision exclusively for rental real estate activities may permit a moderate-income real estate investor to offset other income with up to $25,000 in excess losses from rental real estate. The potential deduction is limited to a maximum of $25,000 per tax year for all real estate investment properties combined. Real estate investors can take a rental property loss deduction of up to $25,000 against other income in the current tax year as long as their adjusted gross income doesn't exceed $100,000. If the adjusted gross income exceeds $100,000, the real estate investor will be denied 50¢ of the loss allowance for every dollar over $100,000, so that the entire $25,000 loss allowance disappears at an adjusted gross income of $150,000. In order to be able to take this deduction, the following four requirements must be met:

- **The properties must qualify.** Certain types of properties don't qualify, including net leased properties and vacation homes in a rental pool.
- **The taxpayer must own a minimum of 10 percent of the property based on value.** Interestingly, the IRS allows a taxpayer to include the interests held by their spouse even if they don't file a joint return.
- **The taxpayer must actively participate in the management.** This doesn't mean the real estate investor can't utilize a management firm. A real estate

investor can meet the active participation requirement by simply communicating with his management company about the approval of new tenants, determining the rental terms, approving repairs or capital improvements, or making other similar decisions.

- **The taxpayer must file her tax return as an individual.** Corporations, certain trusts, and other forms of ownership aren't allowed to take this special deduction.

Any losses disallowed in one year are called *suspended losses* and can be saved and applied to reduce rental or other passive income in future years. If the suspended losses can't be used in this manner, the real estate investor will be able to use them when she sells the rental property to effectively reduce the taxable gain. Thus, the losses will ultimately benefit the investor, but the time value of money concept tells us that the ability to use the losses now is worth more than some time in the future.

Qualifying as a real estate professional

The IRS passive loss rule states that all real estate rental activities must be treated as passive income with only two possible exceptions:

- The maximum of up to a $25,000 deduction for some taxpayers as discussed in the "Understanding passive and active activity" section earlier in the chapter.
- The relatively small number of individuals that can meet the IRS requirements to be classified as real estate professionals.

Beginning in 1994, if a taxpayer meets the eligibility requirements relating to his real estate activities, the rental real estate activities in which he participates aren't subject to the $25,000 limitation. Real estate investors who can be classified as real estate professionals are permitted to deduct all of their rental real estate losses from their ordinary income, such as current employment income (wages, commissions), interest, short-term capital gains, and nonqualified dividends.

The IRS has defined a *real estate professional* as an individual who materially participates in rental real estate activities and meets *both* of the following requirements:

- More than 50 percent of her personal services or employment were performed in a real property business or rental real estate activities, including acquisition, operation, leasing, management, development, construction or reconstruction, and brokerage,
- These activities represented at least 750 hours per tax year. (Work hours as an employee don't qualify unless the taxpayer is at least a 5 percent owner of the employer.)

These individuals are considered *active investors* and are allowed to claim all their real estate loss deductions in the year incurred, to offset positive taxable income or offset gains at the time of sale. But the IRS considers each interest of the taxpayer in rental real estate to be a separate activity, unless you choose to treat all rental real estate interests as one activity. This is an important step. Consult with a tax advisor to determine if aggregating your rental real estate activities is advantageous and, if so, to make sure you properly make the required election when filing your tax return.

But qualifying as an active investor is complicated. The IRS now allows the taxpayer to qualify as a real estate professional by combining hours spent on rental and nonrental real estate activities. For example, even a part-time real estate broker or property manager may be able to demonstrate over 1,000 hours in a typical year in qualified real estate activities such as listing and selling, leasing and managing rentals, and renovation or construction. So meeting the 750 hours isn't a problem but the 50 percent test requires that the 1,000 real estate activity hours be more than 50 percent of all work hours in a year. This can be a problem if you have other extensive nonqualified work activities and a new calculation must be made each year. If you do qualify, carefully document your activities and the hours spent in each through appointment books, calendars or narrative summaries.

How depreciation and tax shelters have changed

Because depreciation is a noncash item and can be a significant deduction, real estate investors have often been able to report a loss for income tax purposes even though the actual cash income was equal or greater than the cash expenses. These losses could then be used to offset or lower taxable income from other sources. This was referred to as a *tax shelter.*

However, in 1986, Congress passed new tax regulations that eliminated most tax shelters for individuals and placed strict limits on a taxpayer's ability to apply deductions, credits, or losses from one business or investment to another unrelated business or investment. The boom in real estate syndications and limited partnerships in the early and mid-1980s had been primarily driven by the ability of high-income wage earners to take large real estate deductions against their wages and other income to significantly reduce their taxable income. The sudden change in the tax regulations dramatically impacted the economics of most rental real estate investments and the syndication and limited partnership market came to a screeching halt.

Before the tax law change, the real estate market had become so distorted that investors didn't even look at the actual cash flow or appreciation potential of a property but simply wanted to know what deductions they could generate. However, most real estate investors have learned to play by the new rules, and real estate retains some favorable tax treatment — cash flow and appreciation are once again important criteria in evaluating prospective real estate investment opportunities.

A potentially useful real estate investment strategy for married couples is to have the stay-at-home spouse become an active real estate agent or property manager and accumulate at least 50 percent of their employment or business time with a minimum of 750 hours per year selling and managing the family rentals. With the real estate professional qualification met, their rental activities are now "active" and they can deduct all of their rental real estate losses. However, lawyers can't get a break as the IRS has specifically ruled that real estate attorneys can't qualify.

Material participation, which requires the real estate investor to be involved "in a regular, continuous, and substantial manner," shouldn't be confused with active participation (which we define in the "Understanding passive and active activity" section, earlier in the chapter).

Exit Strategies

A successful investment strategy doesn't simply involve buying and operating properties. The *disposition* or *exit strategy* has a significant impact on overall success. What good is a real estate wealth-building plan if you put little or no thought into the end game? Begin your exit-strategy planning while you're acquiring property. That is, develop a game plan to work towards before you buy the asset. You can always change or modify your plans, but knowing your exit strategy prior to acquisition is good practice.

You do your homework, buy the right property at the right price, and add value by maintaining and improving the property and obtaining good tenants. So, why undo your good work by selling the property for less than it's worth or paying too much in taxes because you failed to explore ways to defer your capital gains (which can keep more of your money working to keep your portfolio growing)?

When you're looking to buy rental real estate with upside potential, seek those properties that have deferred maintenance and cosmetic problems that will allow you to buy them at a good price. When you go to sell your property, you want to get full value, so before you begin to list or show your available property, scrutinize the curb appeal and physical condition, looking for those items that need attention. Don't rely on your own eye; ask a trained professional real estate agent or property manager who isn't familiar with the property to give you some feedback. Recently, individuals and companies are popping up offering their services (called *staging*) to reduce the required marketing time and maximize the value of the property being sold.

We thoroughly cover the purchase agreement and other issues involved in a real estate transaction in Chapter 11. Because we firmly believe that the proper and ethical way to conduct business in real estate is to use standardized forms and practices, there's no need to present new forms or tactics that are slanted to favor your position as the seller. In the long run, you benefit by treating people fairly in your real estate transactions. If you build a reputation for being ethical, you receive many more opportunities than if you use one-sided methods designed to take advantage of others.

When it's time to sell the property, you have several options, but not all of them will have the same tax consequences.

Outright sale

One exit strategy is to simply sell the property and report the sale to the IRS. With the new lower capital gains tax rates, this strategy may work for taxpayers who are nearing the end of their prime real estate investing years and are looking to slow down and simplify their lives.

In an outright or all-cash sale, the seller simply sells the property, reports the sale to the IRS, and determines whether there is a taxable gain or loss. If there's a gain, then taxes are due, and if the property has been held for at least 12 months, the new lower capital gains tax rates of 5 percent or 15 percent apply. (Seller financing isn't considered an all-cash sale, nor is an installment sale, which we cover later.) Don't forget the 5, 15, or 25 percent tax rate on cost recovery deduction that'll be triggered on the sale.

Although an outright or all-cash sale is fairly straightforward, real estate investors are often interested in postponing the recognition of their gain on sale so that they can postpone the payment of taxes due. This is where an installment sale or an exchange (discussed later) can be useful.

Although the sale of a property can make sense, remember that refinancing an investment property with substantial equity is a great alternative way to free up additional cash for additional real estate acquisitions or other investments or purposes.

Calculating gain or loss on sale

As we indicate in Chapter 15, it's extremely important to prepare and retain accurate records from the initial purchase of your rental property and throughout the ownership because the sale of a real estate investment property must be reported to the IRS.

There are several factors that go into the required calculation to determine whether there's a gain or loss on the sale which can either increase or reduce the overall income:

- The sales price is a major factor.
- Any capital improvements made to the property should be included.
- Accumulated depreciation taken during the holding period increases your taxes when it's recaptured.
- Also, if the property had operating losses that couldn't be taken in prior tax years, then those suspended losses will be used to increase the adjusted basis and lower the potential taxable gain (or increase the loss available to shelter other income).

Table 16-2 outlines the following gain (or loss) on sale calculation.

Step 1: Determine the net sales proceeds.

The *net sales proceeds* are the gross sales price minus the selling expenses (see Table 16-2). The *selling expenses* are all costs incurred to consummate the sales transaction such as real estate commissions, attorney and accountant fees, settlement and escrow fees, title insurance, and other closing costs.

Table 16-2 Calculating Total Gain or Loss on Sale

Gross sales price	**$1,500,000**
Minus selling expenses	(50,000)
Net sales proceeds	**1,450,000**
Minus adjusted basis (see Table 16-3)	(700,000)
Total gain (or loss) on sale	**$750,000**

Step 2: Determine the adjusted basis for the property.

When the property is just acquired, the *basis* is simply the original cost of the property (the equity down payment plus the total debt incurred to finance the property plus closing costs, appraisal, and environmental reports). If the owner didn't purchase the property, the basis is:

- The fair market value at the time of transfer for property received as an inheritance
- The carryover basis if the property is received as a gift
- The substituted basis if the property was acquired in a tax-deferred exchange.

However, the basis isn't static and changes during the ownership period. To adjust the original basis, three factors are taken into account (see Table 16-3 for the sample calculations):

- **Capital improvements:** During the holding period, owners often make some capital improvements or additions to the property. *Capital improvements* are defined as money spent to improve the existing property or construct new property. The adjusted basis is increased by capital improvements. (The capital improvements are added to the original acquisition cost to determine the adjusted basis.)

  Routine and normal repairs required to keep the property in good working order over its useful life are deductible expenses during the tax year in which they're incurred. They're not capital improvements for the purpose of the adjusted basis calculation. For example, replacing a few shingles or even re-roofing a portion of the property is a repair, but completely replacing the roof is a capital improvement. A newly constructed addition that increases the rentable square footage of the rental property is a capital improvement. The capital improvement includes all costs incurred such as contractor payments, architect fees, building permits, construction materials, and labor costs.

- **Cost recovery:** At the same time, the straight-line depreciation taken each tax year is accumulated and reduces the adjusted basis of the property. Note that the total accumulated depreciation is included in the overall calculation of the gain or loss upon sale as part of the adjusted basis but will be reported separately and is taxed at a different rate on the taxpayer's tax return.

- **Casualty losses taken by the taxpayer:** Casualty losses can result from the destruction of, or damage to, your property from any sort of sudden, unexpected, or unusual event such as a flood, hurricane, tornado, fire, earthquake, or even volcanic eruption.

Table 16-3 Adjusted Basis Calculation

Original acquisition cost or basis	**$750,000**
Plus capital improvements	50,000
Minus accumulated cost recovery	(100,000)
Minus any casualty losses taken	0
Adjusted basis	**$700,000**

Step 3: Determine the total gain or loss on the sale.

The total gain or loss is determined by taking the net sales price and subtracting the adjusted basis (see Table 16-2).

Step 4: Adjust the total gain by factoring in accumulated cost recovery and suspended losses.

If you have suspended losses reported on the taxpayer's tax returns during the ownership period, deduct them from the net sales proceeds (see Table 16-4). The *suspended losses* are those losses that the taxpayer couldn't use in prior tax years because the taxpayer didn't meet the strict IRS requirements. See the "Understanding passive and active activity" section earlier in the chapter, for more info. That figure is the *capital gain from appreciation.*

Table 16-4 Capital Gain from Appreciation

Total gain on sale (from Table 16-2)	**$750,000**
Minus straight-line cost recovery	(100,000)
Minus suspended losses	(75,000)
Capital gain from appreciation	**$575,000**

Step 5: Determine total tax liability.

The net gain on sale is taxed as ordinary income unless the property was held for more than 12 months. Fortunately, most real estate investors hold the property over 12 months and can qualify for the lower long-term capital gains tax rates. In fact, if the property has been held less than 12 months, all cost recovery that has been taken will be recaptured as ordinary income.

For tax purposes, the net gain on sale must be allocated between the capital gain from appreciation and the recapture of the accumulated depreciation. The seller doesn't automatically get the benefits of the lower flat 15 percent maximum capital gains tax and may even have to pay the maximum depreciation recapture tax rate of 25 percent if they're in a higher income tax bracket as is the investor in our example. (The depreciation recapture rate is based on your ordinary income tax bracket but won't exceed 25 percent.)

In Table 16-4, the total gain on sale of $750,000, is reduced by $100,000 in accumulated depreciation and suspended losses of $75,000 for a gain from appreciation of $575,000. In Table 16-5, we break the taxation of the capital gain down between capital gain from appreciation and depreciation recapture. The accumulated depreciation is recaptured at 25 percent, resulting in a tax liability of $25,000. The gain from appreciation was taxed at the maximum capital gains flat rate of 15 percent, resulting in a tax liability of $86,250. So, the total tax liability is $111,250.

Table 16-5	Total Tax Liability Calculation
Straight-line cost recovery	$100,000
Times tax rate on recapture	25%
Total tax due for recapture	$25,000
Capital gain from appreciation	$575,000
Times tax rate on capital gain	15%
Total tax due on capital gain	$86,250
Total tax liability	**$111,250**

If the sale of the property results in a net loss, the loss must first be applied to offset net passive-activity income or gains. If there are none, or after they're exhausted, the net loss can be applied to reduce the income or gains from nonpassive activities such as earned income or wages.

Installment sale

An *installment sale* is the disposition of a property in which the seller receives any portion of the sale proceeds in a tax year following the tax year in which the property is sold. The time value of money tells us that it is generally better to have the use of money today than in the future. Knowledgeable real estate investors seek ways to minimize or defer the taxes that they need to pay. One way to accomplish this goal is using the *installment sale method* — within specified IRS limits, the sellers of real estate can report their receipt of funds as actually received over time rather than as a lump sum at the time of the sale.

A taxpayer who sells his property on the installment method is able to report only the pro rata portion of the proceeds actually received in that tax year. The advantage is that the taxable gain is spread over several years and can be reported in years in which the taxpayer may have a lower tax bracket. This is ideal for property sellers who don't need to take their equity at the time of sale because they have other sources of income or want to minimize taxes or both.

This includes transactions in which the seller provides the financing and will receive payments over time. When financing is difficult for buyers to obtain, sellers may offer to take a mortgage note from the buyer for some (or even all) of their equity in the property. As discussed in Chapter 3, having the seller take a note for equity is a common no-money-down strategy.

An installment sale can be an effective way for a seller to assist the buyer in making the purchase as well as to defer the recognition of income and thereby reduce the capital gains tax.

Here's how it works: A real estate investor sells a property for $1,500,000 that has an adjusted basis of $700,000. The buyer makes a down payment of $250,000, assumes the current loan balance of $500,000, and accepts seller financing of $750,000. The terms of the installment sale require the buyer to pay the principal balance of $750,000 owed to the seller at $250,000 each year over the following three years, plus interest. The buyer will report the gain according to the timing of the principal payments.

The amount of the gain that must be reported in a given tax year is equal to the total principal payment multiplied by the profit ratio. The profit ratio is calculated as:

Profit Ratio = Gross Profit/Contract Price

The *gross profit* is the sale price minus the selling costs and adjusted basis.

Sale price	$1,500,000
Minus costs	$50,000
Minus adjusted basis	$700,000
Gross profit	$750,000

The *contract price* is the sale price minus the current loan balance.

Sale price	$1,500,000
Minus loan balance	$500,000
Contract price	$1,000,000

Therefore, in this example, you figure the profit ratio as follows:

Profit Ratio = Gross Profit/Contract Price

Profit Ratio = $750,000/$1,000,000

Profit Ratio = 75%

With the profit ratio, you can compute the gain that must be reported each year.

Year of sale: $250,000 – 75% =	$187,500
Year two: $250,000 – 75% =	$187,500
Year three: $250,000 – 75% =	$187,500
Year four: $250,000 – 75% =	$187,500

Thus, the seller will report $187,500 as the gain in the year of sale, plus $187,500 for each of the next three years. The interest paid by the buyer to the seller on the deferred principal payments is reported by the seller as ordinary interest income.

If this were an all-cash sale, the seller would report the entire $750,000 gain in the year of sale, but the installment sale allows her to report the gain as the principal payments of $187,500 are received each year for four consecutive years. There's no difference in the total gain, simply the timing of the reporting of the gain.

Although there are many proponents of the buying-and-flipping real estate investment strategy, they often overlook the fact that flipping properties for a quick profit can have significant and expensive tax implications. If the IRS sees that you routinely buy and flip properties, they'll classify you as a *dealer* — a taxpayer who buys property (called *inventory* in this case) with the intention of selling it in the short run — as opposed to an *investor* — a person who purchases properties seeking appreciation and income from long-term ownership. It's possible for real estate investors to simultaneously hold some properties for long-term investment while the IRS could classify some properties as inventory where the owner is deemed to be a dealer. The dealer label comes with two drawbacks:

- Dealers aren't allowed to use the installment sales method to spread the recognition of their gain over multiple tax years. The entire profit must be reported and fully taxed in the year of the sale.
- Profit from the sale of a property is considered earned income and is taxed as ordinary income at your personal income tax rate — even if you hold the property for longer than 12 months. (If you hold a property for longer than 12 months, it's typically eligible for the long-term capital gains tax rate, and a dealer would thus lose this benefit.)

Using tax-deferred exchanges

The concept behind a *tax-deferred exchange* is that an investor can transfer the built-up equity in one property to a new property and maintain, essentially, the same investment except that the asset is different. In fact, the IRS actually considers a qualified tax-deferred exchange to be one continuous investment and thus no tax is due on the profit from the sale of the relinquished asset as long as the investor invests all proceeds into the replacement property.

Tax-deferred exchanges are often referred to as 1031 exchanges — the name comes from Section 1031 of the IRS Code that covers them. And there are actually three different types of 1031 tax-deferred exchanges:

- A straight exchange in which two parties trade properties of approximate or equal value.
- A three-party or multiparty exchange, which involves three or more parties buying, selling, or exchanging properties. This happens when one party in an exchange doesn't want a property owned by the other party but prefers the property currently owned by a third party. These transactions can actually involve any number of owners and can be quite complex. They should only be done with the ongoing advice and consultation of an experienced tax professional.
- A *delayed exchange* — sometimes also referred to as a *Starker exchange* — which allows the sale of the relinquished property and the purchase of the replacement property to occur at different times as long as strict rules are followed. This exchange is by far the most used 1031 exchange. (*Reverse Starker exchanges* can also be completed when an accommodator, on behalf of the taxpayer, acquires a replacement property first and then sells the relinquished property at a later date.)

The capital gains tax is deferred, not eliminated. If you sell your property during your lifetime and don't qualify for a tax-deferred exchange, then you'll pay tax on both the capital gain and the recapture of the total depreciation taken since the original investment.

Meeting your goals

A *tax-deferred exchange* is an important tool if you're looking to increase the size of your real estate holdings. Tax-deferred exchanges can be effective tools to postpone the recognition of a gain on real estate investments. They allow the investor to transfer equity to a larger property without paying taxes. Plus, there's no limit to how often or the total number of times that a taxpayer can use an exchange. Therefore, you can keep exchanging upward in value, adding to your assets over your lifetime without ever having to pay any capital gains tax.

The tax-deferred exchange is particularly useful for real estate investors who specialize in buying and renovating properties and would like to reinvest their profits into a larger property rather than sell the property and run the risk of being classified by the IRS as a dealer. A tax-deferred exchange can also help the investor achieve other goals such as:

- Trading for a property in a better location.
- Acquiring a property with better cash flow.
- Making better use of the significant equity that can exist in properties held for many years. Plus, those properties have typically exhausted their depreciable basis, and an exchange can enhance that.

Following the rules

As with any transaction that involves those three letters — IRS — you must play by the rules for the 1031 exchange:

- **The relinquished property and the replacement property must both be investment real estate properties located in the United States.** Actually, the majority of all tax-deferred exchanges involve properties domestically, but the IRS does allow a tax-deferred exchange of a foreign property for another foreign property. The key is both properties must be domestic or foreign and no mixing and matching is allowed!
- **The real estate investor must trade only *like kind* real estate.** *Like kind real estate* means property held for business, trade, or investment purposes. The broad definition of *like kind* doesn't mean *same kind.* It allows real estate investors to use a Section 1031 exchange, for example, to defer taxes when they sell an apartment building and buy raw land, or vice versa; or exchange a single-family rental home for a small office building; and so on. But neither your personal primary residence nor property held as inventory where the investor is defined as a dealer (see the "Installment sale" section, earlier) qualifies.
- **An exchange must be equal to or greater in both value and equity.** Plus any cash or debt relief received is considered to be boot (any receipt of money, property, or reduction in liability owed) and is taxable. For example, if you want to complete a tax-deferred exchange and the property you'll relinquish is valued at $1,000,000 with a loan balance of $500,000, then the replacement property must be purchased for more than $1,000,000 and the equity has to be equal to or greater than $500,000.
- **A neutral third party should be involved.** This neutral third party, called a *facilitator, exchanger,* or *accommodator,* should be appointed prior to the closing of any escrow; an exchange agreement must be signed; and the neutral third party must hold the proceeds unless the properties close simultaneously.
- **The potential replacement property must be clearly and unambiguously identified in writing within 45 days from the close of the relinquished property.** The IRS has limitations on how many replacement properties may be designated or taxpayers would simply identify a long list of potential replacement properties. There are three specific tests to meet this requirement which can get quite technical, but typically the most commonly used is the *three property rule.* Under this rule, the taxpayer can designate a maximum of three replacement properties of any fair market value and the taxpayer must purchase one or more of those properties.

- **The closing of the replacement property must occur within 180 days of the close of the relinquished property.** Meeting this requirement isn't as easy as it may sound, as we detail in the next section.

Counting (and countering) complications and risks

The 1031 tax-deferred exchange has some complications and risks. Our experience is that the identification of the replacement property within 45 days can be a real challenge, especially because only a limited number (usually three) of properties can be identified. In a tight or competitive real estate market, the real estate investor can quickly find himself unable to actually complete the purchase of the replacement property within the 180-day limit, in which case the sale becomes a taxable event.

Real estate owners looking for a replacement property (commonly called an *upleg*) are often tempted to chase a property and overpay. They rationalize that the capital gains deferral is so valuable that they can justify overpaying for the property because they'd otherwise have to pay taxes of the recognized gain. But such investors should realize that this isn't a tax-free exchange, only a deferral of a gain that may be taxable in the future.

In 2000, the IRS issued new guidelines that clarify the proper use of the *reverse Section 1031 exchange*. A reverse 1031 exchange can be complicated and should only be done with the guidance of an experienced tax advisor. Essentially, it allows real estate investors to have an accommodator purchase and hold their new investment properties while they then follow the 1031 guidelines to sell the relinquished property. The advantage is that the real estate investor is sure to have the replacement property in hand; one of the major challenges to a 1031 exchange is the risk involved in having to identify the replacement property within 45 days and complete the acquisition within the 180-day limitation. You should have a written exchange agreement, and title to the replacement property must be taken in the name of the accommodator until your relinquished property is sold.

Calculating the substituted basis

The calculation to compute the basis of the new property can be very complicated if anything other than the property is exchanged. In an exchange, the tax is deferred and the potential gain is carried forward by calculating the substitute basis for the new replacement property. An example of a substitute basis calculation without any boot is shown in Table 16-6. This substitute basis would be used in the event you sell the property during your lifetime without doing a tax-deferred exchange and have a taxable transaction. See your tax specialist to deal with any additional variables in the transaction.

Table 16-6	Substituted Basis Calculation in an Exchange
Value of property exchanged	$1,500,000
Minus basis of property exchanged	700,000
Gain on property exchanged	$800,000
Value of property acquired	$3,000,000
Minus gain on property exchanged	$800,000
Substituted basis on property acquired	**$2,200,000**

Using the capital gains exclusion

Another great tax benefit available for homeowners and real estate investors alike is the capital gains exclusion under Internal Revenue Code 121. Many investors have found that the principal residence capital gains exclusion can be the core of a profitable (and tax-free) investment strategy known as *serial home selling.* (For more information on this topic, see Chapter 2.) Simply buy and move into a property that can be renovated and sell it after a minimum of two years and you can earn a tax-free gain of up to $500,000.

Prior to 1997, the gain on the sale of a principal residence was taxable with two exceptions. The most commonly used was the Internal Revenue Code 1034 rollover statute that required the owner to buy a replacement home of equal or greater value. Seniors over 55 often used the Internal Revenue Code 121, which allowed a one-time capital gains exclusion of up to $125,000 on the sale of a principal residence.

Since legislation passed in 1997, the gain on the sale of a principal residence is tax free up to $250,000 for individual taxpayers and up to $500,000 for married taxpayers who file jointly if they meet some simple requirements:

- The seller must own and have occupied or used the home as his or her principal residence for a total of 730 days (24 months) in the last 60 months — ending on the date of sale or exchange. The occupancy doesn't have to be continuous and the home doesn't need to be the seller's principal residence at the time of the sale or exchange. Only one spouse needs to legally hold title, but both must meet the use test.

  The factors considered by the IRS to determine whether a property meets the principal residence use test include

  - Is the residence used as the address of record for driver's license, tax returns, utilities, credit card bills and other billed items, and the address of record for employment purposes?

  - Is this residence where you actually reside and where your furniture, furnishings, and clothes are kept?

- Generally, the seller can only use the exclusion once every two years. Vacations and short absences count as usage for the two-year use test.

In 2004, the IRS issued new guidelines that provide partial principal residence exemptions for sellers who don't qualify for the full exemption. The partial exemption is based on the number of actual months the seller qualified divided by 24 months. A partial exemption will be allowed for:

- **Work reasons:** For instance, a change in employment where the home seller's new job location is at least 50 miles farther away from the old principal residence than the former job location.
- **Health reasons:** For instance, the need to move to care for a family member or a broad range of health-related reasons. Consult with your tax advisor, because you can meet this requirement in many ways — particularly if recommended by a physician.
- **Unforeseen circumstances:** Examples run the gamut and include a divorce or legal separation, engagement break-up, death, incarceration, multiple births, large increase in assessment dues, lost job or demotion, becoming ineligible for unemployment compensation, and so on. Many circumstances could qualify as unforeseen circumstances, so see your tax advisor for more information about your specific situation.

The taxation of real estate is complicated and constantly changing, so we have just covered the tip of the proverbial iceberg here. If you want in-depth details and advanced real estate tax strategies, we strongly recommend Vernon Hoven's *The Real Estate Investor's Tax Guide* (Dearborn Financial Publishing). Vern has a master's degree in taxation. He teaches accounting and tax professionals all of the new laws at his popular seminars. This excellent book has over 300 pages dedicated to explaining all of the ins and outs of real estate taxation with many examples that bring the material down to an understandable level.

Looking at lease options

Investors can use the lease option to increase cash flow and also sell their properties without paying the usual brokerage commissions. A *lease option* is really a real estate rental transaction combined with the potential of a real estate sales transaction and financing technique. The seller can generate additional cash flow because a lease option generally consists of a monthly rental payment that's higher than the market rent, with a portion of the additional payment being applied to the option purchase price. And a savings can be realized on the brokerage commission because the transaction is usually completed without the full services of real estate brokers. But it's a good idea to have either an experienced broker or real estate attorney review the transaction documents, which will be a minor (but worthwhile) expense.

The typical lease option combines a standard lease with a separate contract giving the tenant a unilateral option to purchase the rental property during a limited period of time for a mutually agreed upon purchase price. The rental property owner has agreed to sell the property during a limited period of time; however, the tenant is not required to exercise the option. (For more on lease options, see Chapter 3.)

Working through an example

Each lease option is unique, but here's an example of how a deal may be structured: An investor owns a rental home with a current market rent of $1,000 per month and a current market value of $120,000. Real estate forecasts indicate that appreciation will be 4 percent, or approximately $5,000, in the next 12 months.

The tenant signs a 12-month standard lease and agrees to pay $1,200 per month with $1,000 in rent and $200 as a nonrefundable option fee that will be applied to the down payment. The owner and tenant also enter into an option-to-purchase agreement that offers the tenant the right to buy the property within 12 months of the lease for $125,000 (the agreed upon estimated fair market value of the property by the end of the option period).

The owner receives an additional cash flow of $200 per month. If the tenant exercises the option, the tenant receives a credit toward the down payment of $200 per month for each month that he paid the option fee. If the owner has used her standard lease form and the lease option documents are drafted properly, the owner will still have the right to evict the tenant for nonpayment of rent or any other material lease default.

In most cases, tenants won't exercise the purchase option because they won't have accumulated the money required for the down payment and their share of the closing costs. In the meantime, you'll have increased your monthly rental income by $200 and had a good tenant. At the end of the option, the tenant is aware that he has paid an additional $2,400 in rent that would've been applied to the down payment or purchase price if he'd exercised his option. You can either renegotiate an extension of the purchase option with the tenant or you can negotiate a new lease without the purchase option.

Proceeding with caution

Avoid long-term lease options. Real estate appreciation can be unpredictable. Don't provide a set option purchase price for any longer than one or two years, or include a clause that the purchase price will increase by an amount equal to the increase in the average median home price in your area.

If you're interested in using a lease option, have a real estate attorney with extensive experience in lease options review the lease and option contract in advance. Lease options can have serious business and even ethical problems if not properly drafted. If not structured properly, your lease option could be considered a sale with the following negative consequences:

- A lease option could trigger the due-on-sale clause with your lender, and they could force you to pay off the entire outstanding loan balance.
- If the property is deemed a sale by the IRS, you can no longer use your tax benefits of depreciation and deductible expenses.
- Your property could be reassessed for property taxes. In many parts of the country, reassessment is based on a change in ownership. An aggressive tax assessor could use the lease option to increase the assessed value. Investigate local reassessment policies in advance.
- You could be liable for failure to comply with seller disclosure laws. There are severe penalties if you don't make the legally required disclosures, including those found on the Transfer Disclosure Statement (TDS) as discussed in Chapter 12.
- You could be prevented from evicting the tenant even if they default on the lease. The courts may consider that the tenant is really a buyer and that a traditional eviction action doesn't apply because the lease option is essentially a contract to purchase real estate. This could require expensive and lengthy court proceedings.

Ethically, keep the nonrefundable option fee reasonable, so if the value of the property declines or your tenant doesn't exercise her option for any reason, you can feel comfortable that the tenant has been treated fairly. Or you may want to renegotiate or consider offering an extension.

Gifts and bequests

A property given as a gift carries the same tax basis from the seller to the new owner. For example, if the tax basis of the property is $100,000, even though the fair market value at the time of the gift is $500,000, the recipient's tax basis remains $100,000. If the recipient were to immediately sell the property, he would have a taxable gain of $400,000. Thus, gifting property to heirs during your lifetime may not be the best strategy.

But death provides a tax-free transfer of real estate. Some investors are determined to avoid paying tax completely and have adopted a strategy of buy and hold for life. They use the 1031 tax-deferred exchange for years to rollover their gains into larger and larger properties and then completely avoid paying tax by never selling. Real estate transferred to your heirs upon death receives a full step up in basis. So in the example above, the party inheriting the real estate with a fair market value of $500,000 now has a tax basis of $500,000 and will only owe taxes on any future gain. So, if you want to make your real estate wealth creation strategy span multiple generations, consider taking advantage of these tax benefits!

Part V
The Part of Tens

"Evidently, he made millions flipping real estate in Japan."

In this part . . .

This part contains chapters of ten-somethings that don't fit elsewhere in this book. Topics that we cover in this section include ten proven ways to enhance the value of a property and our top ten favorite real estate wealth-building strategies.

Chapter 17

More than Ten Ways to Increase a Property's Return

In This Chapter

- Increasing cash flow
- Encouraging equity build-up
- Taking advantage of tax benefits
- Appreciating appreciation

As we cover in Chapter 10, there are essentially four basic ways that you can receive a return on your real estate investments — cash flow, equity build-up from loan paydown, tax benefits, and property appreciation. A great aspect of real estate is that the investor can buy properties according to his particular financial and personal needs. Different properties are geared more toward achieving one of these types of return than another. For example, an investor with significant earned income may focus on properties with tax benefits and not worry as much about cash flow. Investors nearing retirement will prefer properties with cash flow. And all investors look forward to appreciation.

Successful real estate investors continually ask themselves: How can I improve the returns on my real estate investment in each category? In this chapter, we highlight more than ten of the best ways that you can enhance your return on investment with rental properties.

Raise Rents

Although most rental properties have other sources of income, the largest source is almost always the rents. So real estate investors wisely begin with an understanding that rent increases lead to greater cash flow.

However, setting the proper rent and maintaining the optimum market level rents on turnover is one of the most common challenges faced by property owners. Many rental property owners are reluctant to raise rents, because they're concerned that their good tenants will leave. This is a valid concern but shouldn't prevent you from getting rents to market level — one of the fastest and simplest ways to improve your cash flow. Of course, you should always look for cost effective ways to improve the property and make sure that your rents are competitive and a fair value.

We recommend raising the rental rate modestly each year rather than waiting for two or three years and then hitting your tenants with a major increase all at once. Tenants are less likely to move as they understand that the costs of operation are rising slightly each year.

If your rents are already at market levels, look to make upgrades to the property to justify higher rents. Maybe the addition of a combination microwave/exhaust vent unit above the stove or the addition of a deck or awning will be an improvement that justifies higher rent. Any improvements that enhance the quality of living or bring the property to a level similar to higher priced properties in the area can lead to increased market rents.

Reduce Turnover

The single most important factor in determining the expenses of most rental properties is turnover. In both residential and commercial properties, tenant turnover is simply bad for the bottom line. A tenant moving out almost certainly means a loss in rental income, plus you're hit with the increased expenses (maintenance and repairs and capital improvements) to make the rental unit or suite available to show a prospective tenant. Signing long-term leases with qualified tenants, continually maintaining the property in top condition, and being responsive to the tenants can help reduce tenant turnover, which directly improves the net operating income and cash flow.

Another effective tool to reduce the loss of rent during tenant turnover is to prelease the rental unit or tenant suite. If you can prelease the rental to a new tenant only a few days or weeks after the current tenant vacates, you'll dramatically reduce your lost rent and increase your cash flow. After you receive a tenant's notice to vacate, immediately seek permission to enter and determine what you'll need to do to make the property ready for the next tenant. Also begin advertising for a new tenant and gain the cooperation of the departing tenant to show the property.

Consider Lease Options

A *lease option* is an agreement that allows the tenant the right to purchase the leased property at a predetermined price for a certain period of time. Sellers typically use lease options in slow real estate markets to create additional interest in the property — even a potential buyer without a down payment has the opportunity to eventually become a homeowner.

There are many other benefits to the rental property owner willing to offer a lease with an option to purchase the property. The landlord/seller is often able to sell the property for a value above the current market, and the lease option usually requires a one-time option fee that the seller can keep if the buyer can't exercise the option. Also, the renter/buyer will typically pay a higher monthly rental payment with a lease option because a portion of the payment is applied to the ultimate purchase price. The higher monthly payments can be beneficial to the owner if the cash flows for the property are currently negative. Check out Chapter 3 for more on lease options.

Develop a Market Niche

For example, Robert has had success in Las Vegas (of all places!) with smoke-free apartments. After a long day at work in a smoke-filled environment, a health-conscious nonsmoking resident doesn't need to have smoke wafting into their rental unit from their neighbor. Although there are additional costs up front in thoroughly cleaning, completely repainting, and installing all new flooring and window coverings, the demand (and thus the occupancy) for these units is high. Rental properties catering to seniors have always been popular, and the demographics clearly support continued attention to this dynamically growing market niche.

According to a recent study by the National Multi Housing Council (NMHC), student housing is also a great opportunity with the "Echo Boomers" (those born between 1976 and 1994) coming of age and going to college in record numbers. Management of student housing can be difficult for the uninitiated, but with the majority of private (and much of the university) housing being 30+ years old, some real estate investors find the market ripe for renovating rental units for the upscale tastes and surprisingly affluent desires of college students. They'd rather have a private rental unit with their own bathroom facilities and a high-speed Internet connection than a traditional dorm.

Maintain and Renovate

The curb appeal or first impression that your property gives is critical to your overall success. Far and away the easiest way to increase cash flow and increase value is to simply clean up and address the deferred maintenance found in most properties. One of the fundamental rules of real estate is simple supply and demand. If your property really stands out and looks much better than comparable properties, then you generate high demand; your rental will stay full at top market rents. That's what cash flow is all about.

Besides the simple deferred maintenance, another great way to increase cash flow (and value) is to renovate the property. The key here is to spend money only on items that enhance the property and provide a quick payback.

For residential rentals, the best return on investment inside the units is found in updating the baths and kitchens. Access control for parking and building entry can also be a positive enhancement in urban areas, because crime is a concern for many tenants. For commercial properties, upgrading dated interior common areas with higher-quality materials and fixtures generally offers the greatest return.

One of the most cost-effective ways to increase the aesthetics and curb appeal of any type of property is through landscaping improvements. Often you can simply replace dead plantings. If you want to do more, have your landscaping maintenance firm make suggestions or contact a landscape architect. Be sure to look into the installation of an automated, water-conserving, drip irrigation system.

Cut Back Operating Expenses

One of the first steps to take after you purchase a rental property is to evaluate current operating expenses. You want to see whether there's room for improvement, particularly without negatively impacting your tenants.

Asking the local utility companies to perform an energy audit can pinpoint ways for you to reduce expenses. New technology is making the use of solar energy and hydronics systems extremely attractive. The rapidly increasing costs for water and sewer services in many areas of the country have made the installation of submeters cost effective for allocating and recouping the cost from each tenant based on her actual usage.

For larger residential and commercial properties, ask each of the current contractors and service providers to present a proposal or bid. Find other comparable firms and ultimately give your business to those firms that are insured and offer good value. As your real estate empire grows, you'll find that contractors and service providers offer discounts based on volume.

The dangers of cutting corners

Although carefully screening your expenses can have a significant positive impact on your cash flow, don't go overboard and cut expenses too much. Always use licensed professionals where required and secure proper building permits.

Also, be sure to routinely inspect and repair your rental properties or you risk having a tenant withhold rent or even commence litigation claiming a breach of the lease for failing to maintain the property. Many of the current mold lawsuits seek to hold the owners responsible on a theory that they didn't properly inspect and maintain the property — which lead to the propagation of mold.

Another great way to reduce your operating costs without any reduction in value is to combine your various rental properties under one insurance policy. Contact your insurance broker for details.

Scrutinize Property Tax Assessments

A review of the expenses for most rental properties will indicate that the property tax expense is often one of the largest costs in owning real estate. In many parts of the country, property taxes are tied to the value of the real estate. If that's true for your area and real estate values decline, contact your local assessor and inquire about getting a reassessment. A lower assessment will lead to a direct reduction in your property tax bill and a corresponding increase in your cash flow.

You may feel helpless against the bureaucracy, but remember that tax assessors have been known to make clerical errors or to fail to take all factors into account when valuing rental property. If you feel that your assessment is too high, contact your assessor. She may be willing to make an adjustment if you back up your opinion with careful research and a good presentation. Or you may need to make a formal property tax protest. Protests are often first heard within the assessor's office or a local board of appeal. If a dispute continues, appeals may be taken to court in many states.

Refinance and Build Equity Quicker

Although you may have little control over interest rates and will be at the mercy of your lender unless you have a fixed-rate loan, don't forget that refinancing to a lower rate can have a tremendous impact on your cash flow. Of course, going with an interest-only loan or a 40-year amortization can also reduce your debt service payment and increase your cash flow, but these options are extremely risky and not advised.

Equity is the silent wealth builder. Although cash flow and appreciation get much of the attention, equity buildup passively increases the investor's net worth. One of the basic principles of real estate investing is that your tenants are essentially paying your mortgage, and over the course of time you will eventually own your rental property free and clear. Just the equity buildup alone on several small rentals can provide a nice nest egg for retirement.

You can enhance your equity buildup through refinancing to a shorter-term loan. When you first purchase a rental property, your net operating income to service the debt is typically very tight and you need to use financing with 20-year or even 30-year amortization terms. But after you've owned the property for several years, you may find that the cash flow has improved to the point that the property can handle a higher mortgage payment. That is when you refinance your long-term mortgage to a shorter-term mortgage, so that the amount of principal reduction paid with each payment dramatically increases.

Another way to achieve similar results is to arrange to make additional payments designated as principal reduction. This can significantly reduce the total amount of interest paid over the remaining life of the loan and bring the loan payoff date much closer because the interest paid on the loan is a function of the outstanding principal balance.

Before refinancing or making additional principal payments, make sure that your loan doesn't have a prepayment penalty. Lenders count on a certain return on their money, and the early payoff of a loan results in additional costs, so they may include a penalty in the first few years of the loan.

Take Advantage of Tax Benefits

The tax benefits received from real estate vary from investor to investor, but most rental property owners find tax benefits to be a boost to their return.

Even novice real estate investors can take advantage of the generous tax savings with the capital gains exclusion for their principal residence. This exclusion allows sellers to completely eliminate any income tax on their capital gain of up to $500,000 if they meet the simple requirements outlined in Chapter 16. For investors willing to live in the property during renovation, the serial homeselling investment strategy can be used every couple of years to produce tax-free profits.

Real estate investors in large residential and commercial properties routinely use a simultaneous or tax deferred exchange, which allows them to keep their money working rather than paying taxes. The more money you have invested in real estate, the better your cash flow and your accumulation of wealth.

As covered in Chapter 16, depreciation or cost recovery allows the owner to take a noncash deduction that reduces the taxable income from the property. Land isn't depreciable, so the amount of depreciation is determined by the value of the buildings. One way to maximize real estate's potential tax shelter is to be aggressive in allocating as much of the acquisition cost of the property to the buildings to generate a larger deduction for depreciation.

Depreciation deductions are a noncash item, so they often result in a taxable loss even though the actual cash flow for the property is positive. Even if you can't immediately use a taxable loss to offset other earned income, you can use it in years that you have passive income such as a profitable taxable sale of another rental investment property.

Be Prepared to Move On

When most people think about real estate, they correctly determine that appreciation is where the real money is made. Over time, real estate has proven to be an investment that retains and increases in value. Even an average annual rate of appreciation of 5 percent dramatically increases your net worth over time.

However, appreciation can be heavily influenced by outside forces, such as the condition of the neighborhood and the local economy. That is why real estate investors need to perform a thorough due diligence review as discussed in Chapter 8. But even after you buy a property, you can't simply sit back and let the investment ride as the area deteriorates around you. If the neighborhood you're in starts to take a downward turn, be prepared to sell and reinvest in a more dynamic area that offers more upside potential.

Add Value Through Change in Use

The entrepreneurial spirit of real estate investors is also rewarded when they're able to increase the return from real estate by adding value through a change in use. A change in use is taking land that isn't currently being used optimally or, as appraisers phrase it, for its *highest and best use* and repositioning the property in a manner that will result in the highest value. There are several common ways to achieve this, including

- **Entitlements:** The process of gaining the necessary approvals to put land to a more productive use is an extremely powerful way to increase the value of real estate. In nearly every city or town in the country there are land uses, typically agricultural, that become less productive (or inadequate) as the area is developed. Taking the steps to get this land approved as residential or commercially zoned property can dramatically enhance property value.
- **Conversion of use:** The conversion of real estate to another use isn't a new idea, but real estate entrepreneurs have increasingly practiced the concept in recent years. There are many other examples of change in use: the redevelopment of apartment rentals to for-sale housing or the modification of old warehouses to residential lofts and offices.
- **Lot split:** Traditionally, this is the dividing of a larger parcel of raw land into several smaller parcels. The sum total received for the individual parcels will be much greater than the value of the original parcel. Another strategy is to develop or locate a residential rental property that can be split into multiple lots with each parcel containing one to four units, because apartments with four or fewer units receive more favorable financing. You can then offer these investment properties to individuals at a price significantly higher than what the entire property would go for.

- **Assemblage:** The other side of the lot split strategy is *assemblage* — the purchase of two or more smaller parcels with the intent to combine them into a larger parcel that can be more efficiently developed. This method of adding value to real estate can be quite lucrative, particularly in older built-out areas that are ripe for redevelopment. This often happens in areas (like beach communities) where there's high demand and increasing population. Real estate investors buy several individual contiguous lots and then sell the property to a developer who builds a small multifamily apartment building.

Improve Management

Management is the one aspect of owning real estate that offers owners an advantage over other types of investments. You can't call Bill Gates and tell him to change his company's product or pricing, but superior management of your own rental properties can have a direct impact on your results.

The ability to control and immediately implement different management strategies can lead to more satisfied tenants and longer-term tenancies. Some owners are very hands-on with their properties, while others prefer to let a professional handle the day-to-day challenges, but a savvy investor knows that the best returns on investment go to owners that have top management.

Chapter 18

Ten Steps to a Real Estate Fortune (Or a Great Second Income)

In This Chapter

- Traditional approaches to real estate investing
- The get-rich-right strategy of real estate investing
- Ten steps to a real estate fortune

Many real estate infomercial gurus and seminar kings make it sound really easy for anyone to make a fortune in real estate overnight. Buying foreclosures or properties with no money down can provide handsome returns, and there's no doubt that the acquisition of real estate below its intrinsic value will enhance your chances of financial success.

This is simply the traditional sage advice (buy low, sell high) applied to real estate. And if it can be done routinely and without problems with title, devastating physical problems, or the negative tax consequences of being declared a dealer by the IRS, then it can be quite fruitful.

However, finding well-located, physically sound properties that are available at below market prices isn't simple. Our experience is that most sellers know the value of their property and don't simply give away a great property. We often think that the old saying "You get what you pay for" was coined by a real estate investor who just bought a foreclosure only to find it has a large unrecorded tax lien or a cracked slab.

In our experience, successful real estate investors tend to be savvy, hard working, conscientious individuals who enthusiastically perform comprehensive due diligence before buying a property. They don't reinvent the wheel with each deal, because they know their market niche, personal skills, and available resources. They have a vision and use their tried-and-true game plan for each property. If you develop these talents, then you can uncover unique properties with value-added potential that are often missed by your competitors.

Robert refers to this method of real estate investing as the get-rich-right strategy. The best news of all for new real estate investors is that this plan can be undertaken anywhere and initially can be done part-time.

There are times when the local market conditions will be conducive to acquiring properties that are distressed and are available as foreclosures or on favorable terms with seller financing. These can be great buying opportunities that shouldn't be missed. Just be sure that you have thoroughly checked out the property, stay disciplined and don't overpay, and then implement your value-added and disposition plans.

Then there are times when you'll encounter available properties that seem fully valued and offer only incremental opportunities to quickly make physical improvements or enhance cash flow through superior management and a better tenant profile. But these properties are still great additions to your real estate portfolio and should be acquired when they have a strategic location or are located in the path of progress and are poised for long-term stable growth in rental rates. These are the cornerstones of your real estate empire — the keepers.

The ultimate goal of the get-rich-right method is to build a sustainable real estate portfolio through opportunistic buying. There are times when a buy-and-flip opportunity will arise and there are times when the best plan is a buy and hold.

You take your monthly cash flow and look to build that up to cover the down payment on your next property. Meanwhile, you seek opportunities to make a quick profit through a buy-and-flip property and then reinvest the proceeds through a tax-deferred exchange into another investment property. Then you use the equity built up over time in your long-term hold properties by refinancing to pull cash out to further your real estate investments.

General real estate cycles and the economic conditions in your local market area dictate which approach is appropriate at any given time. The key is to have a long-term plan to continually reinvest your proceeds back into the acquisition of more properties unless the market conditions are so unfavorable that all local properties are overvalued. Then you want to reinvest your proceeds into improvements of your current properties or seek real estate investments in other markets where the prices aren't unrealistic.

The ultimate goal of the get-rich-right strategy is to use the short-term, quick profit and the long-term, steady appreciation strategies to build your real estate holdings into a larger portfolio of real estate properties. Ultimately, you can consolidate your real estate holdings into a portfolio of quality properties and utilize the buy-and-hold-for-your-lifetime strategy to create a comfortable lifestyle.

We suggest that you begin investing in real estate with small residential properties for several reasons. For one, almost everyone has been a renter at some point and thus the responsibilities of a residential landlord are easy to understand. Also, the initial capital requirements are generally lower. After you've mastered residential real estate investing you'll want to seriously consider investing in large residential apartment buildings and commercial properties because they offer higher sustained returns.

The secrets to making money in real estate are really quite simple — buy right, add value, reinvest, and ultimately consolidate into larger properties. In this chapter, we give you ten methods to achieve a real estate fortune using the get-rich-right method.

Build up Savings and Clean up Credit

We disagree with some who imply that you can begin your real estate investment career without any cash. Our experience is that the best opportunities and the most options are available to the real estate investors who have both cash and good credit.

Even if you can find properties where the seller provides all the financing, you can't escape certain out-of-pocket expenses or the opportunity cost of lost income as you expend your time and energy tracking down properties and performing the due diligence. We have yet to find a top-notch real estate inspector or escrow company that works for free. Plus, sellers aren't likely to provide financing to a buyer with a poor credit history.

Because the purchase of real estate virtually always necessitates the borrowing of funds, make sure that your credit report is as accurate and as favorable as possible. Your credit score is a key element in not only qualifying for real estate loans, but also in getting the best terms to maximize your use of borrowed capital.

Get a copy of your credit report and correct any errors — today. Charges that were actually paid or a department store credit card account that shows late payments when the amounts are disputed can all contribute to a significant reduction in your credit score. At the very least, ask the credit bureau to place a letter in your file with your version of any disputes. If legitimate delinquent balances appear, formulate payment plans and send the credit reporting bureau updates showing the balance was paid.

Investing in real estate requires a long-term commitment and strategy and initially may require some sacrificing — especially when building a cash nest egg for the down payments and incidental costs of acquiring properties.

The new real estate investor should develop additional sources of income while holding or preferably even cutting current expenses. Most people generate wealth and achieve a higher standard of living through sacrifice and living below their means in the short-term. Maybe you can live with your current vehicle for a couple of years, or you can pass on the luxury apartment community with recreational facilities and amenities that you won't use anyway. For more ideas on how to track and reduce your expenses, pick up a copy of the latest edition of Eric's *Personal Finance For Dummies* (Wiley).

Sustained success in real estate requires you to have cash and good credit. So don't procrastinate — begin working on this step right now.

Buy Property in the Path of Progress

Locate properties that are in the *path of progress* — areas that will continue to improve through new investment and economic activity (see Chapter 8). You can't realistically move your property, so your analysis of the location and its future potential is critical. After you locate the best cities or neighborhoods, there are commonly two types of underachieving real estate assets for you to look for:

- Those income properties that are tired and worn and have extensive deferred maintenance
- Those that are physically sound but poorly managed

Your preference will depend on your specific talents and resources. Robert favors well-located, physically sound properties that simply have underperformed due to poor management. He's able to use his skills and expertise as a property manager to upgrade the properties, bring in new tenants, and increase the rents. So Robert is always looking to buy basically sound properties in good locations with upside potential due to poor management. Particularly attractive properties are those where the current owner or manager hasn't kept rents at the market level.

One of his partners is a builder of brand-new luxury apartments and condos in beach communities. He looks for physically distressed properties that are available for purchase at less than the land value where he can scrap the existing structures and redevelop the well-located property.

Buy the Right Property at the Best Price Possible

Always buy property for the best possible price. This is simple and makes a lot of sense, but may be easier said than done. We suggest following certain guidelines. A real estate investor using the get-rich-right method doesn't buy a new or fully renovated property, unless it's in the path of progress or a prime location, because the value-added or upside has already been taken by the current owner. These properties may be solid investments but you'll be limited to the market increases in rent and value only.

However, in some special situations, buying a new or fully renovated property *is* a good investment alternative. For example, buying a residential rental property in the first phase of an oceanfront community or another unique location that's difficult to replicate could be a great investment in the long run. The pricing in first phases of new developments is often very favorable because the developer must presell a certain number of the units before his permanent loan kicks in.

Infrequently, you may have the opportunity to buy a property from someone whose personal situation requires an immediate sale at significantly below market value. Life happens, and it can create many opportunities to pick up properties on a fire sale basis. This is where having cash reserves and/or a line of credit can give you a real advantage. Don't miss these opportunities, but don't count on them either!

As a general rule, most of your real estate acquisitions should be in the fixer-upper category and priced accordingly. You want to buy those properties that offer specific challenges that match your personal talents so you can use your skills to upgrade and enhance the value of the property and increase the net operating income over time.

Be sure to prepare your own income and expense pro formas from scratch and don't rely on operating results or projections presented by the seller or her broker. Sellers are likely to overstate income and understate expenses — and claim ignorance when the actual results vary. Developing an accurate projection of income and expenses requires the real estate investor to research the market and determine in advance what the cash flow will be upon the implementation of his investment and management plan. This is the only way to know the investment value or what the property is worth to you.

Two important characteristics of successful real estate investors are discipline and the ability to predetermine the maximum price they'll pay for a property to ensure plenty of room for upside potential. You don't want to simply lower your purchase price by the cost of the repairs, because the value you add to the property should be significantly higher than your out-of-pocket expenses.

Renovate Property Right

The get-rich-right strategy depends on finding properties that are well located in the path of progress and then renovating them to increase cash flow and value. But don't overspend on physical improvements. You only want to make those renovations or upgrades that increase the desirability of the property to your target market. Your property is a rental unit, not your own home. You may want to put premium countertops and appliances in your home, but you can't get a good return on your investment if you overimprove your rental property.

Improvements should allow you to increase the rent or add to the property value so that you receive a return of $2 for every $1 spent on the improvements. The best fixer-upper properties for most novice real estate investors are those with simple fixes: Painting, landscaping, and minor repairs generally offer excellent results for only minor costs. These simple repairs are also within the skill set of most real estate investors — who may have developed and perfected their talents by maintaining and upgrading their own homes.

Although doing the work yourself is typically cheaper, don't forget to look at the time factor. It makes no sense to have a rental property off the market for three weeks while you spend evenings and weekends painting in a misguided attempt to save the $1,000 that a contractor would charge for painting that would take two days.

If you use contractors, get three comparable bids from licensed, competent professionals. However, if you already know you have a competitive bid, you can expedite the process by asking the contractor if she can lower the price by 10 percent — then you won't have to go out and get additional bids.

Whether you do the work yourself or hire a contractor, make sure to obtain all required permits and that all improvements meet the applicable building and occupancy codes.

Keep Abreast of Market Rents

One of the biggest challenges for most rental property owners is determining the proper rent to charge tenants for newly renovated rental units. This aspect of property ownership and management simply requires some homework and research. Every property is unique, but your best indications of the market value of your renovated property can be found through a market survey of comparable properties.

After you've acquired and upgraded your new rental property, immediately test the new rental rate structure by offering your vacant rental units or space at the higher market rates you determined in your rental survey. The response you receive from prospects will let you know if you're asking too much or if you still have some upside on your rents. After you install new tenants paying the higher rents, you can then make similar improvements for existing tenants and increase their rents to similar levels.

We recommend that you keep the rent level slightly below the full market rent for existing long-term tenants to show your appreciation for their long-term tenancy and to encourage them to stay. For more on this topic, check out *Property Management For Dummies* (Wiley) by Robert.

Recover Renovation Dollars Through Refinancing

One of the key elements of the get-rich-right strategy is to keep your capital working and use leverage reasonably while maintaining sufficient equity to weather the ups and downs of real estate cycles and local economic challenges.

Acquiring and renovating your rental property required cash, but you also have increased the income, which has created additional value. You can now use this increased value to refinance the property to cover your initial costs of acquisition and renovation.

Although we're always quick to advise against borrowing too much and overleveraging your real estate investments, you also don't want to be too conservative and underestimate your cash needs. The cost of refinancing is such that you don't want to refinance the property more than once and if you were to need cash to overcome some unanticipated problems, the costs of short-term funds could be high. Borrow extra money to allow for reserves.

It can be extremely tempting in a strong real estate market to leverage over-aggressively, but don't get carried away. Don't borrow all of the equity in your own personal residence to go out and buy investment real estate.

You should always own your own home and have a good cushion of equity before looking to acquire investment real estate. The lessons of a falling real estate market are difficult for all investors but are totally devastating to those few investors who borrow too much against their own homes.

Remember that real estate markets have and will continue to have cycles, and you don't want to be too aggressive and find that your real estate empire collapses to the point that you yourself can't even afford to rent one of the apartments you used to own!

Reposition Property with Better Tenants

One of the best ways to increase the income and value of your newly renovated real estate investment is to reposition the property with new, more financially qualified tenants. So look to upgrade your tenants by marketing to a new target tenant profile and re-leasing the property.

Often your renovation efforts will displace your current tenant anyway, but you probably don't want to renew the current tenants' lease even if you're able to work around them. The current tenants may be the reason that the previous owner sold the property and it's in need of a complete renovation! Such tenants aren't likely to suddenly change their ways and will continue to use and abuse the property without any regard for your investment.

Robert advises not to renew the lease and provide brand-new carpeting in a rental unit occupied by a tenant with a pet that destroyed the current flooring. Likewise, you don't want to continue the tenancy of a tenant who won't be able to comfortably pay the higher rent that your fully renovated property is now worth.

This is often one of the toughest challenges for rental property owners — having to stand up to the current marginal tenant and not renew his lease. Although you may occasionally find that the current tenants are financially qualified and will treat the property as their own, the harsh reality is that most repositioned properties should start with a clean slate of tenants. At a minimum, require the current tenants to complete a rental application. Go over the lease renewal exactly as you would for a new tenant and use the same financial criteria.

Another way to improve the stability of your cash flow and minimize the chance of problems with your tenants is to increase the security deposit. However, remember that market conditions usually restrict the amount you can charge for the security deposit.

Superior Management Increases Income and Value

Superior management makes the difference between average and excellent returns in the long run. After you renovate and reposition a property with new tenants at higher rents, you need to retain the tenants and minimize turnover. You can also further enhance net operating income by effectively and efficiently controlling expenses.

Even if you have just acquired your new rental property, you need to consistently work your long-term investment strategy by operating and managing the property effectively to achieve maximum value as if you were going to refinance or were preparing the property for sale.

Your target buyer is going to be someone that wants to buy a *turnkey property* (one that's operating optimally and doesn't require renovation or a change in tenants) for personal use or as a prime rental unit or *coupon clipping* investment (steady, highly predictable stream of income like bond investors receive). Real estate appraisers will determine a higher value for properties with a strong track record of solid net operating income. Remember that to achieve maximum value, you need to have consistent income with rents at market rates, stable tenancy, and reasonable expenses. But don't go for lower expenses at the risk of decreasing curb appeal due to deferred maintenance.

Refinance or Sell and Defer Again

With the appreciation that has occurred over the past decade throughout much of the country, many rental property owners find that they have a considerable amount of equity tied up in their property. Having some equity in the property is good and keeps you from faltering should the local real estate economics take a hit, but too much equity just sitting in a property lowers your overall returns.

Our get-rich-right strategy recommends that you use the equity in your current properties to expand your real estate holdings by investing in additional properties with a view toward diversifying to reduce your overall risk. You can access that equity to generate the cash you need in one of two ways: Either refinance your rental property or look to sell the real estate investment in a tax-deferred exchange.

The best option depends on market conditions. We suggest that you take advantage of favorable financing terms when available to refinance your stabilized long-term properties. You can use the proceeds to restock your capital account in order to invest in additional rental real estate or even make other investments. The best news of all is that you can pull the cash equity from your properties tax-free. Borrowing isn't dangerous if done in moderation.

Or you can sell the property and use the 1031 tax-deferred exchange to keep your equity working. Besides excess or *lazy* equity, some owners prefer the tax-deferred exchange option because they can enhance their use of depreciation to shelter their real estate income. A competent accountant or tax advisor can assist you in making the right choice between refinancing and a tax-deferred exchange.

Consolidate Holdings into Larger Properties

Fortunately, many real estate investors are able to master the concepts of buying and renovating rental real estate. However, they often become so successful that their real estate empire begins to control their lives.

Although owning a diversified portfolio of rental properties has some inherent advantages, the day will come when your extensive real estate holdings create management burdens. Most long-term real estate investors find that they reach the point where their management responsibilities and duties no longer conform to the lifestyle that they can afford. They'll often decide to simplify their lives and hire professional property managers so that a property manager can deal with tenants, turnover, toilets, and trash.

But finding and paying for a qualified property manager for a diversified portfolio of small rental properties isn't easy or cost-effective. Instead, look to the tax-deferred exchange and consolidate your real estate holdings into one or a handful of larger properties that can be professionally managed. You will still enjoy the benefits of real estate ownership without having to deal with the day-to-day challenges of management.

Anyone can build wealth through real estate. Don't wait; get started today!

Appendix

Sample Purchase Agreement

STANDARD RESIDENTIAL PURCHASE AGREEMENT

DEFINITIONS

BROKER includes cooperating brokers and all sales persons. ***DAYS*** means calendar days, midnight to midnight, unless otherwise specified. ***BUSINESS DAY*** excludes Saturdays, Sundays and legal holidays. ***DATE OF ACCEPTANCE*** means the date Seller accepts the offer or the Buyer accepts the counter offer. ***DELIVERED*** means personally delivered, transmitted by facsimile machine, by a nationally recognized overnight courier, or by first class mail, postage prepaid. In the event of mailing, the document will be deemed delivered three (3) business days after deposit; in the event of overnight courier, one (1) business day after deposit; and if by facsimile, at time of transmission provided that a transmission report is generated and retained by the sender reflecting the accurate transmission of the document. Unless otherwise provided in this Agreement or by law, delivery to the agent will constitute delivery to the principal. ***DATE OF CLOSING*** means the date title is transferred. ***TERMINATING THE AGREEMENT*** means that both parties are relieved of their obligations and all deposits will be returned to Buyer. ***PROPERTY*** means the real property and any personal property included in the sale.

AGENCY RELATIONSHIP CONFIRMATION. The following agency relationship is hereby confirmed for this transaction and supersedes any prior agency election:

LISTING AGENT: ______________________________ is the agent of (check one):
(Print Firm Name)

☐ **the Seller exclusively; or** ☐ **both the Buyer and the Seller.**

SELLING AGENT: ______________________________ (if not the same as the Listing Agent) is the agent of (check one):
(Print Firm Name)

☐ **the Buyer exclusively; or** ☐ **the Seller exclusively; or** ☐ **both the Buyer and the Seller.**

Note: This confirmation DOES NOT take the place of the AGENCY DISCLOSURE form (P.P. Form 110.42 CAL) required by law

______________________________ hereinafter designated as BUYER, offers to purchase the real property situated in ______________________, County of ______________________, California, commonly known as ______________________________,
FOR THE PURCHASE PRICE OF $______________ (______________________________ dollars) on the following terms and conditions:

☐ Buyer does ☐ Buyer does not intend to occupy the property as his or her residence.

1. **FINANCING TERMS AND LOAN PROVISIONS.** (Buyer represents that the funds required for the initial deposit, additional deposit, cash balance and closing cost are readily available.)

   A. $______________ **DEPOSIT** evidenced by ☐ check, or ☐ other: ______________________ held uncashed until acceptance and not later than three (3) business days thereafter deposited toward the purchase price with ______________________.

   B. $______________ **ADDITIONAL CASH DEPOSIT** to be placed in escrow ☐ **within** _____ **days after acceptance**, ☐ upon receipt of Loan Commitment per Item 2, ☐ Other: ______________________.

   C. $______________ **BALANCE OF CASH PAYMENT** needed to close, not including closing costs.

   D. $______________ **NEW FIRST LOAN:** ☐ CONVENTIONAL, ☐ FHA, ☐ VA, ☐ Other financing acceptable to Buyer:
   ☐ FIXED RATE: For _____ years, interest not to exceed _______%, payable at approximately $___________ per month (principal and interest only), with the balance due in not less than _____ years.
   ☐ ARM: For _________ years, initial interest rate not to exceed _________%, with initial monthly payments of $___________ and maximum lifetime rate not to exceed ________%.
   ☐ Buyer will pay loan fee or points not to exceed ___________.
   ☐ Lender to appraise property at no less than purchase price prior to loan contingency removal.
   ☐ If FHA or VA, Seller will pay ________% discount points. Seller will also pay other fees and costs, as required by FHA or VA, not to exceed $_______________.

   E. $______________ **EXISTING FINANCING:** ☐ ASSUMPTION OF, ☐ SUBJECT TO existing loan of record described as follows: ______________________

   F. $______________ **SELLER FINANCING:** ☐ FIRST LOAN, ☐ SECOND LOAN, ☐ THIRD LOAN, secured by the property.
   ☐ Seller Financing Addendum, P.P. Form 131.1-3 CAL, is attached and made a part of this Agreement.

   G. $______________ **OTHER FINANCING TERMS:** ______________________

   H. $______________ **TOTAL PURCHASE PRICE (not including closing costs).**

2. **LOAN APPROVAL.** (Please check one of the following):

   A. ☐ **CONTRACT IS NOT CONTINGENT** upon Buyer obtaining a loan.

   B. ☐ **CONTRACT IS CONTINGENT** upon Buyer's ability to obtain commitment for new financing, as set forth above, from a lender or mortgage broker of Buyer's choice, and/or consent to assumption of existing financing provided for in this Agreement, **within** ________ **days after acceptance**. Buyer will in good faith use his or her best efforts to qualify for and obtain the financing and will complete and submit a loan application **within five (5) days after acceptance**. Buyer ☐ will, ☐ will not provide a ☐ prequalification letter, or ☐ preapproval letter from lender or mortgage broker based on Buyer's application and credit report **within** ________ **days after acceptance**. In the event a loan commitment or consent is obtained but not timely honored without fault of Buyer, Buyer may terminate this Agreement.

Buyer [_______] [_______] and Seller [_______] [_______] have read this page.

Page 1 of 7
FORM 101-R.1 CAL (09-2003)
Form generated by: TrueForms™ from REVEAL SYSTEMS, Inc. 800-499-9612

Source: Professional Publishing/TrueForms.com

Property Address: ____

3. **BONDS AND ASSESSMENTS.** All bonds and assessments which are part of or paid with the property tax bill will be assumed by the Buyer. In the event there are other bonds or assessments which have an outstanding principal balance and are a lien upon the property, the current installment will be prorated between Buyer and Seller as of the date of closing. Future installments will be assumed by Buyer WITHOUT CREDIT toward the purchase price, EXCEPT AS FOLLOWS: ____

____

This Agreement is conditioned upon both parties verifying and approving in writing the amount of any bond or assessment to be assumed or paid **within ten (10) days after receipt** of the preliminary title report or property tax bill, whichever is later. In the event of disapproval, the disapproving party may terminate this Agreement.

4. **PROPERTY TAX.** **Within three (3) days after acceptance**, Seller will deliver to Buyer for his or her approval a copy of the latest property tax bill. Buyer is advised that: (a) the property will be reassessed upon change of ownership which may result in a tax increase; and (b) the tax bill may not include certain exempt items such as school taxes on property owned by seniors. Buyer should make further inquiry at the assessor's office. **Within five (5) days after receipt** of the tax bill, Buyer will in writing approve or disapprove the tax bill. In the event of disapproval, Buyer may terminate this Agreement.

5. **EXISTING LOANS.** Seller will, **within three (3) days after acceptance**, provide Buyer with copies of all notes and deeds of trust to be assumed or taken subject to. **Within five (5) days after receipt** Buyer will notify Seller in writing of his or her approval or disapproval of the terms of the documents. Approval will not be unreasonably withheld. **Within three (3) days after acceptance**, Seller will submit a written request for a current Statement of Condition on the above loan(s). Seller warrants that all loans will be current at close of escrow. Seller will pay any prepayment charge imposed on any existing loan paid off at close of escrow. Buyer will pay the prepayment charge on any loan which is to remain a lien upon the property after close of escrow. The parties are encouraged to consult his or her lender regarding prepayment provisions and any due on sale clauses.

6. **DESTRUCTION OF IMPROVEMENTS.** If the improvements of the property are destroyed, materially damaged, or found to be materially defective as a result of such damage prior to close of escrow, Buyer may terminate this Agreement by written notice delivered to Seller or his or her Broker, and all unused deposits will be returned. In the event Buyer does not elect to terminate this Agreement, Buyer will be entitled to receive, in addition to the property, any insurance proceeds payable on account of the damage or destruction.

7. **EXAMINATION OF TITLE.** In addition to any encumbrances assumed or taken "subject to," Seller will convey title to the property subject only to: [1] real estate taxes not yet due; and [2] covenants, conditions, restrictions, rights of way and easements of record, if any, which do not materially affect the value or intended use of the property.
   Within three (3) days after acceptance, Buyer will order a Preliminary Title Report and copies of CC&Rs and other documents of record if applicable. **Within five (5) days after receipt**, Buyer will report to Seller in writing any valid objections to title contained in such report (other than monetary liens to be paid upon close of escrow). If Buyer objects to any exceptions to the title, Seller will use due diligence to remove such exceptions at his or her own expense **before close of escrow**. If such exceptions cannot be removed before close of escrow, this Agreement will terminate, unless Buyer elects to purchase the property subject to such exceptions. If Seller concludes he or she is in good faith unable to remove such objections, Seller will notify Buyer **within ten (10) days after receipt** of said objections. In that event Buyer may terminate this Agreement.

8. **EVIDENCE OF TITLE** will be in the form of a policy of title insurance, issued by ____________________ paid by ☐ Buyer, ☐ Seller, ☐ Other ____________________. **NOTE:** In addition to coverage under a standard OLTA policy, the ALTA Owner's Policy, or CLTA Homeowner's Policy of Title Insurance may offer additional coverage for a number of unrecorded matters. Buyer should discuss the type of policy with the title company of their choice at the time escrow is opened. In the event a lender requires an ALTA lender's policy of title insurance, ☐ Buyer, ☐ Seller will pay the premium.

9. **PRORATIONS.** Rents, real estate taxes, interest, payments on bonds and assessments assumed by Buyer, and homeowners association fees will be prorated as of the date of recordation of the deed. Security deposits, advance rentals, or considerations involving future lease credits will be credited to Buyer.

10. **CLOSING.** Full purchase price to be paid and deed to be recorded ☐ **on or before** ________________, **OR** ☐ **within** ______ **days of acceptance.** Both parties will deposit with an authorized escrow holder, to be selected by Buyer, all funds and instruments necessary to complete the sale in accordance with the terms of this Agreement. ☐ Where customary, signed escrow instructions will be delivered to escrow holder **within** ______ **days of acceptance.** Escrow fee to be paid by ______________. County/City transfer tax(es), if any, to be paid by ________________. Homeowner association transfer fee to be paid by ______________. Unless the transaction is exempt, the escrow holder is instructed to remit the required tax withholding amount to the Franchise Tax Board from the proceeds of sale.
    THIS PURCHASE AGREEMENT TOGETHER WITH ANY ADDENDA WILL CONSTITUTE JOINT ESCROW INSTRUCTIONS TO THE ESCROW HOLDER.

11. **PHYSICAL POSSESSION.** Physical possession of the property, with keys to all property locks, alarms, and garage door openers, will be delivered to Buyer (check one):
    ☐ On the date of recordation of the deed, not later than ________ ☐ a.m., ☐ p.m.;
    ☐ On the ________ day after recordation, not later than ________ ☐ a.m., ☐ p.m.;
    In the event possession is to be delivered **before or after recordation**, such possession is conditioned upon the execution by both parties of a written occupancy agreement on P.P. Form 103 CAL or 104 CAL, or comparable form, **within** _____ **days after acceptance.**

Buyer [_______] [_______] and Seller [_______] [_______] have read this page.

Source: Professional Publishing/TrueForms.com

Property Address: ____

12. **FIXTURES.** All items permanently attached to the property, including light fixtures and bulbs, attached floor coverings, all attached window coverings, including window hardware, window and door screens, storm sash, combination doors, awnings, TV antennas, burglar, fire, smoke and security alarms (unless leased), pool and spa equipment, solar systems, attached fireplace screens, electric garage door openers with controls, outdoor plants and trees (other than in movable containers), are included in the purchase price free of liens, EXCLUDING: ____

13. **CONDITION OF PROPERTY.** Seller agrees that upon delivery of possession to the Buyer: (a) all built-in appliances included in the sale, and the electrical, plumbing (excluding irrigation systems), heating and cooling systems will be in working order and free of leaks; (b) the roof will be free of leaks; (c) all broken or cracked glass, including mirrors and shower/tub enclosures and broken seals between double-pane windows, will be replaced; (d) and existing window and door screens that are damaged will be repaired. **Unless specifically excluded, all of the above are the obligation of the Seller regardless of any disclosures made or conditions discovered by the parties or their agents.** The following items are specifically excluded from the above: ____
____.
Seller's obligations under this provision are not intended to create a duty to repair an item that may fail after possession is delivered. Buyer and Seller acknowledge that Broker is not responsible for any alleged breach of these covenants.

14. **INSPECTIONS OF PHYSICAL CONDITION OF PROPERTY.** Buyer will have the right to retain, at his or her expense, licensed experts including but not limited to engineers, geologists, architects, contractors, surveyors, arborists, and structural pest control operators to inspect the property for any structural and nonstructural conditions, including matters concerning roofing, electrical, plumbing, heating, cooling, appliances, well, septic system, pool, boundaries, geological and environmental hazards, toxic substances including asbestos, mold, formaldehyde, radon gas, and lead-based paint. Buyer, if requested by Seller in writing, will promptly furnish, at no cost to Seller, copies of all written inspection reports obtained. Buyer will approve or disapprove in writing all inspection reports **obtained within fifteen (15) (or ______) days after acceptance.** In the event of Buyer's disapproval, Buyer may, within the time stated or mutually agreed upon extension, elect to terminate this Agreement, or invite Seller to negotiate repairs. (See P.P. Form 101-M, Addendum Regarding Removal of Inspection Contingencies.)

15. **ACCESS TO PROPERTY.** Seller agrees to provide reasonable access to the property to Buyer and inspectors, appraisers, and all other professionals representing Buyer.

16. **MAINTENANCE.** Until possession is delivered, Seller will maintain all structures, landscaping, grounds, and pool in the same general condition as of the date of acceptance or physical inspection, whichever is later. Seller agrees to deliver the property in a neat and clean condition with all debris and personal belongings removed.

17. **PERSONAL PROPERTY.** The following personal property, on the premises when inspected by Buyer, is included in the purchase price and will be transferred to Buyer free of liens and properly identified by a Bill of Sale **at close of escrow.** Unless itemized here, personal property is not included in the sale. No warranty is made as to the condition of the personal property: ______________________.
____

18. **TRANSFER DISCLOSURE STATEMENT (TDS).** Seller will comply with Civil Code §1102 by providing Buyer with a completed Real Estate Transfer Disclosure Statement (P.P. Form 110.21-23 CAL). The completed statement will consist of disclosure by Seller, Listing Agent, and Selling Agent.
☐ Buyer has received and read the completed TDS.
☐ Seller will provide to Buyer the completed TDS **within ______ days after acceptance.**
Buyer and Seller agree that any new reports or other disclosure documents received by Buyer from the Seller after receipt of the TDS are automatically deemed an amendment to the TDS. If any disclosure or a material amendment of any disclosure is delivered by the Seller to the Buyer after the execution of an offer to purchase, Buyer will have **three (3) days** after delivery in person or **five (5) days** after deposit in the mail to terminate his or her offer by delivery of a written notice of termination to Seller or Seller's Agent.
Seller agrees to hold all Brokers in the transaction harmless and to defend and indemnify them from any claim, demand, action or proceedings resulting from any omission or alleged omission by Seller in his or her Real Estate Transfer Disclosure Statement or supplement.

19. **SUPPLEMENT TO STATUTORY DISCLOSURE STATEMENT. Within ______ days after acceptance, or earlier if required by law,** Seller will provide the following or comparable disclosure supplement(s) to Buyer:
☐ P.P. FORM 110.27 CAL, NATURAL HAZARD DISCL.
☐ 3RD PARTY NATURAL HAZARD REPORT BY ______________________
☐ P.P. FORM 110.31-33 CAL, SUPPLEMENT TO TDS
☐ P.P. FORM 110.35-36 CAL, COMMON INTEREST DISCLOSURE
☐ P.P. FORM 110.72, ADDENDUM-SEPTIC SYSTEMS
☐ P.P. FORM 110.90-92 CAL, STANDARD DISCLOSURES AND DISCLAIMERS
☐ P.P. FORM 110.74, LEAD-BASED PAINT DISCLOSURE (for dwellings constructed prior to 1978 - must be delivered prior to acceptance.)
☐ P.P. FORM 110.81 CAL, SMOKE DETECTOR/WATER HEATER CERTIFICATION
OTHER ____

20. **SAFETY BOOKLETS.** By initialing below, Buyer acknowledges receipt of the following booklets:
[_____] [_____] *Homeowner's Guide to Environmental Hazards and Earthquake Safety*, including earthquake hazard disclosure form required for homes constructed prior to 1960, and the lead-based paint pamphlet.
[_____] [_____] *Commercial Property Owner's Guide to Earthquake Safety*, required for certain unreinforced masonry buildings built prior to 1975.

Buyer [_______] [_______] and Seller [_______] [_______] have read this page.

Page 3 of 7

Source: Professional Publishing/TrueForms.com

Property Address: ______________________________

21. **WALK-THROUGH INSPECTION.** Buyer will have the right to conduct a walk-through inspection of the property within _____ days prior to close of escrow, to verify Seller's compliance with the provisions under Item 12, FIXTURES, Item 13, CONDITION OF PROPERTY, Item 16, MAINTENANCE, and Item 17, PERSONAL PROPERTY. This right is not a condition of this Agreement, and Buyer's sole remedy for an alleged breach of these items is a claim for damages. Utilities are to remain turned on until transfer of possession.

22. **COMPLIANCE WITH LOCAL LAWS.** Seller will comply with any local laws applicable to the sale or transfer of the property, including but not limited to: Providing inspections and/or reports for compliance with local building and permit regulations, including septic system inspection reports; compliance with minimum energy conservation standards; and compliance with water conservation measures. All required inspections and reports will be ordered **within three (3) days after acceptance** and will be paid by ☐ Seller, ☐ Buyer. If Seller does not agree **within five (5) days after receipt** of a report to pay the cost of any repair or improvement required to comply with such laws, Buyer may terminate this Agreement. It is understood that if Seller has given notice that necessary permits or final approvals were not obtained for some improvements, Seller will not be responsible for bringing the improvements into compliance unless otherwise agreed.

23. **OPTIONAL PROVISIONS.** The provisions in this Item **23, IF INITIALED BY BUYER** are included in this Agreement.

23-A. [____] [____] MAINTENANCE RESERVE. Seller agrees to leave in escrow a maintenance reserve in the amount of $__________. If, in the reasonable opinion of a qualified technician, any of the equipment listed under Item 13, CONDITION OF PROPERTY, is not in working order, Buyer will furnish Seller a copy of the technician's inspection report and/or submit written notice to Seller of non-compliance of any of the terms under Item 13, CONDITION OF PROPERTY, **within five (5) days after occupancy is delivered.**

In the event Seller fails to make the repairs and/or corrections within **five (5) days after receipt of said report or notice**, Seller authorizes the escrow holder to disburse to Buyer against bills for such repairs or corrections the sum of such bills, not to exceed the amount reserved. Said reserve will be disbursed to Buyer or returned to Seller **not later than fifteen (15) days after date occupancy is delivered.**

23-B. [____] [____] HOME PROTECTION CONTRACT, paid for by ☐ Buyer, ☐ Seller, will become effective **upon close of escrow** for not less than one year at a cost not to exceed $______________. The Brokers have informed both parties that such protection programs are available, but do not approve or endorse any particular program. Unless this provision is initialed, Buyer understands that such a protection plan is waived.

23-C. [____] [____] COMMON INTEREST DEVELOPMENT DISCLOSURE. Within ten (10) days after acceptance, Seller, at his or her expense, agrees to provide to Buyer the management documents and other information required by California Civil Code §1368. **Within five (5) days after receipt**, Buyer will notify Seller in writing of approval or disapproval of the documents and information. In case of disapproval, Buyer may terminate this Agreement.

Any delinquent assessments including penalties, attorney's fees, and other charges that are or could become a lien on the property will be credited to Buyer at close of escrow.

23-D. [____] [____] PROBATE/CONSERVATORSHIP SALE. Pursuant to the California Probate Code, this sale is subject to court approval at which time the court may allow open competitive bidding. An "AS IS" Addendum (P.P. Form 101-AI) ☐ is, ☐ is not attached and made a part of this Agreement.

23-F [____] [____] RENTAL PROPERTY. If checked ☐, property will be vacated no less than five (5) (or ☐ _______) days prior to close of escrow. If not checked, Buyer to take property subject to rights of parties in possession on leases or month-to-month tenancies. **Within five (5) days after acceptance**, Seller will deliver to Buyer for his or her approval copies of the following documents: (a) existing leases and rental agreements with tenants estoppel certificates; (b) any outstanding notices sent to tenants; (c) a written statement of all oral agreements with tenants; (d) existing defaults by Seller or tenants; (e) claims made by or to tenants; (f) a statement of all tenants deposits held by Seller; (g) a complete statement of rental income and expenses; (h) and any service and equipment rental contracts with respect to the property which run beyond close of escrow. Seller warrants all of this documentation to be true and complete.

Within five (5) days after receipt of documents, Buyer will notify Seller in writing of approval or disapproval of the documents. In case of disapproval, Buyer may terminate this Agreement. During the escrow period of this transaction Seller agrees that no changes in the existing leases or rental agreements will be made, nor new leases or rental agreements longer than month to month entered into, nor will any substantial alterations or repairs be made or undertaken without the written consent of the Buyer. Security deposits, advance rentals, or considerations involving future lease credits will be credited to Buyer in escrow.

23-F. [____] [____] RENT CONTROL ORDINANCE. Buyer is aware that a local ordinance is in effect which regulates the rights and obligations of property owners. It may also affect the manner in which future rents can be adjusted.

23-G. [____] [____] TAX DEFERRED EXCHANGE (INVESTMENT PROPERTY). In the event that Seller wishes to enter into a tax deferred exchange for the property, or Buyer wishes to enter into a tax deferred exchange with respect to property owned by him or her in connection with this transaction, each of the parties agrees to cooperate with the other party in connection with such exchange, including the execution of such documents as may be reasonably necessary to complete the exchange; provided that: (a) the other party will not be obligated to delay the closing; (b) all additional costs in connection with the exchange will be borne by the party requesting the exchange; (c) the other party will not be obligated to execute any note, contract, deed or other document providing for any personal liability which would survive the exchange; and (d) the other party will not take title to any

Buyer [________] [________] and Seller [________] [________] have read this page.

Source: Professional Publishing/TrueForms.com

Property Address: ___

property other than the property described in this Agreement. It is understood that a party's rights and obligations under this Agreement may be assigned to a third party intermediary to facilitate the exchange. The other party will be indemnified and held harmless against any liability which arises or is claimed to have arisen on account of the exchange.

24. CONTINGENT ON SALE. (Please check one of the following):

A. ☐ **CONTRACT IS NOT CONTINGENT** upon the sale or close of any property owned by Buyer.

B. ☐ **CONTRACT IS CONTINGENT** on Buyer's Property at ___ which is in escrow and concerning which all contingencies ☐ have, ☐ have not been satisfied, closing on or before ___. If Buyer's escrow is terminated, abandoned, or does not close on time, this Agreement will terminate without further notice unless the parties agree otherwise in writing.

C. ☐ **CONTRACT IS CONTINGENT** on Buyer accepting an offer for his or her property at ___ **within** ___ **days after acceptance** of this Agreement, and that sale closing on or before ___. Seller will have the right to continue to offer the property for sale. When Buyer has accepted an offer on the sale of his or her property, Buyer will promptly deliver a written notice of the sale to Seller. If Buyer's purchase agreement is subject to the sale of another property, it does not qualify without the written consent of Seller. Upon delivering notice of the qualified sale, this Agreement will still be contingent on Buyer's property closing as specified in this Item 24-C. If Buyer's escrow is terminated, abandoned, or does not close on time, this Agreement will terminate without further notice unless the parties agree otherwise in writing.

If Seller accepts a bonafide written offer from a third party prior to Buyer's delivery of notice of acceptance of an offer on the sale of Buyer's property, Seller may give Buyer written notice of that fact. **Within three (3) days of receipt of the notice**, Buyer will waive the contingency of the sale and close of his or her property, or this Agreement will terminate without further notice. In order to be effective, the waiver of contingency must be accompanied by reasonable evidence that funds needed to close escrow will be available and Buyer's ability to obtain financing is not contingent upon the sale and/or close of any property.

25. DEFAULT. In the event Buyer defaults in the performance of this Agreement (unless Buyer and Seller have agreed to liquidated damages), Seller may, subject to any rights of Broker, retain Buyer's deposit to the extent of damages sustained and may take such actions as he or she deems appropriate to collect such additional damages as may have been actually sustained. Buyer will have the right to take such action as he or she deems appropriate to recover such portion of the deposit as may be allowed by law. In the event that Buyer defaults (unless Buyer and Seller have agreed to liquidated damages) Buyer agrees to pay the Broker(s) any commission that would be payable by Seller in the absence of such default.

26. ATTORNEY FEES. In any action, arbitration, or other proceeding involving a dispute between Buyer and Seller arising out of the execution of this Agreement or the sale, whether for tort or for breach of contract, and whether or not brought to trial or final judgment, the prevailing party will be entitled to receive from the other party a reasonable attorney fee, expert witness fees, and costs to be determined by the court or arbitrator(s).

27. EXPIRATION OF OFFER. This Offer will expire unless acceptance is delivered to Buyer or to ___ (Buyer's Broker) on or before (date) ___ (time) ___ ☐ a.m. ☐ p.m.

28. COUNTERPARTS. This Agreement may be executed in one or more counterparts, each of which is deemed to be an original.

29. CONDITIONS SATISFIED/WAIVED IN WRITING. Each condition or contingency, covenant, approval or disapproval will be satisfied according to its terms or waived by written notice delivered to the other party or his or her Broker.

30. TIME. Time is of the essence of this Agreement; provided, however, that if either party fails to comply with any contingency in this Agreement within the time limit specified, this Agreement will not terminate until the other party delivers written notice to the defaulting party requiring compliance **within 24 hours after receipt** of notice. If the party receiving the notice fails to comply **within the 24 hours,** the non-defaulting party may terminate this Agreement without further notice. It is understood that neither the making of deposits nor the close of escrow is a contingency.

31. LIQUIDATED DAMAGES. By initialing in the spaces below,

[_____] [_____] **Buyer agrees** [_____] [_____] **Buyer does not agree**

[_____] [_____] **Seller agrees** [_____] [_____] **Seller does not agree**

that in the event Buyer defaults in the performance of this Agreement, Seller will retain as liquidated damages the deposit set forth in Items 1-A and 1-B, and that said liquidated damages are reasonable in view of all the circumstances existing on the date of this Agreement. If the property is a dwelling with no more than four (4) units, one of which Buyer intends to occupy as his or her residence, the liquidated damages will not exceed three percent (3%) of the purchase price and any deposit in excess of that amount will be refunded to Buyer. In the event that Buyer defaults and has not made the deposit required under Item 1-B, or refuses to execute liquidated damage provision with respect to additional deposits, then Seller will have the option of retaining the initial deposit(s) that have been made, or terminating the obligations of the parties under this Item 31 and recovering such damages from Buyer as may be allowed by law. The parties understand that in case of dispute mutual cancellation instructions are necessary to release funds from escrow or trust accounts.

Buyer [_____] [_____] **and Seller** [_____] [_____] **have read this page.**

Source: Professional Publishing/TrueForms.com

Property Address: ______________________________

32. **MEDIATION OF DISPUTES.** If a dispute arises out of or relates to this Agreement or its breach, by initialing in the "agree" spaces below the parties agree to first try in good faith to settle the dispute by voluntary mediation before resorting to court action or arbitration, unless the dispute is a matter excluded under Item **33-ARBITRATION**. The fees of the mediator will be shared equally between all parties to the dispute. If a party initials the "agree" space and later refuses mediation, that party will not be entitled to recover prevailing party attorney fees in any subsequent action.

[_______] [_______] **Buyer agrees** [_______] [_______] **Buyer does not agree**

[_______] [_______] **Seller agrees** [_______] [_______] **Seller does not agree**

33. **ARBITRATION OF DISPUTES. Any dispute or claim in law or equity between the Buyer and Seller arising out of this Agreement will be decided by neutral binding arbitration in accordance with the California Arbitration Act (C.C.P. §1280 et seq.), and not by court action except as provided by California law for judicial review of arbitration proceedings. If the parties cannot agree upon an arbitrator, a party may petition the Superior Court of the county in which the property is located for an order compelling arbitration and appointing an arbitrator. Service of the petition may be made by first class mail, postage prepaid, to the last known address of the party served. Judgment upon the award rendered by the arbitrator may be entered in any court having jurisdiction. The parties will have the right to discovery in accordance with Code of Civil Procedure §1283.05.**

The parties agree that the following procedure will govern the making of the award by the arbitrator: (a) a Tentative Award will be made by the arbitrator within 30 days following submission of the matter to the arbitrator; (b) the Tentative Award will explain the factual and legal basis for the arbitrator's decision as to each of the principal controverted issues; (c) the Tentative Award will be in writing unless the parties agree otherwise; provided, however, that if the hearing is concluded within one (1) day, the Tentative Award may be made orally at the hearing in the presence of the parties. Within ten (10) days after the Tentative Award has been served or announced, any party may serve objections to the Tentative Award. Upon objections being timely served, the arbitrator may call for additional evidence, oral or written argument, or both. If no objections are filed, the Tentative Award will become final without further action by the parties or arbitrator. Within thirty (30) days after the filing of objections, the arbitrator will either make the Tentative Award final or modify or correct the Tentative Award, which will then become final as modified or corrected.

The provisions of C.C.P. §128.5 authorizing the imposition of sanctions as a result of bad faith actions or tactics will apply to the arbitration proceedings. A prevailing party will also be entitled to an action for malicious prosecution if the elements of such cause of action are met.

The following matters are excluded from arbitration: (a) a judicial or non judicial foreclosure or other action or proceeding to enforce a deed of trust, mortgage, or real property sales contract as defined in Civil Code §2985; (b) an unlawful detainer action; (c) the filing or enforcement of a mechanic's lien; (d) any matter which is within the jurisdiction of a probate court, bankruptcy court, or small claims court; or (e) an action for bodily injury or wrongful death. The filing of a judicial action to enable the recording of a notice of pending action, for order of attachment, receivership, injunction, or other provisional remedies, will not constitute a waiver of the right to arbitrate under this provision.

NOTICE: By initialing in the ["agree"] space below you are agreeing to have any dispute arising out of the matters included in the "Arbitration of Disputes" provision decided by neutral arbitration as provided by California law and you are giving up any rights you might possess to have the dispute litigated in a court or jury trial. By initialing in the ["agree"] space below you are giving up your judicial rights to discovery and appeal, unless those rights are specifically included in the "Arbitration of Disputes" provision. If you refuse to submit to arbitration after agreeing to this provision, you may be compelled to arbitrate under the authority of the California Code of Civil Procedure. Your agreement to this arbitration provision is voluntary.

We have read and understand the foregoing and agree to submit disputes arising out of the matters included in the "Arbitration of Disputes" provision to neutral arbitration.

[_______] [_______] **Buyer agrees** [_______] [_______] **Buyer does not agree**

[_______] [_______] **Seller agrees** [_______] [_______] **Seller does not agree**

34. **SURVIVAL.** The omission from escrow instructions of any provision in this Agreement will not waive the right of any party. All representations or warranties will survive the close of escrow.

35. **ENTIRE AGREEMENT/ASSIGNMENT PROHIBITED.** This document contains the entire agreement of the parties and supersedes all prior agreements or representations with respect to the property which are not expressly set forth. This Agreement may be modified only in writing signed and dated by both parties. **Both parties acknowledge that they have not relied on any statements of the real estate Agent or Broker which are not expressed in this Agreement.** Buyer may not assign any right under this agreement without the prior written consent of Seller. Any such assignment will be void and unenforceable.

36. **ADDENDA.** The following addenda are attached and made a part of this Agreement:

☐ Addendum No. ______ ______________________________

☐ Addendum No. ______ ______________________________

37. **ADDITIONAL TERMS AND CONDITIONS.**

____

____

____

____

____

Buyer [_______] [_______] **and Seller** [_______] [_______] **have read this page.**

Source: Professional Publishing/TrueForms.com

Property Address: ______________________________

NOTICE: The California Department of Justice, sheriff's departments, police departments serving jurisdictions of 200,000 or more and many other local law enforcement authorities maintain for public access a data base of the locations of persons required to register pursuant to paragraph (1) of subdivision (a) of Section 290.4 of the Penal Code. The data base is updated on a quarterly basis and a source of information about the presence of these individuals in any neighborhood. The Department of Justice also maintains a Sex Offender Identification Line through which inquiries about individuals may be made. This is a "900" telephone service. Callers must have specific information about individuals they are checking. Information regarding neighborhoods is not available through the "900" telephone service.

LIMITATION OF AGENCY: A real estate broker or agent is qualified to advise on real estate. If you have any questions concerning the legal sufficiency, legal effect, insurance, or tax consequences of this document or the related transactions, consult with your attorney, accountant or insurance advisor.

The undersigned Buyer acknowledges that he or she has thoroughly read and approved each of the provisions of this offer and agrees to purchase the property for the price and on the terms and conditions specified. Buyer acknowledges receipt of a copy of this offer.

Buyer ______________________ Date ____________ Time ____________

Buyer ______________________ Date ____________ Time ____________

Address ______________________ ______________________

ACCEPTANCE

Seller accepts the foregoing Offer and agrees to sell the property for the price and on the terms and conditions specified.

NOTICE: The amount or rate of real estate commissions is not fixed by law. They are set by each Broker individually and may be negotiable between the Seller and Broker.

38. COMMISSION. Seller agrees to pay in cash the following real estate commission for services rendered, which commission Seller hereby irrevocably assigns to Broker(s) from escrow:
_______% of the accepted price, or $____________, to the listing Broker: ______________________, and
_______% of the accepted price, or $____________, to the selling Broker: ______________________
without regard to the agency relationship. Escrow instructions with respect to commissions may not be amended or revoked without the written consent of the Broker(s).

If Seller receives liquidated or other damages upon default by Buyer, Seller agrees to pay Broker(s) the lesser of the amount provided for above or one half of the damages after deducting any costs of collection, including reasonable attorney fees.

Commission will also be payable upon any default by Seller, or the mutual rescission by Buyer and Seller without the written consent of the Broker(s), which prevents completion of the purchase. This Agreement will not limit the rights of Broker and Seller provided for in any existing listing agreement.

In any action for commission the prevailing party will be entitled to reasonable attorney fees whether or not the action is brought to trial or final judgment.

39. PROVISIONS TO BE INITIALED. The following items must be "agreed to" by both parties to be binding on either party. In the event of disagreement, Seller should make a counter offer.

Item 31. LIQUIDATED DAMAGES **Item 32.** MEDIATION OF DISPUTES **Item 33.** ARBITRATION OF DISPUTES

Seller acknowledges receipt of a copy of this Agreement. Authorization is hereby given the Broker(s) in this transaction to deliver a signed copy to Buyer and to disclose the terms of purchase to members of a Multiple Listing Service, Board or Association of REALTORS® at close of escrow.

40. IF CHECKED ☐ ACCEPTANCE IS SUBJECT TO ATTACHED COUNTER OFFER DATED ____________

Seller ______________________ (Signature)　　Seller ______________________ (Signature)

______________________ (Please Print Name)　　______________________ (Please Print Name)

Date ____________ Time ____________　　Date ____________ Time ____________

Address ______________________

____

Rev. by ____________
Date ____________

Page 7 of 7
FORM 101-R.7 CAL (09-2003) PROFESSIONAL PUBLISHING
Form generated by: TrueForms™ from REVEAL SYSTEMS, Inc. 800-499-9612

Source: Professional Publishing/TrueForms.com

Index

• Numerics •

• A •

• B •

• C •

• D •

• E •

• F •

• G •

• H •

• I •

• J •

• K •

• L •

• M •

• N •

• Q •

• R •

• S •

• T •

• U •

• V •

• W •

• Y •

• Z •

BUSINESS, CAREERS & PERSONAL FINANCE
Investing For Dummies
0-7645-5307-0
Home Buying For Dummies
0-7645-5331-3 *†
Also available:
Accounting For Dummies † 0-7645-5314-3
Business Plans Kit For Dummies † 0-7645-5365-8
Cover Letters For Dummies 0-7645-5224-4
Frugal Living For Dummies 0-7645-5403-4
House Selling For Dummies 0-7645-5425-5
Mortgages For Dummies 0-7645-7192-3
Mutual Funds For Dummies 0-7645-5329-1
Personal Finance For Dummies * 0-7645-2590-5
Property Management For Dummies 0-7645-5330-5
Resumes For Dummies † 0-7645-5471-9
Selling For Dummies 0-7645-5363-1
Small Business Kit For Dummies *† 0-7645-5093-4
HOME & BUSINESS COMPUTER BASICS
Windows XP For Dummies
0-7645-4074-2
Excel 2003 All-in-One Desk Reference For Dummies
0-7645-3758-X
Also available:
ACT! 6 For Dummies 0-7645-2645-6
iLife '04 All-in-One Desk Reference For Dummies 0-7645-7347-0
iPAQ For Dummies 0-7645-6769-1
Mac OS X Panther Timesaving Techniques For Dummies 0-7645-5812-9
Macs For Dummies 0-7645-5656-8
Microsoft Money 2004 For Dummies 0-7645-4195-1
Office 2003 All-in-One Desk Reference For Dummies 0-7645-3883-7
Outlook 2003 For Dummies 0-7645-3759-8
PCs For Dummies 0-7645-4074-2
TiVo For Dummies 0-7645-6923-6
Upgrading and Fixing PCs For Dummies 0-7645-1665-5
Windows XP Timesaving Techniques For Dummies 0-7645-3748-2
FOOD, HOME, GARDEN, HOBBIES, MUSIC & PETS
Feng Shui For Dummies
0-7645-5295-3
Poker For Dummies
0-7645-5232-5
Also available:
Bass Guitar For Dummies 0-7645-2487-9
Diabetes Cookbook For Dummies 0-7645-5230-9
Gardening For Dummies * 0-7645-5130-2
Guitar For Dummies 0-7645-5106-X
Holiday Decorating For Dummies 0-7645-2570-0
Home Improvement All-in-One For Dummies 0-7645-5680-0
Knitting For Dummies 0-7645-5395-X
Piano For Dummies 0-7645-5105-1
Puppies For Dummies 0-7645-5255-4
Scrapbooking For Dummies 0-7645-7208-3
Senior Dogs For Dummies 0-7645-5818-8
Singing For Dummies 0-7645-2475-5
30-Minute Meals For Dummies 0-7645-2589-1
INTERNET & DIGITAL MEDIA
Digital Photography For Dummies
0-7645-1664-7
Starting an eBay Business For Dummies
0-7645-6924-4
Also available:
2005 Online Shopping Directory For Dummies 0-7645-7495-7
CD & DVD Recording For Dummies 0-7645-5956-7
eBay For Dummies 0-7645-5654-1
Fighting Spam For Dummies 0-7645-5965-6
Genealogy Online For Dummies 0-7645-5964-8
Google For Dummies 0-7645-4420-9
Home Recording For Musicians For Dummies 0-7645-1634-5
The Internet For Dummies 0-7645-4173-0
iPod & iTunes For Dummies 0-7645-7772-7
Preventing Identity Theft For Dummies 0-7645-7336-5
Pro Tools All-in-One Desk Reference For Dummies 0-7645-5714-9
Roxio Easy Media Creator For Dummies 0-7645-7131-1

SPORTS, FITNESS, PARENTING, RELIGION & SPIRITUALITY

0-7645-5146-9 0-7645-5418-2

Also available:

- Adoption For Dummies 0-7645-5488-3
- Basketball For Dummies 0-7645-5248-1
- The Bible For Dummies 0-7645-5296-1
- Buddhism For Dummies 0-7645-5359-3
- Catholicism For Dummies 0-7645-5391-7
- Hockey For Dummies 0-7645-5228-7
- Judaism For Dummies 0-7645-5299-6
- Martial Arts For Dummies 0-7645-5358-5
- Pilates For Dummies 0-7645-5397-6
- Religion For Dummies 0-7645-5264-3
- Teaching Kids to Read For Dummies 0-7645-4043-2
- Weight Training For Dummies 0-7645-5168-X
- Yoga For Dummies 0-7645-5117-5

TRAVEL

0-7645-5438-7 0-7645-5453-0

Also available:

- Alaska For Dummies 0-7645-1761-9
- Arizona For Dummies 0-7645-6938-4
- Cancún and the Yucatán For Dummies 0-7645-2437-2
- Cruise Vacations For Dummies 0-7645-6941-4
- Europe For Dummies 0-7645-5456-5
- Ireland For Dummies 0-7645-5455-7
- Las Vegas For Dummies 0-7645-5448-4
- London For Dummies 0-7645-4277-X
- New York City For Dummies 0-7645-6945-7
- Paris For Dummies 0-7645-5494-8
- RV Vacations For Dummies 0-7645-5443-3
- Walt Disney World & Orlando For Dummies 0-7645-6943-0

GRAPHICS, DESIGN & WEB DEVELOPMENT

0-7645-4345-8 0-7645-5589-8

Also available:

- Adobe Acrobat 6 PDF For Dummies 0-7645-3760-1
- Building a Web Site For Dummies 0-7645-7144-3
- Dreamweaver MX 2004 For Dummies 0-7645-4342-3
- FrontPage 2003 For Dummies 0-7645-3882-9
- HTML 4 For Dummies 0-7645-1995-6
- Illustrator CS For Dummies 0-7645-4084-X
- Macromedia Flash MX 2004 For Dummie 0-7645-4358-X
- Photoshop 7 All-in-One Desk Reference For Dummies 0-7645-1667-1
- Photoshop CS Timesaving Techniques For Dummies 0-7645-6782-9
- PHP 5 For Dummies 0-7645-4166-8
- PowerPoint 2003 For Dummies 0-7645-3908-6
- QuarkXPress 6 For Dummies 0-7645-2593-X

NETWORKING, SECURITY, PROGRAMMING & DATABASES

0-7645-6852-3 0-7645-5784-X

Also available:

- A+ Certification For Dummies 0-7645-4187-0
- Access 2003 All-in-One Desk Reference For Dummies 0-7645-3988-4
- Beginning Programming For Dummies 0-7645-4997-9
- C For Dummies 0-7645-7068-4
- Firewalls For Dummies 0-7645-4048-3
- Home Networking For Dummies 0-7645-42796
- Network Security For Dummies 0-7645-1679-5
- Networking For Dummies 0-7645-1677-9
- TCP/IP For Dummies 0-7645-1760-0
- VBA For Dummies 0-7645-3989-2
- Wireless All In-One Desk Reference For Dummies 0-7645-7496-5
- Wireless Home Networking For Dummie 0-7645-3910-8